The Ice Broken

Studies in the History of Church and Theology

Edited by
Andreas J. Beck, Leuven

In cooperation with
Ulrich L. Lehner, Milwaukee
Kenneth P. Minkema, New Haven
Richard A. Muller, Grand Rapids
Peter Opitz, Zurich
Ulrike Treusch, Giessen

VOLUME 3

1. Pieter L. Rouwendal, *Predestination and Preaching in Genevan Theology from Calvin to Pictet.*
2. Antonie Vos, *John Duns Scotus. A Life.*

Willem J. op 't Hof

# The Ice Broken

Puritan Influences on the Netherlands in the Seventeenth Century

Volume 1

Dedicated to the Restored Reformed Church of the Netherlands

This edition was made possible by the generous donations of:
Restored Reformed Church of the Netherlands
Stichting Deddens-Koppefonds

Cover design: Brainstorm
Typesetting: Gewoon Geertje

ISSN 2543-0777
ISBN 9789492701091

Copyright © Summum Academic Publications, Kampen, The Netherlands.
All rights reserved. No part of this publication may be reproduced, translated, stored in a retrieval system, or transmitted in any form by any means, electronic, mechanical, photocopying, recording or otherwise, without prior written permission from the publisher.

# CONTENTS

| | | |
|---|---|---|
| | PREFACE | 7 |
| | INTRODUCTION | 9 |
| | MAP OF THE UNITED PROVINCES<br>Denoting places mentioned in the text | 21 |
| 1. | KNOWN ONLY IN TRANSLATION<br>Translations of six unpublished Puritan manuscripts | 23 |
| 2. | CAUSE BEATEN BY CONSEQUENCE<br>Three Puritan books published in translation prior to the<br>text even coming into print | 75 |
| 3. | SCRIBAL PIETY<br>The role of manuscripts in the international<br>dissemination of Puritanism and Pietism | 99 |
| 4. | LEARNED AT HOUSEHOLD SEMINARIES<br>The significance for European Pietism of Puritan household<br>seminaries | 129 |
| 5. | DUTCH CHURCHES IN ENGLAND AS CHANNELS<br>BETWEEN PURITANISM AND DUTCH PIETY<br>The significance of Dutch churches in England for Dutch<br>translators of Puritan works | 181 |
| 6. | LATENT CITATIONS<br>Hidden Puritan content in Dutch Pietist works | 251 |
| 7. | PURITAN PREACHING BY<br>DUTCH MINISTERS<br>Puritan content in Dutch sermons | 277 |

8. MILITARY AND PIETY
   English and Scots soldiers and their Puritan influence in the
   Dutch Republic                                                287

9. SHOPS OPENED ON EASTER
   MONDAY 1673
   An unique instance of further reformation
   at Sluis                                                      307

10. A SCOTS HANDMAID AT SLUIS
    The Sluis handmaid Barbara Jobs
    in light of her wills                                        339

BIBLIOGRAPHY                                                     363

ACKNOWLEDGEMENTS OF PHOTOGRAPHS                                  403

INDEX OF PERSONS                                                 404

INDEX OF SUBJECTS                                                423

INDEX OF PLACES                                                  434

INDEX OF BIBLE TEXTS                                             440

# PREFACE

This is an enormously important volume of essays. It has become increasingly apparent to early modern religious, political, cultural and book-historians that translations provide badly neglected but unique and invaluable insights into the processes of cultural change and exchange in this period. This is a field in which Prof. Op 't Hof has been a distinguished pioneer, and in the area of Anglo-Dutch religious translations in particular he is the acknowledged and undisputed authority. His work is path-breaking in its empirical research and interpretative insights, deeply learned and definitive in its critical analysis, and extraordinarily significant in its broader implications. The only problem hitherto has been that his work has generally not been available in the English language, with the result that scholars working on book-history and puritanism in England and the USA have been sadly unaware of the ways in which Prof. Op 't Hof has revolutionised the field. What has been desperately needed for a long time is a translated collection of his articles, and this volume is therefore a work that is both timely and of enormous importance. It should have a major and lasting influence on many areas of research in Europe and the USA. The assembling of this distinguished body of research is also a fitting testament to a distinguished scholarly career.

This is definitive scholarship that provides a wealth of precious insights into the whole process of translation. So many crucial aspects of the phenomenon – the often hidden identities and backgrounds of translators, their possible connections with authors, the ways in which translations were instigated, the print runs, latent citations of translated work, the ways in which readers responded to the texts or incorporated their messages into preaching and pastoral activity – are ones where historians expect to be able to do little more than shrug their shoulders. In all these areas, through painstaking and pioneering scholarship, Prof. Op 't Hof not only addresses the problems head-on but has located and critically assessed a surprising volume of precious information and striking examples. As a result, the articles shed invaluable light on early modern scholarly practices and careers, cultural exchange and relations, the book trade, and the religious politics of the Dutch Republic. They also make quite clear that the Dutch translation of English puritan works, and the ways in which this was carried out, are absolutely crucial to understanding the origins, nature and development of the Dutch Second Reformation.

It is impossible in a short preface to mention all the striking discoveries and insights in these articles – the countless conundrums and bibliographical mysteries that have been painstakingly solved with exquisite care and judgment, the new discoveries, and the fresh attributions. Beyond the purely bibliographical issues, other chapters provide major insights in other areas. Chapter 4 on household seminaries, for example, is a work of major importance on a neglected aspect of the practice of piety and cultural relations in the Reformed world. Chapter 9 is a wonderfully rich case study of the impact of the Further Reformation in opposing the observation of feast days and use of a set liturgy. Chapter 10 is a splendid and fascinating example of how the meticulous study of wills can illuminate a relatively humble religious life and distinctive Further Reformation religious practices. The contract discussed in chapter 7 to extract sermon materials from English works is a jaw-dropping discovery: precisely the sort of thing that one suspected might have been happening but would never dream of being able to find recorded in such extraordinary detail and with such candour.

It is an undiluted pleasure, therefore, to welcome to the English-reading scholarly world this remarkable body of work by a master of the field. Not only does it enrich our understandings of book history, translation, cultural exchange, and religious politics in the Dutch Republic, but it will provide an invaluable point of reference for future research on these issues in other countries.

Anthony A. Milton

# INTRODUCTION

It was Wim Janse who, as the then Dean of the Faculty of Theology and Vice-Rector of VU University Amsterdam, urged me to bundle together a number of my articles previously published in Dutch for this English volume to draw to international notice the findings of my decades-long inquiry into the influence of Puritanism on the Netherlands, particularly in the seventeenth century. The original intention was merely to bring up to date several already-published articles, but once I began putting these together as requested, the natural completion suggested itself: to write new chapters to complement them. Consequently, the work has expanded so much that it has had to become a two-volume edition.

This first volume is made up of ten chapters, each of which is an article on a theme of its own, so that the ground each covers is well-defined. The golden thread binding them all together is not hard to spot: it is the influence exerted by English and Scottish Puritanism upon the United Provinces. Each of these contributions indicates in its own thematic way the importance of that influence. Moreover, the unity of these various topics is accentuated by the many cross-connections that there are between the chapters.

The research underlying the articles was carried out at a range of levels and for different original purposes, which has given rise to variation. As dictated by the nature of the chapter in question, the methods have involved research into books, archives and the scholarly literature. The first three chapters revolve around the manuscript issue. In the context of research into devotional material, that is pretty much virgin territory. Our first chapter describes six manuscripts that never appeared in print in their original language; they were published only in translation. The second examines three translations that were published *before* the original came out. The third sets out general research into the role played by manuscripts in the international transmission of practical divinity. In this third chapter, we penetrate the geographical boundary set by the subtitle of this book by foraging further afield than the Netherlands: here, Denmark and Germany come into view.

The fourth chapter focuses on Puritan household academies as nurseries of Dutch and other Continental trainee ministers of the Gospel where they underwent the practical phase of their homiletic and pastoral education. This is another chapter that takes more of Europe into its scope than the Netherlands alone. Chapter five is devoted to the question of what mediating role the Dutch congregations in England played in the transmission of

Puritan thinking and practice to the United Provinces; the dominant note here is sounded by translators.

The sixth chapter enquires into the phenomenon of latent borrowings from Puritan sources in Dutch Pietist writing and into the reasons why the sources were not acknowledged; it also calls the reader's attention to how widespread a practice it also was in Continental countries beyond the Netherlands to quote Puritans without giving them credit.

Chapter seven constitutes an initial attempt to gain a general impression of the Puritan content of Dutch sermons. Surprisingly, an archival source of a legal nature has furnished the most, and the most useful, information in this regard. The eighth chapter demonstrates that the combination of military service with pious inclinations was by no means as unheard-of or impossible as one might imagine. The final two chapters relate to the fortified border town of Sluis: chapter nine shows us that nonconformist influence could lead to a small-scale revolt and social unrest locally,[1] and the last chapter brings out how the influence that is the theme of this whole book was able to penetrate to the humblest classes of society and that it can be traced through source material in archives that Dutch researchers have hitherto completely omitted to consult.[2]

Except in the final two chapters, the author has in view new thematic approaches to research in this field of study. That being so, the present contributions cannot typically offer more than an initial, and hence preliminary, scan of the horizon and of discoveries. In contract, the last two chapters are intended by the author to demonstrate that the most unprepossessing of archival sources can sometimes deliver spectacular results for this avenue of research. The author hopes that other researchers will tackle and resolve the newly-arisen issues and that they will also include non-ecclesiastical archives in their research more than has been the practice heretofore. Furthermore, it is his firm conviction that much of the ground covered in this volume is also applicable to other countries where Puritanism left its mark, in some cases a deeply-carved one. The significance of the present study extends beyond the relationship between Great Britain and the Netherlands.

It is for three reasons that this book limits its purview to the seventeenth century. Firstly, the authors whose translated works were in terms of quantity the most popular in that century were conspicuous by their total or near-total lack of readers by the eighteenth century. Secondly, the absolute zenith of these translations in quantitative terms falls around the midpoint

---

1 This chapter is an augmented version of an article published in Dutch on the events of 3 April 1673 at Sluis: Op 't Hof [1999-2].
2 This chapter was originally published in Dutch: Op 't Hof [2002].

of the seventeenth century.³ The third reason will be discussed later in this introduction. Despite those observations, this temporal limitation has not been imposed absolutely: the first chapter makes summary reference to post-seventeenth-century editions. These details were deliberately included to give the reader a sense of how Dutch aficionados have continued with some degree of regularity to publish translations of this kind down to the present day, whether or not linguistically updated, and that even the twentieth and twenty-first centuries have witnessed the production of fresh

# OPERA
Ofte alle de
## THEOLOGISCHE
# WERKEN,

Meest betreffende de Praktijke der Godtzaligheidt / en den Wandel van een Christen / in de plichten nevens Godt en zijne Even-naasten:

Van den zeer Geleerden, en Godtzaligen

## THOMAS GOODWIN.

Uyt het Engels getrouwelijk vertaelt en van Nieus overzien

Door

Mr. JACOBUS KOELMAN,

Bedienaar des Goddelikken Woorts tot Sluys in Vlaanderen.

Met twee nodige Registers verzien/
Noit soo by malkanderen gedrukt.

t'AMSTERDAM,

By JAN HENDRIKSZ. BOOM, Boek-verkooper, op de Cingel, by Jan-Roon-Poorts-Toorn, in 't af-gaan van de Sluys, in de Boek-binder, 1664.

---

3 Van Lieburg [1989], 74–78.

translations of the genre. This inclusion serves to disabuse readers of the impression which they might otherwise form that the subject of this volume should somehow be the exclusive preserve of the seventeenth century or that it should be a matter of purely historical interest. In actual fact, the Dutch have never ceased translating or publishing the material in question, and it is in quite rude health in our own day, albeit not in the quantities seen in the seventeenth century.

The main title of this study is taken from a clause deployed by the Sluis preacher Jacobus Koelman[4] (1631–1695) in the preface to his collected translations of the works of Thomas Goodwin (1600–1680): *Opera ofte alle de theologische werken, meest betreffende de praktijke der godtzaligheidt, en den wandel van een christen, in de plichten nevens Godt en zijne evennaesten* [Opera, or all the theological works primarily concerning the practice of piety and the Christian's walk in his duties toward God and his neighbour]. Koelman begins that preface by remarking that his national church has been richly blessed, and continues to be so in his day, by the practical works of English ministers. The Dutch ought to be grateful to God for this, he writes. He grants that the Dutch writers on the practicalities of theology are not a whit behind Englishmen in intellect or skill, and can imagine that they might actually excel them one day, but adds that it cannot be denied "that the English divines have gone before us, broken the ice, shown the way, given us material and method".[5]

*The passage in the original*

> dat de Engelſche Theologanten ons hebben voorgegaan, het ys gebroken, de wegh geweeſen, ſtoffe ende Methode gegeven

Given the context, what Koelman means by their having "broken the ice" is that Dutch devotional literature would have been inconceivable in the absence of its English counterpart. With their writings, the Puritans have, icebreaker-like, pioneered a route for Dutch Pietists and their devotional authors to follow in. English devotional material arose earlier in time, setting the tone for its Dutch equivalent, and it was in English that the genre was shaped as to its direction, topics and manners of treatment, which the Dutch genre would continue to observe. To corroborate his assertion,

---

4 Krull; Van Lieburg [1990]; Meeuse [1990, 2008]; Op 't Hof [2013-1], 237–268; Groenendijk [2017].
5 Goodwin [1664], (*)4r.

Koelman has only to point to the collected works of Goodwin in the very book that he is prefacing.

The passage quoted constitutes a stipulation by Koelman that there was a relationship of dependence between Dutch and English devotional book production, and that the former had grown up as pupil to the latter. Yet this master-pupil relationship did not, to him, imply of necessity that the pupil movement could never surpass its pedagogue, but rather that the pupil would remain always in a debt of gratitude even if he did manage to scale greater heights by standing on his forerunner's shoulders. The value to be assigned to a perception of this kind is determined by one's answer to the question of what position the observer took regarding the observed. In Koelman's case, it is obvious that he was not merely a great admirer of English (and later of Scots) devotional matter but that his very convictions were almost entirely moulded by those writings. Hence, his judgement is not objective in the matter, and we ought to assume from this consideration alone a notable degree of exaggeration in his statement. Nevertheless, the choosing of Koelman's phrase to headline this whole volume is the author's preferred way of signalling that he is of the opinion that this seventeenth-century preacher had indeed got to the nub of the matter. The reader will have to determine for himself at the end of this study whether or not the presentation of the material given here has induced him to agree with that assessment.

There is still one word in our subtitle that calls for further elucidation: 'Puritan'. Why has that adjective been chosen, rather than plumping for the safer 'devotional', as we have (for tactical reasons) done thus far in this introduction? The key drawback with 'devotional' as an adjective is that it is restricted in scope to the *inward* aspect of the personal life of faith, whereas the works considered in the present volume tackle the *outward* expressions of faith besides, as well as addressing collective piety in its many and diverse manifestations. Moreover, 'devotional' is a term freighted with at least as much pre-Reformational significance, if not even more, than with seventeenth-century connotations. The advantage of using our chosen word, 'Puritan', is that it relates to an historical movement of the sixteenth and seventeenth centuries. This helpfully does away with the inapplicably universal and timeless cachets of the word 'devotional'; moreover, 'Puritan' quite decisively denotes the confessional allegiance of the works treated of in this study, namely the Reformed confession. Whereas the term 'devotional' will not admit of any doctrinal exclusivism, 'Puritan' does. A final reason for terminating this study at the close of the seventeenth century is the fact that Puritanism as an historical movement ended with that century.

A final, and not insignificant, reason to choose the word 'Puritan' is historiographical. Study of the theme of this book has thus far been an almost exclusively Dutch preserve, and the literature of that discipline has consistently deployed the noun *Puriteinen* and the adjective *Puriteins*.[6] Admittedly, one of these studies did use the term *Piëtist* and its derivatives instead, but made clear that what was meant thereby was *Pietist Puritanism*.[7] The only twentieth-century academic to have written in English on this research topic was the American Keith L. Sprunger, who produced two substantial monographs which likewise couched the study entirely within the frame of Puritanism.[8] In this new century, we have already had two Anglophone researchers who have summarised some of the findings of Dutch studies of the influence of English Reformed piety on the seventeenth-century United Provinces. The first of these to go into print was an American, Philip Benedict, whose view of the matter is set out in a succinct overview that he gives of that influence, in a section which he entitled "The Puritan Manner of Godliness".[9] He has been followed by the Englishman Anthony Milton, who devotes a chapter of the *Cambridge Companion to Puritanism* to "Puritanism and the continental Reformed churches".[10] It was felt that to have veered away from that terminology in this collection would have generated far more questions and problems than sticking to it would.

Many as the advantages of the word 'Puritan' are, we are saddled with one major objection to it: it covers a multitude of meanings.[11] Hence, it is essential that we resolve right at the outset what is meant *here* by Puritanism. While the term has ended up as a catch-all for all manner of distinct meanings, it is well enough established that a focus upon piety was from its very inception a defining characteristic of the historical movement of Puritanism[12] and that this remained a constant, despite all the vagaries of political, ecclesiastical and social circumstances. Indeed, there is no shortage of researchers who regard that as being nothing less than Puritanism's key char-

---

6   To list all the publications in question would take up too much space, so we must content ourselves here with an overview of the most important of them. First and foremost is the journal *Documentatieblad Nadere Reformatie*, published since 1977, which has played host to many dozens of articles over the years, typically going into detail on some aspect or other of the influence we are considering here. Chief among the books in this literature are: Van der Haar [1980]; Groenendijk [1984-1]; Alblas; Op 't Hof [1987-1, 2001-1]; Van 't Spijker et al., 155–202; Op 't Hof et al. [2009], 41–84, 107–214, 237–258; Op 't Hof and Huisman [2013], 123–208, 235–402; Groenendijk [2017].
7   Op 't Hof [1987-1].
8   Sprunger [1982, 1994].
9   Benedict, 518–526.
10  Milton, 118–119.
11  Coffey and Lim.
12  Collinson [1983], 1–17; Hughes; Webster [1997], 3–4, 95–121; Bozeman, 64–68; Haigh, 46–47, 104, 122–123, 128.

acteristic.[13] Nor is this a post-hoc academic interpretation or construct: it is altogether of a piece with the view taken by seventeenth-century Puritans of themselves.[14] It is, then, entirely justified that the first chapter of the third part of the *Cambridge Companion to Puritanism* deals with practical divinity and spirituality.[15] The more precise term 'Pietist Puritanism'[16] denotes not so much one of many *strands* of Puritanism as it does one of its key *qualities*, if not its most important characteristic of all as a movement.

Never in history has an attempt been made to define the term 'Puritanism' in terms of that movement's outworkings in non-English-speaking countries. The theme of this study lends itself ideally to such an attempt. With the number of publications that have now come out on the influence exerted upon the Netherlands by Puritanism, it has become incontrovertible that the decisive factor in that influence was piety in the broadest sense of the word. Certainly, there was an impact in the dogmatic and ecclesiological domains too, but these pale into insignificance compared with the amount of transference of ideals and practices of piety.[17] It is for this critical reason that the present volume treats Puritanism as meaning *Pietist Puritanism*. Whenever in this study the words 'Puritanism' and 'Puritan' occur, then, they are to be understood in the Pietist sense of the word.

This study speaks of English and Scottish Puritanism. The existence of such a phenomenon as English Puritanism has never been called into question, but the same could not be said of Scottish Puritanism. In an intriguing article, Margo Todd problematises Scottish Puritanism.[18] Can the term 'Puritanism' actually be applied to Scotland? Her answer is, "yes and no—but then again yes".[19] This response by such a discerning researcher would be sufficient in and of itself to justify the use of the term, but Todd's argument has spurred the present author to air a few matters anyway. Todd argues as follows. The Scots church was the most Puritan of all Reformed churches of its age. There had been nothing half-baked about the process of reformation north of the border as there had been in the case of the Church of England. Therefore, there was a total absence in Scotland of that distinctive feature of Puritanism, ecclesiastical opposition. Even so, Todd pleads

---

13 For example, Hambrick-Stowe [1982], 5–8, 23, 38, 53, 113; Cliffe [1984], 2; Morgan, 18; Packer, 28; Mullan, 4–5; Schwanda, 9.
14 Cliffe [1984], 5; Spurr, 9a.
15 Hambrick-Stowe [2008].
16 The term was coined by Stoeffler as a variation upon a term used by Heppe and Lang, 'Puritan Pietism': Stoeffler, 28; Heppe, 14; Lang, 75.
17 Op 't Hof [2001-1], 373–374.
18 Margo Todd.
19 Margo Todd, 175.

for the use of the term "Scottish Puritanism", albeit with a view to something more specific: Puritan spirituality or the experimental religion that characterised the Scots Church of the sixteenth and seventeenth centuries.

Todd's plea lands her very close to the Pietist understanding of Puritanism that is observed in the present study. However, there is the major difference that in this book, piety is defined not only inwardly and experimentally: this author understands the *practice* of piety, in the sense both of individual striving to make one's calling and election sure and collective forms of sanctification, to fall under that term also. Both forms of sanctification imply the exercise of religious duties such as Bible reading, prayer, meditation, sung praise, fasting, godly conversation and household instruction. Todd may well be right to have flagged up that the Church of Scotland was one in which the Puritan ideals of church life had in formal and official terms largely been implemented at all echelons, but even a superficial survey of the manuscript minute books of Kirk sessions, presbyteries and synods will reveal that the lived reality of the Scots church not infrequently contradicted those ideals and that its percolation through to families and personal lives remained limited to a small minority of the national church.[20] In other words, Puritanism was far from being superfluous to requirements in Scotland, in Todd's purely organisational-ecclesiastical definition of its essence. Something far weightier than that consideration, however, in this connection is that Puritanism was an oppositional movement not merely vis-à-vis the Church establishment, but every bit as much vis-à-vis the spiritual lives of families and individuals. This twin understanding forms an extra, and decisive, reason to concur with Todd's plea that we can indeed speak of Scottish Puritanism.

On top of that, David George Mullan's 2000 study of Scottish Puritanism has already set the tone for the academic terminology of this field in the twenty-first century.[21] This being so, it is revealing that not only in Todd, in her 2008 article, but in John Coffey too, in his 2006 article on the problem of Scottish Puritanism,[22] do we see positive attitudes towards the use of the term.

Not only in the two realms of Great Britain, but across the North Sea too, an analogous piety movement was well under way in the last quarter of the sixteenth century. It is known to scholarship as Dutch Reformed Pietism.[23] Within that movement, a related tendency began to distinguish itself from 1608 onwards: the Further Reformation.[24] What the Further

---

20 Cf. Coffey, 80.
21 Mullan.
22 Coffey.
23 Op 't Hof [2005-1], 52–59.
24 Beeke [1991], 383–413; Van Lieburg [1994]; Graafland *et al.*

Reformation was about was transposing the Pietist desire for devotion into programmatic activity. Without neglecting the aspect of inward experience, the advocates of the Further Reformation concretised Pietist formulations and grievances as deeds; by developing elaborate programmes that identified which ecclesiastical, political, social and familial affairs were in need of reform and by what various means; and furthermore by submitting these programmes to the appropriate bodies of church, state and society as specific reform proposals.

Reformed Pietism embodied itself in various national manifestations on the Continent. We may, with a degree of caution, speak of there having been a Pietist tendency within seventeenth-century Reformed Protestantism in France.[25] From the 1590s onwards, the same is seen even in Switzerland and Germany,[26] and besides that there is every reason to speak of a distinct German Further Reformation in its own right.[27] Finally, around the mid-seventeenth century, Reformed Pietism took on native garb in Hungary and Transylvania.[28] It was Puritan-tinted to the extent that it has in fact been called Hungarian Puritanism.[29]

All the chapters of this book are the author's own work, but he is keen not to do down the very valuable help that he received from Frans W. Huisman MA, a researcher at the Study Centre for Protestant Book Culture at VU University Amsterdam.[30] Huisman has, in the interests of the Further Reformation Study Foundation, developed an online bibliographical database, Pietas, that gives both bibliographical and content descriptions of the editions of all Dutch-language Reformed Pietist works. It must be borne in mind that Pietas remains a work in progress and hence is still a growing database. The delightful aspect of the project for the purposes of this study is that the entire sum of all Dutch translations of Puritan writings can be found in Pietas already.[31]

There is in fact another website that hosts a retrospective Dutch bibliography, Short-Title Catalogue Netherlands (STCN),[32] but it has three shortcomings compared with Pietas. The most fundamental of these is that its data is drawn exclusively from public libraries, whereas Pietas is also informed by the

---

25 Op 't Hof [2005-1], 49–52.
26 Op 't Hof [2005-1], 61–66.
27 Op 't Hof [2008-1], 504–512, 520–523; Van de Kamp [2012-1], 155–156.
28 Op 't Hof [2005-1], 69–73.
29 Murdock [2004].
30 For the following, see Huisman [2011].
31 Since 17 May 2011, Pietas has been searchable online: http://www.pietasonline.nl/pietas. As of April 2019, it contained 7,724 entries.
32 http://picarta.pica.nl/DB=3.11.

Netherlands' most significant private collections of Reformed piety material, and also by some domestic and foreign public libraries passed over by the STCN. The import of this is revealed in the fact that Pietas houses 32% more listings than STCN![33] In addition, Pietas includes page or folio numbering details (which STCN does not), and unlike STCN includes rich data such as printing privileges and patents accorded to a work, the prior ownership chain, and differentiated subjects within books.

Huisman, and also Dr Jan van de Kamp, did the author the great favour of giving the drafts of these chapters a read through and providing constructive criticism, which was taken with gratitude. The same is true of Leen van Valen, whom I am supervising for doctoral studies on piety relations between Scotland and the Netherlands largely in the period 1660–1690; he was good enough to furnish the sections on Scots authors with his comments. Dr Willem Heijting and Dr Nelleke Moser receive my thanks for their kind involvement with the first three chapters. My thanks also to Alexander Thomson MA for translating my manuscript into fluent English, for compiling the place-names for the map that follows this introduction, and for proofreading the text. I am equally thankful to my friend Jan Rozendaal for kindly providing the illustrations. Finally, I am extremely grateful to my denomination, the Restored Reformed Church of the Netherlands, and to the Stichting Deddens-Koppefonds for their generous donations.

Before we proceed to the study itself, a few words are in order on methodological formalities. Where this book mentions a translation without specifying the target language, then it is always a translation into Dutch that is meant. After the title of a translation in italics, the title of the English original is given (likewise in italics) in parenthesis; only where the original title is unavailable has the title been back-translated into modern English.

When we come to totalling up numbers of translations in book form, we are opening up a can of worms. What constitutes a translation? Is it each individual instance of an edition with a unique title page and/or its own collation formula? This study understands 'a translation' to mean a unit which is declared to constitute a unit on its first title page or in the dedication (in the first of them, if there is a plurality) or in the preface. In practice, then, one 'translation' within the meaning of the present volume can encompass more than one work by the same author, or even more than one work by more than one author. Where books incorporate a bundle of separate parts—sermons, for instance—from distinct sources, we can sometimes have to do with a plethora of entries in the bibliographies in English. Reprints do not count towards the translation totals, except where they con-

---

33 Huisman [2011], 14.

tain substantial new Puritan texts. Where we have to do with a combined edition of previously-published translations, then the new product is counted as an edition if it features one or more previously-unpublished Puritan texts. In some instances, more than one translator each produced his own Dutch version of a given Puritan text independently. Where this is so, each translator's effort is notched up as one translation for our totals. That is not the approach that has been taken for modernisations of the language of prior translations, however. Where a translation forms part of a series, each volume that appeared is counted as a translation in its own right, except where it is evident that the publisher's original intent had been to combine the parts into a single book.

The first mention of a given historical personage in the main body of the text is accompanied by his birth and death years, where known, in parentheses. Personages not from Britain or America are, where possible, supplied with footnotes by their surnames pointing the reader to literature about them. Historical personages from the English-speaking world can be looked up in biographical dictionaries and in the literature in English; only in special cases is reference made to a predominance of Dutch literature. The same applies to the English source-texts of the translations that can be found in English-language bibliographies.[34] The author has presumed that these characters are so familiar to his readers that they need no special annotation. Nor are bibliographical data given for the translations: these can be looked up on Pietas. References in the footnotes are kept as brief as possible; copious information is reserved for the Manuscript Sources and the Bibliography. The bibliography of post-1800 publications gives the names and surnames of authors and editors in the form in which they appear on the title page of their work. The same applies to the listing there of all book titles. Where books published prior to the nineteenth century are cited, the year of publication is always given in parentheses after the author's surname, or in the case of an anonymous work, after the title.

An article by Vivienne Larminie has recently appeared, embedding the subject of this study in a European context. Her finding that "Anglo-Dutch pathways are relatively well-trodden"[35] is entirely justified in that regard, yet it could give rise to the erroneous notion that the Anglo-Dutch connection might have little more potential yield and that it might therefore not be a subject that suggested itself for further research. The present author hopes that this collection of research will demonstrate how wide of the mark such a conclusion would be. This is a subject well worthy of continuing and thoroughgoing study.

---

34 Pollard *et al.*; Wing.
35 Larminie, 3.

# MAP OF THE UNITED PROVINCES

denoting places mentioned in the text

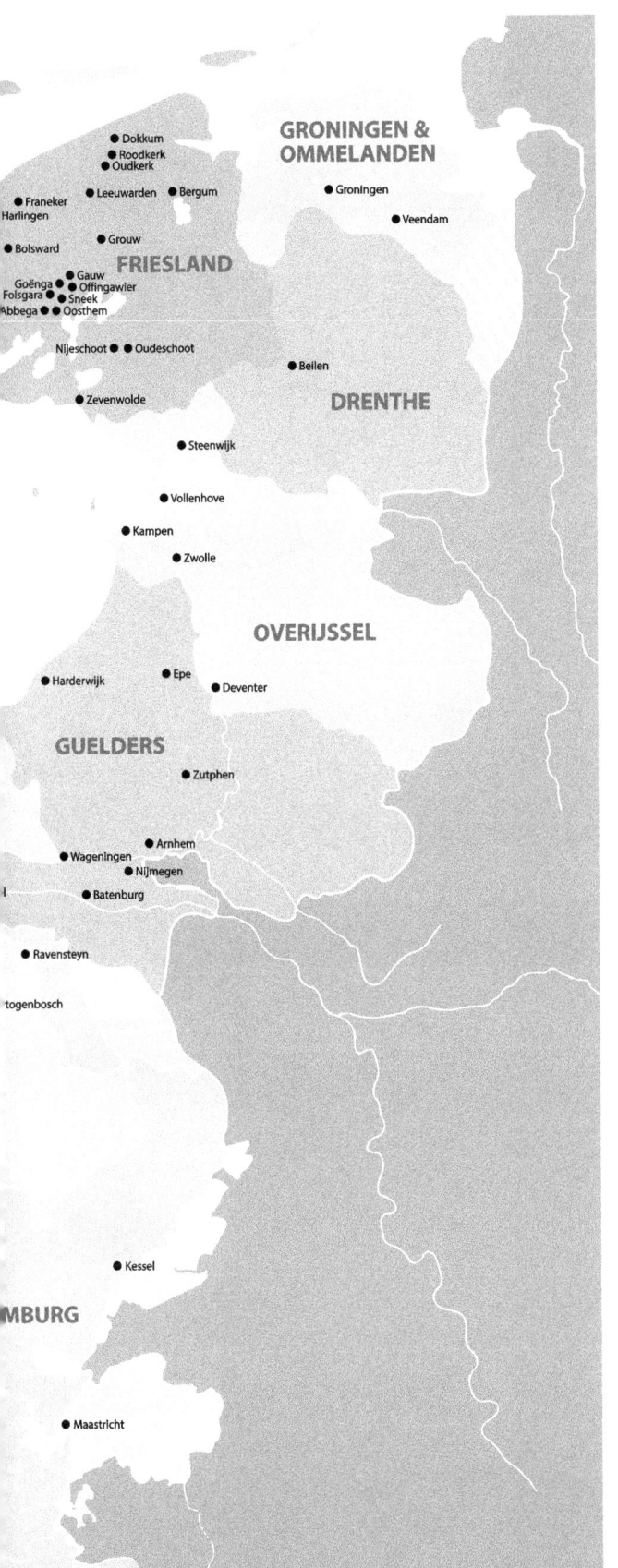

# 1. KNOWN ONLY IN TRANSLATION

## Translations of six unpublished Puritan manuscripts

*Research into seventeenth-century translations of Puritan works that has progressed over the past decades in the Netherlands has yielded rich and varied findings.*[1] *Perhaps the most surprising of all these is that there are at least six Puritan works that are not known in their original language from a single extant copy—not even by citation in secondary literature—and that these works are accordingly very unlikely ever to have been published in their English originals. This being the case, we are obliged to infer that the contents of these works have been preserved only in translation. This phenomenon is at the very least an extremely rare occurrence in the history of culture and books: reason indeed for attention to be dedicated to this remarkable phenomenon.*

*The present author is aware of only one other seventeenth-century instance of the phenomenon, and, tellingly, that instance concerns a pronouncedly anti-Puritan work:* A treatise of the sabbath and the Lords-day *(1636) by David Primrose. The manuscript underlying this book edition had been written by Primrose in French when he was a preacher at Rouen. Writing it had been his response to a request by his father Gilbert Primrose (d. 1642), minister of the French Church in London, to commit to paper his thoughts on the Sabbath. A controversy was raging in England at that time on the theory and practice of Sabbatarianism, with the issue of ecclesiastical festival days also coupled to the debate. The reason for Primrose senior's request was that he wished to see Puritan views and practices of the Sabbath and festival days refuted. Having left his son's French manuscript lying around for three years, he finally found time to involve himself in the raging debate and—without his son's knowledge—translated it and had it printed. He then sent his son a copy, and Primrose junior sent him back a number of corrections, which were added to the edition. Like several of the translations*

---

1 Van der Haar [1980]; Op 't Hof [1981, 1985]; Schoneveld; Alblas; Op 't Hof [1987-1], 4; [1993-3, 1996-2, -3]; Meeuse [1996]; Op 't Hof [1997]; Van 't Veld; Op 't Hof [2001-2, -3]; Op 't Hof and Huisman [2002]; Den Ouden; Op 't Hof [2005-3]; Op 't Hof et al. [2009]; Van de Kamp [2010]; Op 't Hof [2011-3, -4]; Op 't Hof and Huisman [2013]; Koopman. In their guide to the seventeenth-century Dutch book trade, Pettegree and der Weduwen are thus quite right to devote special attention to this phenomenon, under the title "Borowed plumes": Pettegree and der Weduwen, 135–140.

*that will be considered in due course*, A treatise of the sabbath and the Lordsday *enjoyed a modest international success. Two Leiden preachers, Bernardus van Wijngaarden (1613–1682) and Samuel Althusius*[2] *(1600–1669), onward-translated Primrose's book into Dutch, incorporating the corrigenda into the body of the text itself. Their translation was published in 1659.*

*Given how highly remarkable it is for a published translation to have an unpublished source-text, it is high time that we pay dedicated attention to the six unpublished Puritan manuscripts.*

*There is an additional reason for us to consider the translations of the aforementioned unpublished manuscripts. A consultation of the Oxford Dictionary of National Biography entries for the Puritan original authors in question reveals that their biographers apparently had no inkling of the most intriguing and compelling fact that each of the authors whom they were describing had written a work that in all probability never saw the light of day in English. Evidently, the matters raised in this present contribution are unknown to non-Dutch researchers, or alternatively have been considered of such slight importance that no attention has been paid to them.*[3] *Should the latter be the case, this article will seek to demonstrate that, in their Continental translations, the six works in question assuredly are of research interest.*

*This article will consider the relationships between the authors and their translators; the aims that the authors had in composing their manuscripts; the functions that the manuscripts performed; the circumstances in which the translations came into existence; the intentions that the translators had with their productions; and the number of reprints and particular impacts that the translations had. Additionally, because the texts would otherwise remain unknown to researchers who lack knowledge of Dutch, their contents are summarised here. The translations will first be considered in chronological order of their year of initial publication before conclusions are drawn regarding their significance for our knowledge of the devotional relations between Pietist circles in England and Scotland on the one hand and the Netherlands on the other.*

---

2 De Bie and Loosjes, 1: 106–107.
3 The only published figure to have shown any familiarity with this phenomenon, the nineteenth-century researcher William Steven, records in a footnote that the work of Robert McWard that we shall consider below had never been published in the original English: Steven, 81, footnote. However, not a single Dutch researcher followed up on this clue. Stevens also back-translates the Dutch title of the work into English and states in the following terms the impression that the work made upon him: "His *Solemn Appeal to Preachers in the times of spiritual declension*, struck me as an awakening and touching address.": Steven, 81.

### William Whately, *Corte verhandelinghe van de voornaemste christelicke oeffeninghen,* Middelburg, 1609

The earliest translation that we shall examine was made by Willem Teellinck[4] (1579–1629). As his biography is covered in Volume II, only such details as are essential for an understanding of the background to the translation are provided here. Teellinck was in England from the last quarter of 1603 until the first quarter of 1606. He underwent a radical conversion while living among Puritans in early 1604. Later that year, he married an Englishwoman, and he spent around three quarters of a year at Banbury, a hub of Puritanism in central England, in 1605. It was here that he came under the lasting influence of the practices of strictly-prescribed family devotions and Sabbatarianism, and also here that he felt the vocation to the ministry rising within him. Upon his return to his native land, brief theological studies of around three months at Leiden were followed by his installation as the minister of the united parishes of Haamstede and Burgh on the Zeeland island of Schouwen-Duiveland in November 1606. Both his career and his sixty written works furnish ample proof that he was not only the Father of the Further Reformation[5] but that he remained thoroughly influenced for life by Puritanism and that he never gave over in his enthusiasm to introduce and enculturate the thinking of that English piety movement in his homeland.[6]

Against this background, it is no wonder that Teellinck's output consisted not solely of his own works but additionally of three translations of Puritan works. The first of all his publications was a translation of a little work by William Perkins (1558–1602), the Father of English Puritanism; both his fourth and his (posthumous) fifty-first publications were translations of writings by the vicar of Banbury, the Puritan William Whately (1583–1639).[7] It will probably never be established whether author and translator had ever met before 1605, when the latter was staying at Banbury. At any rate, the two men were soulmates at Banbury. This friendship continued after Teellinck's return to his native land and found its expression in correspondence between the men, as we shall see anon.

The work under present consideration was Teellinck's fourth publication and the second of his published translations: William Whately, *Corte verhandelinghe van de voornaemste christelicke oeffeninghen* [A brief

---

4 Beeke [2003]; Op 't Hof [2008-1, 2011-1, 2015-1].
5 Beeke [1991], 383–413; Van Lieburg [1994]; Graafland *et al.*
6 Op 't Hof [2008-1], 562–564; Op 't Hof [2011-1], 221–226.
7 Op 't Hof [1993-1], 27, 31, 118.

treatment of the chief Christian exercises].[8] It was published at Middelburg in early 1609 and amounted to 122 pages in octavo format. In the book's dedication, dated 6 February 1609, Teellinck recounts that Whately had sent him several manuscripts during the course of 1607 and that the latter had dedicated the present writing, now appearing in published translation, to Teellinck in a covering note. It was after letting a few of his closest friends read the manuscript, and having heard from them that they had found it most instructive, that Teellinck had decided to bring it out in print. Teellinck adds in his 1609 dedication that if the book is well received, he intends to publish the rest of Whately's manuscripts. He emphasises the fact that Whately, being an expert in spiritual experience, had written the actual content.

Teellinck devotes the largest part of the dedication to a description of the exemplary life of the family of townsfolk with whom he had lodged at Banbury. It can be discerned from the address of the dedication whom Teellinck had in mind as those who should model themselves after this example, namely Dutch candidate ministers and congregations. It was his firm conviction that the Puritan family worship and the simplicity of Puritan preaching for which he expressed such esteem, coupled with intensive pastoral care, would form the basis for the improvement of Dutch spiritual life.

Teellinck asks the reader to pray for him and for his dear friend Whately, who, Teellinck reports, is preparing to write a work in Latin on the practice of theology.[9] Teellinck rounds off his dedication by heartily recommending that candidate ministers read *Sacra theologia* [Sacred theology] by Dudley Fenner (d. 1587). He greatly regrets that this work, although universally available, appears to be little consulted. Although there is much in the book that might stand in the way of the reader's acceptance, such as its Ramistic method of inquiry, Teellinck argues that it is still very much worth acquiring and reading, since it treats of so many aspects of the practice of theology. Teellinck adds that he is making this recommendation because he himself has found the work to contain a treasure and is keen for others to delight in it similarly.

*Corte verhandelinghe* is divided into ten chapters, each subdivided into sections. It was the translator who added these divisions. Chapter 1 gives an overview of the content of the work by breaking it down into

---

8 Op 't Hof [1977].
9 Whately may have written this, but in any case it is not known to be extant and therefore in all likelihood was never published: Pollard *et al.*, 2:449b–450b, nos. 25296–25324.

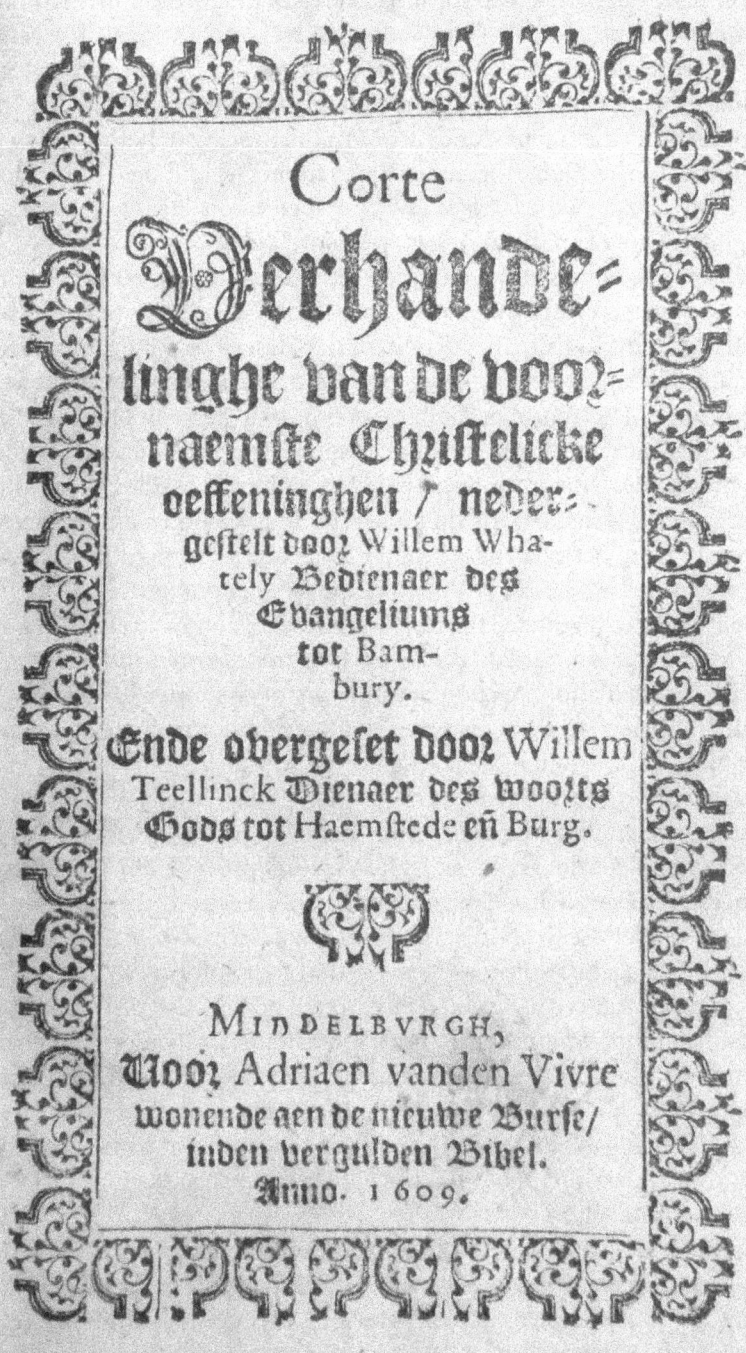

constituent categories. The spiritual exercises that every Christian ought to conduct to promote piety are either general or occasional. The general duties are to be divided into private and public. The private category includes the reading of Scripture; meditating upon it; prayer; and Christian conversation. The public duties are both the hearing of both reading and preaching of the Word; the use of the sacraments; and the observance of the Lord's Day. Two exercises are described upon emergent occasions: religious fasting and the making of religious vows.

Chapter 2 covers the reading of the Word. Its first section demonstrates from Scripture that every Christian is obliged to read the Bible regularly; daily, in fact. The second section describes three fruits of Bible reading. The third section teaches that four things are to be eschewed if one is to read Scripture profitably. Section four describes the two inner habits that must be striven for while reading. The fifth and final section of the chapter describes four outward attitudes for the reading of Scripture.

Chapter 3 considers meditation. The first section demonstrates its necessity from Scripture; the second discusses its twofold fruit. Section three clarifies what exactly meditation is; section four examines the proper times to meditate. The fifth section sets out how to arrive at a subject for meditation. Section six covers how to keep one's thoughts on the matter for mediation. Section seven treats of the order to follow when meditating. Section eight proposes that in order to meditate on an issue, one must have a sound knowledge of its substance and of what issues cohere with it. The ninth and final section advises the reader on how to attune his heart and affections to the matter.

Chapter 4 considers prayer. Its first section proves from Scripture references that every Christian must pray daily. Section two identifies the fruits of prayer for the body; section three describes how prayer aids in the struggle against spiritual foes. Section four informs the reader that many spiritual gifts can be obtained through prayer. The fifth section contains the author's definition of prayer. Section six provides rules for the content of prayer; rules for the manner of prayer are given in section seven. The eighth section gives rules for focusing upon God in prayer; the ninth, for being attentive to the brethren; the tenth, for being mindful of one's own situation. Finally, the eleventh section suggests four means for praying as one ought.

Chapter 5 covers Christian conversation. The first section demonstrates its necessity from Scripture. The second describes three of its fruits. Section three sets out four rules for Christian conversation; section four identifies four means of gaining competence in the art of discourse.

Chapter 6 covers the public reading and preaching of the Word. The first section proves its necessity from Scripture. Section two teaches what three things are necessary if one is to hear the Word profitably. Section three distinguishes several preparations that are to be made before hearing the Word. The fourth section considers hindrances to hearing profitably. The fifth section discusses love of and belief in the Word. Section six considers the particular self-preparation that is necessary immediately before attending preaching. Section seven covers preparation for preaching upon exceptional occasions. The eighth and ninth sections of the chapter discuss proper behaviour while hearing the Word preached or read.

Chapter 7 treats of the sacraments. After a definition in its first section of what a sacrament is, section two covers the ministry of the sacraments. Section three considers baptism in particular; section four, the Lord's Supper.

Lord's Day observance is the theme of Chapter 8. Section one proves that the Sabbath is a commandment of the moral law and thus everlastingly in force. Section two contains rebuttals of objections raised against the Sabbatical commandment. The third section determines the times of day at which the day of rest commences and ends. Section four treats of the four duties that inhere in preparation for the Sabbath. Section five introduces the matters of rest upon, and sanctification of, the Sabbath. Section six considers resting from one's work duties. Sections seven to nine consider, in turn, resting from recreational activities, worldly discussions, and earth-bound thoughts. The tenth section considers the question of who is required to rest. Finally, section eleven considers how the Sabbath is to be sanctified.

Chapter 9 covers fasting. Its first section proves from Scripture that fasting is a duty even in the Gospel dispensation. Section two identifies four fruits of fasting. The third section considers abasement; section four defines what reconciliation consists of. Section five identifies occasions opportune for fasting. Section six states three things that the author holds it necessary to observe when fasting.

Vows are the subject of Chapter 10. Its first section asserts that the keeping of vows is a duty incumbent upon the believer in the Gospel age, and also defines what a vow is. Section two sets out the rules for the content of vows; the third section provides rules for the manner of making them. The fourth section defines three purposes inherent in a vow. Section five covers the obligation to make good the vow.

Given the unstructured nature of Whately's manuscript, it is all but certain that the manuscript was initially intended for private use. This need not necessarily mean the author's own exclusive use; it could equally be the case that some of his friends or congregants read it. They will have been allowed by him to have read the manuscript if they wished, and perhaps to have copied it. The other manuscripts sent in the parcel will not have had any other intended purpose than this manuscript. Nothing can be said with any degree of certainty on the question of whether the manuscripts sent to Teellinck were the autographs or copies. The fact that Whately dedicated the original English text underlying *Corte verhandelinghe* to Teellinck would suggest that Whately—presumably without saying as much explicitly—was thereby suggesting that his Dutch friend might care to publish the text. Teellinck grasped the meaning of Whately's having sent the manuscript, but proceeded to publish his translation only once he had had a few of his most trusted friends read and warmly acclaim it. As will become evident below, the translator's eldest brother Eeuwout Teellinck[10] (1573–1629) was without doubt one such test-reader.

Sales of *Corte verhandelinghe* are likely to have disappointed both translator and publisher, since no second edition was called for during Teellinck's lifetime. Later in the seventeenth century, two reprints did come out, both at Dordrecht, in 1649 and 1658.[11]

To measure the success of an edition by the number of copies printed is a yardstick that plainly suggests itself. The more editions of a given book appeared, the greater that work's influence will have been. Yet this logic falls short in some instances, and *Corte verhandelinghe* is a case in point. One might expect that the sole edition of the translation would indicate that the book left little or no trace behind it in the early decades of the seventeenth century, yet the historical reality was quite the opposite.

In the first place, we must consider Teellinck's brother Eeuwout, who held high provincial office as Comptroller of the States of Zeeland. Eeuwout wrote 22 religious works, most of them pamphlets. Largely tying in with developments and current events in politics, the military and the church, Eeuwout in these publications made a fierce and impassioned assault on Remonstrant and Roman Catholic doctrines and practices on the one hand, and on the other hand incessantly and with all his faculties urged a further reformation of all areas of life. In these tracts, he was in such close agreement with the aims of his younger brother Willem that he can be seen as his twin brother in a spiritual sense. Historically, this closeness is bound up with the strong probability that Eeuwout was exposed to

---

10 Op 't Hof [1989, 1999-1].
11 Op 't Hof [1993-1], 31–32.

Willem's zeal when the latter returned home in 1606 with English Puritan fire in his bosom.

These facts explain why Eeuwout in his writings frequently bestows lavish praise on his brother and quotes at length from his work. Willem's translation *Corte verhandelinghe* is no exception in this regard. Various of his brother's expressions taken from *Corte verhandelinghe* are incorporated both in Eeuwout's *Christelicke clachte van eenige godsalige luyden over hare onvruchtbaerheydt in het ware christelicke leven* [Christian grievance of some godly folk at their unfruitfulness in real Christian life] (1618), and his chief work *Vyer ende wolck-calomne, lichtende nacht ende dach, om het Israel Godes, by eenige algemeene regels, nae een gesette ordre ende mate, in elck deel des daeghs, ende daed des levens, van stap tot stap door de grousame woestenie deses werelts, tot in het hemelsche Canaan te leyden* [Pillar of fire and cloud, burning night and day, to lead the Israel of God, by some general rules, to a determined order and degree, in each part of the day and act of life, from one step to the next, through the dreary desert of this world into the heavenly Canaan] (1622), a complete body of ethical teaching. The noteworthy aspects of his incorporations are considered in Chapter 6, since Eeuwout does not acknowledge Willem as his source in these borrowings.[12] Although *Christelicke clachte* was printed only once, his main work *Vyer ende wolck-calomne* was reprinted at Utrecht in 1649 and again in 1660.[13] These two editions are accompanied by a foreword by the man responsible for publishing them, to whom we now turn our gaze.

Gisbertus Voetius[14] (1589–1676), who was later to assume the professorship of theology at Utrecht and to be a mainstay of the Further Reformation, notifies the reader in his foreword to Willem Teellinck's posthumously-published *De worstelinghe eenes bekeerden sondaers* [The struggle of a converted sinner] (1631) that it was especially through the instrumentality of Teellinck's dedication in his second translation that the attention of many a minister and congregant was drawn to matters that they had previously paid scarcely a thought to and that were not otherwise written about. Indeed, Voetius declares that the work had exerted nothing less than a shock effect upon a good number of its readers. Their consideration of that book had given them an appreciation of the necessity of further reformation and had won them over to endorse the means that needed to be applied in order to accomplish it. Later in the same

---

12 This study, 252-253.
13 Op 't Hof [1988-1], 28, 36–37.
14 Duker; Van Oort *et al.*; Andreas J. Beck.

foreword, Voetius intimates that he himself was one of those many whose eyes Teellinck had opened to the vital concern of the practice of piety.[15] The year of publication of *Corte verhandelinghe* allows us to conclude that the about-face in his spiritual attitudes and efforts took place while he was still a student at Leiden.[16]

We shall see in Chapter 6 how the structure of *Corte verhandelinghe* provided the template for Voetius' academic manual for the practice of piety, *TA ΑΣΚΗΤΙΚΑ sive exercitia pietatis* [Ascetics, or the exercise of piety] (1664).[17] This work represents the fruits of Voetius' forty years' experience as a lecturer to numerous Dutch and foreign students of theology. The English Puritan manuscript in question, then, indirectly played a notable role in the academic teaching of theology on the Continent. Whately's convictions doubtless resonated with and served as a model for the practice of piety in the Netherlands and further afield.

There is hard evidence that *Corte verhandelinghe* exerted influence beyond the Netherlands. In 1706, the heirs of Friedrich Lanckischen published at Leipzig a work by Johann Georg Hoffmann in praise of the usefulness of English preachers, *Geistlicher engeländis. Redner, worinne die Schrifften der engeländischen Prediger untersuchet, gegen die evangelische Prediger-Methode gehalten, und überall, daß es damit nicht allein auff euserliche Moden und Ohren-juckende Zierathen, sondern auff Beweisung des Geistes und der Krafft des göttlichen Worts ankomme, vermittelst der Theologiae exeget. & pathologicae bewiesen wird: wobey ein sonderbarer Vorbericht von der Beschaffenheit und Nutz solcher Schrifften, nebst etlichen nach engeländischer Art elaborirten Predigten zu finden* [The spiritual English orator: in which the writings of English preachers are examined, held up against the evangelical[18] method of preaching, and it is comprehensively proven that what is at stake is not merely external fashions and ear-tickling ornaments, but the demonstration of the Spirit and of the power of the Word of God by means of exegetical and affective theology; to which is prefaced a special message on the nature and use of such writings, as well as some sermons worked up in the English manner]. At the publisher's request, a Lutheran senior rector, Johann Martin Schamelius[19] (1671–1742), comprised a list of the English writings of the type treated

---

15  Teellinck [1631], 2*3r., 2*4r.
16  Op 't Hof [1989], 94–96, 102.
17  This study, 254.
18  i.e., Lutheran.
19  Lindner.

in the book that had appeared in German translation.[20] In fact, translations of Italian, French and Dutch works also crop up on the list, and one of the Dutch authors mentioned is Teellinck. Among the translations of works by Teellinck that Schamelius lists is one entitled *Vornehmste Ubung der Christen* [Chief exercise of Christians]. This evidently refers to a manuscript related to the content of *Corte verhandelinghe*; the German translation must have been made during the seventeenth century. The notable aspect is that this onward translation had gained such traction among German Lutherans that it was still being discussed as the eighteenth century opened.

### John Archer, *Twee god-vruchtighe meditatien*, Arnhem, 1643

The second translation that we shall consider was done by Daniel van Laren[21] (b. 1585). As Volume II dedicates a chapter to van Laren, we will not explore his life and significance here. Only two things need be borne in mind. Van Laren was a minister at Arnhem, the capital of the large eastern Dutch province of Guelders, from 1625 to 1651. Second, a consideration regarding his translations: van Laren matches Willem Teellinck in that there are three translations that bear his name. Arthur Hildersham (1563-1632) was the author of the first two source-texts for these; van Laren's last translation will now be considered.

The translation of John Archer's (d. 1642) *Twee god-vruchtige meditatien* was published at Arnhem in 1643. Its full Dutch title is: *Twee god-vruchtighe meditatien allen christenen ter saelighyed ten hooghsten noodigh. D'eerste. Van t'ghevoelen der sonden. De tweede. Van t'remedie tegens de sonden. Door den wijsen hoogh-geleerden ende seer godsaelighen heer, Joan Archer laetst pastor in de Engelsche kercke tot Arnhem alwaer hy is begraven. Ende uyt het Engels in Nederduyts vertaelt door D. van Laren* [Two devotional meditations most needful to all Christians for their salvation, the first on sensibility of sins, the second on the remedy for sins; by the wise, most learned and very godly gentleman John Archer, late pastor of the English church at Arnhem, where he lies buried, and translated out of English into Low Dutch by D. van Laren]. The work was issued in duodecimo and covers 298 pages. The researcher of English bibliography will discover that not a hint of the original text of this book has ever been thrown up, which warrants the conclusion that the work was probably never laid to press in English.[22]

---

20  Hoffmann [1706], g1r.-h4v.
21  Op 't Hof [2016-3].
22  Wing, 1: 135 nos. A3612–3620.

The Arnhem publisher responsible for this book[23] was unwilling to see his name associated with that of Archer due to the latter's dubious reputation as a millenarian. Consequently, he published the work anonymously. Given this decision by the publisher, it is all the more surprising that van Laren did opt to associate his name publicly with that of his controversial English colleague. His foreword indicates that he acquired the manuscript after Archer's death, that he was obliged to edit and amplify the text substantially, and that both the translation and its publication were undertaken at his own initiative. Given all this, there is no other conclusion to draw than that van Laren was a close friend of Archer's and that this translation was his way of honouring the memory of his brother minister.

We now face the intriguing issue of the relationship between Archer and van Laren. Archer had arrived in the Netherlands in 1637 at the head of ten or a dozen families; more than a hundred English religious refugees in all. The families were unwilling to conform to the high-church ceremonies introduced into the Church of England by Archbishop William Laud (1573–1645). Several of these nonconformist exiles were noblemen, on account of which the English Church in Arnhem gained the greatest status of any of the English or Scots congregations in the Netherlands. Archer first settled with his flock in the centre of the Netherlands, in Vianen and Utrecht. They informed the alderman of Arnhem on 20 September 1638 of their desire to move to his city if suitable houses could be found for them and if they could be supplied with a building in which to hold Reformed divine service in English. The city fathers were only too glad to welcome these families and allocated the congregation the Broerenkerk to meet in. This congregation was the only English church in the Province of Guelders that was not formed of military recruits.

Archer ministered to the congregation until his death *circa* 1642. He obtained the assistance of two curates during this period: Thomas Goodwin (1600–1680) from 1639–1641, and Philip Nye (1595–1672) from 1639 to 1640 or 1641. This indicates that there was a time of overlap of at least one year in which the English congregation at Arnhem had three clergymen taking it in turns to preach. All three men were inveterate

---

23  The edition lacks any identification of either printer or publisher. There were two printing/publishing firms operating in Arnhem in 1643: those of Jacob van Biesen and Jan Jacobs. Both of these are known to have published works by van Laren. A typographical comparison would establish which of the two firms was responsible for the 1643 edition. Pending the availability of any such scientific evidence, I am inclined to assume that the publication was undertaken by van Biesen: Op 't Hof [2005-2], 119.

Congregationalists. Citing this fact, Keith L. Sprunger writes that the congregation had very little to do with Dutch Reformed churches, nor even with other English churches in the Netherlands, apart from the English Church in Rotterdam, which was as strongly Independent in conviction as itself. The life of the congregation was based upon a church covenant that all members were required to sign. Every applicant for church membership was thoroughly examined before admittance. The congregation assembled twice each Sunday and held communion every Sunday. Many innovations were introduced into the life of the congregation, including the anointing of the sick, the laying-on of hands, solo singing, prophecies, and the holy kiss. In England, Archer was posthumously accused of harbouring fantastical notions about the fate of the soul after death and of holding that God was the author of sin; reason enough for the Westminster Assembly, together with Parliament, to issue a condemnation of one of his works and burn it publicly. Also, Archer and Goodwin at Arnhem were responsible for the rise of millenarian views among the English Puritans.[24]

However isolated the English congregation in Arnhem was in its Independency, van Laren's involvement with Archer's manuscript is a proof that the former at least managed to build a warm rapport with him during Archer's four or so years in the capital of Guelders. This friendship must also call into question the accuracy of the claims voiced in England that Archer was an out-and-out heretic.

*Twee god-vruchtighe meditatien* is a working-up of a pair of sermons on two different Bible texts. The first text is Luke 5:31-32—*And Jesus answering said unto them, They that are whole need not a physician; but they that are sick. I came not to call the righteous, but sinners to repentance.* The second text is John 6:35—*And Jesus said unto them, I am the bread of life: he that cometh to me shall never hunger; and he that believeth on me shall never thirst.*

The first of these sermons sets out that to feel one's sins is essential to coming to the grace of God in Christ. Archer derives two doctrinal points from the text. The first is that Christ imparts His grace to those only who are profoundly sensible of their sins and wretchedness. This wretchedness makes the wrath of God very terrible, makes sin a thing bitterer than anything else on earth, allows the subject no respite or satisfaction in worldly pursuits, makes Christ sweet and lovely above all things, and makes man small and lowly in his own sight. These are the five hallmarks of a thoroughgoing conviction of sin, a work effected by the Holy Ghost

---

24 Sprunger [1982], 226–232; Op 't Hof [2005-4].

after He has removed six hindrances to conviction: 1. ignorance; 2. slothfulness of heart; 3. the fancy that one is better than others; 4. the state of being unperturbed by affliction; 5. an unjustified appeal to God's mercy; 6. the paucity of preachers who insist upon one's having a thorough knowledge of his own sinfulness. In pastoral vein, the author offers, in the doctrine of this sermon, comfort to those who imagine themselves insufficiently humbled and those who have despaired through believing that there is no salvation with God for their own soul. He emphatically states that nothing may be posited as occurring between one's humbling before God and one's believing on Christ, such as, for instance, the claimed godly hallmark of desiring to be freed from sin more than from the punishment it entails. While some theologians classify this as part of the believer's preparation, Archer regards it as the outworking of a justifying faith that is still too weak to accept Christ. He states two differences between the humbling of the elect and that of the reprobate: the former is a permanent state, even where there is faith, and does not permit its subject to rest until the soul is united with Christ. What a humbled soul stands in need of is not so much a continued humbling, but rather faith in Christ.

Archer's second doctrinal point, which in contrast to the first is only very summarily considered, is that Christ brings to repentance all those to whom He shows mercy. In the author's view, some Biblical references to repentance concern the preparation to actual metanoia while others refer to the metanoia itself. Repentance is a turning-around of the whole man, from all sins, to the whole law of God. He who is unwilling to repent is unfit for Christ.

Archer's second sermon, on John 6:35, expounds that since Christ is the only Bread of Life, He is the sole remedy against sin. Christ is that Remedy in the union of His humanity with His godhood. As there is such a Remedy, those who feel their sins and wretchedness are not to despair, since Christ is for hungry souls alone. To develop such a hunger, one should unburden oneself of sins and of the world by considering the vanity and damage they represent, and should kindle an inner yearning for Christ by considering law and gospel.

Second, one obtains Christ by coming to Him; that is, believing in Him. On this point, Archer cites Martin Bucer[25] (1491–1551), who writes that coming to Christ is accepting Him as Saviour and trusting oneself entirely to Him. Coming to Christ is inextricably linked with trusting in Him. There is yet a much stronger trust in Christ, one founded upon the

---

25  Greschat.

knowledge of sharing personally in Him. This is the full confidence of salvation. He who accepts Christ must accept Him not partially but in all respects; not only as his Priest, but equally as his King and Prophet. The basis of belief is God's free and bountiful offer in the Gospel. This free offer must never lead to a sinful life, nor to the notion that it is easy to be saved, for to give oneself over to Christ is a supernatural deed. The devil sets two traps for mankind: the first is to imagine oneself to have faith while evincing none of the fruits of faith; the second is to work to humble oneself without believing. Archer repudiates the notion that one has to perceive something of holiness within oneself before feeling that it is safe to believe. Faith can only be grounded upon God's free promise.

Third, Archer sets out that Christ is freely available to all, on the sole condition that they believe in Him. Fourthly, he discusses the glorious fruits of faith. It is through faith that a person shares in Christ and God. Once he does so, he will no longer hunger or thirst after sin, nor after permitted worldly things, nor even after grace. There are four reasons given for this last argument: 1. grace cannot be lost; 2. the believer has received, as a gift of grace, its fulfilment in himself; 3. the believer possesses a fullness of grace as regards its components, but not as regards its degrees; 4. the believer has fulfilment in Christ. The extent of this fulfilment will be perfect in the life to come. In the application of this sermon, Archer quotes from John Calvin's[26] (1509–1564) commentary on James 2:5, which states that he who feels the lack of anything has no faith and he who has faith lacks nothing. Archer uses the image of the pail to illustrate faith: it is the pail wherewith one draws from the well of Christ and His promises.

From what van Laren reports about his treatment of the manuscript, it is evident that it was composed of notes that Archer had made in connection with two sermons that he was preparing to deliver. Archer apparently had no further designs for these papers. When he died, van Laren will have obtained the manuscript from Archer's heirs, whether or not it was the case that he solicited it. His relationship with the Englishman was obviously strong enough for him to wish to honour his memory with a publication. So it was that the manuscript was put to a use that the author himself could never have dreamt of.

After van Laren's death, his translation of Archer's work had a second edition. This printing was attended by very remarkable, if not unique, circumstance: that the Arnhem publisher Jacob van Biesen[27] (d. 1677)

---

26  Backus and Benedict.
27  Op 't Hof [2013-3], 219–234.

> **Twee Godtvruchtighe**
> # MEDITATIEN,
> **Allen Christenen ter saligheyt**
> ten hooghsten noodigh.
>
> *DE EERSTE,*
> Van 't Ghevoelen der Sonden.
>
> *DE TWEEDE,*
> Van 't Remedie tegen de Sonden.
>
> Eerst in 't Engelsch beschreven
> *Door den Wijsen, Hoogh-geleerden ende seer Godtsalighen Heer,*
> Mr. ARTHUR HILDERSHAM, **Predicant in de Provintie van Leicester.**
>
> Ende in de Nederlandtsche Sprake gebracht
> *Door*
> DANIEL van LAREN, **in sijn leben Bedienaer des H. Euangeliums tot** ARNHEM.
>
> Een seer deughdelijck Tractaet, ende daerom op 't nieuw ten driedenmael gedruckt, en van veel Druck-fauten verbetert.
>
> *Tot* ARNHEM,
>
> Gedruckt by Jacob van Biesen, Ord. Drucker
> van den Ed. Hove van Gelderlandt. In 't Jaer 1669.

attributed Archer's work to Arthur Hildersham.[28] A modernised-Dutch version of this second edition appeared in a small print run in 2010, while the following year a photographic reprint of it was brought out, also in a small quantity.[29] In other words, there is an unmistakable—if small—recent revival of interest in this work.

---

28  Op 't Hof [2013-3], 224–226.
29  Archer; Hildersham.

John Livingstone, Robert Trail, John Nevay, John Hog, James Gardiner, John Brown, *Getuygenis en verklaringe van eenighe predikanten uyt Schotlant, woonende hier te lande, tegen de opinien en practijcken van mr. Jean de Labadie en synen aenhangh: mitsgaders een kort en oprecht verhael van het danssen, kussen, en omhelsen van mr. Jean de Labadie en sijn geselschap geschiet binnen Erfort, na datse het heylige Avondtmael hadden gehouden en oock op andere tijden, uytgegeven door Jacobus Borstius*, Rotterdam, 1671

The third translated work that we shall consider begins with a jointly-written repudiation by six Scots ministers, exiled to Rotterdam, of the teachings and practices of Jean de Labadie[30] (1610–1674), the controversial French Reformed minister who had been in the Netherlands from 1666 to 1670 before establishing a house-church at Herford, Westphalia. The authors of the English original are John Livingstone (1603–1672), Robert Trail (1603–1678), John Nevay (d. 1672), John Hog (d. 1692), James Gardiner, and John Brown (1610–1679).[31]

The title page proclaims that the book was edited by the Rotterdam minister Jacobus Borstius[32] (1612–1680). From another source, we know that he was also the translator of this compendium. In the anonymous biography of him that is provided in his posthumous *Vyftien predicatien* [Fifteen sermons] (1696), we read: "The Scots brethren were motivated by a concern for the peace of the Church, and being loth to lay the affair bare before the whole world, they wrote against the schism-crazed and profiteering l'Abadie; and Borstius took on the pains of translating their work."[33]

Some details on Borstius are in order here. Born in the relatively wealthy Purmerland district of the Province of Noord-Holland on 25 July 1612, he attended the Latin schools at Haarlem and further afield at 's-Hertogenbosch before enrolling at Leiden University as a theology student on 2 February 1633, aged 20.[34] In his student years, Borstius swam

---

30   Saxby.
31   In one of his works, dating from 1684, Jacobus Koelman informs us that five of these six had already died some years previously and that four of them were not only so learned but also so godly that "all Scotland speaks of them with high esteem" (*heel Schotlant met hooge estime van haar spreekt*). He gives the names of the four whom he means by this compliment as Livingstone, Trail, Nevay and Brown: Koelman [1684], 160. As we know that Hog was still living in 1684, the fifth deceased contributor meant in the Dutchman's comment must be Gardiner. Evidently, he was a lesser-known figure and one who made less of an impression upon Koelman.
32   Exalto [1975], 141–156; Florijn [2015-2].
33   Borstius [1696], E4r.
34   *Album Studiosorum Academiae Lugduno Batavae*, 249.

into the orbit of the minister of the English Church in Leiden, Hugh Goodyear (1589/90–1661), whose godliness impressed him so greatly that he began to regard him as a second father. It was from Goodyear that he learnt his English, becoming accomplished enough to preach in the language several times later in life, in Dordrecht, Rotterdam and Leiden. Goodyear also introduced him to English devotional books, for which he acquired a lifelong taste.

In 1638, Borstius was inducted as minister of the united parishes of Wormerveer and Zaandijk in his native province. Here, he devoted his efforts to church-building. Six years later, he became minister of the major Zuid-Holland port of Dordrecht, where his eloquence ensured that the Great Church filled up hours before he was due to preach. A sermon of his on I Corinthians 11:14, printed by someone in the congregation, triggered a veritable avalanche of papers debating the proper length of men's hair, when published without his consent in 1645. Even professors joined in the mêlée. Other sermons by Borstius were published in the same period. His two-part *ars moriendi* was likewise popular, going through six editions. Borstius' Puritan sympathies yielded him a close spiritual association in Dordrecht with the minister of the city's English church, Robert Paget (d. 1684), a friendship ended only by death.

Borstius enjoyed similar cordiality with Godefridus Udemans[35] (1581/2–1649), minister of the major Zeeland port of Zierikzee and a key figure[36] in the Further Reformation. This association had been forged as far back as 1630, in 's-Hertogenbosch, capital of the southern Dutch province of Brabant, when Borstius was still a grammar school boy and Udemans had two stints as a supply preacher in the city from 1630 to 1632. Their acquaintance blossomed into close friendship in Borstius' Dordrecht years because Udemans called by regularly to oversee the printing of his writings by Dordrecht printer and publisher François Boels[37] (1591–1656). In the foreword to his published sermon on—or, rather, against—luxuriant male locks, Borstius acknowledges that he is beholden to Udemans for the latter's weighty and penetrating critique of that fad, published by Boels in 1643. Borstius adds some fulsome praise of Udemans for good measure. The fact that the two men were subsequently lumped together by society at large for fierce criticism and vituperation during the polemics on men's hair will only have served to strengthen their mutual esteem. It is telling that Udemans, shortly before his death,

---

35  Meertens; Fieret; Exalto [1989]; Schutte [1989], 301–302, 310–311; Uil [2016-2].
36  Graafland *et al.*, 171.
37  Heijting [1999, 2011].

offered Borstius during their last encounter in 1648 to act as witness at the baptism of Borstius' child, which he saw in its mother's lap.[38]

In the same year, 1648, Boels seized upon the occasion of the formal ending of the Eighty Years' War with the Habsburgs to bring out the third edition of *Timotheus*, a work by Willem Teellinck (who, as noted above, was the Father of the Further Reformation). In *Timotheus*, Teellinck warns the Reformed against going sightseeing in Roman Catholic churches or cloisters when in Roman Catholic districts.[39] It was very probably at Boels' instigation that Borstius wrote the foreword for this edition, in which he offers the following description of Teellinck:[40]

> that the Author was a most Godly Minister, quite irreproachable as to his life, even towards his very bitterest foes, who were never able to find anything shameful or scandalous about him, however much they might have manipulated and fished for just that.[41]

No fool was Boels, then, in inviting Borstius to pen the foreword! Borstius' esteem for Teellinck, his intimacy with Udemans, the contents of his writings and his close contacts with Puritans resident in the Netherlands are sufficient arguments to regard him as a representative of the Further Reformation.

Borstius moved from Dordrecht to Rotterdam in 1654. In his Rotterdam years, a range of other devotional titles appeared from his hand. The best-known is his little catechism *Kort begrijp der christelijke leere* [A brief comprehension of Christian doctrine], reprinted countless times until and including the twenty-first century and used in several Dutch Reformed denominations to this day as the basis for catechism, even appearing among the liturgical appendices to many Dutch Bibles. *Kort begrijp* was used in the mission field, too, being translated into Malay. The zenith of Borstius' publishing endeavours at Rotterdam was his trilogy of works on the Lord's Supper: *Bedenckingen en gebeden over de voorbereydinghe tot het heylige Avondtmael* [Meditations and prayers on preparation for Holy Communion] (1665). Seven years after that work, *De vermakelijke wandeling na den hemel* [The delightful path to heaven] came into circulation, as did his later much-reprinted *Verscheyde consideratieën over den tegenwoordigen toestant van ons lieve vaderlant* [Various

---

38  Op 't Hof [1987-3].
39  Op 't Hof [1978].
40  Op 't Hof [2008-1], 461, 471.
41  Teellinck [1648], *2r.

considerations regarding the present condition of our dear fatherland]. This latter work is a pro-Orange assault on John de Witt[42] (1625-1672), Grand Pensionary of Holland (the western and most powerful of the United Provinces of the Netherlands), with whom he had previously been on friendly terms while still in Dordrecht.

At Rotterdam, Borstius struck up a circle of Puritan exile acquaintances just as he had previously. These included the Englishman Thomas Cawton (1605-1659) and several Scots: Alexander Petrie (d. 1662), Robert McWard (d. 1681), Livingstone, Nevay, Trail and Brown. The last five of these deeply affected him by their piety, being Scots Covenanters driven from their native soil for the sake of their principles. They remained in Rotterdam for the rest of their lives, as the Stuart monarchy bore them no good will whatsoever. On Borstius' deathbed in 1680, a last visit paid by McWard is recorded to have cheered him greatly.

Borstius was a stalwart defender of the Covenanting cause in any way he knew how, translation being one of his contributions to the effort. It was in his translation that a Scottish church history was published in 1668, entitled *Historie der kerken van Schotland tot 1667* [History of the churches of Scotland up until 1667]. Although there is no acknowledgement in the publication itself that Borstius had done the translation, it was he and none other that made this work accessible to a Dutch readership. We can be so sure of this thanks to another Dutch translator on whom this chapter will soon focus, Jacobus Koelman[43] (1631-1695), who at one point in his prolific oeuvre identifies Borstius as the translator.[44]

In 1670, another book translated by Borstius was published: *Onderwys van het scheyden van de gereformeerde, en 't oprichten van een suyvere kercke* [Instruction in departing from the Reformed church and founding a pure church]. In the literature on Borstius, this latter work is always credited to his name, the scholars in question evidently taking their cue from the book's title page. Yet in his dedication, which is addressed to his Dordrecht colleague Henricus Dibbets[45] (1603-1673), Borstius clearly informs us that the book is a reworked translation of parts of a work by Samuel Rutherford (d. 1661), together with a translation of parts of a work by James Durham (1622-1658).[46] Livingstone had handed Borstius

---

42 Rowen; Panhuysen.
43 Krull; Van Lieburg [1990]; Meeuse [1990, 2008]; Op 't Hof [2013-1], 237-268; Groenendijk [2017].
44 Koelman [1680], 149.
45 Schotel [1841], 1: 385-389.
46 Borstius [1670], *2r.

these books with the request that he translate the sections now appearing in the work in question. Livingstone's intention, Borstius explains, had been that these extracts would be suitable reading material for warning the Dutch away from Labadism and that they would additionally help demonstrate what was wrong with the standpoints of Separatism and of Independency. Both of these translations were presented to the public by Borstius' son, the Rotterdam publisher Johannes Borstius. A second edition was published in Wesel. It was by way of a follow-up of sorts to *Onderwys van het scheyden van de gereformeerde, en 't oprichten van een suyvere kercke* that the work currently under consideration was brought out by the same publisher in 1671.

The three translations done by Borstius are expressions of how great an impression the Covenanters who had settled in Rotterdam had made upon him, particularly in their piety. There is every reason to suppose that the initiative of translating these works was actually more of a public-relations exercise by the Scots than it was a spontaneous action of his own. If the Dutch were to acquire an appreciation of the Covenanting stance and to muster sympathy for the position in which the men now found themselves in their land of exile, it was essential that an informative book should come out in Dutch to describe what had been done by the Crown to their brethren who had remained in Scotland. In Borstius, the Scots found a man both able and—perhaps after a little cajoling on their part—willing to take on the task of publication. Given the sensitivities of the subject matter (including considerable diplomatic pressure from the Stuart monarchy upon the United Provinces to extradite the Covenanter refugees), it is easy to appreciate why Borstius was not keen to leave any trace evident of his having been the translator. Koelman's letting the cat out of the bag twelve years later could do Borstius no harm; he was just deceased when the revelation was made.

The views of the Scots Covenanters appeared to be similar on many points to those of de Labadie, certainly as far as outsiders would have been concerned, and was it not de Labadie whose separatist drive had shaken not just the church but the state in the Netherlands to the core? Moreover, the Covenanters had been very sympathetic towards this Huguenot when he had arrived in Middelburg (just as the Further Reformation men had been), before he had revealed his separatist inclinations. It was to assure their position in the Netherlands, then, that the Scotsmen found it prudent to formulate and put on record their opposition to de Labadie's course. But if their plan was to succeed, they would need a translator—with Borstius, once again, fitting the bill. Given that the two translations in question could offer little offence, Borstius had no objection this time to placing his name in the editions.

The translation under consideration in this article was published in 1671 with the full title *Getuygenis en verklaringe van eenighe predikanten uyt Schotlant, woonende hier te lande, tegen de opinien en practijcken van mr. Jean de Labadie en synen aenhangh: mitsgaders een kort en oprecht verhael van het danssen, kussen, en omhelsen van mr. Jean de Labadie en sijn geselschap geschiet binnen Erfort, na datse het heylige Avondtmael hadden gehouden en oock op andere tijden. Uytgegeven door Jacobus Borstius* [Testimony and declaration of some preachers from Scotland living in this country, against the opinions and practices of M[aste]r Jean de Labadie and his followership; together with a brief and straightforward account of the dancing, kissing and embracing by M[aste]r Jean de Labadie and his fellowship that went on at Herford after they had held Holy Communion and also at other times; edited by Jacobus Borstius]. It therefore contains two separate writings. The above title is explicit enough that it was the Scotsmen who drafted the rebuttal of Labadism in the first of these tractates, but can we be sure that this applies likewise to the second? Once again, it is Koelman who illuminates the matter for us. In his above-mentioned book, after having informed the reader of the fact that he and Brown travelled to Amsterdam in June 1671 to take down a widow's eyewitness account of the scandalous goings-on in Westphalia, and that he worked this up into a written report, he adds:

> Six Scots Preachers, among them *Broun*, expressing themselves opposed to the opinions and practices, and in particular the [written] protestation and Confession, of *Labadie* and his adherents, thought it good to add thereto a brief and sincere account of the dancing, kissing, and embracing done by *Labadie* and his fellowship at *Herford*, being the same in substance, and almost [the same] in words, as I wrote there[on].[47]

We must therefore assume that the essence of the second work in this book derives ultimately from Koelman. His Scots colleagues—and here we must take our cue from Koelman's account to conceive of Brown in a leading role—thus reworded the content somewhat into their own idiom and topped and tailed it with words of their own. This information on the authorship of the work is grounds enough to allow us to regard the second work, as well as the first, as a production of the six Covenanters.

---

47 Koelman [1684], 159. My thanks to Mr Leen van Valen of Dordrecht for this detail.

> Getuygenis en Verklaringe
> Van eenighe Predikanten uyt Schotlant, woonende hier te Lande,
> Tegen de Opinien en Practijcken van
> # M.ʀ JEAN DE LABADIE
> EN SYNEN AENHANGH:
>
> Mitsgaders een kort en oprecht Verhael van het
> *Danssen, Kussen, en Omhelsen van*
> M.ʀ JEAN DE LABADIE en sijn Gesel-
> schap geschiet binnen Erfort, na datse het Heylige Avondtmael hadden gehouden en oock op andere tijden.
>
> *Uytgegeven door* JACOBUS BORSTIUS.
>
>
>
> Tot ROTTERDAM,
> By JOANNES BORSTIUS, Boeckverkooper op den hoeck van de groote Marct. 1671.

As is inevitably the case in books authored by a committee, one of them must have volunteered to be penman and assumed responsibility for the manuscript. Brown's direct involvement in making further inquiries about the events at Herford makes him the likeliest man to have performed this role. That this is so is also suggested by the order of authors' names as given in the publication: Brown's name appears last, which we may ascribe to humility on his part. It is to be assumed that from the outset, Brown produced these two manuscripts with the deliberate aim of disseminating them to the public at large by means of publication. When Borstius declared his willingness to serve as translator, Brown will have handed him the autographs of both manuscripts.

The original texts never resulted in English-language editions, so far as is known. No wonder either, as the commotion around de Labadie barely registered in British minds, let alone having any connection with England or Scotland.

The translation runs to 61 pages in quarto format; the first of the two works, by far the longer, takes up pages 3 to 53. In this first work, the writers declare that they started out entirely of one mind with de Labadie, when as yet he was showing no separatist inclinations, and that they even leapt to his defence against Dutch detractors, but that he now peddled un-Reformed views and practices. They have reached this conclusion not from hearsay but from de Labadie's own published words and from Heinrich Schlüter's book.[48] The works of de Labadie himself that they cite the most are *Protestatie nopende het oprechte geloof, de suyvere en gesonde leer, ende der algemeene orthodoxy* [Testimony concerning genuine faith, pure and sound doctrine, and general orthodoxy], Amsterdam, 1669, and *Verklaringe van de suyverheyt des geloofs* [Declaration of the purity of (the) faith], Amsterdam, 1671. On several of the points that now follow, the Scots are so cautious that they repeatedly remind the reader that de Labadie and his followers have not expressed themselves entirely unambiguously and that they would appreciate it if they were to clarify their positions further.

De Labadie teaches, they note, that the children of Christian parents are not members of the visible church and that they therefore ought not be baptised; he also deems it necessary that a schism should occur within the established church and a new denomination be set up. He gives strong cause to suspect that he wishes to preach the Word exclusively to regenerate Christians and to pastor such people only. He holds that the Church consists of the regenerate, thereby committing the error of conflating the visible church with the invisible Church. He arrogates to himself the right to judge of a person's spiritual state. In addition, while de Labadie does

---

48 A book had been published at Amsterdam in 1670 entitled: *Ken-teeckenen van de weder-geboorte. Vermeert met eenighe brieven van kerckelijcke consideratien* [Hallmarks of the new birth, supplemented by some letters on ecclesiastical considerations]. Despite what the Scots believed, however, its author was not Schlüter but Jan Backhuys. Schlüter, a ministerial candidate, had started out as a disciple of de Labadie but later distanced himself from the movement. He ensured that Backhuys' work appeared in print, giving it a Labadist framework so that de Labadie's notions would achieve broader dissemination: Van den End, 195; Saxby, 183.

preach that the covenant of grace was established with Christ, he is silent on the obligation on man, pursuant to that covenant, to believe and repent. On the other hand, he says that the believer must fulfil the covenant through the grace of Christ. Moreover, he denies that the covenant made with Abraham was the covenant of grace, and insists that the Abrahamic covenant was abolished anyway with the coming of Christ. He propounds that only the born-again belong to the new covenant and that only those who excel in grace may serve as ministers of the Gospel. It would seem, the Scots write, that de Labadie's is a doctrine that leaves no room for the children of God to bewail their continuingly sinful nature, for in his view, Christ is at all times recognisably Master in the hearts of His people.

The authors are intrigued to know whether or not de Labadie believes that a married woman who alone adheres to his congregation should not rather follow her husband's lead in where to attend worship. Or might he judge it best for her to be divorced from her husband in such a case? Another query that they have for him is whether someone should deny his blood relatives the communication of his worldly goods in order to share them exclusively with fellow Labadists. If community of goods is one of the prerequisites for joining de Labadie's church, then in this regard his arrangements are no longer any different from those of Roman Catholic cloisters. Finally, the Covenanters name a number of teachings of de Labadie's that come close to being, or are even identical with, the doctrine of the millenarians. They challenge him, in as many words, to state whether he believes that a thousand-year kingdom of peace on earth will precede the Day of Judgement. On this point, they state emphatically that only one more parousia of Christ is to be expected, namely His return in final judgement. Approaching the end of the work, the Scots conclude that many of de Labadie's views and practices are suspiciously similar to those of the Anabaptists and Antinomians. At the very end of this tractate, they warn their readers not to content themselves with externalities but to seek the kernel of the Gospel, namely Christ.

The second little work in the book, occupying pp. 54–61, provides an account of what went on after a celebration of Holy Communion, and also at other times, in de Labadie's congregation at Herford. The authors inform the reader that after the first work in the book had been translated and taken to press, one of them[49] travelled to Amsterdam with Koelman to speak to a widow who had herself been at Herford. They recount that she and other ladies who had sojourned with the Labadists had become

---

49 Namely, John Brown (see above), whose declining to name himself here is a further indication that he was the scribe of the work.

embroiled in a heated dispute with their visitors over whether the dancing practised at Herford was Biblical or not. The ladies had prayed in aid the record of David's dancing (II Samuel 6:14), but the Scotsman had retorted that we do not read of David dancing with women, much less embracing and kissing them. When the ladies then fell back on the case of Miriam leading the dance (Exodus 15:20), the minister replied that the Scripture in question was clear that this was certainly no instance of mixed dancing.

The following day during the Amsterdam visit, the Scots and Dutch ministerial duo paid a call on de Labadie's disciple Pierre du Lignon (d. 1681). The Frenchman informed them that he likewise saw no harm at all in the Labadists' practice of danced worship, and that de Labadie had taken part in it himself, as had Anna Maria van Schurman[50] (1607–1678). When, during the conversation, du Lignon mentioned de Labadie's personal approval of the dance, the Scots preacher proposed to set out his moral grievances against de Labadie in a Latin letter, on condition that du Lignon undertook to deliver it to his master in person and that he saw to it that de Labadie replied. Du Lignon was unwilling to agree to this. To conclude their account, the authors write that it still remains to be seen how the Labadists will turn out in the end.

Turning over the leaf after reaching the end of this second tractate, we find, bizarrely, an unnumbered new page announcing an appendix to the foregoing work. It bears the text: "*[Melchisédech]* Thévenot on the account of his travels in the Levant, page 102". This supplement describes the religious dance practices of Turkish dervishes!

The editorial history of the translation poses a minor conundrum. The second tractate that we have just been considering was separately published by the same publisher in the same year, in the same typeface. The crucial question is the chronology. Koelman's understanding (as cited above), namely that the Scots ministers added their account of the events at Herford to their repudiation of de Labadie's views and practices, warrants the interpretation that it was the separate edition that was second of the two versions to be published. We may posit that Borstius in his publishing capacity made the calculation that the second brief work would attract a far greater readership on its own, given its sensational nature, and that he for that reason presented the market with a separate edition of it a short while after the bundled edition in the hope of achieving a little bestseller. However, if that was his expectation, it was hardly if at all met, for only this one edition of the separate pamphlet is known.

---

50 Van Beek.

**Robert McWard, *De wekker der leeraaren*, Vlissingen (Flushing), 1674**
Our fourth translation was done by Jacobus Koelman, the then minister of Sluis in States-Flanders. Koelman's life and work may be largely left aside here, as they will be described in Volume II. He began from 1669 onwards to make more of Scots Puritanism than of its English variant. His contact with Brown in 1671, discussed above, is convincing evidence of this. Given this latter fact, we can appreciate why it was that Koelman had a translation of his published at Vlissingen in 1674 whose full title was *De wekker der leeraaren. In tijden van verval met aanwijzingh van den plight der vroome, ten goede van haer leeraars* [The ministers' alarm in times of falling-away, with mention of the duty of the godly, for the good of their teachers]. This was an octavo edition; the body of the text took up 156 pages. The original work is by McWard, a Scots Puritan, but the translator was uncertain of this at the very least, if not entirely unaware of the author's identity. Such is evident because his foreword, of no fewer than 42 pages, commences with the announcement that he once borrowed the English source-text from a pious maiden of Utrecht and that he has sought in vain to apprise himself with certainty of its authorship. For that reason, Koelman presents the work as anonymous.[51]

Four years later, a Koelman translation of a work by Hugh Binning (1627–1653) was published: *Ettelijcke gronden van de christelijcke religie* (1678), whose original title is *The common principles of the christian religion, clearly proved, and singularly improved; or, a practical catechism* (1660). In this case, Koelman sketches the life of the author before the actual translation begins.[52] He makes it clear at the outset that some of his information here is taken from details that McWard gave him in 1676. Koelman conversed with McWard several times during the course of the year that the latter was minister of the Scots Church in Rotterdam. Apart from this, Koelman adds, he later asked McWard by letter, passed via a Scots acquaintance, to write down and send him biographical details on the life and death of Binning. McWard made his best efforts to oblige, and Koelman now presents the resulting information in translation.[53]

The foregoing makes it clear that Koelman exchanged thoughts several times with McWard at Rotterdam in 1676. It can hardly be surmised that Koelman's translation *De wekker der leeraaren* did not come up in conversation on those occasions, whether we are to assume as one possibility that the translator had ascertained in the interim that McWard was

---

51 [McWard] [1674], *2r.
52 Binning [1678], 2*2r.–6*2v.
53 Binning [1678], 2*2r.–2*3r.

the author and now wished to notify him of how matters had progressed, or alternatively that McWard clarified his authorship for Koelman. Whatever the case may have been, this was the juncture at which Koelman made the personal acquaintance of a man whose book he had translated into Dutch a couple of years previously.

However, we ought not to lose sight of the fact that we do know that the biographical sketch of Binning incorporated by Koelman into *Ettelijcke gronden van de christelijcke religie* arose from the personal acquaintance with McWard that Koelman had—by that time—made. The remarkable, even unique, aspect of this section of the book is that it owes its existence to the specific request of a Dutchman and that it can only be consulted in its Dutch version. Accordingly, this biographical piece is a perfect example of the theme of this chapter.

The most striking aspect of *De wekker der leeraaren* is that any indication of the original English text ever having been published is entirely lacking. This implies that Koelman was working from a manuscript of the source-text. We are left, then, with two possibilities: either he had access to the autograph, or the lady of Utrecht had furnished him with a copy. This latter scenario is a real possibility, given the extensive practice in the seventeenth century to copy out texts—typically religious and in particular devotional texts—longhand.

As already noted, Koelman wrote a lengthy foreword to his translation. In it, besides describing how he came by the manuscript he has translated and stating that he is uncertain of its authorship, he draws the Dutch reader's attention to a biting turn of phrase used by the author. This concerns the assertion that Satan was the author of the act that obliged the use of formulaic prayers. Koelman asks that the reader understand that this very controversial turn of phrase is rooted in the English and Scottish context, for an understanding of which he recommends the reading of the Borstius-published Dutch edition of the Covenanter tract *Naphtali, or, the wrestlings of the Church of Scotland*, which he cites as "*Naphthali, ofte de worstelingen van Scotlandt &c. ofte Historie der Kerken van Schotlandt tot het jaar 1667, gedruckt tot Rotterdam by Ioh. Borstium*"[54]. Koelman also seeks in the foreword to recast for the reader the contents of the manuscript in his own compelling words, with reference to the discussion of the necessity of addressing shortcomings in the church as presented in Willem Teellinck's Further Reformation blueprint, *Noodwendigh vertoogh* [Necessary exposition] (1627)[55].

---

54 [McWard] [1674], *2v.–*3r.
55 [McWard] [1674], 4*1r.

# De Wekker der LEERAAREN.

### In tijden van Verval

Met

Aanwijzingh van den plight der Vroome, ten goede van haer Leeraars.

Voorgestelt in een BRIEF, eerst in 't Engels Beschreven / door een yveraar Godts;

### En Vertaalt

Door JAKOBUS KOELMAN, Die- naar van de Heere Jesus in sijn Gemeynte tot Sluys in Vlaanderen

Tot VLISSINGEN,

Gedruckt by Abraham van Laren, Or- dinaris Stadts-drucker op de Beurs 1674.

The work proper begins with McWard's pronouncement that many preachers are not shaking sinners out of their soul-slumber by suspending them above the pits of hell, and that they are not comforting tormented souls aright by sending them to Jesus. McWard brings this complaint to life largely by causing such a character to level two accusations from beyond the grave against this type of preacher: that he was prepared to let him go to hell with a false heaven in his imagination, and that due to this, the preacher himself seriously risks following him in his fate. A preacher unacquainted with either hell or heaven will not be much loss to hell, nor much of an enrichment of heaven. He ought to know for himself the terrors of hell and the sweetness of communion with God in Christ. Yet many ministers give cause to suspect that they have no experimental knowledge of these matters. They are, McWard adds, neglecting to preach the solemnities of the law, particularly where members of high social status are concerned. They are serving dying congregants dishonestly. For ten pages of the translation, McWard lets his character of the soul on the way to perdition heap reproach after reproach upon unfaithful preachers. The guilty servants are called upon by the author to preach earnestly and Biblically; to build their study-chamber above the clouds in heaven; to represent Jesus in His loveliness such that their hearers will feel that He is their souls' Beloved; to pray zealously for the assistance of the Holy Ghost while preparing their sermons and, being so prepared, to touch hearts; and finally to declare law and Gospel accurately to their various hearers.

Having preached, the minister should ensure that he does not negate his own words through his manner of life; that he prays, meditates and looks for fruit from the preaching; and that he will weep and make supplication if he sees that there is little or no fruit. It is at this point that McWard sets off his tirade against the use of the Book of Common Prayer, as follows. He who uses those formularies to pray will have to ditch his Bible when he preaches. The use of set prayers quenches the Spirit. The advocates of formulaic prayer often persecute those who seek God more earnestly than they themselves do. Satan was the author of the act that obliged the use of formulaic prayers. He who prays coldly will not preach warmly.

Godly ministers pray and fast for their hearers in secret, too, and set a good example in their manner of life. The author urges ministers to be faithful about their pastoral visitations and to keep up the same methods here as in the pulpit. To highlight the urgency of the matter, he sketches the character of a terrified sinner under conviction of the wrath of God and causes him to address a lackadaisical minister in earnest, emotional terms. McWard then writes against the use of the church calendar. The feast days are of human invention, for Christ never instituted them. What is more, they are of Roman origin. Many preachers who in theory would take the point that the church ought not to celebrate any feast days nevertheless preach on those days in practice.

Next, the author addresses the hearers of preaching. He states in emphatic terms that he is not setting out to alienate them from preaching or to put it about that there are no faithful ministers left whatsoever. It is, however, his conviction that there are very few left, and it is to be feared that God in His righteous anger will further reduce that remnant, for faithful preachers of Christ are now suffering persecution. Congregation members are then urged to bear in mind that even the best of preachers have their flaws and their sins. Having set out this as his background, the author calls upon congregations to see to two things.

Firstly, congregations ought to warn their preachers of their faults and sins and punish those that they see, but cautiously, agreeably and with a great deal of respect for their office, and while also confessing their own guilt. Secondly, they must play their part in helping their preachers by coming to church hungry and thirsty, by putting what they have heard into practice, and by encouraging faithful ministers. On the first of those points, just as if a suckling child drinks poorly its mother's breasts will dry up, so it is in spiritual matters between a preacher and his hearers. The more spiritual hunger and thirst, the more the Lord will grant spiritual gifts to the preacher in his ministration, even if he started with only five loaves and two fishes. Faithful preachers need encouragement, because: they are at all times subject to the attacks and temptations of the devil; they come to experience how little they know of God; and they are often persecuted by civil government and briefed against by carnal pulpiteers who are keen to make them out to be enthusiasts. Even if congregants are mocked for it, they ought to travel serious distances to hear preachers who are anointed with the Spirit of God.

Next, McWard laments how many preachers are opposed to conventicles and even submit requests to the civil power to break up such conventicles. On this point, he spends two pages describing how a preacher spoke on Matthew 5:6 at such a meeting—*Blessed they which do hunger and thirst after righteousness: for they shall be filled.* Another subject he touches upon here is the ethos and content of the theological training given at universities. These courses are so unspiritual and at odds with godliness that McWard calls them a plague upon the church. The universities are churning out candidate ministers who deny the moral nature of the Fourth Commandment, who claim Christian liberty in its place, and who accuse those who pursue holiness of being unduly precise.

The author charges his readers to make much intercession for the few faithful servants of God that there are. Many ministers preach toothlessly because they have never known the power of the Word for themselves. Congregants are to pray for the Spirit to be with their ministers, that they would be taught in the heavenly academy. Intercession should above all be made for preachers who encourage conventicles. The intercession ought to focus on the sermons and prayers that the preachers utter. The prayer-book should be prayed out of their hands. Once all these steps have been taken, the congregations must wait upon the Spirit of God. They should regard the preached word as if it were spoken by God Himself. Even in cases where preachers have no experimental knowledge of the Word that they are expounding, it is still the Word of God.

We may make the following remarks about McWard's manuscript on the basis of what is known to us. The content of the text is such that McWard will not have intended it for personal use. However, he appears to have lacked the resources (possibly financially) to have the work published. Those of his friends who had interest in the work will have made copies. One of these was lent to Koelman by the pious woman of Utrecht. However, it appears that she was at such a remove from McWard that she was not able to supply Koelman with the name of the author. McWard will have been far more astonished that his work appeared in Dutch translation courtesy of Koelman than that the Dutchman had managed to ascertain that he was its author.

In 1680, Koelman asked the favour that McWard's work be republished, but even after his death, it was necessary to publish an average of two new editions per century, so that there are currently nine Dutch editions known. The Rotterdam publisher of the third edition (1733), Hendrik van Pelt[56] (1704-1773), appended to the text of *De wekker der leeraaren* the text of another Koelman work: *Neerlandts ondergang, gedreigt, en naby* [The Netherlands' fall threatened and at hand]. Petrus Henricus Dorsius (b. 1711), the editor, wrote its dedication to Maarten Vlaardingerwoud, former alderman of Rotterdam, in that city on 4 June 1733. In this dedication, Dorsius states that many faithful ministers not only saw God's judgements coming but that they had warned of them both from the pulpit and in print. McWard and Koelman were such ministers, sound in doctrine and godly and exemplary in life. He adds that it is because he knows Vlaardingerwoud will take the content of both works to heart that he has dedicated this edition to him.

---

56  Op 't Hof [2016-8].

Two years later, in 1735, Dorsius enrolled as a theological student at the University of Groningen, and in 1736 he continued his studies by matriculating at Leiden.[57] After graduation, he departed for Pennsylvania, where he served as a minister of the Gospel, before returning to his homeland later. The van Pelt edition of 1741 calls itself on its title page the fifth edition. This makes it most probable that van Pelt himself had brought out the fourth edition some time between 1733 and 1741. Two further editions were brought out in the latter half of the twentieth century: one *circa* 1970 and one in 1996. The first was a reprint of the 1733 edition. The Dutch text of the second was modernised by T. Benschop of Lopik in the Province of Utrecht, the whole being preceded by a foreword of recommendation by the minister of the Netherlands Reformed Congregation at Yerseke in Zeeland, Christiaan van den Poel, dated April 1997 [sic!]. If we include the non-extant fourth edition in our count, we arrive at ten editions.

For the sake of completeness, we may add finally that Koelman's foreword was issued separately in a rewritten and updated form during the Dutch ecclesiastical upheavals of 1834, under the title *Gedachten over den toestand van vele hervormde leeraren* [Thoughts on the condition of many Reformed ministers].[58] This was the year in which the first batch of conservative believers, known in Dutch parlance as *orthodox-gereformeerden*, left the Reformed Church. It is beyond question that this edition was directly occasioned by the schism of 1834, known in Dutch as the *Afscheiding* [Secession]. As an additional detail, the publisher of this pamphlet version was T.E. Mulder[59] of Veendam in the north-eastern province of Groningen. Mulder was a former sea-captain and one of the regular publishers used by Hendrik de Cock[60] (1801–1842), the leader of the *Afscheiding* in the northern provinces of the country, where it had much of its initial momentum and met stiff opposition from magistrates and churchmen.[61] De Cock himself, then, was probably behind the republishing of Koelman's foreword.

Of the four translations considered thus far of works whose original English texts were almost certainly never published, this work of McWard enjoyed the most extensive and lasting influence. Indeed, its success was

---

57 *Album Studiosorum Academiae Groninganae*, 184; *Album Studiosorum Academiae Lugduno Batavae*, 963.
58 Meeuse [2008], 107; Imminkhuizen, 56 no. 430.
59 Van der Laan, index.
60 F.L. Bos.
61 Van der Haar [1984], 61.

far greater than has been related until now. Koelman could never have imagined it, but his translation of McWard was onward-translated from Dutch into no fewer than three other languages. At least as important as this is the fact that all three onward translations were done in the context of another confession, namely Lutheranism.

Firstly, the Lutheran rector of Tüttleben near Gotha in Thuringia, Georg Michael Laurentius, a Pietist, rendered Koelman's translation of McWard's work into German at the turn of the eighteenth century. The resulting book was printed by the press of the renowned orphanage in Halle (the German centre of Lutheran Pietism) that had recently been founded by the prominent Lutheran clergyman August Hermann Francke[62] (1663–1727). It made such an impact in Lutheran circles that it was twice reprinted by the orphanage press, in 1711 and 1712 respectively.[63] In 1753, the German version of the work saw the light of day for the fourth time, now as a component of *Drey geistreiche Schrifften* [Three spirit-rich works] by the Lutheran Pietist Theophilus Großgebauer[64] (1627–1661).

Laurentius' translation not only had a wide readership in Germany but also permeated abroad. The close relations between the centre of German Lutheran Pietism and Danish Lutheran Pietists account for the fact that a Danish onward translation was brought out at Copenhagen in 1740. Its translator is unknown, but the fact that this is a publication of the university printer and publisher Jacob Preusses is an indication that this was an officially-prepared edition and that the church hierarchy wished to use the translation to improve the spirituality of Danish Lutheran preaching.[65] Another Danish edition was published in 1853. In the same century, a Swedish onward translation of Laurentius' Danish version was put into circulation. It appeared in the name of Peter Lorenz Sellergren[66] (1768–1843), the revivalist Lutheran rector of Hälleberg in the diocese of Växjö. This richly gifted man had experienced a Pietist conversion while already in Gospel ministry and had since played a major role in the renewal of Lutheran Pietism in southern Sweden. He stood consciously in the piety traditions of Johann Arndt[67] (1555–1621), Philipp Jakob Spener[68] (1635–1705) and Francke. Under the influence of the Herrnhuter Brethren, he progressively became less legalistic and more evangelical during his life.

---

62 Beyreuther; Obst.
63 Van der Haar [1997], 167 nos. 7–9.
64 Strom, 195–221; Van de Kamp [2016], 267–277.
65 Huisman [2008], 218–219, 242b–243a; [2009-2], 144–145, 175.
66 Stenvall; Laasonen, 333.
67 Schneider.
68 Grünberg; Wallmann.

### Robert Fleming, *Josuaas verkiesinge*, 1683

The final translation that we shall consider is of a work by Robert Fleming senior (1630–1694), a Scots Presbyterian who succeeded McWard as minister of the Scots Church in Rotterdam in 1677. Unlike his predecessor, Fleming did not assume an inimical stance against Charles II of Scotland and England. He gave account of his political opinions in 1681 in a publication levelled against the extreme views of his brother minister Brown, who had also served the Scots Church in Rotterdam, albeit briefly and in the capacity of an assistant minister.

It was in 1683 that the Dutch translation of Fleming, entitled *Josuaas verkiezinge; ofte de geresolveerde christen* [Joshua's choice, or the resolute Christian], was published. The work draws on Joshua 24:15—*And if it seem evil unto you to serve the LORD, choose you this day whom ye will serve; whether the gods which your fathers served that [were] on the other side of the flood, or the gods of the Amorites, in whose land ye dwell; but as for me and my house, we will serve the LORD.* The published *Josuaas verkiezinge* comprises 307 pages of text in octavo format. It is an obscure edition: it lacks a printer's name, publisher's name and even place of publication. However, we may infer from the fact that Fleming lived and ministered in Rotterdam, and that those to whom the work was dedicated also resided there, that this was the city in which the book was written and published. There is no indication whatsoever that Fleming spoke Dutch, so the work must be understood as a translation of an English original. Here again, then, we have to do with an original unknown as a publication,[69] hence the inclusion in this chapter of Fleming's work. Nothing in the published text mentions a translator even tangentially, so anything written regarding the identity of such will inevitably be speculative. It can at least be noted that the translation is of poor quality: the meaning of the Dutch is on occasion hard or impossible to grasp. This most probably indicates that it was a Scot who translated Fleming's work.

The authorial dedication is dated 15 August 1683 and is addressed to Herman van Zoelen[70] (1636–1702), director of the Dutch East India Company; Willem Schepers[71] (1620–1704), Lieutenant-Admiral of the

---

69 Steven gives as the title of the original: "*Joshua's Choice: or the confirmed Christian*, 1684. This was previously printed the same year at Amsterdam, in Dutch": Steven, 111. However, not a trace can be found of a work entitled *Joshua's Choice*. Given that Steven's information on the publication of the translation is out by one year, we may posit that his assertion as to the original published English text is likewise founded upon a misconception.

70 Engelbrecht, 209–210.

71 Engelbrecht, 230.

Admiralty College at Rotterdam; Jacob Muys de Brauw[72] (1636–1702); and Adriaan Boon[73] (1653–1718), director of the Dutch West India Company, and additionally to the aldermen and councillors of Rotterdam. The dedication expresses Fleming's gratitude for all the kind favours he has received from the men. The work itself is an amplified book version of several sermons that Fleming had preached to his congregation.

Following the dedication, we encounter a lengthy foreword, running to several dozen pages. Both here and in the body of the tractate itself, the author writes largely in the first person singular, lending a personal touch to the overall work. The contents of the foreword are as follows. The author laments sorely that, 1,600 years into the progress of the Gospel, most people seem not to dare trust the veracity of Scripture. He states his six aims as being to demonstrate that: 1. the experience and practice of piety brings about assurance; 2. faith is characterised by the certainty of the Word of God; 3. true faith consists in a knowledge of the truth and a sure confidence; 4. any rejection or making light of Christ's own testimony springs not from the man's intellect but from his will; 5. sincere Reformed faith is not self-serving but works exclusively in the service of God; 6. the Roman Catholic doctrine that one can never be assured of one's salvation is to be repudiated.

Fleming goes on to state four premises: 1. that there is now more cause than ever to expect a great falling-away from Christian faith, for it is to be feared that most Christians are unregenerate; nevertheless, Rome is beginning to fall and spiritual dawn has already broken; 2. that there is more atheism in the present day than ever before; 3. that many, under the influence of Socinianism, are exalting their intellects above revelation; and 4. that people typically confess the Christian faith outwardly without being able to explain the faith to others, and concomitantly that an assent to the truth does not in and of itself constitute that faith which unites the believer with Christ. He then writes that the condition of the church and of religion necessitates the taking of the following series of steps. Firstly, instead of disputations and dissensions, a simple little book ought to be drafted and published to discuss and prove the first principles of the Gospel without speculation or quibbling. Fleming judges that it would be preferable for such a booklet not to be bundled together with other catechisms. Secondly, a work ought to be brought out that will set out the necessity of a Holy Ghost-worked experimental familiarity with the truth.

---

72 Engelbrecht, 253–254.
73 Engelbrecht, 253.

Thirdly, Fleming urges that a book of remembrance be composed to recount God's mighty deeds in history since Christ. Fourthly, he calls upon his readers to desist from unedifying arguments and disagreements within the church, and instead to bear witness to God's wondrous providences concerning her.

In the next section of his foreword, Fleming identifies several reasons why many Christians doubt the veracity of the Christian faith. The first of these is that it is supposedly difficult to defend the credibility of the Reformed religion: citing Martin Bucer, the author argues that on the contrary, the believer's obligation is always to proclaim Christ with all boldness. The second reason given is that the church will overcome great tribulations and persecutions. The third is that God often refrains from immediately punishing ungodliness. The fourth consists of the consideration that whereas popery and the Saracen are making progress in great strides, the church is being riven by partisanships. The author proceeds to refute that latter consideration, using the following six arguments: 1. the Spirit of God prophesied the power of the Ottoman Empire in Revelation 9:14 ("the four angels which are bound in the great river Euphrates"); 2. the same Scripture accounts for the reason behind the Turks' power, namely their committing the idolatry of image-worship with the antichrist; 3. the rise of Mohammed in the Orient was coeval with the Occidental development that the Pope manifested himself as antichrist, and that this correlation answers to the quick succession in the Book of Revelation of the fifth trumpet judgement (the stinging locusts arising from the smoke of the fallen star) by the sixth trumpet judgement (the 200 million horsemen); 4. both popery and Mohammedanism originate in a falling-away from the truth of the Gospel, both refuse to have their doctrinal claims subjected to a testing by the Word of God, and both inflict violence and cruelty to perpetuate their religion; 5. Revelation 9:14 teaches that popery and Mohammedanism are instruments for the execution of God's judgement on the earth; 6. the fact that Christ is acknowledged in the Qur'ān as a great prophet proves the truth of Christianity.

Scripture thus warrants the expectation that the church has a future. The author refrains, however, from outlining that positive future in specific terms.

The foreword is followed by an appendix, in which Fleming feels obliged by his own sentiments, as well as by the requests of others, to defend the nonconformist position. Their standpoints are almost universally misrepresented and the assertion is being made that they depart at fundamental points from the Reformed, or that their doctrine brings nothing but disorder. The behaviour of certain figures in Scotland has provoked the latter accusation. The culprits Fleming has in mind are those of the radical Presbyterian party.

Fleming sets out the following fundamentals of nonconformism: 1. everything in it is subject to Scripture as the sole standard; 2. a private person has no right to arrogate to himself the powers proper to the civil magistracy, to corroborate which doctrine he cites Martin Luther (1483–1546); 3. it is not out of fear but for conscience sake that temporal government should be afforded all reasonable honour and obedience; 4. the supreme lordship of Christ will never have to defend itself against the authority of civil government; 5. those who concur on the fundamentals of the truth are not at liberty to separate from each other; 6. church discipline is always to be exercised congregationally, never privately; 7. church authority ought to be exercised in such a way as to be of service and to be spiritual; 8. sanctification is characterised by cautious considerateness and by edification of one's neighbour, without doing down the truth; 9. on secondary issues, the believer must make himself the least among his brethren; 10. truth will only stand by virtue of its mighty working upon souls.

Rounding off his foreword, Fleming bewails three current developments: 1. the calumnies being poured out upon the nonconformists, even by the Reformed; 2. the apparent determination that men have not only to bring about schism within the church but also to sow discord between church and state; 3. the insistence upon despising the nonconformists despite the following considerations: a) even their detractors are obliged to concede that they are zealous and sincere Christians both in matters of doctrine and in their living; b) they seek to be exercised above all else in the most essential points of Christianity, and in secret individual communion with God; c) they try to maintain peace with all men, insofar as is possible; d) the extent of the disputes over nonconformism is being exaggerated, which is having the effect of splitting the Reformed church at a time when popery is engaged in a scathing assault.

In the body of the work, Fleming draws two doctrines out of his Bible text: 1. it is no easy thing for a person to take a stand determining to serve the Lord and to embrace the confession of the truth; 2. confirmation in the truth must be preceded by earnest testing and a carefully-weighed decision.

The author argues that the following matters must be examined in order to arrive at a better familiarity with assurance of the truth: 1. the nature of assurance and what great store God sets by it; 2. the plainly-seen confirmation of assurance; 3. the inward excellences of the truth; 4. the greatness of experiencing the truth of the Gospel; 5. the role of the Gospel

# JOSUAAS VERKIESINGE;

## Ofte de geresolveerde

# CHRISTEN,

Na sijn *grondig ondersoeck* en *beproevinge der waerheit.*

Waer in de weg getoont word om in dese bekommerlijcke tijden, met kennisse ende versekeringe des Gemoeds, God te dienen ende hem na te volgen.

*Voorgestelt uyt JOSUÆ Cap.* 24. *vers* 15.

Door

R. FLAMINIUS,

Bedienaer des H. Euangeliums in de Schotse Gemeente tot ROTTERDAM.

Doe naderde Elia tot den gantschen Volcke, en seyde: Hoe lange hinkt gy op twee gedachten? Soo de Heere God is, volget hem na; en soo 't Baal is, volget hem na: maer het Volk antwoorde hem niet een vvoord. 1 Koning. 18: 21.

Dese vvaren edelder dan die te Thessalonica vvaren, als die het Woord ontfingen met alle toegenegentheyt, ondersoeckende dagelijks de Schriften of dese dingen alsoo vvare. 1. Actor. 17: 11.

Gedrukt in 't Jaer 1683.

as the power of God unto salvation; 6. the conflicts of the Gospel; 7. the earnest of salvation and the first fruits of heavenly glory; 8. the perceptible revelation of the reality of hell; 9. the fact that there are now more attestations to the truth of the Gospel than there were in the early centuries of Christianity.

Under point 1 of the above considerations, Fleming states that assurance is grounded not upon an audible voice from heaven but upon the truth of the Word. Most often, faith has to live upon the promises alone. Under point 2, he states that all the Messianic promises and foreshadowings are fulfilled in Christ. The author writes under point 3 that truth renews the believer and that communion with God humbles people to receive an inner peace and liberty as well as causing them to lead a godly life such as will be thought upon even after their death. Under point 4, Fleming explains that there is no extraneous cause for the consolations that the Christian feels, that the Christian rejoices in afflictions, that he experiences a spiritual peace and that his prayers are heard. He also points to acts of God that are inexplicable from natural causes, to the testimonies of His dying children, and to the unanimity of witness voiced by God's children in all times and places. Under the fifth point, the author argues from the fact that the Kingdom of God grows in the face of every repression; emphasises that this growth is solely due to the Spirit of God and His power; outlines how, through the Gospel, people turn away from ungodliness and idolatry and willingly take upon them Christ's yoke, not even shirking from martyrdom. Under point 7, he declares with reference to deathbed testimonies that the Christian's spiritual growth, peace and joy are his earnest of future glory. Under the eighth point, Fleming dwells upon the realities of the consequences of earthly sin, of the witness of conscience (such as upon one's deathbed), of blasphemies, and of severe punishments that God visits upon people in earthly life. Under the ninth and final of these points, he sketches the great extent of the church, her long continuance in spite of the power of antichrist, and the fact that the Gospel has penetrated nearly every corner of the whole world.

Fleming's third lesson from the Bible text is that one ought to serve God. He considers, in sequence, the quality and easiness of this service and particular motives for such service. Service of God flows from newness of life; it largely concerns the inner man; and it sets its sights upon Christ, Who is both its Fountain and its Example. This service is a labour of love and has the promise of eternal glory. The motives that Fleming names are the glorious fruits of the service of God.

His fourth lesson is that one must seek the welfare of one's neighbour. Joshua was keen to bring his household, as a father and lord, and his people, as a magistrate, to a service of the Lord. Every person is obliged to use the gifts he enjoys to extend the Kingdom of God, but sadly this is little exercised. Fleming calls upon the Reformed to recommend their Reformed faith to Roman Catholics: in doing so, they must eschew fleshly and political aids as well as scholastic habits of reasoning, merely giving a simple account of the hope that is in them. This duty is the more incumbent upon the Reformed because the Roman Catholics are out to lead the Reformed astray through their Congregation for the Propagation of the Faith and because now is still the time in which the Lord is saving people from the clutches of Rome. The author urges the Reformed to dispense with their internal disagreements and apply themselves concertedly to this aim. He also expresses the wish that the Reformed would spread the Gospel among Jews, both in the Netherlands and in countries where Dutchmen were engaged in trade. After all, there is a promise of a future conversion of the Jews. In the third place under this lesson, Fleming insistently urges mission among the heathen. The discovery of new continents, and the new trade, has smoothed the way for such mission. The opportunity is certainly present, given that the Christian government of the Netherlands not only permits mission but even itself engages therein.

Christians ought to bear witness to God's providences, particularly to their descendants. The author praises the habit of keeping a journal of personal spiritual experiences. One's deathbed is an outstanding opportunity to bear witness. God's wondrous deeds in history, including church history, are eminently worthy of being proclaimed and documented, too. Fleming concedes that tomes of church history and of martyrdoms already exist, but is of the opinion that it is highly desirable that a book would appear that described the miraculous ways in which God had led His church, as a counterpoint to atheism.

One of the chief ways in which God can be served is in prayer. Fleming cites the advice of Albertus Crantzius (1448–1517) to his fellow-monk Luther: "Brother, repair to your cell and say, 'O Lord, have mercy on me.'" The power of the church reposes especially in prayer and intercession: it is high time that men stood in the breach. Fleming describes four breaches that need prayerful filling: 1. indifference; 2. speaking ill of the truth; 3. schisms within the national church; 4. a general lukewarmness among the proponents of the truth. Under point 1, he quotes a Christian author of some centuries earlier who stated that while the early church strove to bring the world to Christianity, the only zeal left nowadays is to bring Christianity to the world. This inversion brings God's judgement over those who so act. The author quotes Elizabeth I's secretary of state, Sir Francis Walsingham (d. 1590), in this regard. Under point 2, Fleming urges his readers to live a consecrated and careful life, giving no occasion for schism in the church. Point 3 contains his warning that Christians should make for concord in matters fundamental to the faith, and act cautiously and meekly in cases of disagreement, restricting themselves to Scriptural expressions. On this point, he cites Philip Melanchthon (1497–1560): "I seek not my own honour, but the truth." In the next section, in which Fleming urges the necessity of witnessing, he again mentions Luther. He also writes that he was pleasantly surprised when he heard that a good friend of his renowned for his godliness, since deceased, had banded together with likeminded persons to spread the knowledge of Christ via a proto-mission that he calls a "planting abroad".[74] Personally, Fleming expects a great extension of the Kingdom of God in the future.

Fleming then derives from the Bible text the doctrine that one must first be firmly grounded in the truth before being able to confess it. He believes that it is now harder to make people into confessors of the truth than it was in centuries past to convert the heathen: no false religion has such lukewarm people as the Reformed Church counts among its adherents. The new birth is indispensable to being a Christian; moreover, the believer must distinguish himself from the world in his life and actions. There can only be said to be a firm grounding in the truth where one has first earnestly examined one's own mind; where the accepting of the truth was not first prompted by an external motive; and where the glorious matters of the Lord are sealed in power to the soul. A sincere embracing of the truth yields many wonderful fruits, such as peace in the soul; a gladness in well doing; assurance in tribulations and in the face of death; and even riches.

Fleming teaches that the present day is a time in which the Lord is allowing His judgement to fall upon the Reformed churches and in which men can more easily be diverted into error than kept within the bounds of confession of the truth. The fact that the Church of God is under almost universal persecution is a proof that judgement begins at the house of God (I Peter 4:17). Yet Satan has but a short time left, the author adds.

Before proceeding to give his defences of the truth of the Reformed confession, Fleming sets out the following eight considerations. 1. despite all the disagreements on secondary issues, there is still only one saving faith; 2. he who admits of the existence of God is also bound to acknowledge the truth of Christianity; 3. the truth is revealed in the Holy

---

74 This may be a reference to the Frankfurter Kompanie, which founded a Christian colony in Pennsylvania and whose aims were advocated by Benjamin Furly of Rotterdam: Hull; Deppermann, 329.

Scriptures; 4. Scripture makes it plain that there must be an antichrist; 5. the matters of contention between the Reformed and Roman churches are unbridgeable; 6. he who has no part experimentally in the Reformed faith can make no fitting confession thereof; 7. the dispute between the Roman and Reformed churches is of momentous importance; 8. the Reformed faith is the same today as ever she was.

The author now provides his six reasons why the Reformed faith, and not the Roman Catholic, is the truth. His first reason is Scripture itself. The second is a juxtaposition of various characteristics proper to the Reformed faith, such as that nothing is kept from the common people; that it is a faith that abases man and exalts God; that Christ is the only Foundation; that sin is not excused; that it avails itself not of violence but of reason to convince men; and that peace, not distress, is its effect in men. The third reason he gives is that the Roman Catholic religion shuts off the intellect. The fourth reason is that the characteristics of the true church are set out in Scripture. Fifthly, God has in the Reformation freed His own church from the power of antichrist. Among the men whom the author counts here as forerunners of the Reformation are Regiomontanus[75] (1436-1476), Rudolphus Agricola[76] (1443-1485), Wessel Gansfort[77] (1419-1489), Petrus Mosselanus (1493-1524) (whose dying words he quotes), Capnie (d. 1521) and Desiderius Erasmus[78] (d. 1536). He proceeds to relate some of the events of the Reformation from the church history of Johan Hendrik Hottingerus (1620-1667), from *Geneva restituta* [Geneva restored] by Friedrich Spanheim[79] (1632-1701), and from *III boecken van de vier monarchien: XXVI boecken van den staat der religie ende gemeijne welvaert onder keyser Carel V* [Three books on the four monarchies; 26 books on the state of religion and general welfare under Emperor Charles V] by Johannes Sleidanus[80] (1506-1556). As his sixth reason, Fleming describes the glorious condition of the Reformed church since the Reformation. She withstood gruesome persecutions to assert her existence in a number of countries between 1521 and 1560[81]: Germany, France, Switzerland, the Netherlands, Denmark, Sweden, England and Ireland. The author considers in some detail the salutary warning

---

75 Mett.
76 Akkerman and Vanderjagt.
77 Akkerman *et al.*
78 Van Ruler and Verbrugh.
79 Nauta [1983-2].
80 Kess.
81 He may have chosen 1560 as his cut-off point because it was the year of the official Reformation of his homeland.

provided by the life of the renowned Italian renegade, Franciscus Spira (1502-1548). Fleming believes that there have been three miraculous periods in history: 1. the Exodus and entry into the Promised Land; 2. the expansion of Primitive Christianity; 3. the growth of the Reformed churches since the Reformation. His seventh reason derives from God's dealings with each of the national Reformed denominations. He begins his review with Bohemia, quoting the testimonies of the Roman Catholic authors Aeneas Silvius, the later Pope Pius II[82] (1404-1464) and the Italian humanist Poggius[83] (1380-1459), before surveying the progress of the Reformed cause in France, England, Scotland and the Netherlands. The eighth and final reason that Fleming provides is the unspiritual, cunning and Satanic attacks perpetrated on the Reformed faith by the church of Rome. In tracing these, he mentions Pierre Jurieu[84] (1637-1713), who since 1682 had been an immediate preaching colleague of his as minister of the French Reformed congregation at Rotterdam.

In order to determine whether the Roman or Reformed confession is the true religion, one should compare them both with the doctrine of the apostolic church; discern which principles are the most useful for the propagation and defence of the Christian faith; and consider which confession can best refute atheism, and which of the two is more comforting at the hour of death. Fleming then cites several examples of a Christian deathbed faced with assurance, citing, *inter alia*, a work by Melchior Adam (d. 1622). The figures he names are Jacobus Bergerus (d. 1602), John Selden (1584-1654), Francis Bacon (1561-1626), Hugo de Groot[85] (1583-1645), John Wilmot, Earl of Rochester (d. 1680), Olympia Fulvia Moreta (1526-1555), and an unnamed high-born Englishwoman.

Fleming concludes his work with a postscript, in which he first describes the execrable present state of the Reformed churches: 1. only a few Christians are able to give a personal testimony of the truth; 2. only a few Christians trust to the Lord for their earthly life; 3. not many Christians are earnestly engaged in the things that make for their everlasting peace; 4. there are few evidences of the Holy Ghost at work in those who confess Christianity; 5. many Christians feel no need of experience; 6. few Christians communicate of their goods to others. He proceeds to set out that the church of Rome is determined to bring down the Reformed churches. Finally, Fleming offers the following six encouragements: 1. no

---

82 Ady.
83 Walser.
84 Knetsch.
85 Nellen.

religion banishes the fear of death like Reformed Christianity; 2. the author, following Calvin, regards God's past judgements executed upon the enemies of His church as entailing promises of future aid; 3. Rome's fall is sure; 4. every instance of redemption of the church since the Reformation has been preceded by a nadir—a. Philip II (1527–1598) and the Duke of Alva (1507–1582), b. Bloody Mary (1516–1558), c. the loss of the Palatinate and Bohemia; 5. there are yet more to be ushered in to the multitude of those that are saved; 6. even if believers balk at devoting their lives to the truth, deliverance will arise for the church from another place.

Even after this conclusion, Fleming provides 48 further succinct theses congruent with the foregoing contents of his work.

It is anything but a pleasant and easy task to peruse this work. The structure of its argument is rather involved; logic is lacking in the flow of propositions; and there is no shortage of repetition of certain of the author's insights and thoughts. All in all, then, the book is a wearying read. It is, however, clear that the subjects covered in the work are entirely consistent with those of Fleming's published English works.

It can hardly be surmised that a work such as this was not intended by its author for publication. The fact that it nevertheless failed to appear in print in the original presumably has to do with an inability to find any publishers who regarded an English edition as a profitable undertaking. Fleming must have had recourse to translation of the work as a matter of necessity. The resulting Dutch publication is unlikely to have had much, if any, diffusion outside Rotterdam. Moreover, the fact that only one extant copy is known at the time of writing this article implies that the print run was not extensive, and the consideration that that copy has remained in Rotterdam to this day is an indication of the geographical limitations of its dissemination.

## Conclusions

In the history of books in general, it is a remarkable event when it appears almost certain that a given manuscript was never laid to press but that it nevertheless achieved prominence through translation into another language. Since this did occur in the work of translators who made seventeenth-century Puritan works accessible to their monoglot Dutch countrymen, this fact alone would suffice to make their translations a highly interesting and compelling field of inquiry.

There are various reasons why there were six Puritan manuscripts that are known only as five translations. As a first consideration, there was a great plethora of translations of Puritan writings overall in the seventeenth century. The digital bibliographical repository Pietas reveals the total number of such translations fairly accurately: currently, 382 translations are known. Given that total figure, the number of five such exceptional cases is not so remarkable as it would be if the set of all known translations were smaller.

Second, and more significantly, the six manuscripts in question indicate the existence of a very close relationship between the authors and their translators. Teellinck spent at least nine months in 1605 in the immediate circle of Whately at Banbury, and the two continued a written correspondence for years thereafter, with the Englishman sending his Dutch friend manuscripts. Van Laren and Archer were fellow ministers at Arnhem from 1638 to 1642, and their friendship was such that van Laren did all he could to have the Englishman's manuscript published, even if Archer was not entirely uncontroversial—or perhaps precisely because he was controversial. Borstius had years of close association with the six Scots preachers in Rotterdam. Koelman had fairly close contact with McWard in Rotterdam in 1676, after which he corresponded at least once more with the Scot. As regards the fifth translation, nothing is known of the translator's identity, but we can be entirely confident that the translator was a good acquaintance of Fleming's at the least, if not a friend. There is a direct connection between the fact that all but one of the authors were religious refugees in the Netherlands from England or Scotland and the fact that they enjoyed close relations with their translators. There is a probability bordering on certainty that it was also in the Netherlands that eight of these authors—all bar one of them—wrote their English manuscripts. The same considerations will also serve to explain that, as far as is currently known, there are unpublished Puritan texts that are known only in Dutch translation.

The authors of the two earliest of these manuscripts had no intended channel of publication; however, matters changed in the case of Whately, when he sent Teellinck the first manuscript. In both instances, it was the translator who saw to the publication of the work. The latter four of the manuscripts to be written *were* firmly intended by their Scots authors to be published, but they were not able to find a publisher willing to take on the task. In McWard's case, it was Koelman who ensured publication. In contrast, it appears to have been the Scotsmen themselves who took the initiative of having *Getuygenis en verklaringe van eenighe predikanten uyt Schotlant* and Fleming's work published.

A slightly more difficult question to answer is that of the nature of the manuscripts that underlay the translations. In the cases of Archer, the six Scots ministers and Fleming, it will have been the author's autographs that were used; this also appears likely in the case of Whately's little tractate. Koelman, by contrast, had a copy of the original available to him when translating McWard's work.

Whately sent Teellinck his manuscript, so in this case no mediator was necessary, save for the man who delivered the parcel. In the case of van Laren, it appears that he received Archer's manuscript from the latter's heirs. Borstius was handed Brown's manuscript by Brown himself. We know for a certainty that the manuscript of Koelman's translation reached the translator via a third party, namely a pious woman of Utrecht. It was only subsequently that author and translator made each other's acquaintance and struck up a friendship. For Fleming's work, the assumption is warranted that it was the author himself who handed the translator his manuscript.

The years of publication of the five translations are reasonably evenly spread across the whole of the seventeenth century: one translation per quarter-century, with the exception of the third quarter, when two were published. It is also to be noted that all the authors were ordained ministers, as were all the (known) translators: accordingly, authors and translators were professional associates.

Nothing of research value can be concluded as to how the translations were done, since the original texts are not to hand. It can, however, be pointed out that the translation of Fleming does not bear the hallmarks of having been done by a native Dutch speaker. It was most probably the work of a Scotsman long resident in the Netherlands. The translators appear not to have adapted the text of any of the manuscripts of the Scots authors, whereas that is the case with Teellinck and van Laren in their translations of Whately's and Archer's manuscripts respectively. Teellinck structured the translation of the entire work with a division into chapters and sections; van Laren took even more pains and time about his translation, improving and amplifying the patchy text of the original.

Turning our attention to the content of Teellinck's and van Laren's translations, we note that they are congruent with both men's reforming efforts and that both works were aimed at ministers and trainee ministers, who were accorded the key role in the Further Reformation that the men were working to achieve.[86] The two works by the six Scots authors are also connected with reforming aims, albeit in another sense: they were written to demonstrate that the Scottish brand of reformation was not separatist, as de Labadie's had been, but that it rather fitted entirely within the national-church contours of Reformed Christendom. Yet Van

---

86 Graafland *et al.*, 141.

Laren's translation is experimental in nature, in the sense that it dwells upon the inner spiritual life. The translation of Fleming serves as a protest against lukewarmness within Reformed Christendom, one in which anti-popery and an optimistic near-future eschatology are evident. Given the nature of three of the five translations, it is only logical that they were undertaken by major proponents of the Further Reformation. This corroborates the hypothesis that Puritanism was one of the characteristics of the Dutch piety movement.[87] There is, however, a shift discernible within this translational aspect of that movement: whereas the two translations from the first half of the seventeenth century were of works by English Puritans, the three that date from the second half of the century were based on Scots Puritan texts. The Scots Puritans in question were Presbyterians in exile in the Netherlands. It is of note that Archer too, an Englishman, had sought religious refuge in the Netherlands from the policies of Charles I.

The size of these translations was anything but compendious. The shortest of all were the two works translated from the six Scots, which totalled 61 quarto pages. The works of Whately, Archer and McWard were also very modest in length, totalling 278 octavo pages and 298 pages in duodecimo format. The longest work was Fleming's tractate, which itself came to 307 octavo pages in translation.

While the translation of the two works of the six Scots and that of Fleming failed to achieve much effect in the Netherlands, the same cannot be said of the remaining three translations. The weakest influence among these three was that achieved by the translation of Archer's work, which was reprinted only once. It is true that two further editions of it were recently published, but their small print runs indicate that they were of very slight significance. The translation of Whately's work was printed twice during the seventeenth century itself after initial publication, but it enjoyed an influence many times greater than one might expect from its mere three editions. As Voetius has it, the first edition of the translation of Whately opened the eyes of many a Dutch preacher and congregant to the necessity of further reformation. Voetius counted himself as one such convert; Eeuwout Teellinck can be reckoned as another. This being the case, *Corte verhandelinghe van de voornaemste christelicke oeffeninghen* formed a not inconsiderable plank in the construction of the Further Reformation.

The significance of Koelman's translation was realised not so much immediately as in the fullness of time. It was reprinted only once during

---

87 Graafland *et al.*, 149–150.

the seventeenth century. The fact that it was reprinted with some regularity up to the late twentieth century, twice being supplied with a new dedication or foreword, indicates that the work has since its first appearance been regarded over the centuries as a suitable means of spreading the conviction that preaching has not been what it ought to be. Such a conclusion is supported by the fact that Koelman's foreword to the translation was separately published in 1834 in support of the *Afscheiding*.

A truly remarkable aspect of the effect that the translations in question had is their international reach. Teellinck's translation was translated onward into German by a person unknown, and this German manuscript circulated so widely that it was still known at the opening of the eighteenth century. It is Koelman's translation, however, that achieved the greatest success beyond the Netherlands: it was not only translated onward into German but published in that language. The German version was reprinted no fewer than three times during the eighteenth century. As if that achievement were not fascinating enough in and of itself, there is yet more to say about the success of the work: the German translation served as the source-text for both an eighteenth-century and a nineteenth-century Danish and a nineteenth- century Swedish onward translation. Accordingly, McWard's work has been made available to Continental readers in four languages, yet British readers do not have it in the original language in which it was written! Such are the remarkable vagaries to which a book can be subject in history.

The most unexpected and intriguing aspect of two of the total of five translations that we have been considering is their interdenominational appeal. Puritan works are Reformed in nature, yet in Germany, two of the translations leaped the barrier between the Reformed and Lutheran confessions.[88] It must be added that it is reasonable to posit that Teellinck's translation was onward-translated by a German Reformed adherent and that it will originally have been intended for German Reformed readers, but the fact that it is cited in a Lutheran work demonstrates that its influence spread beyond those bounds. The three non-Dutch translations of McWard's work were all done by Lutherans, and moreover all the editions of these onward translations were published by Lutheran adherents. What is highly significant in this regard is that the translators were without exception Pietists and that the translations took their place at the heart of the Lutheran Pietist movements in Germany, Denmark and Sweden. The considerable influence exerted by Koelman's translation of McWard's work among Lutheran Pietists in these three countries is one of the major

---

88 Sträter, 38–57.

arguments to support the hypothesis that international Reformed Pietism was of undeniable significance for its corollary, international Lutheran Pietism.[89]

---

[89] Op 't Hof [2001-1], 377–378; [2005-1], 96–100; Deppermann; Huisman [2008], 223; Van de Kamp [2012-1], 150–152; Op 't Hof [2016-1].

## 2. CAUSE BEATEN BY CONSEQUENCE

Three Puritan books published in translation prior to the text even coming into print

*The most surprising finding of the research into seventeenth-century translations of Puritan manuscripts revealed in the previous chapter was that six Puritan manuscripts were almost certainly never published in English, even though they appeared in print in Dutch. That is to say, the historicity of these English writings can be established only on the basis of their appearance in a foreign language—Dutch—and their contents are likewise accessible to us exclusively in translation. Yet this field of research has more surprises in store. There were at least three Puritan works in the seventeenth century that appeared in translation earlier—in some cases, far earlier— than the original English text did. Although a less exceptional phenomenon than the subject of the first chapter, this is nevertheless a very remarkable and striking eventuality in its own right.*

*This fact remains next to unknown outside the circle of Dutch researchers of the history of piety, as evidenced by the entries for the Puritan authors in question in the Oxford Dictionary of National Biography. However, in the case of John Brown (1610-1679), the matter might have been more widely known heretofore, for William Steven (1796-1857) described it explicitly in his history (1833) of the Scots Church in Rotterdam.[1] Over half a century later, Andrew L. Drummond transmitted this detail in his study of the ecclesiastical relationship between Scotland and the Continent. It has been noted again in the present century, by Alastair J. Mann in his overview of the Scottish book trade from 1500 to 1700.[2]*

*This chapter will consider the same aspects of the persons and writings in question as the first chapter did, with the exception that the contents of the works are now not summarised, as they are available to the researcher in their English editions. The methodology followed in this chapter is identical with that of the first: a chronological discussion of the three published Dutch translations is followed by conclusions, in which account is taken of the findings of the previous chapter.*

---

1 Steven, 72–73; 80 footnote.
2 Drummond, 102; Mann, 85.

### John Cotton, *Salomons prophetie*, Middelburg, 1633

The chronologically earliest translation that we shall consider was made by Johannes de Swaef[3] (1594-1653), a schoolmaster in Middelburg, the provincial capital of Zeeland, where he lived all his life. In print, he appears as a poet, an author and a translator[4]. In his authorial capacity, he made his mark as the writer of the first parenting handbook in Dutch (1621), entitled *De geestelycke queeckerye van de jonge planten des Heeren* [The spiritual nursing of the Lord's young plants]. It is a work with a strong focus on the practice of piety. The same focus is evident in his second work, *Mardachai* (1631), which sets out to provide spiritual guidelines for the practical life of the believing citizen as modelled in the Book of Esther. His book dedications indicate that de Swaef's friends included two major figures of the Further Reformation[5], the brothers Willem Teellinck[6] (1579-1629) and Eeuwout Teellinck[7] (1573-1629), as well as the politician and poet Jacob Cats[8] (1577-1660), a man not entirely devoid of Pietist sympathies either.

De Swaef made his translating debut in 1617 with his rendering of a work by the French Calvinist Lambert Daneau[9] (1530-1595). The book considers what constitutes proper apparel for the Christian, launching a volley of attacks on the prevailing immodesty, show and excess of contemporary costume. Under Willem Teellinck's influence, de Swaef fell for the charms of Puritanism. As a consequence, his translations thereafter almost exclusively concerned Puritan works. With an eye to the promotion of catechising in the family, a practice he had extolled in his pedagogical magnum opus, de Swaef translated a catechism by Paul Baynes (d. 1617) in 1622. Two years later, there followed a translation by him of a work by Nicholas Byfield (1579-1622) stating rules for a holy and godly life. Taken together, all the above is ample reason to consider de Swaef one of the most significant lay promoters of the Further Reformation in its first phase.

De Swaef's last publication was also his final translation: *Salomons prophetie*, by John Cotton (1585-1652), the renowned Puritan minister of the two Bostons. This translation was both printed and published at Middelburg in 1633 and contains 187 pages in octavo format. The work is

---

3 Groenendijk [1990]; Op 't Hof [2016-13].
4 For this latter aspect, see Op 't Hof [1979].
5 Beeke [1991], 383-413; Van Lieburg [1994]; Graafland *et al.*
6 Beeke [2003]; Op 't Hof [2008-1, 2011-1, 2015-1].
7 Op 't Hof [1999-1].
8 Ten Berge; Op 't Hof [2015-11].
9 Félice; Fatio.

# Salomons Prophetie,
## DAT IS,
# Het Liet der Lie-
## deren / verklaert /

Door *Mr. J. Cotton*, Prediker des Goddelijcken Woordts binnen LONDEN.

Uyt het Engels vertaelt, door *I. d. S.*

TOT MIDDELBURGH,
Ghedzuckt voo2 Anthony de Latre.
Boeck-vercooper op den Burght / 1633.

an exposition of the Song of Solomon, voicing the conviction that in that Bible book, Solomon typifies what the condition of the church of God will be from the author's own day until the Last Judgement. The exposition is one that dwells on salvation history. In accordance with that focus, Solomon's bride is not viewed as representing the soul of the individual believer, but rather as the church.

There is a remarkable aspect to the book history of *Salomons prophetie*. The original appeared in print only in 1642, at London, under the title *A brief exposition of the whole book of Canticles, or Song of Solomon*—and this without Cotton's knowledge![10] This leaves us with no other conclusion to draw but that de Swaef was working from manuscript when he translated the work. From whom had he obtained the manuscript? Some light is shed on the matter in de Swaef's dedication to Cats, a man whose life as well as his oeuvre had a Pietist dimension, who subsequently became Grand Pensionary of Holland (the most powerful of the United Provinces of the Netherlands), and who enjoyed the greatest popularity of any Dutch poet in the seventeenth and eighteenth centuries. The dedication states that the translation had been made at the request of the Teellinck brothers, Eeuwout and Willem.[11] Given Willem's connections with England, he is the likeliest figure to have handed de Swaef the manuscript of Cotton's work. The question remains, however, of how Teellinck came by it.

Again, this step of the investigation reveals a web of detail. The minister of the Dutch Church in London, Timotheus van Vleteren[12] (d. 1641), whose calling to England was facilitated by Willem Teellinck and his eldest son (and fellow minister) Maximiliaan Teellinck[13] (1605–1653),[14] wrote Cotton a letter on 26 October 1629. In it, he reports that he had received papers from the Netherlands from Maximiliaan Teellinck, together with a request to forward them to Cotton. Van Vleteren introduces himself to Cotton as a spiritual intimate of Maximiliaan from their time at school and university together, informing him that he and Maximiliaan were near neighbours at the commencement of their respective preaching careers, that Maximiliaan had studied at Cotton's household seminary in Boston together with van Vleteren's successor as minister at

---

10   Emerson, 39.
11   Cotton [1633], A3r.
12   Op 't Hof [2016-20].
13   Brienen [1993]; Op 't Hof [2016-16].
14   Op 't Hof [2008-1], 356–358.

Zoutelande on Walcheren, Isaac Bisschop (d. 1661), and that Maximiliaan had handed van Vleteren a number of manuscripts of Cotton's.[15]

Cotton's reply, dated 16 December 1629, indicates that Maximiliaan had brought him, via van Vleteren, a letter and a memorial poem upon his father's death. The most interesting information in it, however, concerns Cotton's request that van Vleteren ask Maximiliaan what had become of a manuscript that Cotton had been urged to write by Willem Teellinck, whom Cotton incidentally says he had never met in person. He wonders in the letter whether the delivery might have gone astray, since he has never had acknowledgement of receipt of the manuscript that he had sent Teellinck.[16]

It is beyond dispute that the contact between the Father of the Further Reformation and Cotton, one of the foremost English Puritans, was brought about by Maximiliaan, who as a young man had been among Cotton's household seminary students and who may also have attended university conferences of a devotional nature.[17] Evidently, that contact blossomed into a correspondence and a relationship of trust; Teellinck's request and Cotton's positive response admit of no other explanation. We may deduce from the known circumstances that Cotton sent the manuscript of his treatise in late 1628. Whether or not it ever reached Teellinck is a question likely to remain unresolved for all time, since the latter died in early April 1629.

It is via his son Maximiliaan that William Teellinck will have received the manuscript of Cotton's exegesis of the Song of Solomon. He will then have lent it to his like-minded elder brother Eeuwout to read. Both brothers will have concluded that the manuscript was worth translating, and hence asked de Swaef to do so. The date of Willem Teellinck's death makes it certain that this occurred no later than early 1629. It is reasonable, therefore, to assume that de Swaef finished his translation during 1629 at the latest. Yet the translation was not immediately published. de Swaef's dedication, dated 22 September 1633, informs us that publication ensued rather later and was undertaken at the strong insistence of several preachers.

---

15 These writings had not as yet been published, so they must have existed in manuscript form only.
16 Bush, 133–136.
17 Webster [1997], 21.

Two further aspects command our attention. The first can be dealt with briefly. The title page of the translation identifies the author of the original work as a "London preacher". Yet there is a mistake here as to Cotton's place of ministry: he only ever had a congregation in Boston, albeit on both sides of the Atlantic—first in Lincolnshire (1612–1633), then in the eponymous settlement in New England (1633–1652). In no sense did he ever minister in the capital of England. We must ascribe this error to one of two men: either the printer or the translator himself. de Swaef is the likelier source of the error, since he was readily available to read the proofs, living as he did in the city where the work was printed. Consequently, it appears that de Swaef himself had little or no acquaintance with the author.

The second aspect is that of whether the published text of the 1642 English edition is identical with the source-text of de Swaef's translation. No differences are apparent in the first few pages, but as the work progresses, one sees fairly regularly that the two versions are not in full agreement. In the majority of places where they differ, the published English text is more extensive than the Dutch translation. The disagreements are largely trivial or no more than a couple of lines long, but there are instances where a longer section of text, even an entire paragraph, is different or missing in de Swaef.[18]

The difference between the two texts is most evident in applicatory sections. For instance, compared with the translation's seven applications of Cant. 1:5–9[19], the English text is not only lengthier[20] but also contains fully nine applications. The points of application not found in de Swaef's version, numbers 4 and 5 in the 1642 edition, contain Cotton's teachings that it is God Himself Who sends the church the calamities she faces, and that it is sinful to reject the church and separate oneself from her. In the Dutch, the text of Cant. 1:10–17 is afforded twelve applications,[21] as against eleven in the English.[22] Although this is an instance of an additional point in the Dutch, the English text is still more extensive in this section than in the Dutch version. The point of application not found in the English edition is the teaching that idolatry is not to be tolerated even in the wife or mother of a prince; she is to be deposed. There are more

---

18  Examples include (the pagination here refers to the English text): entire paragraphs on pp. 12, 22, 31; the greater part of a paragraph on 31–32; and part of a paragraph on 32.
19  23–25.
20  31–35.
21  32–36.
22  43–49.

applicatory sections besides this where the English text is longer than the Dutch; sometimes considerably longer.[23] There is one more place where the published English text has more applications than the Dutch translation, namely the second set of applications drawn from Cant. 3. Here, the English has nine applications to the six of the Dutch. Those not found in the Dutch are numbers 2, 7 and 8 in the English.[24]

More than in the foregoing, however, it is in the following two sections that it becomes obvious that the English source-text of de Swaef's translation was actually a different version of the work than that published in English in 1642. One of these sections is the exposition of Cant. 4:7–11, which has seven points in the Dutch as against six in the English.[25] When the anticipated conversion of the Jews is discussed, de Swaef's translation gives a reference in parenthesis to a fuller treatment of the matter in the last sermon on another text (Jer. 31:20)[26]—the parenthesis that gives this reference not being reflected at all in the 1642 edition.[27]

Even though there are unmistakable differences between the translation and the published English text of 1642, they do not constitute any developments or discrepancies in the contents. This must mean that the text of Cotton's exposition of the Song of Solomon that found its way to the Netherlands as of 1629 (Willem Teellinck's year of death) or earlier was subsequently revised by Cotton himself, and that these revisions were largely amplifications, albeit that the added matter did not represent any change of views or new insights.

An intriguing question is what relationship the manuscript circulating at Middelburg by 1629 bore to the manuscript underlying the English publication of 1642. Was the Middelburg manuscript an apograph of the 1642 source-manuscript (which we would then posit to be Cotton's autograph and subsequently amplified in his hand), or was the same handwritten copy used for the production of both the Dutch and the English

---

23  On Cant. 2:1–7, applicatory points 1, 2, 6, 7 and 8 (English [hereinafter 'E.']: 60–65 and Dutch [hereinafter 'D.']: 44–46); on Cant. 2:8–17, points 1, 2, 3, 6, 7, 8 and 9 (E:73–80 and D:54–55); on Cant. 3, points 1, 2, 3, 4 and 5 of the first set of applications and most of the points in the second set, in so far as they match (E:92–98 and D:63–66); on Cant. 4:1–6, the third and fourth points of application (E:113 and D:77–78); on Cant. 4:7–11, points 1, 2, 3, 4, 5, 7 and 8 (E:124–129 and D:87–90); in the concluding series of applications, the text is on most points slightly more extensive, except on points 10, 11 and 13, where it is very much more extensive (E:257–264 and D:184–187).
24  95–98.
25  D:78–79 and E:144.
26  145.
27  202.

books? If the latter is the case, it must have been returned to Cotton from the Netherlands once it had been used for the translation and will later have had Cotton's additions written on it. Given the intensity of Cotton's relationship at this stage of his life with the Further Reformers, especially those of Zeeland, this latter hypothesis cannot be ruled out. That notwithstanding, there is a piece of information to incline us strongly towards the former hypothesis. Thanks to the efforts of Sargent Bush, the editor of the correspondence of John Cotton, it is known that students at Cotton's household seminary were set to work by their master copying manuscripts.[28] It is therefore very tempting to assume that a Dutch student—and if so, Maximiliaan Teellinck would be the likeliest copyist—wrote out Cotton's study on the Song of Solomon while staying in his household and that he brought it home for his father and uncle to read.

The translation as a whole bears indications that de Swaef was an amateur who did not always grasp the right meaning of the English source-text. Moreover, he evidently gave little attention to overseeing the publication of his translation. To ascribe to him a more professional or involved role than that would make it difficult to account for the fact that he at one point turns the civil magistrate into the church[29] or that in the exposition of the knocking at the door in Cant. 5:2, one of the two sections found in the published English text is missing altogether[30] in the Dutch.[31] Given that the translation introduces that single section with "1.", it is evident that de Swaef either overlooked the other during translation or failed to spot the printer's error during proofreading. At one point, his translation mentions play-actors,[32] a concept lacking in the 1642 text. It is impossible to work out whether this represents an interpolation of the translator's own or whether there really was an underlying word for it in the English manuscript that he had to hand.

The fact that Cotton had his writings disseminated via copies written out by students at his household seminary, rather than via the printing press, will presumably have had to do with his nonconformist and Congregationalist persuasion. In other words, although Cotton did intend for his works to make his views known and have them exert influence, he avoided the conventional means. That Dutch seminary students should take home copies of several of his manuscripts will have been something

---

28  Bush, 68–71.
29  D:187 and E:262 (tenth point of application).
30  102.
31  145–146.
32  186.

that he was certainly encouraging: witness the fact that he composed and sent a little treatise to Willem Teellinck at the latter's request even though he was not otherwise acquainted with him. Moreover, Cotton will certainly not have had any objections to his exposition of the Song of Solomon having been translated and published for Dutch readers. Textual comparison of the 1633 Dutch print edition with the 1642 English print edition reveals that Cotton had lightly revised, and above all supplemented, the original form of his work himself in the intervening years.

De Swaef's translation cannot have made much inroads into the Dutch reading public, as there was never a second edition.

**John Brown, *Christus de wegh, de waarheidt, ende het leven* and *Christus de hoop der heerlijkheidt in de geloovige*, Rotterdam, 1676**
The translator of the second work under consideration for having been published in Dutch before English was Jacobus Koelman[33] (1631–1695). His career, catalogue of publications and historical significance will not be described here, since he was a subject of attention in the first chapter[34] and since a dedicated chapter in Volume II will go into detail on those aspects.

In 1676, a year after Koelman's ejection from his living as minister at Sluis in States-Flanders (now Zeeland-Flanders), a combined publication came out of two translations by him of works by John Brown, under the title *Christus de wegh, de waarheidt, ende het leven* [Christ the way, the truth, and the life]. This overall title was actually the title of the first of the two works in the volume, the title of the second work being *Christus de hoop der heerlijkheidt in de geloovige* [Christ the hope of glory in the believer]. It was an octavo edition totalling 549 pages. This was not the first Koelman translation of Brown to come out in the Netherlands: 1675 had seen the publication of Koelman's original Dutch work *Reformatie nodigh ontrent de feest-dagen* [Reformation needful regarding the festival days], supplemented by his translation of a generous extract from Brown's tractate *Causa Dei contra antisabbatarios* [The cause of God against the Anti-Sabbatarians], running to fully sixty pages. The extract is Chapter 13 of Part II of the work, which tackles the question of whether the church is at liberty to decree annual festivals.[35] However, in his 1676 combined translation, Koelman presents the Dutch reader with a work on the per-

---

33 Krull; Van Lieburg [1990]; Meeuse [1990, 2008]; Op 't Hof [2013-1], 237–268; Groenendijk [2017].
34 This study, 50-57.
35 Koelman [1675], 243–302.

# CHRISTUS

De WEGH, de WAARHEIDT,
ende het LEVEN.

Een

## TRACTAAT

Vertoonende,
Hoe men CHRISTUS tot alles, en byzonder tot *Heiligmaking*, zoude gebruiken.

In 't Engelsch beschreven door
Mr **JOHANNES BROWN**,
Dienaar des H. Euangeliums.

En vertaalt door
**JACOBUS KOELMAN**.
*Leeraar* der *Gemeinte* van *Sluys* in *Vlaanderen*.

Noch is hier bijgevoeght een ander

TRACTAAT

van den zelven Autheur,
Over COLOSS. 1: Vers 27.

Tot Rotterdam, Gedrukt bij Henricus Goddæus,
Boekdrukker in den Oppert. Anno 1676.

sonal inner life of faith, a theme not broached in the earlier work. It appears, then, that Koelman had become taken with Brown's Puritan convictions on the Sabbath and the inner life of faith.

Koelman's preface to this combined translation is signed Rotterdam, 17 July 1676. It commences with a reference to a translation he made eight years previously, *Het groote interest van een christen* [*The christians great interest* (1659)], by another Scot, William Guthrie (1620–1665). Koelman explains that Brown's *Christus de wegh, de waarheidt, ende het leven* may be seen as a sequel to that work, since Guthrie's book concerns justification and Brown writes on sanctification. Koelman adds that little has been written at all and even less in the Netherlands regarding Christ's being the Source of sanctification, and that not much is being preached on that theme either. He himself has never found such an outstanding book on the subject as this, and it is for this reason that he has translated it even before it has been published in English.[36] He expects much fruit from his translation: even preachers will be able to benefit greatly from it, who have until now often been presenting the Gospel legalistically, whether from ignorance or inexperience. However, Koelman adds, it is above all pious lay readers whom he has in mind with this translation. He hopes that they will not remain suspended in their doubts, crises of confidence and weaknesses, but that they now will be enabled to learn joyfully how to draw the water of grace from the Fountain of salvation.

Koelman then expresses the yearning that those more experienced in grace will communicate to feebler brethren at conventicles the thoughts central to Brown's work. To this end, he urges in the strongest terms that such meetings be held, well knowing as he does the opposition that they arouse. He adds some rules for conventicles: no persons may be slandered and no separation from the Church promoted, but rather the attenders are to pray together, sing, discuss sermons they have heard, read the Scriptures, share spiritual experiences and pose their questions about the practice of piety, whether a minister is present or not. He adduces no fewer than 25 arguments for the holding of such conventicles. He trusts that the reader who appreciates his translation will recompense his efforts by praying not only for him but also for the persecuted church in Scotland and England. In particular, Koelman urges the reader to be mindful of the situation north of the border, citing the text of a royal decree against conventicles promulgated at Edinburgh on 1 March 1676. For all that the persecution in Scotland is terrible, Koelman writes, the saving work of the Holy Ghost is no less mighty there: many are coming

---

36  Brown [1676], *2r-*3r.

to faith. He concludes his preface with the remark that he translated the work particularly with his beloved former congregation at Sluis in mind. It may be in connection with this remark that the preliminaries to the edition are rounded off by two spiritual songs by his fellow Sluis minister and ally in the advocacy of a general reformation of morals, David Montanus[37] (d. 1687).

We are faced with the question of whether Koelman and Brown were acquainted with each other when the former received the pair of manuscripts from the latter in 1676 for translation. We must conclude that they were, for how would Koelman otherwise have known—as he states in his preface—that the English manuscript of the first of these works was (shortly) to be sent to press? In a later work, Koelman relates that he travelled to Amsterdam together with Brown in July 1671 to interview a widow who had fallen under the influence of Jean de Labadie[38] (1610–1674), seeking first-hand information from her as to what exactly had happened in May of that year at de Labadie's commune at Herford, Westphalia.[39] What had transpired was that de Labadie and his followers—men, women and maidens—had become in some sense spiritually crazed and had started dancing and kissing each other. This episode explains why Koelman had, as far back as his Sluis years, been a close spiritual associate of Brown. The bond was not diminished by Koelman's later ejection from his living: as noted above, even in 1675, when staying at Rotterdam immediately after his banishment, Koelman supplemented his work on the reforming of ecclesiastical festivals with a translated extract of Brown's treatise on the Sabbath. As regards Brown, it is at least documented that he was residing at Rotterdam during 1676,[40] so there should be no doubt that Koelman was handed Brown's manuscripts by the author in person. Subsequently, in 1679, Koelman was, together with Robert McWard (1633–1687) and Brown, one of the ministers to lay hands upon Richard Cameron (d. 1680) at Cameron's ordination at the Scots Church in Rotterdam. Cameron was sent over to Scotland, where he would be executed a year later during a Covenanter uprising.

Koelman's high words of praise for Brown's works give us cause to suppose that it was the Dutchman's initiative to translate and publish them. So warm was the two ministers' friendship that Brown had no objection to his work appearing in Koelman's translation before his own

---

37 Ros [1995]; Op 't Hof [2016-6].
38 Saxby.
39 Koelman [1684], 154. My thanks to Mr Leen van Valen of Dordrecht for this detail.
40 Sprunger [1982], index, under Brown, John.

original came out. The hypothesis might also be defensible that the positive reception that this translation enjoyed with the Dutch—to be detailed below—actually helped secure the English publication of the work.

A second edition of *Christus de wegh, de waarheidt, ende het leven* appeared at Amsterdam in 1679, with three appendices. The first of these is a translator's admonition to the reader,[41] in which Koelman states that his translation of the first of the two works in the volume came out a year before the publication of the English original and makes clear that his translation was based on the author's manuscript. Koelman clarifies that he has followed the authorial manuscript with the second of the works, too.[42]

In fact, the latter work did not appear in print in English until 1694, published at Edinburgh under the title *Christ in believers the hope of glory*. The first of the tractates, *Christ the way, and the truth, and the life*, had meanwhile been published at London in 1677. Comparison of the Dutch text with the English reveals that there are no discrepancies of note between Brown and Koelman in either of the works, an indication of Koelman's skill and experience as a translator.[43]

This first appendix to the 1679 edition is entitled an Admonition because it contains Koelman's caveat that the opinions expressed by English Puritan Richard Baxter (1615-1691) in *Het huys-boeck der armen* [*The poor man's family book* (1674)], as it appeared in Dutch translation at Utrecht in 1678, are suspect. According to Koelman, Baxter preaches Christ merely as the Example of sanctification, never as its Author. Consequently, Koelman finds this book of Baxter's a legalistic presentation of the Gospel.

The second appendix is a translation of the text of Brown's dedication to Lady Strathnaver and Brown's original preface, both of which are rendered as found in the English edition *Christ the way, and the truth, and the life* (1677).[44] The translation of this appendix merits some remarks. Koelman, having decided to run together Brown's dedication and preface, left the last paragraph of the former and the first page of the latter[45] untranslated for the sake of flow; moreover, the first section that follows this omission is not literally translated. Sometimes, short clauses of the

---

41  Brown [1679], 340-342.
42  Brown [1679], 340.
43  This concurs with the conclusions of van de Kamp [2013].
44  Brown [1679], 343-360 and 360-368 respectively.
45  E:D3r.

preface are not rendered in the Dutch;[46] on occasion, larger units of text are left out.[47] Noteworthy also is the translator's omission of the following sentence about the sermon outlines that Brown includes in his work: "*The persvvasion vvhereof did induce me to publish the follovving heads of some sermons, after they had been translated into* dutch*, and published here*".[48]

The third appendix is a translation of McWard's preface to the English edition.[49] Again, the Dutch text is shorter than the original:[50] some of the abridgements are longer than mere clauses or short passages and amount to extensive sections,[51] including the omission of a list of the names of authors and a bibliography[52]. Also omitted by Koelman is McWard's statement to the reader that Brown's work

> hath been turned into dutch, and that it hath not onely met with great acceptation, amongst all the serious and Godly in these parts, who have seen it; but it is much sought after; and they professe themselves singularly thereby edified, and set a going after God, by its efficat[i]ous perswasivenesse, with a singing alacrity.[53]

We may infer that Koelman was quite deliberate in deciding not to stick closely to the source-texts for these appendices and to allow himself to abridge some sections, both shorter and longer.

*Christus de wegh, de waarheidt, ende het leven* itself is a 29-chapter exposition of how the believer must appropriate Christ for his sanctification. As the title indicates, the work is based on John 14:6—*Jesus saith unto him, I am the way, the truth, and the life: no man cometh unto the Father, but by me.*

The other work that Koelman combines with this work, *Christus de hoop der heerlijkheidt in de geloovige*, is not subdivided into chapters and

---

46  D:360 = E:D3v.; D:361 = E:D5v.; D:361 = E:D6r.; D:362 = E:D6v.; D:362 = E:D7r. (twice); D:363 = E:D7v.; D:363 = E:D7v–D8r.; D 366 = E:D10v.; D:366 = E:D11r.; D:368 = E:D12v.
47  D:360 = E:D4r.–D5r. (two pages); D:361 = E:D5r.–D5v. (one page).
48  D 361 = E:D6r.
49  Brown [1679], 369-199[=399].
50  For example, D:369 = E:B1r. (twice); D:372 = E:B2v.; D:379 = E:B8r.–v.; D:381 = E:B9v.–B10r.; D:384 = E:B12r.; D:387 = E:C3r.
51  D 372 = E:B3r.–B4r. (more than two pages); D:382 = E:B10v.–B11v. (a page and a half); D:387 = E:C2r.–v. (a page and a half); D:390 = E:C4v.–C8v. (no fewer than eight pages); D:396 = E:C12r.–D1v. (almost three pages).
52  E:C4v.–C7r.
53  E:D1r.

# CHRISTUS
*De*
Hoop der Heerlijkheidt
*In de*
# GELOOVIGEN:
Aangewesen in ettelijke *Predikatien*, in 't *Engels* gedaan door

Mr. JOHANNES BROWN.

En vertaalt door

JACOBUS KOELMAN.

COLOSS. I. VERS 27.
*Christus in u de Hoop der Heerlijkheidt.*

t'AMSTERDAM,
By *Jan Bouman*, Boekverkooper, in de Kalver-
straat, over de Kapel. 1679.

is a treatment of Colossians 1:27— *to whom God would make known what is the riches of the glory of this mystery among the Gentiles; which is Christ in you, the hope of glory.*

As we have already seen, it was not until 1694 that the original text underlying *Christus de hoop der heerlijkheidt in de geloovige* was made available to the English-speaking reader. The anonymous author of the 1694 preface—presumably its Edinburgh publisher, John Reid—offers the reader not only an account of how the work came about but also some remarkable information about both the English text and its Dutch translation. The passage is worth quoting in its entirety for the significance of its details:

> *they are only some Notes of Sermons preached in the time of the Authors trouble, at* Utrecht, *for the most part in his own Chamber; Which after his Death, came to the hand of the Reverend Mr.* James Koolman, *Minister of the Gospel at* Sluis *in* Flanders, *and by him were published in* Dutch, *as an Appendix to the* Dutch *Translation of the Authors Book, intituled,* CHRIST the Way, the Truth, and the Life, *And now are only translated out of* Dutch, *at first intended for the private use of some particular Persons, but afterward by the Solicitations of some, who had the occasion to read them, they were diligently compared with the* Dutch *Translation, and committed to the Press, the Original not being extant, so far as I know, that this present Translation may be compared with it, and therfore any Defects that may appear in this little Book, cannot in Justice be ascribed to the Author, but to the Translators, who yet have used very great Diligence and Faithfulness in what they have done.*[54]

We learn, then, that Brown had originally preached the text as sermons, most of which he preached in the room that he rented in a house in Utrecht. The audience for these sermons will therefore have been a select group of like-minded Scots and perhaps English expatriates in Utrecht. Given that Brown handed Koelman the manuscript before 17 July 1676, he must have spent a little while in Utrecht that year.[55] It is to be hoped that the 1694 information about the origin of the work itself is more reliable than the details about the translation, since the latter information is clearly wrong in claiming that Koelman obtained the manuscript after Brown's death. This is impossible, since the latter died in 1679 and Koelman's translation was published in 1676! It appears to be only on this

---

54  Brown [1694], A4r.–v.
55  Cf. Sprunger [1982], 435–436.

point that the Edinburgh preface is mistaken; in other respects, it is correct regarding the translator and the translation.

The details given about the English edition of the work have a surprise in store. One might expect that what the Scots publisher had obtained and published would be the original manuscript, yet the above passage as good as states that this was unobtainable and that the text now appearing was an English back-translation of the Dutch. This might in fact be a phenomenon unique in history!

Drawing on the rest of what is known about the English translation and edition, we may reconstruct the following. A Scotsman who had lived long enough in the Netherlands as a religious exile to have a reading knowledge of the language will have purchased a copy of Koelman's translation from a Dutch bookseller. After his return to Scotland following the downfall of the Stuart dynasty, he will have commended the book warmly to those spiritually likeminded with him, and they will have urged him to make the book accessible to them. He evidently did so, such that a number of people came to know of its contents; this culminated in requests for publication, which Reid undertook in 1694.

*Christus de wegh, de waarheidt, ende het leven* is a devotional work that continues down to the present to appeal to a Dutch readership as it did when it first appeared. It went through no fewer than ten editions in the Netherlands up to and including the twentieth century. Koelman himself lived to see the third edition go to print, in 1686. However, sales of the Dutch book were not evenly-paced. Both the second and the third editions appeared in a title edition, in 1680 and 1686 respectively. Interest in the work peaked in the first half of the eighteenth century, with five of the total of ten editions appearing in the space of just 23 years—1718, 1724 (twice), 1734, and 1741. A title edition of the latter was brought out as late as 1749.

We must account, then, for this strong concentration of editions in the early eighteenth century. In his article on Dutch Pietist reading material in the seventeenth and eighteenth centuries, which continues to be a valuable contribution to research, Fred van Lieburg expresses his puzzlement that the supply of devotional reading matter plummeted in the latter half of the eighteenth century and remained at a low ebb until at least the schism from the Dutch Reformed Church in 1834, the *Afscheiding*. Van Lieburg voices the possible explanation that the ructions in the book market and among the reading public that were brought about by the dissemination and popularisation of Enlightenment ideas did not fail to have an impact on Pietist reading culture.[56] Indeed, this is doubtless

---

56   Van Lieburg [1989], 78.

the main reason for the sharp drop in demand for devotional works in that era, but this consideration does not offer a positive reason to account for the repeated publication of the work in question earlier in the eighteenth century. Koelman's preface may supply the key. As we have already seen, it is largely taken up with commendations of the holding of conventicles. It was none other than Koelman who was responsible for the flowering as never before of this expression of Pietism in the Netherlands. It seems only logical, then, that as long as the conventicle continued to be a concept in high demand, Koelman's translation of Brown's two works continued to be sought-after, and equally that as soon as the popularity of holding such fellowship meetings began to flag, under the influence of the Enlightenment, demand likewise fell away for devotional reading matter such as translations of Brown. Not only is this a plausible explanation of the accumulation of editions of these works at that time; it also accounts for the steep rise in Dutch Pietist original works and for the gentler growth in the number of Dutch translations of the Puritans.[57]

A second possible explanation, one very much congruent with the foregoing, has to do with the Christocentric nature of sanctification as it is presented in *Christus de wegh, de waarheidt, ende het leven*. The focus upon Christ in sanctification found far more acceptance in the eighteenth century than in the seventeenth. Significant in this regard is the history of the reception in the Netherlands of the highly prescriptive piety manual of the Welsh Puritan Bishop Lewis Bayly (d. 1631): while the seventeenth-century editions of *De practycke ofte oeffeninghe der godtzaligheydt* [*The practise of pietie* (1612)] total 51, there were a mere two Dutch editions in the eighteenth century![58]

After the 1741 edition of Koelman's bundled translations of Brown, it was nearly a century and a half before another came on the Dutch market, in 1882. The most recent republication came just short of a further century later, in 1979. To ease publication, this edition was a photomechanical copy of its 1882 predecessor. Thus, demand for Koelman's translation has not entirely dried up in the last two and a half centuries; it continues to drip very slowly but steadily.

**Conclusions**

The great importance of translations of this genre, and how very interesting and intriguing a field of research this can be, is not only seen in the evidence of the first chapter that there were seventeenth-century Dutch

---

57  Van Lieburg [1989], 76.
58  Huisman [2009-1].

translations of six Puritan manuscripts which we may be practically certain were never published in the English original; it is equally apparent in the present chapter's research finding that in that same country and century, translations came out of three further Puritan manuscripts that as yet had not been published in their source language.

The existence of no fewer than three such exceptional cases—within the compass of just two translated publications—can be accounted for along the same lines as in the foregoing article. On the one hand, it is a reflection of the large number of translations of Puritan writings that were in circulation in the seventeenth-century Dutch Republic; on the other, it is a manifestation of the closeness of contact between the translators and the authors—and, in one of the instances, of contact between instigator and author. At first sight, this interpretation might seem entirely misplaced in the case of the translation of Cotton. De Swaef had so little knowledge of the author he was translating that he quite wrongly assumed him to be a London preacher. But what of the instigator, Willem Teellinck? Although Jan van de Kamp considers it quite possible in theory that Teellinck made Cotton's acquaintance in England before 1606, such an early acquaintance is ruled out by Cotton's own letter to Timotheus van Vleteren, minister of the Dutch Church in London, on 16 December 1629, in which he states that he has never met Teellinck in the flesh.[59] Nevertheless, the correspondence that Cotton built up with Teellinck via the latter's son Maximiliaan evidently reached such a level of trust that the request was sent from Middelburg to Boston to compose a treatise on a dogmatic issue and Cotton acceded. In point of fact, Cotton's manuscript took two intermediaries to reach de Swaef, namely Teellinck junior and senior. Maximiliaan copied it from Cotton's autograph in Lincolnshire, took it back with him over the North Sea, and let his father and uncle read it, who in turn persuaded de Swaef to translate it.

In contrast, the contact between Koelman and Brown was personal and direct. By 1671 at the latest, they had come to know and appreciate each other. In 1676, the Scotsman gave the banned Dutch minister his two manuscripts to the end that he should translate them. This is the third case we have seen of authors personally handing translators their manuscripts, fully conscious of the intended aim: the first such instance was that of the manuscripts of the six Scotsmen, and the second was Fleming's passing of his manuscript to a translator unknown to us. Both of these have been described in the first chapter. Concerning the first translation considered in that chapter, we have strong grounds for positing that

---

59  Van de Kamp [2010], 37 and 39 respectively.

Whately deliberately dedicated his manuscript to Teellinck in order to encourage him to translate the work. If this was indeed Whately's intention, then we have a situation in which two-thirds of the instances considered consisted of the deliberate handing over of a manuscript by its author for it to be translated.

Just as in our chapter on unpublished Puritan texts, so also here in the case of Puritan texts appearing in translation before their originals, there are no known instances of this phenomenon ever having occurred other than in the Dutch language.

As regards the translators' sources, de Swaef was obliged to make do with a copy of the original manuscript, whereas Koelman was granted the author's own manuscripts. While Cotton straightforwardly did not intend for his exposition of the Song of Solomon to appear in print, it was subtler in the case of Brown, who did intend the first but not the second of those manuscripts of his that eventually were translated to be published. Only nine years after its Dutch edition was Cotton's exposition of the Song of Solomon published, and even then without his knowledge! The edition was based on a manuscript that contained changes and additions as compared with the one that de Swaef had translated from. The first and longer of Brown's manuscripts took only one year after Dutch publication to appear in print in English; both of the translations of his works were made from his own manuscripts. The second of them, consisting of sermon notes, had not been intended by Brown for publication. It will have been at Koelman's urging that the Scotsman handed over these notes for Dutch translation and dissemination. Consistent with the above, it took fully eighteen years for this work to see the light of day in English. What may very well be unique about this edition is that the published English text is not that of the original English manuscript—which had been lost—but a fresh English retranslation from the Dutch edition. This new English version arose from requests from the friends of the Scottish translator after they had heard from him the merits of the work. He was familiar with it from his years of exile in the Netherlands during the persecutions of the Non-Indulging Covenanters. The fresh translation was read in manuscript in a wider circle of acquaintances than before; this resulted in a clamour to publish it as a book.

None of the three manuscripts considered in this chapter was exceptional in length. Together, they took up 736 pages in octavo format. Two of the three manuscripts come from the middle of the second half of the century; only one dates from the latter end of the first half. Two of the three were experimental in their spirituality; the third was exegetical in nature. Both of the translators were adherents of the Further Reformation,

Koelman as a key figure in the movement and de Swaef as a foot soldier.[60] If we include the five translated books of the previous chapter in our considerations, then the Further Reformation slant to these translations is still seen to be no less pronounced: five of the seven books were translated by men of the Further Reformation.

In this connection, it must not be disregarded that a third of the overall number of manuscripts considered in these first two chapters were translated by Koelman. His predominance is explained by several factors. Firstly, Koelman occupies top place in the ranking of those who translated the most Puritan works into Dutch in the seventeenth century. Secondly, there can be few Dutchmen who kept up such intensive and influential channels of communication with Puritans as Koelman did. The fact that his contacts on this front were almost all Scotsmen is, then, the reason why two-thirds of the nine manuscripts we have been considering thus far were written by Scots Covenanters. Finally, Koelman's substantial share of the total indicates something of the Puritan essence of the Further Reformation, that being the movement of which Koelman was such a leading advocate.

It may seem odd to some that the Teellinck brothers wished to see Cotton's work appear in Dutch, as it had no Further Reformation or Pietist content as such. In order to understand the reason, one must bear in mind that both brothers took a keen interest in the political and religious developments of their day and that they expected the near future to herald a whole series of epoch-making and even apocalyptic events. This series of events would culminate in the church enjoying a more and more glorious future. It was from this perspective that the Teellincks were interested in historicist Bible exposition.[61]

The strongly expository character of Cotton's work is without doubt the reason why de Swaef's translation did not see more than one edition, the average Christian reader being keener on devotional material than on exegesis. It was by the same token that Koelman's combined translation of Brown's two treatises met with such acclaim: not only did the focus of Brown's writings play a role in their success, but more particularly it was the warm, pastoral Christocentrism that saturates the works that was valued. Of all seven books we have considered thus far, it was Koelman's translation of Brown that was reprinted the most. It will not have been by chance that five of the ten reprints in all of the book were undertaken

---

60 Graafland *et al.*, 171.
61 For Willem, see Op 't Hof [2011-1], 199–203; for Eeuwout, see Op 't Hof [1999-1], 64–67.

during the heyday of the conventicle, not least when we consider Koelman's praise of the practice in his preface to the Dutch reader. Unfortunately, little research has been conducted into the subjects that were on the agenda at these conventicles. If evidence were available on that question, it could serve to confirm or negate the explanation offered above for the temporal concentration of reprints.

Very much in contradistinction to the six manuscripts considered in the first chapter, the three described in the present chapter have left no trace of an impact. That this obtains for de Swaef's translation is unsurprising enough, but the fact that it is also true of the ten editions of Koelman's translations gives food for thought. After all, it was in the nature of the conventicle scene that it generated little, if any, documentation. One might therefore expect that the lack of a demonstrable effect of these works in the Netherlands would imply that they had no impact whatsoever in other countries.

Yet it is on just such points as this that the course of history can thwart the laws of logic and reason. The translation of the second of Brown's works was used in the last decade of the seventeenth century as the source-text for the first-ever publication of the work in its original language, and that fully eighteen years after the translation had been published. In amongst all manner of apparently unremarkable facts, then, a fact is thrown up that if not unique is at the least extremely rare. This detail demonstrates in its own way what a vital role translations played in the seventeenth-century international cultural milieu.

There is one more fact that allows the translations of Puritan works to be placed in a broader, international context. The works of the German Lutheran spiritual mysticist Jacob Böhme[62] (1575–1624) were disseminated largely in manuscript form during his own lifetime: they were copied by hand countless times over. These writings were collected in manuscript by the Amsterdam merchant Abraham van Beyerlandt (1587–1648), who then translated them into Dutch and had the translations published. It is telling that the three German editions of Böhme's collected works were all based on manuscripts assembled by van Beyerlandt.[63]

That it should have been in the Netherlands that Böhme's oeuvre was published stands to reason: his views were so controversial in the German states themselves that publishers dared not touch them, while in the Netherlands, and certainly in Amsterdam, such tolerance prevailed—to practical intents—that his works could be printed and disseminated

---

62 Lemper.
63 Brecht [1993-2], 213; Van Ingen.

without much hassle. The same explanation may be applied to eight of the nine Puritan manuscripts considered in these first two chapters. It was with good reason that Archer, the six Scots ministers, McWard, Fleming, Cotton and Brown had all left their native lands by the time their works came out in Dutch. Their ecclesiastical and spiritual views were not tolerated at home by the Crown. Save for Cotton, who had thrown in his lot with the American colonies, it was in the Netherlands that all these authors had sought refuge. We conclude, then, that it was not only the spirit of publishing tolerance in the Netherlands that accounted for the publication of these works in Dutch, but more particularly the fact that this country was their new home and field of ministry.

# 3. SCRIBAL PIETY

## The role of manuscripts in the international dissemination of Puritanism and Pietism

*The previous chapters have considered how seventeenth-century published translations of Puritan manuscripts were not based exclusively on book editions of the authorial manuscript but rather almost certainly drew upon at least nine actual autographs or copies of those manuscripts. This fact in and of itself demonstrates the great role that manuscripts played in the international dissemination of Puritanism. This consideration gains in importance in light of the fact that heretofore, special attention has never really been paid by academic researchers to the significance of manuscripts in the international spread of Puritanism from Britain. One contribution that has been made in this regard is that Frans W. Huisman focused on the Danish translations in manuscript of Puritan and Pietist writings, in an article published several years ago in both Dutch and Danish versions; this was followed by an article in Dutch by Jan van de Kamp discussing or otherwise listing some of the data that follows in the present chapter.[1]*

*It is not so very surprising that researchers have had a blind spot for manuscripts that underlay translations, since the same oversight is common to more general academic disciplines such as the history of books, of literature and of translation. In the United Kingdom at least, this lacuna in scholarship cannot be blamed on any lack of awareness of the relevance of manuscripts to seventeenth-century history, for manuscript research has been a discipline in its own right at British universities since the 1980s, one that has yielded many studies already.[2] There is even a dedicated series of*

---

1 Huisman [2008, 2009-2]; Van de Kamp [2010].
2 Beal [1980]; Love [1993]; Marotti [1995]; Beal [1998]; Brown; Anderson; Marotti [2000]; Love [2000, 2002]; Ezell; cf. Collinson *et al.*, 30; Burke [2007], 21–22; Greengrass and Freeman. The subtitle of *Print, Manuscript and Puritanism in England, 1580–1720* rather seemed to promise new information on the role of manuscripts in Puritanism, but sadly disappointed in that respect: Cambers, 171–180, 232–233. In contrast, another author makes exemplary use of manuscripts as sources of citations in his study of English preachers and their audience: Hunt. However, this is perhaps only to be expected, as he is a Curator of Manuscripts at the British Library.

*published studies on manuscript research, in print since 1989:* English Manuscript Studies 1100–1700. *Despite this specialism, the phenomenon of translations made from unpublished manuscripts has been all but ignored. The present writer is aware of only a single exception that proves this rule.*[3] *Even a trawl of works in English on other branches of historical research, such as the history of media and the history of translation, nets no findings on this phenomenon.*[4]

*Unlike in the United Kingdom, there is no tradition in the Netherlands of research on seventeenth-century manuscripts. While Willem Heijting did pay particular attention to the significance of media other than printed books, including manuscripts*[5]*, his plea for these kinds of communications to be researched has not yet resulted in any concrete findings.*[6] *Hardly surprising, then, that the standard work on Dutch book history has not a word to say about the theme of this present chapter.*[7] *Even the rich tradition of research on the Further Reformation and Dutch Reformed Pietism has next to nothing to offer on the subject. As far as the present author is aware, only one scholarly paragraph has ever been written on this topic.*[8]

*This yawning gap in research would be more readily explained if it were the case that no translations based on the manuscript of the source-text had ever been published beyond the field of Puritan texts. However, the number of manuscripts of Puritan texts that served as source for Dutch translations even in just the seventeenth century, now totalling nine to our knowledge, makes it vanishingly unlikely that this form of transfer was unknown to other sectors of the international exchange of scientific, religious, literary and cultural insights. In the first chapter, we have already briefly considered the English translation of the French manuscript of an anti-Puritan polemic, and in the previous chapter, the fact was mentioned that manuscripts by Jacob Böhme*[9] *(1575–1624) were first published in Dutch translation. It is also known that the unpublished Latin notes of Baruch Spinoza*[10] *(1632–1677) in his own copy of his* Tractatus theologico-politicus *(1670) were*

---

3   Richard Todd.
4   Briggs and Burke; Burke [2005, 2007].
5   Heijting [2010], especially 416.
6   Nelleke Moser has focused on manuscripts for quite some years now, since 2003: Moser [2003-1,-2, 2007, 2008, 2010, 2011, 2013, 2015, 2016-1,-2]. The latest of these publications concerns a Pietist hymnbook in manuscript. Unfortunately, that source falls outwith the scope of this study, as it dates from the latter half of the eighteenth century.
7   Delft and de Wolf.
8   Van Lieburg [1989], 82–83.
9   Lemper.
10  Van Bunge.

published in the French translation of Jan Hendrik Glazemaker (1620–1682) in 1678.[11] Even if these examples were very exceptional, it would still mean that the subject of Puritan manuscripts would take on a far greater importance to cultural history than the present author is aware that it currently commands.

In this chapter, the nine manuscripts considered in the two foregoing chapters are taken as a given and thus not included in the overview of (other) manuscripts. They will, however, crop up again in the chapter conclusions and will be taken into account there.

**Issues at hand**
The uncharted nature of this terrain, as set out above, calls for further exploration. Such inquiry will be conducted in this chapter, even if it cannot amount to more than a *tour d'horizon*. Our main research question is: Did the nine manuscripts underlying the Dutch publications comprise the whole set of their kind, or were they part of a larger whole? That is to say, are there more manuscripts of Puritan texts that ended up in foreign hands besides these nine and which, unlike these nine, were not published in translation? Questions proceeding from that main question include: Were the original Puritan texts in question translated or not? How did the transfers come about—directly from author to recipient, or via an intermediary? Did the transfers take place in the country of original production or in the country of reception? Did giver and recipient belong to any particular social group? Was the intention of the giver always that the work be translated and published in the foreign language in question? Did such manuscripts have a demonstrable impact?

Also, with a view to one of the key motives for this study, the phenomenon of Puritan manuscripts in foreign possession can be placed in a far broader context: Are there known examples of manuscripts with Pietistic content ending up beyond the country of their production, or at least in a country that spoke another language, and enjoying any significance or influence there?

The manuscripts considered thus far are *primary* manuscripts; that is, ones written in the hand of the author himself, or otherwise copies thereof, but at any rate such manuscripts of a text as were precursors to and underlay the published book version of a translation of that text. One could also call them pre-publication manuscripts. However, this field of research also includes manuscripts of translations that were copied out from a printed source-text. One could call such artefacts post-publication

---

11   Israel, 305–306.

manuscripts. A drawback of the adjective 'post-publication' is that it can give rise to the following misapprehension. A post-publication manuscript of necessity follows after the publication of the original text, but in many instances it will actually pre-date the publication of the *translation* as a book. Hence, quite often a 'post-publication' manuscript is equally a *pre*-publication manuscript! For this reason, it is preferable to denote this category of manuscripts as *secondary*, and we shall be using the nomenclature of primary and secondary manuscripts for the rest of the present chapter. For clarity, we state here that the primary manuscripts contain the English source-texts, and the secondary manuscripts the translations into languages other than English.

Many of the research questions we have just formulated for the primary manuscripts are also applicable to the secondary manuscripts, and will accordingly have to be addressed in that section of the chapter also.

**Puritan primary manuscripts**
Given the total lack of dedicated published material on the phenomenon under consideration, we shall commence with an overview of what van de Kamp's article has to say on the subject and of what else can be gleaned from smatterings in the literature, supplemented by such knowledge as the present author has acquired. The Puritan primary manuscripts are first considered, then the Puritan secondary manuscripts, all arranged in chronological order.

*William Whately*
The first manuscript in our survey is connected with a figure we are already familiar with from previous chapters, namely Willem Teellinck[12] (1570–1629). In 1633, a translation of his was published posthumously at Middelburg under the title *Cana Galileæ, oete houwelijckx predicatie. Neerghestelt om de bittere wateren, (daer mede den houwelijcken staet veeltijdts besprenght wort) te versoeten, ende in wijn te veranderen. [...] Noch een gulden cleynoot, behelsende twaelf christelijcke plichten, om de ziele van een christen inwendich te vercieren* [Cana of Galilee, or a wedding sermon, penned to sweeten the bitter waters wherewith the estate of marriage is often strewn, and to change them into wine [...] Further, A golden treasury, encompassing twelve Christian duties to ornament inwardly a Christian's soul].[13] This was a 148-page book in duodecimo format.

---

12  Beeke [2003]; Op 't Hof [2008-1, 2011-1, 2015-1].
13  Op 't Hof [2003].

## CANA GALILEÆ, OETE **Houwelijcke Predicatie.**

Neerghestelt **Om de bittere wateren,** (daer mede den Houwelijcken staet veeltijdts besprenght wort) te versoeten, ende in wijn te veranderen.

Uyt het Enghels in het Nederduytsch overgeset, door W. *Teellinck*, in sijn leven Dienaer des H. Euangelij, binnen Middelburgh in Zeelant.

NOCH **Een Gulden Clepnoot,** behelsende twaelf Christelijcke Plichten om de ziele van een Christen inwendich te vercieren.

Tot Middelburgh. Gedruct voor Iacob vande Vivere, Boeckvercooper, 1633.

---

*Cana Galileæ* consists of two parts. The first is a wedding sermon, in which Whately sets out the duties of spouses from Ephesians 5:23. He separates them into major and less important duties. The former category includes chastity and cohabitation, which are discussed in turn. Breakers of wedlock ought to be capitally punished by the government. Both adultery and wilful desertion are just causes for divorce; the wronged party may remarry in such cases. The less important duties concern either the overall relationship between the spouses or their sexual congress. Whately closes his work with two conclusions: 1. that marriage is not to be entered into lightly but ought to be preceded by thorough preparation; and 2. that the spouses must each concentrate on fulfilling their own duties and not busy themselves with the failings of their husband or wife.

The second part of *Cana Galileæ* consists of three texts that have nothing to do with the subject matter of the first part. The first of the three texts, *Een gulden cleynoot* itself, sets out twelve Christian duties as described in the aforementioned title. It is followed by *Een ander cleynoot. Bestaende uyt twee douzijn costelijcke medaelien ofte christelijcke plichten* [A second treasury, of two dozen precious medals or Christian duties]. The last three pages of the volume are a separate text again: *Betrachtinge van een godsalich man, ontrent zijn gheloove* [Meditation of a godly man on his faith]. None of the parts of this book has its author listed on the title page, although it is announced that Teellinck translated the wedding sermon from English. This was the third translation he had made of a Puritan work that had come to be published. The reader is left very much with the impression that the editor, perhaps at the publisher's instigation, cast about to augment the wedding sermon with extra material to obtain a publication of a little more bulk. *Cana Galileæ* was published only once, and there is only a single extant copy of that sole print run.[14]

The preliminaries to *Cana Galileæ* are made up of two texts: a bridal poem and a preface. The bridal poem is signed N.A.V.D. All the evidence would indicate that these refer to the initials of Nicolaas Anthony van der Deliën[15] (b. 1600), who, given the place (Middelburg) and time of his birth, will have been familiar with Teellinck as a preacher in his city. One of the details mentioned in Teellinck's posthumously-issued *Laetste predikatien* [Last sermons] indicates that van der Deliën was a friend of Teellinck's.[16] The author tells us in the preface that his aim in writing this little work has been to acquaint spouses with the duties they owe in their marriage and to inform them on the practicalities of marriage. He also states that he originally delivered the contents orally as a wedding sermon.

The name appearing under this preface resolves the question of who wrote the English original underlying *Cana Galileæ*: it was William Whately (1583–1639), another of whose short works Teellinck had already translated. The preface is dated 20 August 1608. Surprisingly, an English bibliographical search for Whately indicates that no work of his from the year 1608 is known and that the title *Cana Galileæ* is entirely

---

14  Op 't Hof [1993-1], 118.
15  Op 't Hof [2015-13].
16  Teellinck [1647], (3*)12r.

# A BRIDE-BVSH,
## OR
## A WEDDING SERMON:

Compendiously describing
the duties of Married
Persons:

*By performing whereof, Marriage shall
be to them a great Helpe, which
now finde it a little
Hell.*

*Marriage is honourable amongst all men : but Whoremongers and
Adulterers God will iudge.* Heb. 13.4.

Printed at London by *William Iaggard*, for *Nicholas Bourne*, and
are to be sold at his shop at the entrance into the
Royall Exchange, 1617.

missing from the list of his works. However, there is a work of his whose subtitle matches that of Teellinck's translation: *A bride-bush, or a wedding sermon*. The first edition of that work in English dates from 1617. Research of the contents confirms that this is the same text as Teellinck's translation. What is remarkable is that Whately's preface to the 1617 English edition is dated 20 August 1608, just as it is in the Dutch translation. Consequently, the only conclusion we can draw is that Whately already had the text of his wedding sermon ready for press in 1608 and that the publication of that original text did not occur until nearly a decade afterwards.

The second edition of *A bride-bush*, dated 1619, is more than four times as copious as the 1617 edition.[17] Whately included in this edition a dedication to his father-in-law, giving us a number of facts that shed more light on the background and editorial history of this work. He states that it was some ten or eleven years previously (*i.e., circa* 1608) that he had preached a wedding sermon and had let a friend have a copy of it. That copy of the sermon had been published in 1617 without his knowledge, which had induced Whately to publish the current, much fuller version.

Given that Teellinck, the translator of the wedding sermon, had died in 1629, this was a posthumous edition. We are left wondering what it could have been that made the editor and publisher recall from oblivion a translated manuscript on such a topic as this. In seeking an answer to this question, our train of thought will inevitably gravitate towards the theory that there was a particular occasion for the publication. This notion is corroborated by the introductory poem in the volume, which makes clear that this translation was distributed at a wedding. Unfortunately, we are not told whose marriage it was. Although conclusive proof is not forthcoming in the present state of research, it is entirely reasonable to posit that *Cana Galileæ* was published on the occasion of the wedding of the last unmarried offspring of Willem Teellinck, namely his daughter Johanna, who was married to the preacher Petrus Gribius[18] (1602/3–1666) in 1633. The spouses had come to know each other via Johanna's eldest brother, Maximiliaan[19] (1605–1653), who while a theology student at Franeker had been in the same matriculation year as Gribius[20] and who

---

17  For the information in this paragraph, I am indebted to Dr Christopher Godfrey of the University of Manchester.
18  Van der Kamp [2015].
19  Brienen [1993]; Op 't Hof [2016-16].
20  Op 't Hof [1987-1], 499–500.

had travelled to England together with Gribius to be trained in the pragmatics of the ministry by John Cotton (1585–1652) at his household seminary. In light of Maximiliaan's closeness to Gribius, we may suppose that Maximiliaan had a hand in the publication of *Cana Galileæ*.

This reconstruction does throw up one problem, however. Van der Deliën had died in 1630, making it impossible that he could have penned his poem with a view to the impending nuptials of Petrus and Johanna in 1633. A sensible resolution of this conundrum would be that Maximiliaan had come across van der Deliën's epithalamion among his father's papers and thought it would be a fitting enrichment to the edition. Alternatively, it may first have served as van der Deliën's present for Maximiliaan's own wedding, in which case Maximiliaan would have had it in his own possession.

At this juncture, we ought to consider another problem, namely the question of when it was that Willem Teellinck translated Whately's wedding sermon. Given that the first edition of the work in English dates from 1617, it would at first glance seem quite obvious to assume that the translation must have been made between 1617 and 1629. However, there is considerable reason to doubt that, with several remarkable circumstances that combine to imply a very different history.

In the first place, Teellinck had already published a translated work by Whately before, and as we have seen in a previous chapter, he had received the manuscript of that work in the course of 1607, as part of a consignment from the author. From Teellinck's indication of his intention to publish these too once he is reassured that his present translation is well received, we glean that the other items sent were also manuscripts.[21]

In the second place, there is the fact that while the first (unauthorised) edition of the English text of *A bride-bush* dates from 1617, its preface is dated 1608, so that Whately had evidently readied his work for the press at that time but failed to find a publisher. It is therefore plausible that Whately took the same course of action now as he had in 1607, namely sending a copy of the work to his spiritual comrade in Middelburg. If he did do so, then there is a great likelihood that Teellinck had proceeded to translate this book, too, into Dutch before it appeared in print in English in 1617. The foregoing hypothesis also provides a sound basis for explaining the strange total discrepancy between the title of the translation published in 1633 and the title of the English edition of 1617: *Cana Galileæ*, as opposed to *A bride-bush*. The Dutch title might be the original title from 1608, which if so will have been changed to *A bride-bush* in 1617

---

21 This study, 26.

when the first English edition came out without Whately's knowledge. For his own 1619 edition, Whately chose not to change the title.

There is a third aspect of *Cana Galileæ* that lends substance to the hypothesis developed thus far. The second and third parts of the work, treating of Christian duties, remain of obscure provenance. Their author is not named, nor are we informed whether they represent an original Dutch text or a translation from English. Since the wedding sermon is explicitly presented in the volume as a translation from English and the other two parts are not, we might be inclined to suppose that these latter two are Teellinck's own writings. Their content would certainly chime with such an authorship. Yet it is equally possible, given the contents of these sections, that Whately was their author as he was of the first part. It is therefore of interest that the first three parts of *Cana Galileæ* have duties as their theme and that both the first and the second part bear the message that we must have an eye not to other's sins but to our own. The final part of the volume, covering merely the last three pages, will also have been Whately's work if the second and third parts were.

If Whately was indeed responsible for the second, third and fourth parts of the volume, then the source-texts may well have been those aforementioned other manuscripts that Whately sent Teellinck in 1607 or on other occasions. If this was the case, then Maximiliaan will have discovered the translations while preparing *Cana Galileæ* for press and will have added them to the Dutch text of Whately's wedding sermon, in order to pad out the book. Should this reconstruction be correct, then it implies that Teellinck translated the manuscripts he obtained from his English friend rather quickly, regardless of whether he had a publisher interested in them or not. Seen in that light, *Cana Galileæ* might well have been translated in 1608 or shortly thereafter.

The foregoing makes it probable that Teellinck obtained manuscripts with Puritan content from his Banbury friend Whately during 1607 and 1608 and that he proceeded to translate them without much delay. The reason that he did not publish them will have had to do with the fact that he did not live to see demand for a reprint of the 1609 publication of his other translation of Whately, *Corte verhandelinghe van de voornaemste christelicke oeffeninghen* [A brief treatment of the chief Christian exercises]. He will have been disappointed at the sluggish reception of that book, thereby being dissuaded from publishing any more of his English friend's manuscripts. Teellinck might perhaps still have made some efforts to secure a publisher, but if so, he will not have found one prepared to fund the venture.

Whatever the niceties of the matter, it is at least clear that Whately and Teellinck remained in contact for life. A previously unknown piece of evidence supports this claim:[22] on 25 July 1623, a testimonial regarding one Levinus Coolman was read out at the presbytery of Schouwen-Duiveland. This testimony had been penned by Whately, who had had Coolman as a house-guest.[23] Even though the particular circumstances that prompted this testimonial have not (yet) revealed themselves, it is very plausible that it was via Teellinck that Coolman found his way to Whately.

*John Cotton*
The first manuscript considered above had to do with the first Puritan work that was almost certainly never published in English but was published in Dutch. The following manuscripts we shall discuss, on the other hand, are of the oldest known Puritan work that was ever laid to press in Dutch before it appeared in the original English. On 26 October 1629, Timotheus van Vleteren[24] (d. 1641), minister of the Dutch Church in London, wrote a letter to one of the leading Puritans of all, John Cotton, who was then still in Boston, Lincolnshire.[25] Van Vleteren had previously had an incumbency in the Netherlands, at Zoutelande on the Zeeland island of Walcheren, from 1624-1628. He was recommended by Teellinck when the London ministry became vacant in 1627. Together with his eldest son Maximiliaan, Teellinck saw to it that van Vleteren was able to accept the call that was subsequently issued.[26] In his letter to Cotton, whom he had not seen in the flesh, van Vleteren spelled out that he was a spiritual ally of both Maximiliaan Teellinck and Isaac Bisschop (d. 1661), who had both studied in Cotton's household. He had been a friend of Maximiliaan's since boyhood; Bisschop had succeeded him as minister of Zoutelande. Both had told van Vleteren, in words of high praise, of the edifying conversations they had had with Cotton. The following clause in the letter is of crucial significance to the present chapter: "[…] and communicated their writinges from you vnto me namely Catechisme, on the

---

22  I owe this find to the kind negotiating assistance of my colleague, Prof. Fred A. van Lieburg.
23  Zierikzee, Gemeentearchief Schouwen-Duiveland [Municipal Archive of the Island of Schouwen-Duiveland], Archief Classis Zierikzee [Archive of Zierikzee Presbytery], inv. no. 1, Acta Classis Schouwen-Duiveland [Records of the Presbytery of Schouwen-Duiveland], 23 July 1623 art. 1.
24  Op 't Hof [2016-20].
25  Bush, 133-135.
26  Op 't Hof [2008-1], 356-358; Hessels, 3: 1333-1350, 1358-1360.

Canticles, of predestination."[27] Evidently, we have to do here with three manuscripts of Cotton's that had then not yet been published: a catechism, a commentary on the Song of Solomon, and a treatise on predestination. The first of these must refer to a work published only in 1713 (!), entitled *A treatise of I. of faith. II. twelve fundamental articles of christian religion. III. a doctrinal conclusion. IV. questions and answers upon church-government*; the second, a work published in London in 1642, entitled *A brief exposition of the whole book of Canticles, or Song of Solomon*; the third will be *A treatise of Mr. Cottons, clearing certaine doubts concerning predestination*, also published in London, in 1646. Since it is known that Cotton was in the habit of continually revising his own manuscripts[28], the versions referred to in van Vleteren's letter are not likely to agree exactly with the texts as later published. Be that as it may, it is remarkable that Maximiliaan Teellinck and Bisschop took home with them manuscripts of at least three works by their Puritan instructor and that once back in the Netherlands, they lent them to a spiritually like-minded friend to read.

Cotton's reply to van Vleteren, dated 16 December 1629, contains further new leads for the present study.[29] It appears that Cotton had, at Willem Teellinck's request, written a brief treatise demonstrating that the most exacting of human efforts, and any and all forms of common grace, fall short of conversion. Moreover, Teellinck had died more than half a year previously and had not been personally known to Cotton. In the reply, Cotton asks what has become of the resulting work that he sent, since he never heard anything more about it. Unfortunately, no response to this reply is known, but it would not be surprising if Cotton never received his manuscript back again, since none of his published works fits the description given in the reply.[30]

Compiling our data, we arrive at the following reconstruction. During Maximiliaan's residence together with Bisschop at Cotton's household seminary in Boston from 1625 to 1627, he obtained at least three manuscripts from Cotton, which he took home at the end of his studies. He lent them to his close friend and brother minister, van Vleteren. It is impossible to assume other than that he had first of all let his father read them, who since his own conversion in a Puritan environment had a lifelong orientation towards Puritanism. The information that Maximiliaan provided to

---

27  Bush, 134.
28  This study, 81-83.
29  Bush, 135–137.
30  Pollard *et al.*, 1: 263b nos. 5854–5855; Wing, 1: 648–650 nos. C6407–6472.

his father about Cotton will have been prompting enough for Willem to write to the Englishman to seek his opinion on the role that man's efforts and universal grace play in conversion. It is all but certain that this chain of events is linked with the manuscript written by Cotton in 1618 in which he propounds "that those who are condemned are damned for refusing to do what they can do".[31] It was in that Dutch request that Cotton found his leading to draft his brief treatise and to send it to Teellinck. It must be in connection with Willem Teellinck's death in early April 1629 that the manuscript went missing.

**Puritan secondary manuscripts**
Texts written by Puritan authors were translated on a broad scale and in a good many countries. Sometimes, an individual would write a translation for private use; on other occasions, the translation was made with an eye to publication. In the latter case, the translator would typically consign the manuscript to the printer in person and the manuscript itself would have no further role to play, save perhaps at the proofreading stage. Where there was a considerable time lag between translation and publication, or where the secondary manuscript was never published, then it is a possibility that the manuscript in question had a story to tell. That is the aspect that we will now be looking at, considering the Netherlands, Denmark and Germany in turn.

*Netherlands*
The complete works of a Scots Episcopalian of Puritan convictions, Bishop William Cowper (1568–1619), were brought into circulation in Dutch translation during the second and third decades of the seventeenth century. The whole translation, save for part of the commentary on Revelation, was the work of one man: the Hague preacher Johannes Lamotius[32] (d. 1627). One of Cowper's works translated by Lamotius came to bear the Dutch title *Een seer troostelijcke tsaemenspreeckinghe tussschen den Heere ende de siele*. Although it was furnished with its own title page, its page numbering continued from the previous work contained in the volume, which was *Een verachtinge des doodts* [A defiance of death]. Both of these little works came out in 1618. The title page of the dialogue states explicitly that it was translated from the English by Lamotius.[33] The original English text of this brief work had first appeared in print in 1610,

---

31  Bremer [ODNB].
32  Op 't Hof [1987-1], 423–437.
33  Op 't Hof [1987-1], 101.

entitled *A most comfortable and christian dialogue betweene the Lord and the soule*.

We know from the autobiography of Zutphen preacher Willem Baudartius[34] (1565–1640) that he translated the same dialogue into Dutch in 1615.[35] Since the autobiography makes no mention of that translation ever having been published and no trace of such a publication is evident, we may with near certainty presume that this translation never progressed past manuscript stage.

In the seventeenth century, a manuscript was seldom intended exclusively for private use: it would typically be lent to relatives, friends, acquaintances and those showing an interest. Such is likely to have been the case with this manuscript, too. One interesting question that arises in this regard is whether Lamotius might have been among those who read or had sight of Baudartius' manuscript translation of Cowper's dialogue. It is incontrovertible that the two ministers forged a close friendship.[36] Given that friendship, it is notable that Lamotius translated nearly the whole of Cowper's oeuvre between 1612 and 1627, while Baudartius' translation of Cowper's dialogue was undertaken in 1615. The chronology makes it reasonable for us to suppose that it was Lamotius who made his friend and brother minister Baudartius aware of Cowper's work; additionally, it might have well been him who gave Baudartius the English source-text, whether by lending him his own copy or purchasing one for him. Had the reverse been the case, Lamotius would very likely have made mention of his indebtedness in the preface to one or other of his translations.

As has been seen in the previous chapter, the manuscript of Cotton's exposition of the Song of Solomon was translated by the Middelburg schoolmaster Johannes de Swaef[37] (1594–1653), probably in 1629, and came onto the market in 1633 courtesy of a Middelburg publisher. We read most instructively in de Swaef's dedication of his translation to the then Pensionary of the City of Dordrecht (and later Grand Pensionary of the States of Holland), Jacob Cats[38] (1577–1660), that the manuscript translation had by the time of its publication already generated a number of manuscript copies: several preachers had written out de Swaef's

---

34  Broek Roelofs; this study, 201-207.
35  Broek Roelofs, 222.
36  This study, 201 and 205.
37  Groenendijk [1990]; Op 't Hof [2016-13].
38  Ten Berge; Op 't Hof [2015-11].

translation.[39] Thus, there were numerous copies of the translation of Cotton's Song of Solomon commentary in circulation before it came into print. This course of events will certainly not have been exceptional.

A translation by Jacobus Koelman[40] (1631-1695) of *The soules humiliation* (1637) by the Father of Connecticut, Thomas Hooker (1586-1647) of Leicestershire and Cambridge, was published in 1678, entitled *Ziels-vernedering, en heylzame wanhoop*. One of Koelman's two motives for making this translation was that he was implored by several countrymen who had read a Dutch summary of the content of the book to furnish them with a full version. The précis was written by the sometime Utrecht preacher Johannes Theodori van der Wenden (d. 1664), whom Koelman calls an especially godly and holy man. Nor is that description mere fancy: Koelman, who had grown up in Utrecht, had witnessed his life at close quarters. Van der Wenden had given his manuscript to someone who evidently had let others read it. Koelman made his unabridged translation to spare these and other readers the pains of having to copy out the summary time and again.[41] These remarks by Koelman reveal that a manuscript by van der Wende was in circulation that contained a précis of the aforementioned Puritan work and that it was regularly being copied.

*Denmark*
For the following section of this chapter that is devoted to Denmark, I am entirely indebted to an article by Frans W. Huisman.[42] A book was published at Copenhagen in 1704-1706 entitled *Hiertets Selfbedragelse eller Selfbedragelses Hemmelighed, nemlig hvorledes et Menniske udi sin Saligheds Sag sig self bedrager*. It was a Danish translation of *The mysterie of self-deceiving* by the Essex and Cambridge Puritan Daniel Dyke (d. 1614). The translation was by Ludvig Winslow (1674-1712), who wrote an extensive preface to the book, giving many interesting details. For our present purposes, the details of note are those concerning the reception enjoyed by Dyke's work in Denmark and most especially Winslow's remarks about translations circulating in manuscript. Winslow sees fit to tell us that before his present translation, no fewer than seven Danish translations of the same work had been made for private use, which hence

---

39 Cotton [1633], A3v.
40 Krull; Van Lieburg [1990]; Meeuse [1990, 2008]; Op 't Hof [2013-1], 237-268; Groenendijk [2017].
41 Hooker [1678], *2r.
42 Huisman [2008, 2009-2].

were never published. One of these was the effort of a noble lady, Sophia Below (1590–1650), whose daughter was the learned translator Birgitte Thott (1610–1662). The manuscript translation will be discussed in our next paragraph. While Winslow himself was personally aware of seven previous translations of Dyke's book, he goes on to inform the reader that a contemporary Danish professor had said that actually no fewer than twenty [!] different Danes had translated this Puritan text. These translations were intended for personal meditation and also for reworking into sermons.[43]

The unique Karen Brahes Library at Odense,[44] which represents the distillation of the intellectual and spiritual concerns of a social group of noble Danish families through the course of the whole seventeenth century and the first three decades of the eighteenth, harbours not only printed but also handwritten devotional material. The library boasts manuscripts of Danish translations of Puritan books and chrestomathies of Puritan writings that never saw a printing press in Denmark. Inscriptions indicate that there was an intensive exchange of manuscripts carried on between the members of the various noble families. It is not groundless to assert that no country preserves more handwritten translations of Puritan works than Denmark does. The woman responsible for this wealth of material is Anne Gøye (1609–1681), who began assembling her library as far back as her time spent lodging with her uncle, the prominent Danish scholar Holger Rosenkrantz (1574–1642). When she bequeathed her books to her grand-niece Karen Brahe, the collection already ran to a thousand printed volumes and around a hundred volumes of manuscripts![45]

There follows an overview of the Danish manuscripts that contain a Puritan text in translation.[46] As far as has been possible, the below is an alphabetical list by author, title of translation, name of translator, year or period of translation, source-language and finally (in square brackets) title and publication year of the source-text, or alternatively—where the source-language and publication year of the source-text remain unknown—the title and publication year of the earliest known English edition.

---

43 One of the advantages of the medium of manuscript was that the translations eluded the stringent Lutheran censorship exercised on publications.
44 Nielsen; Madsen.
45 Huisman [2008], 201–2; [2009-2], 124–5.
46 I have Frans W. Huisman's kind mediation to thank for access to the following data.

*Anne Goye*

Lewis Bayly, 'En meget skiøn Tractat Om den Sande Christelige Andact. huad den? Om dendz Nødvendighed: Och Huorledes mand den samme Kand bekomme och beholde', Karen Bille sl. Falck Giøes, 1650, German[47] [*Praxis Pietatis*, 1635]

Arthur Dent, 'Den Sande Omvendelses Vey, paa huilken Et Christelig hierte kand rettelige vandre sin gandske lifves tid til Guds Velbehag', Susanne Juel Jens Datter, 1677[48] [*A sermon of repentance*, 1582]

Daniel Dyke, 'Selff Bedrags Hemmelighed', Sophie Below and Birgitte Thott, 1651, English[49] [*The mystery of self-deceiving*, 1614]

Joseph Hall, 'Den fri Fanges Tancker', Birgitte Thott, 1633–1668[50] [*Contemplationes*, 1634]

Joseph Hall, 'Prædiken over Johannes Evangelium Cap. 19. vers 30', Birgitte Thott, 1633–1668[51] [*Contemplationes*, 1634]

Joseph Hall, 'Sattans gloende piile ud', Sophie Thott, 1667, English[52] [*Contemplationes*, 1634]

Joseph Hall, 'Een opbyggelig Tractat kaldet Andægtige Siæel-Sucke med stor andagt", C.M.R., early eighteenth century, Dutch[53] [De suchten van een aendachtighe ziele, *Contemplationes*, 1663, 45-54]

Joseph Hall, 'Een Christen Anatomeret og aabenbaret i sin gandsche Disposition og Omgiengelse', C.M.R., early eighteenth century[54] [*Contemplationes*, 1634]

This list justifies the following conclusions. The temporal concentration of these compositions lies in the latter half of the seventeenth century. This will be a consequence of the fact that the authors concerned had first achieved their fame in Germany through translations[55] and that the degree of popularity that they enjoyed in Denmark was a concomitant of this. In turn, this aspect is connected with the fact that German was the source-text for one of the most extensive of the manuscripts. In this regard, it is striking that one of the shorter texts was a translation out of Dutch, although that fact is also congruent with the discovery that at least

---

47  Riising, A VI, 18 (1–38).
48  Riising, A VI, 30 (1–28).
49  Riising, A VI, 24.
50  Riising, A III, 6 (34–59).
51  Riising, A III, 6 (60–93).
52  Riising, A VI, 22 (64–140).
53  Riising, A VI, 53 (1–31).
54  Riising, A VI, 53 (31–52).
55  Sträter; Van der Haar [1997].

one-third of all known German translations of Puritan works were based on a Dutch source-text.[56]

Something remarkable and characteristic of the Danish translations is that all known translators were female, while in no other land is any instance known of a woman being involved in making a Puritan work accessible to her countrymen. A further distinctive is that the translators appertained to the highest Danish social class.[57] Yet most remarkable of all is the fact that the translators and their readers were Lutherans. The sum of all Danish manuscript translations of Puritan works is irrefutable proof of the absorption of Reformed piety in countries with an established Lutheran church. Given this, there are sound arguments in favour of the position that Puritanism was the manifestation of Reformed piety par excellence that was able to transcend confessions and penetrate through barriers. Puritan piety was so catholic in appeal and so vital in essence that it achieved interconfessional outworkings.[58]

*Germany*
The archive of the Franckesche Stiftungen at Halle houses a manuscript containing four brief passages of Puritan texts in German translation.[59] The first three are in the same hand; the fourth extract was penned by another writer. Unfortunately, the names of the translators and dates of translation are not stated. It appears to be a kind of chrestomathy (collection of texts selected for their exemplariness). The archive description of the manuscript is as follows:

*Die zeitliche Waffen womit ein Christ kan die feurige Pfeile des Satans auslöschen u. bereit sein zur Zeit d. Anfechtung durch Pauli Bayne, Engelsman, versetzt in hollendisch durch L. Lamotium. Ef. 6.10. Zuletzt meine brüd[er] seydt stark in dem H[errn] und in d[er] Macht seiner Stärke.* [The temporal arms wherewith a Christian can quench Satan's fiery darts and be prepared for the time of assailment, by Paul Bayne, Englishman, translated into Dutch by L. Lamotius, Eph. 6:10: "Finally, my brethren, be strong in the Lord and in the power of His might".]
Ein Mensch in Christo oder eine neu Creatur durch Thom. Taylor. 2 Cor. 5,17 Ist jemand in Christo, so ist er eine neue Creatur. [A man

---

56 Sträter, 31; Op 't Hof [2001-1], 350–351; Van de Kamp [2012-1], 147.
57 Huisman [2008], 195–196; [2009-2], 117–119.
58 Op 't Hof [2001-1], 376–377; Huisman [2008], 203, 212, 220–223; [2009-2], 126, 136–137, 146–149.
59 Halle, Archiv Franckesche Stiftungen, A 36.

in Christ, or a new creation, by Thom*[as]* Taylor, II Cor. 5:17: "If any man be in Christ, he is a new creature".]

Robert Boltons Von der Erniedrigung ad Christo auß Act. 2,37. [Of humiliation unto Christ, by Robert Bolton, from Acts 2:37.]

Sol. Loqvia durch Paulus Peine darinnen er eine sonderl. Anweisung v. Aufweckung zu wahrer bekehrung, liebe v. neuen gehorsam gegen Gott entfaltet. [A monologue by Paul Peine, in which is set out a special declaration urging awakening to true repentance, love and new obedience towards God.]

In 1676, *Ein Mensch in Christo oder eine neue Creatur* was published, a work written by Thomas Taylor (1576-1633) and translated by Simon Jodocus Krüger[60] (d. 1706). The title page informs us that Krüger had used the Dutch translation as his source-text, not the English original.[61] This presents us with three possibilities. Either the man in whose hand the first three extracts in the manuscript are written was Krüger himself; or it was an unidentified scribe who in the case of Taylor's work had copied out Krüger's translation; or else it was someone who produced the translations on his own initiative. Since the source-text for the first extract was also the Dutch translation of the passage in question, it would appear that the man behind the first three German texts was, if not a copyist, then a German who understood Dutch but not English. In any event, Dutch versions of the third and fourth extract were already available in the period when this chrestomathy was written, which will have been in the 1670s at the earliest. Detailed further research might be able to throw more light on the question.

No German translations at all are known of the works of Paul Baynes (d. 1617).[62] Accordingly, we conclude that the first and the last of the extracts only ever existed in manuscript. Three works by Robert Bolton (1572-1631) appeared in German translation between 1673 and 1676.[63] The third of the extracts might relate to one of these.

**Pietist manuscripts**
It was not only Puritan works that circulated in manuscript on the Continent; interested readers were able to read non-Puritan Reformed works on piety in the same manner. Currently, one English and several German

---

60  Leurdijk [2015].
61  Leurdijk [2013], 34.
62  McKenzie, 82.
63  McKenzie, 90-91.

# A
# SPARKE
## TOWARD THE
### KINDLING OF
*Sorrow for* SION.

*A Meditation on* AMOS 6. 6.

## BEING THE SVMME OF
A Sermon preached at Sergeants Inne in FLEET-STREET.

By THOMAS GATAKER B. *of* D. and Paſtor of *Rotherhith*.

LONDON,
Printed by *I. H.* for *William Sheffard*, and are to be ſold at the ſigne of the Starre in Corne-hill, and in Popes-head Alley. 1621.

and Danish secondary manuscripts are known, but in light of the above section we ought not to be astonished if future discoveries indicate that such manuscripts were circulating in more countries than these.

*Willem Teellinck*
Teellinck is no less a key figure in this section than in the previous; a further indication that it is not misguided to refer to him as the Father of the Further Reformation. *Weech-schale des heylichdoms* was published in 1621, the seventeenth of his works to go to press.[64] The work became available to English readers the same year, under the title *The ballance of the sanctuarie*. The translator is not stated, but it is known that the renowned Puritan Thomas Gataker (1574–1654), who had become personally acquainted with the Middelburg reformer in the summer of 1620, proofread the translation and was responsible for the final editing. By implication, then, Gataker had the manuscript of the translation in his hands and read it painstakingly. This had unexpected consequences. As Gataker read the manuscript, he recalled that he had his own notes on similar homiletic matter, from a sermon he had preached more than a year previously, still lying around. He now conceived the desire to publish his own notes on the subject in more extensive form. The resulting booklet was *A sparke towards the kindling of sorrow for Sion*, which too was published in 1621. Surely, it was a one-off event that the manuscript of an English translation of a Dutch Further Reformation work thus prompted the publication in England of a Puritan sermon.

The translation of Teellinck's work not only became known in manuscript across the North Sea but also spread in the other direction, eastwards to the German states. His magnum opus was the most comprehensive reformation blueprint ever seen in Dutch: *Noodwendigh vertoogh* [A necessary exposition] (1627). As such, it may be regarded as the major written monument to the piety movement in the Netherlands. This copious volume was finally translated into German in 1674 by the German lawyer Philipp Erberfeld[65] (1639–1709), who had taken his doctorate in law at Franeker in the Dutch province of Friesland in 1668. In his preface to *Leben auß dem Tode* [Life out of death] (1675), his translation of a work by another Dutch Further Reformation man, Guiljelmus Saldenus[66] (1627–1694), Erberfeld includes the plea that he is still seeking a publisher for his translation of *Noodwendigh vertoogh*. Van de Kamp

---

64  For this and the following, see Op 't Hof [2008-1], 225–229.
65  Van de Kamp [2012-1], 69–105.
66  Van den End.

has proposed the intriguing and moreover plausible hypothesis that Erberfeld's failure thus far to secure a publisher had to do with the fact that the Father of Lutheran Pietism, Philipp Jakob Spener[67] (1635–1705), had already published his own reform agenda.

While it is unproven whether or not this had a bearing on Erberfeld's quest, it is a fact that his translation in manuscript of Teellinck's magnum opus was known to more than one preacher in the Ruhr presbytery as of 31 October 1674. That was the date on which an extraordinary session was called by preacher Heinrich Brüggemann with the agenda of drawing up rules of conduct for ministers of the gospel. During this Reformational meeting—the date of 31 October will not have been chosen for nought!—the translation of *Noodwendigh vertoogh* came up in discussion: it was remarked that the content of the book concurred with that of *Christelijcke bedenckingen* [Christian observations] by Godefridus Udemans[68] (1581/2–1649). We conclude, then, that the German translation of Teellinck's work in manuscript, whether or not copies were involved, had not lacked impact already.

If we were to assume, however, that that example constituted the exception that proved the supposed rule that translations were not circulated in manuscript, the following publication we shall consider, from the first decade of the eighteenth century, would correct our misapprehension.[69] In 1706, the heirs of Friedrich Lanckischen at Leipzig brought out a work by the Lutheran superintendent Johann Georg Hoffmann (1648–1706) entitled *Geistlicher engeländis. Redner, worinne die Schrifften der engeländischen Prediger untersuchet, gegen die evangelische Prediger-Methode gehalten, und überall, daß es damit nicht allein auff euserliche Moden und Ohren-juckende Zierathen, sondern auff Beweisung des Geistes und der Krafft des göttlichen Worts ankomme, vermittelst der Theologiae exeget. & pathologicae bewiesen wird: wobey ein sonderbarer Vorbericht von der Beschaffenheit und Nutz solcher Schrifften, nebst etlichen nach engeländischer Art elaborirten Predigten zu finden* [The spiritual English orator: in which the writings of English preachers are examined, held up against the evangelical[70] method of preaching, and it is comprehensively proven that what is at stake is not merely external fashions and ear-tickling ornaments, but the demonstration of the Spirit and of the power of the

---

67  Grünberg; Wallmann.
68  Meertens; Fieret; K. Exalto [1989]; Schutte [1989], 301–302, 310–311; Uil [2016-2].
69  For the following, cf. Op 't Hof [2008-1], 510–511.
70  i.e., Lutheran.

Word of God by means of exegetical and pathological[71] theology; to which is prefaced a special message on the nature and use of such writings, as well as some sermons worked up in the English manner].

At the publisher's request, the Naumburg preacher Johann Martin Schamelius[72] (1671–1742) drew up a list of the English writings of the type treated in the book that had appeared in German translation. This was inserted between the foreword and the body of the text. In fact, translations of Italian, French and Dutch works also crop up on the list, and one of the Dutch authors mentioned is Teellinck. Schamelius enumerates here among Teellinck's works not only those that are known to have been published in German translation but also the German titles *Nothwendiger Vertrag* and *Vornehmste Ubung der Christen*. He must have been referring to manuscripts in those two cases. The first of these is undoubtedly identical with Erberfeld's translation of Teellinck's magnum opus; the latter must refer to *Corte verhandelinghe*, Teellinck's translation of a manuscript of Whately's. Evidently, then, there were various manuscript translations circulating among German Teellinck aficionados! Schamelius' mention of these two manuscripts in 1706 is a strong indication that they were far from having fallen out of favour many decades after their translation.

One of the entries in the Frankfurt Book Fair catalogue for Easter/Autumn 1699, which was published a full year in advance, reads:

> *Teelinck, Wilhelm*: Lust=Garten Christlicher Gebeter in IV. Theilen [...] übersetztet von Christoph Brüßken, Pfarrherrn in Offenbach in 18. Franckfurt bey Joh. David Zunnern. [A pleasure-garden of Christian prayers in four sections [...] translated by Christoph Bruessken, vicar of Offenbach, *[published]* in 18*[mo]* at Frankfurt by Joh*[annes]* David Zunner.][73]

The translator of *Lust-Hof* referred to here, Johann Christoph Brößke, was minister first at Offenbach-am-Main from 1687–1698 and then at Neckerau in the Palatinate.[74] As there is no trace of this edition, we must assume that it proceeded no further than the announcement of the new title and that it remained a translation in manuscript only.

---

71 i.e., expert on the passions of the soul.
72 Lindner.
73 Schrader, 447 footnote 112.
74 Schrader, 438–439 footnote 83.

*Ecce virum, toto cui pulchra modestia vultu*
  *Excubat, et plenus Numine verba facit:*
*Aut vigil æterni condit monumenta laboris,*
  *Fulta quibus pietas, cum pietate fides.*
*Simplicitas oculos, doctam facundia linguam:*
  *Pura verecundus pectora candor habet.*
*Scilicet ante fores tali famulante corona,*
  *Virtutem Dominam quis neget esse domi?*

                                Johannes Westerburg.

## Godefridus Udemans

The foregoing has already made mention of the fact that the Ruhr presbytery meeting of 1674 considered the matter of a translation in manuscript of Udemans' *Christelijke bedenckingen*. However, a decision was also taken at that gathering about the manuscript in question: when the proposal was made to have the translation published, it was resolved that advice first be sought on this from the sister presbyteries and synods. Some things can probably be deduced about the provenance of this manuscript. Given that Swiss preacher Jacob Meyer's translation of the work in question by Udemans was published the same year, it is possible that members of the Ruhr presbytery had access to that manuscript or perhaps copies of it. Whatever the facts in that regard, the minutes of the presbytery session at least indicate that the Dutch Further Reformation was a matter of prime attention by the German Reformed and that manuscripts played a crucial role in these channels.

## Pierre du Moulin

Naturally, the manuscript collection of the aforementioned Karen Brahes Library includes translations of works that can be broadly considered to belong to German Lutheran Pietism. Two authors are represented in the collection, namely Johann Arndt[75] (155–1621) and Martin Moller[76] (1547–1606).[77] It has already been seen that there were also noblewomen among the patrons of Puritan texts. At this point, attention must be paid to the fact that another Pietist work, *Du combat chrétien ou des afflictions* (Of the Christian struggle or afflictions) (1622) by the French Reformed author Pierre du Moulin[78] (1568–1658), was translated into Danish by Birgitte Thott. Indeed, two manuscript copies of the translation survive.[79]

**Conclusions**

This final section draws conclusions from both the present material and the findings of the two foregoing chapters. The very exceptional nature of nine of the manuscripts considered in the first two chapters, and the number of manuscripts mentioned in the present chapter, make it an oddity that there have been only two recent pieces of academic research

---

75 Brecht [1993-1], 130–151.
76 Axmacher.
77 Riising A VI, 15, 16, 17 and 38, 58 respectively.
78 Rimbault.
79 Riising, A VI 22 (1–64), 23 (1–80).

that bear upon Puritan manuscripts and that this field of study has been entirely neglected heretofore in studies of Dutch Reformed piety.

At first sight, it can be a surprise that it was—so far as we presently know—exclusively in the Netherlands that translations of Puritan works appeared that gained a rather exceptional significance and position with respect to the original manuscript. Yet this stands to reason once the unique position of the Dutch Republic compared with other Continental Protestant nations is taken into account: it was the closest of all Reformed countries to the British Isles geographically, had the most intensive trade relationship with England and Scotland, was the country to which more sixteenth-century English religious emigrants moved than to any other, was the almost universal destination of choice for English religious emigrants on the European continent, and not in the least place had seen tens of thousands of Scots and English soldiers serve in its national army. In addition, the Netherlands was the only entirely Reformed polity among neighbouring European nations. It is small wonder, then, that Puritan ideas and practices from Britain took root nowhere else so deeply as they did in this land close by across the North Sea. The above considerations also serve to explain the fact that it was predominantly Dutchmen who had personal and direct contact with British Puritans.

Yet this is not all that must be said about the significance of the Dutch Republic. Given its role in the seventeenth century as the fulcrum of European and even global trade as well as of Protestant (largely theological) academia, this country was also the ideal transit country for the onward dissemination of Puritanism. In this connection, the German and Danish onward translations of Puritan texts, based on Dutch source-texts, are of great indicative value.

Denmark is in many respects a land apart on a European scale. Although it was a thoroughly Lutheran country, relatively many Puritan works were translated there. To the extent that these translations found their way into print, they had undergone dogmatic filtration; despite this, their mere existence remains remarkable and shows us that Lutherans welcomed some element in Reformed piety literature that they found lacking in their own piety tradition. What exactly that element was remains unelucidated for lack of research. Huisman ventures to identify two general currents that were appreciated: the manner of preaching, and the activation of the visible aspects of faith.[80] Doubtless, a thoroughgoing comparison of the piety of the established church in Denmark and that of the Puritan translations would throw up more distinctions. The data pre-

---

80  Huisman [2008], 221; [2009-2], 147.

sented above does suffice, however, for us to posit that Puritan works on the inner spiritual life were translated at least as often as those on the practice of piety.

In which Denmark was unique was that the translations in question were made by non-theologians. This was by no means a well-established practice: in the Netherlands, the only non-theologian to publish a Puritan translation was the schoolmaster de Swaef, and in Germany, his sole counterpart was Erberfeld, a lawyer. Even more unprecedented was that the Danish translators of the Puritan works in question were women and from the highest ranks of the nobility—phenomena that are both without parallel at all in the Netherlands or Germany.

As regards the Netherlands, it is striking that all but two of the manuscripts from the first three decades of the seventeenth century are connected with Willem Teellinck and that of the manuscripts from the latter half of the century, all but one had to do with Koelman. We see, then, that the Further Reformation had overwhelming representation in the translation of Puritan manuscripts. The only translations not associated with that movement were Baudartius' unpublished Dutch version of Cowper's dialogue, the translation of John Archer's (d. 1639) sermons by Daniel van Laren[81] (b. 1585), and the translation of Fleming's work. The dominance of the Further Reformation in the translation scene further manifests itself in the German manuscript translations, which without exception are connected with Teellinck and his fellow Further Reformer, Udemans.

The present chapter has indicated the relative importance of the dominance of manuscripts written by Scots and has nuanced our impression of the period in which they were produced. In this chapter, only one manuscript has been considered that actually harks back to a text composed by a Scot: Baudartius' translation of Cowper's dialogue. While all the other manuscripts with a Scottish background date from the latter half of the seventeenth century, Baudartius' translation is from the first half of the century, and from as far back as its second decade.

The large majority of the nine manuscripts we have considered were intended by their authors for publication. This chapter has demonstrated that this intention did not obtain generally: after all, in most cases it cannot be convincingly suggested, let alone proven, that the translator had a print edition in mind. The minority of cases was made up of the following persons. Whately, in that he sent Teellinck his wedding sermon in manuscript in 1608, must have hoped that his friend in the Netherlands would produce a Dutch version of it, a service he had already rendered Whately

---

81  Op 't Hof [2016-3].

the previous year when given another manuscript. Erberfeld did his utmost to have his own translation of Teellinck's magnum opus published. Gataker only developed this yearning after becoming acquainted with a smaller work of Teellinck's. In contrast, Brößke had the ambition to publish from the outset, albeit an ambition never achieved.

Finally, the provisional nature of this present concluding section must be emphasised. Research into seventeenth-century Dutch Reformed piety has attained such a stage of maturity that there should not be many more surprises in store for us; sadly, this is still far from the case for other parts of Europe such as Germany, Hungary, Transylvania, France and Scandinavia. Definitive pronouncements can only be made once we have more certainty about the role of manuscripts in European piety overall. This notwithstanding, with a view to seventeenth-century global trade relationships and the colonies of the Dutch Republic, it would seem prudent not to restrict our scope to Europe but to extend it worldwide.

What we can posit—in all tentativeness, as urged above—is that within Reformed Protestantism, piety was a subject that lent itself to the use of manuscripts more readily than any other branch of theology, whether dogmatics, catechesis, polemics or others. This being the case, it stands to reason that the maxim that "the best things are kept in mens studies in Manuscripts" has reached us from two piety-minded men: the phrase was coined by the Puritan Thomas Goodwin (1600–1680) and cited approvingly by the pro-Puritan Samuel Hartlib (d. 1662).[82] All the more reason, then, to take piety seriously as an object of research in its own right.

---

82 Greengrass, 317.

# 4. LEARNED AT HOUSEHOLD SEMINARIES

## The significance for European Pietism of Puritan household seminaries

*In 1707, the Middelburg clergyman Jacobus Leydecker[1] (1656–1729) wrote, in the second volume of his defence of the Synod of Dort (1618–1619), the following most intriguing passage:*

> *Indeed, one has beheld remarkably in the Netherlands—when our Church wearied of disputing with the Remonstrants and it became necessary to turn to soul-searching in order to make blessed use of the doctrine of the Synod of Dort (on which point, I do wish that people would consider S. Amama's orations in his* Antibarbarus*)—that students seeking to become preachers often crossed over to England to learn the language and the practice: the ministers would fill their rooms with English writings. Moreover, godly men who understood the language translated them, to the great edification of our congregations, who were thriving more in godliness then than now.[2]*

According to this author, then, theology students wishing to be ordained would often journey to England to learn the English language and the Puritan practice, and ministers filled their studies with English (i.e., Puritan) works; and in addition, godly men translated them, to the great edification of the Dutch churches. We shall consider the key translators in Volume 2. Although no research has (yet) been conducted on the matter, it is known from the scholarly literature that some clergymen did indeed have—sometimes in copious quantities—English originals of Puritan writings in their bookcases.[3] Is it also the case, then, that Dutch theology students really did cross the North Sea to learn English and ministerial practice? This chapter will seek an answer to that question.

---

1 Uil [2016-1].
2 Leydecker [1707], 19.
3 Op 't Hof [1987-1], 628–629; Postema, 170–208; Op 't Hof [2015-2], 48a; [2015-6], 102b; [2015-14], 219a; Zwanenburg, 86a; Van der Kamp [2015]; Op 't Hof [2016-11], 230a; [2016-17], 378a-b; [2016-22], 532a; [2016-24]; Uil [2016-2], 411b.

We have already seen several times in the foregoing three chapters that one of the means of transmission of Puritan ideals and practices to the Continent was that of Puritan household seminaries, also known as house academies.[4] In the seventeenth century, many theology students came over to England from across Europe for a period of acquainting themselves firsthand with Puritan theology. A number of them, chiefly Dutchmen, went beyond simply attending lectures at Cambridge or Oxford: they arranged a stay at one of the household seminaries at which Puritan clergymen gave their trainee colleagues practical instruction in the Puritan way of preaching and pastoral work.

There has never yet been a dedicated study of the phenomenon of the Puritan household seminaries, not even in article form, let alone any specific academic interest in the overseas students who attended them. It makes eminent sense, then, to collate here all the data found scattered through the literature and to seek to sketch a representative picture of the historical reality of Continental students' stays at Puritan household seminaries. This should help bring into its own a subject that has thus far languished in obscurity.

The present chapter first summarises the state of knowledge on Puritan household seminaries and goes on to provide an overview of their Continental participants. Information on the subject is then evaluated for veracity before conclusions are finally drawn.

**Puritan household seminaries**
Although all the chapters on Puritanism in England in the standard English work on that movement devote merely a single sentence to the Puritan household seminaries and contain no references at all to literature on them,[5] John Morgan does spend eight pages on the topic in his 1986 work on godly learning.[6] Those pages may be summarised as follows. It was predominantly, but not exclusively, Puritans who had an abiding interest in the practical formation of trainee preachers as a supplement to their

---
4 For two reasons, the present author prefers the latter term. In the first place, it is a better reflection than the term 'household seminary' of the fact that academic subjects were often taught by the clergymen in these programmes. In the second place, as we shall see anon, not all the students on these courses lodged with the tutor's family. Strictly speaking, then, the term 'household seminary' is inapplicable to such cases. However, the rest of this chapter will continue to use that term as the standard expression, so as to respect the established usage of church historians in English (the only two scholars to use the term 'academy' being Ole P. Grell and Anthony Milton).
5 Webster [1997], 52.
6 Morgan, 293–300.

university studies. They catered to this felt need by arranging for theology students to lodge in the homes of experienced ministers after their graduation from the academic component of their studies so that they could be taught there on the practicalities of gospel ministry. The earliest Puritan known to have trained students practically was the Cambridge clergyman Richard Greenham (d. *c.* 1592). Robert Browne (1550-1633) and Arthur Hildersham (1563-1632) were among his students.[7] Delegates to the Dedham Conference (1582-1589), a Presbyterian gathering in Essex, decided at one of their sessions—in 1584[8]—that theology students ought to be given practical training. Puritans who put Greenham's ideal into practice included the father of English Puritanism, William Perkins (1558-1602); the Oxfordshire preacher and author John Dod (d. 1645); the rector of St Antholin's in London, Charles Offspring (d. 1640); the Boston (Lincolnshire and Massachusetts) minister John Cotton (1585-1652), the President of Queen's College, Cambridge, and Westminster Assembly delegate Herbert Palmer (1601-1647); the logician Alexander Richardson (c. 1565-1621), the Suffolk minister Richard Blackerby (1574-1648); and the founder of Connecticut, Thomas Hooker (1586-1647). One of Dod's practical trainees was Robert Harris (1581-1658), later President of Trinity College, Oxford. Cotton's household seminary men included Samuel Winter (1603-1666) (later Provost of Trinity College, Dublin), John Angier (1605-1677) (who grew up in Dedham and later ministered in Cheshire); Anthony Tuckney (1599-1670) (later Master of St John's College, Cambridge); and Thomas Hill (d. 1653) (later Master of Trinity College, Cambridge).

Palmer was the household seminary teacher of Thomas Cawton (1605-1659), who became minister of the English Church in Rotterdam. Richardson's household seminary men included John Yates (d. 1660) (later a minister in Norfolk), William Ames[9] (1576-1633) (later chaplain to the English soldiers in the army of the States-General and then a theology professor at Franeker in Friesland), Hooker, and Charles Chauncey (1592-1672) (later President of Harvard). Four names are known of men who studied under Blackerby: the Suffolk nonconformist Samuel Fairclough (1594-1677); Nicholas Bernard (d. 1661) (subsequently chaplain to Archbishop James Ussher and later to Oliver Cromwell); Samuel Stone (1602-1663) (who later emigrated to Massachusetts with Thomas

---

7   It was probably Hildersham who, during his stay with Greenham, collated the commonplace book of Greenham's sayings which survives in manuscript: Primus, 9-10.
8   Webster [1997], 24.
9   Visscher; Sprunger [1972]; Van Vliet; Van 't Spijker [2015].

Hooker); and Jonas Proost (d. 1667), who would later serve various Dutch congregations in England. As for Hooker, his known household students were Jeremiah Burroughs (d. 1646) (later teacher of the English Church in Rotterdam); John Beadle (d. 1667) (later rector of Barnstone in Essex); and Nathaniel Rogers (1598–1655) (later pastor of Ipswich, Massachusetts). Often, students would while at a household seminary be given the opportunity to accumulate preaching experience as a lecturer.

Some household seminaries, such as those of Blackerby, Palmer and Thomas Gataker (1574–1654), burgeoned into quasi-official educational institutions that trained two streams of in parallel: one a university preparation course for boys, and the other a practical training stream for academic young men, including a sub-stream of theologians. Gataker's seminary was of sufficient stature to attract foreign students.

Close spiritual friendships were formed among students at household seminaries, and many underwent conversion experiences while studying in them. A cogent observation made by Morgan is that the milieu of household seminaries was overwhelmingly nonconformist, in the sense that the focus lay not so much on reform of ecclesiastical structures as it did on the further edification of the church. The household seminary form of education gradually waned from the 1630s onwards, as it was in that decade that most of their founding educators died.

In his study on clerical friendship in the seventeenth-century Anglo-American Puritan community, published in 1994, Francis J. Bremer devotes just two pages to the phenomenon of the Puritan household seminary, which he moreover denotes with several different names. However, this contribution does add the stock of knowledge:[10] he informs us that it was particularly fellows at the University of Cambridge who referred students to the household seminaries, and that this was a means of preparing them for the Master of Arts degree. In concrete terms, Bremer provides the following additional information to supplement Morgan's research. Blackerby had Stephen Marshall (d. 1655; later a vicar in Essex) at his household seminary; Gataker had at his own household seminary Hugh Peter (1598–1660) (later chaplain to the New Model Army), Joseph Symonds (d. 1652) (later preacher of the English Church in Rotterdam) and the Scotsman Thomas Young (1587–1655) as well as a number of foreign students, including Wilhelm Thilenius (1596–1638), who became minister of the Dutch congregation at Austin Friars in 1624. Young would later train John Milton (1608–1674). John Rogers (d. 1636), lecturer of Dedham, also ran a household seminary. Cotton, too, attracted

---

10   Bremer, 37–38.

students from the Continent. Bremer identifies one of these as Maximiliaan Teelinck[11] (1605-1653), son of Willem Teellinck[12] (1579-1629). According to Bremer, Maximiliaan and his son-in-law were sent to Boston, Lincolnshire, to study under Cotton for a period of three years. John Rulice (1602-1666), a German, was sent to the same household seminary by John Preston (1587-1628).

Bremer also finds that there were seldom more than two or three students at a household seminary at any one time. The intimacy of the environment ensured that close social and spiritual bonds were forged and that the master had an enormous influence upon his students. Even marriages arose from these environments: Fairclough, for instance, married Blackerby's daughter; Cotton introduced Winter to his future wife; and Angier married Cotton's niece Ellen Winstanly.

The fact that the standard English work on Puritanism pays next to no attention to Puritan household seminaries becomes the more baffling when one considers that the author of the chapter in question wrote on the phenomenon in great detail in another of his publications: Tom Webster devotes no fewer than thirteen pages to the subject in his 1997 study on the Caroline Puritan Movement.[13] He also furnishes the researcher with new information. Greenham was not the only Elizabethan clergyman to train theology students in the practice of homiletics and pastoral visitation: a contemporary of his who did the same was Bernard Gilpin (1517-1583). Gataker trained John Grayle (1614-1654) (later rector of Tidworth in Wiltshire) and John Rogers. Other preacher trainers were Thomas Taylor (1576-1633) in Reading, John Ball (1585-1640) in Staffordshire, and Thomas Ball (1590-1659) at Northampton. Hildersham taught the future exorcist of the North Midlands, John Darrell (b. 1562), and also John Brinsley, later schoolmaster at Ashby-de-la-Zouch and lecturer in London, and Simeon Ashe (d. 1662). Francis Higginson (1588-1630), later the first minister of Salem, Massachusetts, had as household seminary students Lazarus Seaman (d. 1675) (later Master of Peterhouse, Cambridge); John Bryan (d. 1676), who later ministered in Warwickshire; Richard Richardson; and Edward Howe. In all probability, it was Offspring's household seminary at St Antholin, Budge Row (Watling Street) that supplied the men for the three to six lectureships that that London congregation maintained in the period. Webster finds it surprising that no household seminaries anywhere were ever (to his knowledge)

---

11   Brienen [1993]; Op 't Hof [2016-16].
12   Beeke [2003]; Op 't Hof [2008-1, 2011-1, 2015-1].
13   Webster [1997], 23-35.

suppressed, hotbeds of nonconformity as they were. Matters become especially intriguing when Webster asserts that a Dutchman named Walter *(sic)* Teellinck was at William Whately's (1583-1639) household seminary and that he penned a vivid description of his time in that seminary.

Generally, a household seminary would close when its master died. An exception to this rule was the case of Dod, whose household seminary was taken over by Harris—who like John Poynter had sat at Dod's feet—after it had been silenced in 1604.

Webster finds that the household seminary as an institution was at its strongest in Essex. It was in that county, at Barking, that Alexander Richardson (d. 1621) was from at least 1607 instructing not only the already-mentioned men but also George Walker (d. 1651), Daniel Cawdrey (1588-1664), John Greenham, John Barlow, John Wilson (d. 1667) and John Yates (d. 1660), who had previously had John Rogers as his instructor. Also, it was in Ashen, on the Essex-Suffolk border, that Blackerby rented a house from *circa* 1605 until 1628, in which he taught the sons of pious gentry, tradesmen and yeomen in secular study and also trained prospective ministers. Besides the aforementioned names, one of the latter category was Christopher Burrell, who married one of Blackerby's daughters. Some of the prospective ministers studying there also came from overseas, including Proost. Thomas Weld (1595-1661) had Thomas Shepard (1605-1649) and John Cullen at his household seminary. One of John Rogers' students was John Fuller; one of Hooker's was John Eliot (d. 1690), the missionary to the Massachusett Indians, who grew up in Nazeing. It is also known that the Cambridge theologian Samuel Collins (1576-1651), Regius Professor of Divinity and later Provost of King's College, trained many future preachers at his household seminary. Richard Rogers (d 1618) and his son Daniel (1573-1652) also took on household seminary students. Marshall trained Hugh Glover, his successor in the role of household seminary master. All the above household seminaries were in Essex. For Webster, the conclusion is inevitable that one of the chief aspects of the work of Hooker—who himself had a household seminary at Little Baddows in Essex—was the coordination of the further education of godly ministers.

Webster ends his overview with a brief assessment of the impact of the household seminary. In his estimation, it was a minority of those training for the ministry that attended one of these institutions. Many became chaplains in the households of gentle professors (that is, Puritan adherents among the nobility) directly after graduating from university; others moved directly into benefices, lectureships or became schoolteachers. Yet those that did attend a household seminary often experienced tremendous spiritual growth and became part of godly society. Also, he finds that the presence of a household seminary was not without its effects on those parishes which provided a home for it. An additional phenomenon was that many of the students ended up marrying the daughters of their mentors.

The reader who has thoroughly digested the foregoing data will not be able to shake off the impression that the image of Puritan household seminaries that emerges from the literature to date is rather preliminary, incomplete and superficial. Such an impression is confirmed at several turns. A cursory research trail through the Oxford Dictionary of National Biography [ODNB] is sufficient to reveal that there more masters and students of Puritan household seminaries are known than are named by Morgan, Bremer or Webster. William Bridge (1600–1671) and Jeremiah Burroughs (d. 1646) were household seminary students of John Rogers while up at Cambridge. Bryan trained young preachers and prospective preachers. Edmund Calamy (1600–1666) received his supervision at the home of Bishop Nicholas Felton (1556–1626). Henry Smith was a student of Richard Greenham; Matthew Newcomen (1610–1669) was a student of John Rogers. Daniel Rogers (1573–1652) taught Martin Holbeach, Tuckney and Wilson at his home. John Higginson (1616–1708) took practical studies under Cotton and other New England ministers. This last fact indicates how the phenomenon of the Puritan household seminary had been transferred to America by emigrating Englishmen. A final interesting detail from the ODNB is that Thomas Hille junior led an academy for training ministers at Findern in Derbyshire up to 1720. The household seminaries were thus not restricted to the seventeenth century, as the literature would suggest, but continued into the first decades of the eighteenth.

Other literature supplements the ODNB with the following facts. Ralph Levett (b. 1600) was another of Cotton's students while the latter was still in England.[14] Once in Massachusetts, Cotton took more household seminary students: his own son Seaborn (1633–1686)[15] and Benjamin Woodbridge (1622–1684)[16]. Sargent Bush demonstrates that in both England and America, Cotton used his household seminary students as copyists for his manuscripts.[17]

---

14   Bush, 34.
15   Bush, 69–70.
16   Ziff, 252–253; Emerson, 28.
17   Bush, 68–71.

A final aspect to be considered is a suggestion made by Ole Peter Grell. In the first quarter of the seventeenth century, a quarterly meal was instituted at Austin Friars with the aim of fostering mutual love among the church officers: the *agapē*. The driving force behind the love-feast was the church minister Simeon Ruytinck senior (d. 1621). In his research into the background of this *agapē*, Grell posits that Ruytinck might have drawn inspiration for the idea from the household seminaries.[18]

From this overwhelming mass of data, we can see how important the Puritan household seminary is as a topic. Yet this mass can also be confusing, which is why we sorely need a dedicated study of the subject.[19] Only equipped with such a study will we have all the Puritans within our purview who were associated with one of these seminaries as tutor and/or student, and will we have a grasp of the geographical and chronological range of the institution. Once the numerical aspects of the seminaries are known, they can also be set against the absolute totals of preachers and theology students in the period. Something else that will have to receive far more attention in such a study than it yet has is the rich variety of the household seminaries. Were these facilities nurseries exclusively for the practical equipping of would-be preachers, or did they constitute a form of education that could equally prepare the young man for university? Were non-theologians, or those not intending to practice in theology, also welcome to attend? Did the students live as family members of their tutor? The variations in the answers to these questions are also applicable to the difficulties we encounter in pinning down the numbers of students involved. In addition, it would be greatly to the benefit of church history research if a list of students per household seminary could be made available, one that also stated their years of study. The presentation of data in this format might make visible some connections that have thus far not suggested themselves. A further aspect that remains unresolved is that of the duties with which household seminary students would busy themselves. Were these limited in scope to study, preaching and pastoral work, or did the students also carry out particular extra tasks, such as manuscript copying? A question to which no attention has yet been paid is that of the financial side of the household seminaries. Was the student required to pay for his attendance at one of these seminaries, and if so, did this take the form of monetary fees exclusively, or could it perhaps also be paid off in kind, by analogy with the sizar system then common among poor university students; by undertaking copying duties, for instance?

---

18  Grell [1996], 198.
19  Cf. Cambers, 22 footnote 51.

Finally, some deep research into the motives that young men had for becoming household seminary students could be expected to clarify a great deal. The picture that is now current is that a student would typically be recommended to a household seminary by a university tutor, but it could well be that the backgrounds of those drawn into these institutions was far broader. Connected with this issue is the question that must continually be asked as to whether, and to what extent, young men might have chosen the household seminary study route due to the poor impression they had of university study courses or of student life in academic circles. That is to say, was the household seminary in some sense an alternative to the university, or rather a supplement to academic studies?

The pressing need for such a study of Puritan household seminaries is underscored when we consider the possibility that the above researchers might perhaps have been tempted in their enthusiasm to label historical persons as mentors or students at household seminaries who did not in reality fulfil such roles. For example, as Morgan would have it, Perkins was among those who took in trainee preachers for a practical course of study at his home,[20] but there is not a trace in history of Perkins' household seminary. Webster operates with the assumption that Whately had a household seminary, and even interprets a document describing the day-to-day religious life in a household associated with Whately as an account of operations at that supposed seminary, yet the following section will demonstrate that this assumption is incorrect. Moreover, we nowhere else in the literature find a household seminary attributed to Whately, and Webster himself provides no hard evidence of such. Did the seminary actually exist? It is high time that clarity be afforded in such doubtful cases.

**Continental students at Puritan household seminaries**
As we have seen in the above section, Morgan knows of Proost as having been a student under Blackerby; Bremer informs us that Thilenus was at Gataker's household seminary and that Maximiliaan Teellinck and Rulice were household seminary students with Cotton; Webster knows of Cotton and Blackerby as the masters of household seminary students from the Continent, including Proost in Blackerby's household; Webster is certain that the Dutchman Teellinck was a student of Whately's; and Larzer Ziff is aware of Cotton's having had Germans among his ministry trainees.

---

20 Morgan, 295 footnote 116, in which he invokes what Samuel Ward wrote of Perkins: "who likewise did exceeding much good by his advise and direction to many Ministers in the Country, who did resort unto him from everywhere": Knappen, 130. This is obviously a misinterpretation of that clause in Ward's journal.

Yet the literature gives us more details than these. In his biography of Ames, Keith L. Sprunger mentions the names of two German students who both studied at Franeker under Ames before crossing the North Sea to move in to Cotton's household seminary: Egbert Grim (1605/6–1636) and Petrus Gribius (1602/3–1666).[21]

In his study of the Dutch Church in London at Austin Friars, Grell quotes, while discussing the church's minister Willem Thilenus (1596–1638), from a work by Samuel Clarke (1599–1683) in which the latter provides ten biographies of Puritan divines.[22] The cited passage is from the section giving the biography of Gataker. In view of its importance to the present chapter, it is given here in full:

> Of Forreigners that sojourned with him, and were as ambitious of being entertained by him as of they had been admitted into a University; these were some, Mr. *Thylein*, who was afterwards a Reverend Pastor of the *Dutch* Church in *London* (whose son was brought by his mother but a fortnight before Mr. *Gatakers* decease, intreating the same good office in the behalf of him, which the Father had with much comfort enjoyed), Mr. *Peters*, Mr. *And. Demetrius*, Mr. *Hornbeck*, Mr. *Rich*, Mr. *Swerd*, Mr. *Wittefrangel*, Mr. *Severinus Benzon*, Mr. *George de Mey*, Dr. *Treschovius*, &c.[23]

> Of Forreigners that sojourned with him, and were as ambitious of being entertained by him as if they had been admitted into a University, these were some, Mr. *Thylein*, who was afterwards a Reverend Pastor of the *Dutch* Church in *London* (whose son was brought by his mother but a fortnight before Mr. *Gatakers* deceafe, intreating the fame good office in the behalf of him, which the Father had with much comfort enjoyed) Mr. *Peters*, Mr. *And. Demetrius*, Mr. *Hornbeck*, Mr. *Rich*, Mr. *Swerd*, Mr. *Wittefrangel*, Mr. *Severinus Benzon*, Mr. *Georg; de Mey*, Dr. *Trefchovius*, &c.

The Dutch researcher J. van der Haar came across this passage independently of Grell and subsequently sought in a brief article of his to identify several of the preachers mentioned in it.[24] He was fully confident of his identifications in only two cases: Wittefrangel is Petrus Wittewron-

---

21 Sprunger [1972], 237.
22 Grell [1989], 58–59.
23 Clarke [1662], 146.
24 Van der Haar [1986].

gel (1609–1662), who later ministered at Amsterdam, and George de Mey (1630–1712) is the man of that name who was later a preacher at Leidschendam near Leiden.

In the standard Dutch work on Puritanism, the author of the section on international influence gives us more clarity on the names. He agrees with Grell that "Thylein" refers to Willem Thilenus. It cannot be ascertained who this man's son was whose mother brought him to Gataker just before the latter's death. It might be that one of Thilenus' older sons was a household seminary student of men including Gataker, for Johannes Thilenus[25] (1627–1692) returned to England for between one and two years, to learn the art of preaching from a number of leading Puritans, in the interval between studying theology at Utrecht and becoming minister of the congregation at Koudekerke on Walcheren.[26] "And. Demetrius" refers to Andreas Demetrius (1619–1687), who was installed as minister at Hontenisse in States-Flanders (now Zeeland-Flanders) in 1648. "Hornbeck" is not the Johannes Hoornbeeck[27] (1617–1666) who later became a renowned professor, as van der Haar concluded,[28] but is that man's namesake cousin (d. 1668), who became minister of Grijpskerke on Walcheren in 1635 and who then served the congregation of nearby Vlissingen (Flushing) from 1645 until his decease in 1668. "Rich" is an Anglicisation of Arnoldus de Rijcke (d. 1665), who began his preaching career at Aagtekerke, also on Walcheren, in 1638 and who was a minister in the provincial capital, Middelburg, by the time of his death. "Swerd" must be Jacobus Sweerd (1610–1646), who was installed as preacher at Hoek in States-Flanders in 1633. "Wittefrangel" and "George de Mey" were correctly identified by van der Haar. This leaves only the names that remained obscure even to the author of the relevant section of the standard Dutch work on the subject: "Peters", "Severinus Benzon" and "Dr. Treschovius".

Later on in his study on the church of Austin Friars, Grell informs the reader that John White enrolled four Palatinate men at his household seminary in 1626: "Mr. Sleer, Mr. Fisher, Mr. Haake and Mr. Hopff."[29]

The editor of the correspondence of Cotton, Sargent Bush, Jr., writes that the Dutchmen Maximiliaan Teellinck and Isaac Bisschop (1598/9–1661) were students of Cotton's household seminary.[30] A very compelling

---

25 Nagtglas [1888], 2:761–763; Op 't Hof [2016-17].
26 Nuttall, 38.
27 Hofmeyr; Op 't Hof [2015-18].
28 Van der Haar [1986], 107.
29 Grell [1989], 181.
30 Bush, 38–40.

deduction that Bush makes is that he determines from a comparison of handwriting that the aforementioned German, Rulice, worked as a copyist for Cotton.[31]

Finally, we may refer to the previously-mentioned standard English work on Puritanism. In his contribution on Puritanism and the Continental Reformed churches, Anthony Milton has an intriguing paragraph about the significance of the household seminaries.[32] He opens the paragraph by telling us that a flock of Continental trainee ministers—especially Dutch—was trained by Gataker. Milton then quotes from a letter of John Ball's to Samuel Hartlib (d. 1662); that correspondence will be discussed at the end of this chapter. He then presents the entirely new thesis that we must seek the fruits of the instruction of overseas students at the household seminaries not so much in the Dutch piety movement of the Further Reformation, but rather in the Puritan movement in Hungary. He goes on to argue that more than a hundred Hungarian Reformed students came to England during the first half of the seventeenth century and that four of them formed a League of Piety in London in 1638.

In connection with that last sentence of Milton's, the present author found the following intriguing paragraph—never before discussed in the literature—in Clarke's biographical section on Palmer:

> He was neither Wastfull nor covetous, but very liberall; doing many acts of Charity (beside what hath been mentioned before) to such as stood in need; bestowing plenteous relief, according as he was able, both by his own hands and the hands of others, so that those who received it knew not oft-times whence it came. And when that eminent work of charity was on foot in *Cambridge,* while he was Fellow of *Queens* Colledge, whereby divers young Scholars, who were forced by reason of the wars to fly out of *Germany,* especially of the *Palatinate,* were sent for hither and educated, partly in the University, and partly under able and godly Divines in the Country, whereby they might be fitted to do God and their Countrey service (when God should give them opportunity to return) having here been educated in the knowledge of our language, and the way of practical Preaching, which hath been no where more eminent then in *England,* (which work succeeded beyond expectation) he was one of the great actors therein, and did contribute liberally thereunto. The like assistance also he afforded to

---

31  Bush, 69.
32  Milton, 119.

divers *Hungarians, Transilvanians*, and other strangers, who came over into *England* for the same reason.³³

**Further research**
Now that we have set out all that is known from the literature, it is time for further research. The first section has already shown that there are reasons to take some of the information found in the literature with a pinch of salt. It might not be expected at first sight that the data on overseas students would be any more reliable than the foregoing on domestic students. Researchers heretofore have known of five Puritan tutors who hosted Continental future preachers: Blackerby, Cotton, Gataker, Whately and White. The household seminaries of each of these will now be considered in turn and subjected to further research. Thereafter, we shall look more generally at the issue of Palatinate, Hungarian and Transylvanian students at Puritan household seminaries.

*Richard Blackerby*
The need for this kind of further research is immediately apparent in relation to the first Continental student mentioned in the foregoing section, Proost, who studied with Blackerby.

Mr Richard Blackerby Dyed in the yeer 1648 in his 74th year
F.H. Van Houe. Sculp.

---

33  Clarke [1677], 200.

> JONAS PROOST

Morgan, Grell and Webster all report that the Jonas Proost in question was minister of the Dutch congregations in Colchester and London successively.[34] They all owe this information to a common source, namely a biographical compendium by Clarke, whose actual words on Proost, while describing Blackerby's life, are:

> Divers young Students (after they came from University) betook themselves to him to prepare them for the Minestry, whom he taught the Hebrew Tongue, to whom he opened the Scriptures, and read Divinity, and gave them excellent advice for Learning, Doctrine and Life; and many eminent persons proceeded from this *Gamaliel*; [...] Mr. *Prosse* Minister of two *Dutch* Congregations, first in *Colchester*, then in *London*.[35]

According to the list of ministers of the Dutch Church in London, Jonas Proost, a native of Colchester, served the London congregation from 1644 to 1667.[36] Before that, one Jonas Proost had been minister of the Dutch Church in Colchester, inaugurated in 1599.[37] This latter (chronologically earlier) Proost had matriculated at the University of Heidelberg in 1588 and subsequently matriculated as a theology student at the University of Leiden on 14 August 1592, where he was recorded as having been born in England.[38] While at Leiden, he conducted a disputation under Franciscus Junius[39] (1545–1602). The same year, he was called to the parish of Akersloot in the Province of Noord-Holland, accepted the call and was installed the following year. He left for Colchester in 1599.[40] It is evident from a superficial consideration that these two men cannot be one and the same Jonas Proost; if they were, Proost would have had 71 years' pulpit service, making him a world record holder among preachers!

There is a second problem here. Whereas the Proost whom we find preaching at Colchester was inaugurated there in 1599, Blackerby did not even open his household seminary until *circa* 1605. The only sensible solution to these two conundrums is that one Jonas Proost succeeded

---

34  Morgan, 296 footnote 125; Grell [1989], 59 footnote 59; Webster [1997], 31.
35  Clarke [1683], 58.
36  Moens [1884], 208.
37  Van Berkel [1983], 17; Moens [1884], 208.
38  Toepke, 2:139; *Album Studiosorum Academiae Lugduno Batavae*, 33.
39  Cuno; Venemans.
40  De Waard, 3:5 footnote 3; Van Lieburg [1996], 1:198.

another. It would be congruent with other such cases known to church history if these two men were in fact father and son. If this generational succession had taken place in London, it would surely be known to history, given the great wealth of documentation from the Dutch Church there. Consequently, it must have been at Colchester that Jonas Proost senior handed over the congregation to his son. This reconstruction is entirely consistent with the fact that Blackerby discontinued his household seminary in 1628.

In the *Journal* of Isaac Beeckman[41] (1588–1637) we read of a Jonas Proost who delivered a speech at the Latin School in Dordrecht in 1627, the day after Beeckman had given his inaugural lecture there.[42] Klaas van Berkel, Beeckman's biographer, regards that Proost as being the namesake son of the minister of the Dutch Church in Colchester, and believes that he was sent by his father to the Latin School in Rotterdam run by brothers Jacob Beeckman[43] (1590–1629) and Isaac Beeckman. He finds it probable that Proost *filius* accompanied Isaac in the latter's move from Rotterdam to Dordrecht in 1627.[44] This interpretation perfectly matches the above suggestion by the present author that the two men were father and son. It is all but certain, then, that Jonas junior was attending Blackerby's household seminary in 1627 and/or 1628 and that he later took over his father's ministry at Colchester.

*John Cotton*
In the current state of research, five foreign students are known to have been educated at Cotton's household seminary: Bisschop, Gribius, Grim, Rulice, and Maximiliaan Teellinck.

*John Cotton*

---

41   Van Berkel [1983].
42   De Waard, 3:5.
43   Van Berkel [2015].
44   Van Berkel [1983], 17 footnote 15; 62–63 footnote 14.

> ISAAC BISSCHOP

Isaac Bisschop was born in Middelburg, the provincial capital of Zeeland, in 1598 or 1599 and matriculated as a student of the Faculty of Letters at the University of Leiden on 23 February 1619 under the Latinised form of his surname, Episcopius.[45] In late 1625 or early 1626, he sat and passed the preaching qualification examination in the Amsterdam presbytery. He was admitted to Walcheren presbytery as a candidate minister on 2 February 1626. It is also known that his first installation as an incumbent was at Zoutelande on Walcheren in February 1627 and that he left for nearby Vlissingen in 1638, dying there in November 1661.[46] Consequently, he will have been a student of Cotton's in 1626.

> PETRUS GRIBIUS

Petrus Gribius (1602/3–1666) was born in the Palatinate and studied theology at Franeker under the Puritan Ames. He matriculated as a student of philosophy at that university on 7 June 1624.[47] He defended no fewer than seven disputations under Ames in 1626[48] and went on to spend some time with Cotton. He must have sailed back to the Continent in spring 1630, for he was the deliverer of a letter from Cotton, dated 12 April of that year, to Hugh Goodyear (1617–1661), minister of the English Church at Leiden.[49] Remaining in the Netherlands, he was curate of the English Church at Amersfoort from 1630–1632. After being dismissed from that post, due to his refusal to conform to the Book of Common Prayer and to rites of the Church of England, he served as chaplain to English troops in 's-Hertogenbosch. Gribius would stay the rest of his life in the Netherlands, apart from a two-year interval. He was installed in the church of Bruinisse on the Zeeland island of Schouwen-Duiveland on 4 July 1638; was welcomed by the English Church at Middelburg on 23 November 1643; and became the successor of Rulice—whom we shall consider below—as minister of the German Church in Amsterdam on

---

45 *Album Studiosorum Academiae Lugduno Batavae*, 140.
46 Van Lieburg [1996], 1:23; Vrolikhert [1758], 112–117.
47 Fockema Andreae and Meijer, 74 no. 2118.
48 Postma and van Sluis, 92–95.
49 Van de Kamp [2010], 41; Bush, 139–141. In this letter, Cotton informs the latter of Gribius' stay with him and also writes that the young man whom Goodyear had recommended to Cotton was taking his meals at Cotton's house but was lodging with a neighbour for lack of space. The literature mistakenly assumes that young man to be Gribius: Veenhoff and Smolenaars, 9.

10 November 1652. He died in that city on 22 March 1666. Between these offices, he had been a preacher in Brazil from 1646–1648.[50]

Gribius was in contact with Samuel Hartlib (d. 1662), who lived his latter years in London after being raised in Prussia and Poland. Hartlib laboured in close association with the Scots theologian John Durie (or Dury) (1596–1680) and the Czech pedagogue and theologian Jan Amos Comenius[51] (1592–1670) to unite the Lutheran and Reformed confessions, to reform education and to convert the Jews. One of the means by which these scholars hoped to bring the Calvinists and Lutherans together was by fostering practical divinity.

As one testimony to Gribius' language skills had it in 1641: "he speaks Netherlandish very well, his tongue being more adapted to English than to High German."[52]

> EGBERT GRIM
The German Egbert Grim (1605/6–1636) is known to have matriculated as a student of theology and philosophy at the University of Franeker on 20 April 1625, to have defended a disputation under Ames in 1626, and to have matriculated as a student of theology at the University of Leiden on 3 August 1629, aged 24.[53] Since he signed in to Cotton's household seminary as having arrived from Franeker,[54] he must have been at that university for some of the years 1626–1629. He also studied at the University of Oxford in the same period. Whatever other parts of his learning came from Cotton, his agreement with the liturgy of the Church of England was not learned in those years: he defended his theses at Leiden in 1629, written in vindication of those formularies. His agreement with the rites of the Church of England was also the reason why he has been described as a fringe member of the English Synod, with reference to his later time as chaplain of an English regiment in the Netherlands in the 1630s. Ames responded to Grim's theses with a letter to him, telling the German that he could agree with all his positions except those that concerned the liturgy of the Church of England. On that point, he upbraided Grim sharply. Cotton and Goodyear notified Grim of their similar opposition to the liturgy of the Church of England in the same manner. Grim

---

50 Stearns, index; Sprunger [1982], index; Schalkwijk, index; Joosse, index.; Van Lieburg [2011], 231–232; Van de Kamp [2012-2], 198–199.
51 Blekastad; Murphy.
52 Hessels, 3:1871; cf. 1891.
53 Fockema Andreae and Meijer, 76 no. 2202; Sprunger [1972], 237 footnote 92; *Album Studiosorum Academiae Lugduno Batavae*, 220.
54 Sprunger [1972], 237.

died at Wesel, just beyond the Dutch border in the County of Cleves, in 1636.[55]

A year before his death, Grim had a two-volume quarto edition of over a thousand pages published at Wesel, *Pauselicke heiligheit* [The papal kind of holiness], in which he prayed a great number of Roman Catholic sources in aid in his attempt to prove that there had been a woman Pope. This publication prompted a debate between him and the Roman Catholic Johannes Stalenus (d. 1631) in nearby Rees. Grim subsequently published a brief account of the debate; this, too, came out at Wesel. Both publications are in Dutch.

> JOHN RULICE

John Rulice[56] (1602–1666) was born at Kirchberg in the Palatinate and studied at Herborn in Hesse from 1623. He then departed for the Netherlands, where a letter of recommendation was written for him by the ex-king of Bohemia, Frederick V[57] (1596–1632), then resident at The Hague, addressed to the Puritan John Preston, the then Master of Emmanuel College, Cambridge. Preston was particularly taken with Rulice and subsequently sent him to Cotton for further study. A letter survives dated 29 November 1628 in which Rulice tells Cotton that he is preparing to take ship for the Netherlands.[58] One gains the impression from the wording of the letter that the writer had not long left Cotton's orbit at the time of writing. Thus, it is at least established that Rulice was at Cotton's household seminary during 1628.

Less than a month after his letter, Rulice enrolled at Leiden as a theology student on 30 December 1628.[59] He then spent some years at Dorchester as assistant to the Puritan John White, who was seeking to bring about a godly reformation in the West Country. Rulice was even ordained in Dorchester by the Bishop of Bristol, Robert Wright, on 16 January 1630. From 1630 onwards, White supervised the emigration of around 20,000 nonconformist Puritans to the New World through the auspices of the Massachusetts Bay Company, which White had founded. When the first

---

55 Stearns, index.; Sprunger [1972], index; Sprunger [1982], 132, 297, 304; Bush, 32 footnote 64.
56 Streiter. However, that author dismisses both the content of Rulice's letter of 29 November 1628 and the date of his matriculation at Leiden as not to be taken seriously. In doing so, he puts forward a chronology of the life of Rulice that diverges from that presented here.
57 Groenveld.
58 Bush, 38–39, 69, 129–33.
59 *Album Studiosorum Academiae Lugduno Batavae*, 215.

batch of emigrants left in 1630, it was Cotton who preached their farewell sermon, entitled *God's promise to His plantation*. Rulice left the county town of Dorset for London on 31 November 1631. He probably did not remain long in London, however, for Gustavus Adolphus of Sweden (1594-1632) liberated the Palatinate at the end of the year, freeing Rulice to return to his home town of Kirchberg. It is likely that Rulice availed himself of this opportunity to visit his relatives. Heidelberg was not conquered until May 1633; not long thereafter, Rulice was installed in the ministry there. It proved to be a brief pastorate: he was dispatched to England in mid-1634 to collect funds for the war effort in his homeland. The Palatinate, and Heidelberg too, was reconquered by Roman Catholic forces in November of that year; after that time, the funds Rulice raised were reapportioned to the aid of Protestant refugees from the Palatinate. After Archbishop William Laud (1573-1645) and Charles I (1600-1649) both granted Rulice permission in spring 1635 to collect funds, he managed to raise about a hundred thousand guilders for the relief effort.

After completing his fundraising mission, Rulice was made assistant pastor of the English Church in Amsterdam on 27 January 1636, serving under John Paget (d. 1638). Once it became clear that this appointment was not working well, the Reformed presbytery of Amsterdam mediated to have him transferred to the German Reformed Church in Amsterdam; both the English and the German congregations were officially subordinate to that Dutch presbytery. Rulice was installed at the German Church on 26 July 1639. Hoornbeeck dedicated his 1646 invective against the Weigelian heresy to Rulice, although the contents of that dedication reveal nothing about the connections between the two men. In 1652, Rulice, succeeded in his post by Gribius, departed for Heidelberg, where he preached for two years. This had been made possible by the Peace of Münster in 1648, since the treaty provided for Charles Louis[60] (1671-1680), who had succeeded his father Frederick V as Elector Palatine, to take possession of the Lower Palatinate.

Why Rulice returned to the Netherlands two years thereafter is unclear, but we find him installed at the Dutch-speaking Reformed Church in Amsterdam on 16 May 1655. It was at Rulice's bidding that Niclaas van Turenout, a Dutchman, onward-translated Theodore Haak's[61] German translation of *Some helpes to stir up to christian duties* (1634) by Henry Whitfield (1597-1657) into Dutch. The Dutch onward translation of the German text, which had been published at Amsterdam in 1638

---
60   Hauck.
61   This study, 165-166.

under the title *Ermunter dich, das ist: kurtze und einfältige Handleitung, wie sich ein jeder zu und in der* Übung *der Gottseligkeit soll erwecken und aufmunteren*⁶²[Encourage thyself; that is, a brief and simple handbook on how one and all can awaken and encourage themselves unto and in the practice of piety], was published in 1655, also at Amsterdam, entitled *Opweckingh ter godtsaligheyt* [A stirring-up to piety]. Rulice once again became minister of the German Church at Amsterdam in August 1666, but not for long: he died in November of that year. It was written about Rulice in 1644 that he spoke no Dutch,⁶³ yet he must have learnt the language in the ensuing decade, for otherwise he would never have managed to become minister of the Dutch Church in the nation's chief city in 1655.

Rulice was in close contact with the Puritan-minded scholar Samuel Hartlib, who busied himself with the collation and dissemination of knowledge in all manner of subjects, developed models for pedagogical and social reform, and collaborated with Durie on the abovementioned project to unite all Protestants. Rulice was also on good terms with one of the wealthiest men of his time, the Amsterdam merchant, banker, proto-industrialist, politician and diplomat Louis de Geer (1587–1652). In addition, in the last decade of his life, Rulice had almost daily contact with Comenius, whom de Geer had fetched to Amsterdam. Comenius dedicated one of his works to Rulice.

> Maximiliaan Teellinck

Maximiliaan Teellinck was a son of Willem Teellinck. After attending Jacob and Isaac Beeckman's Latin School at Rotterdam, he matriculated at the University of Leiden on 19 October 1623 as a theology student, aged 21.⁶⁴ He continued his studies at the University of Franeker under Ames; we find his name noted there on 25 October 1624 as a new student of philosophy.⁶⁵ He defended three disputations under Ames in 1625.⁶⁶ He left Franeker that same year and became a candidate minister in Walcheren presbytery on 8 September 1625. The next firm date we have in his life is that he was welcomed as minister of the English Church at Vlissingen on 11 July 1627. In the meantime, he had been studying at Cotton's household seminary.

---

62 McKenzie, 433 no. 1769.
63 Hessels, 3:1933–1934.
64 *Album Studiosorum Academiae Lugduno Batavae*, 172.
65 Fockema Andreae and Meijer, 75 no. 2162.
66 Postma and van Sluis, 88–89.

Teellinck was inaugurated as minister of the Dutch-speaking congregation in Zierikzee on Schouwen-Duiveland on 6 August 1628, and ended his preaching career at the Zeeland provincial capital of Middelburg, where he was installed on 4 November 1640 and died on 26 November 1653.

*Thomas Gataker*
Gataker instructed a whole flock of overseas students: Benzon, Demetrius, Hoornbeeck, de Mey, Peters, de Rijcke, Sweerd, Johannes Thilenus, Willem Thilenus, Treschovius and Wittewrongel.

> SEVERINUS BENZON
Unfortunately, nothing more is known of this man than that his name implies he was a Dane.

> ANDREAS DEMETRIUS
Andreas Demetrius (1619–1687) was born in Dordrecht in May 1619, the son of preacher Daniel Demetrius. He matriculated at the University of

Leiden on 7 August 1636, reading philosophy.[67] Nevertheless, we find him defending a disputation under Gisbertus Voetius[68] (1589–1676) at Utrecht on 26 October that year.[69] Evidently, he lasted only a matter of weeks at Leiden before transferring to Utrecht. His first incumbency was at Hontenisse in the Province of Zeeland, where he was installed on 3 March 1648. He spent the better part of a year there before moving to Kessel in Noord-Brabant, where he was installed on 30 November 1648. He owed this call the recommendation of him made to the Great Church Assembly at 's-Hertogenbosch (Den Bosch) by the Count of Hoorne, who was lord of Kessel.[70] He was called to the nearby congregation of Ravensteyn in 1653 and remained there until his death in 1687.[71] Demetrius must have attended Gataker's household seminary in the 1640s, and prior to 1648.

> JOHANNES HOORNBEECK

Of the six Dutch preachers to bear the surname Hoornbeeck, only two are of the right generation to be considered as candidates for the Hoornbeeck who was instructed by Gataker. Both had the given name Johannes. One of them, the later professor at Utrecht and subsequently Leiden, is not known ever to have visited England.[72] The other Johannes was born at Middelburg *c.* 1609, matriculated at the University of Leiden on 29 October 1629 as a student of philosophy and theology, giving his age as twenty, and became the minister of Grijpskerke on Walcheren in 1635.[73] Thanks to the publication of the archive of the Dutch Church in London, we may with a high degree of confidence identify which of the two men was meant by Clarke. In the years 1640–1642, the Utrecht professor Voetius proposed as a suitable nomination for the vacancy at that congregation the Johannes who later became a professor.[74] He attested that this Hoornbeeck had a mastery of English.[75] Historical evidence of this mastery is found in the declaration by Anthony à Wood (1632–1695) that Hoornbeeck had added a self-made Latin translation of the Savoy Declaration of the Faith and Order (1658) to Hoornbeeck's *Epistola, ad reverendum &*

---

67  *Album Studiosorum Academiae Lugduno Batavae*, 279.
68  Duker; Oort *et al.*; Andreas J. Beck.
69  Andreas J. Beck, 446.
70  Abels and Wouters, 45.
71  Van Lieburg [1996], 1:47.
72  Hofmeyr, 36–44.
73  *Album Studiosorum Academiae Lugduno Batavae*, 222; Van Lieburg [1996], 1:104.
74  Hessels, 3:1822–1823, 1864–1865, 1870, 1882, 1883, 1891, 1911–1912, 1930; cf. 1933.
75  Hessels, 3:1865.

JOHANNES HOORNBEEK.
S.S. Theologiæ Doctor et primo in Ultrajectina, post in Lugdunensi Batavorum Academia, Professor et Ecclesiæ ibidem Pastor.

*celeberrimum virum Johannem Duraeum Scoto-Britannum, qua respondetur Examini Johannis Beverley, Angli, de independentissimo. Addita est Independentium in Anglia confessio* [A letter to the reverend and most renowned man John Durie, the Scot, in which a response is given to the inquiry of John Beverley of England regarding Independentism; to which is appended the confession of the Independents in England] (1660).[76] Both documents indicate that this Johannes Hoornbeeck spent time in England.

It is no easy matter to determine when Hoornbeeck was in England. He matriculated at the University of Leiden on 14 April 1633 as a student of philosophy and letters, registering himself as having come from Haarlem.[77] Two years later, owing to the plague raging at Leiden, he moved to Utrecht and attended Voetius' lectures until September 1636. He then

---

76   À Wood, 3:967.
77   *Album Studiosorum Academiae Lugduno Batavae*, 252.

returned to Leiden, but departed to move in with his mother in April 1637 after his father had died that February. He became a candidate minister on 24 April 1638 and was installed on 1 March the following year as minister of the Dutch congregation at Mülheim outside Cologne. He felt obliged to leave his first congregation in 1643 due to persecution from Roman Catholics. On 21 December that year, he received his doctorate in divinity at Utrecht; this was followed by the offer of a professorship by that university on 3 May 1644, which he accepted. He moved once again from Utrecht to Leiden in 1654 and remained there until his death on 1 September 1666. There is thus only one period in Hoornbeeck's life in which he could possibly have undertaken his visit to England: April 1637 to April 1638.

> GEORGE DE MEY

George de Mey[78] was christened at Rotterdam on 26 February 1630, the son of wine merchant Jean de Mey, who had most likely been born in Norwich in 1584. He matriculated at the University of Leiden as a theology student in May 1646.[79] From 4 December 1651 until 23 March 1654, he was part of a three-man legation to England and France led by Jacob Cats, dispatched to London to plead for the repeal of the Navigation Act.[80] His first installation as preacher was at Leidschendam on 22 July 1657. His subsequent installations were at Steenwijk in the north of the Netherlands on 29 October 1663; at Gorinchem on 9 June 1666; and finally at Gouda on 19 September 1681. He passed away in that city on 7 February 1712.

Fortunately for the researcher, a letter survives from Gataker to de Mey, dated 19 December 1653.[81] It is apparent from the content of this letter that the Dutchman had already left Gataker by that time, that he had asked him a question about original sin (to which Gataker was responding in the letter in question), that they had formed a friendship, that Gataker was of the opinion that de Mey needed some further study,[82] and that de Mey had stayed with Gataker at the same time as Treschovius

---

78 Wumkes; Engelbrecht, 236–237.
79 *Album Studiosorum Academiae Lugduno Batavae*, 368.
80 We know from a nineteenth-century study that de Mey wrote an account of his travels, but unfortunately it is not currently known where that account is now kept: Schotel [1840], 203–214.
81 Leiden, University Library, BUR F 5:1.
82 Given that it would be another two and a half years before de Mey was ordained, it appears that he did take his old master's advice and entered into deeper theological study first. However, the letter gives us no inkling as to where and in what form he might have undertaken that study.

(who in Gataker's letter is spelt Trescovius). That last detail, then, is a corroboration of the information that Clarke provides about Gataker's students.

When de Mey died, his local brother minister Leonard Beels (1674–1756) preached his funeral sermon. The bond between the two had been very intimate, for Beels stated that he had esteemed de Mey and regarded him as his father in Christ. In the sermon, he told the congregation that de Mey had spent nine months at Gataker's house after his studies.[83] It appears that de Mey was at Gataker's household seminary for three-quarters of a year in 1653.

---

83 Verwijs.

> Peters

Owing to the lack of any extraneous data, there is nothing instructive that can be written on the identity of Peters.

> Arnoldus de Rijcke

Born in Middelburg in 1610 or 1611, Arnoldus de Rijcke matriculated as a philosophy student at the University of Leiden on 10 May 1632.[84] He was ordained to preaching candidacy on 1 April 1638 at Aagtekerke on Walcheren. Remaining on that island for the rest of his life, he was installed at Serooskerke on 1645; at Veere in 1650; and was finally installed at Middelburg on 5 December 1655, ministering there for nearly a decade. He died in July 1665.[85] In all probability, he studied with Gataker in 1637. It was partly due to his knowledge of English that he was one of the names considered in 1644 when a vacancy arose for the third pastoral position that the Dutch Church in London maintained. The opinion ventured by a London elder who had heard de Rijcke in the Netherlands was, "I like his method of preaching, but he is not so precise as some."[86] Accordingly, he was not called to London.

> Jacobus van de Sweerde

Jacobus van de Sweerde was born in Middelburg in 1608 or 1609 and matriculated as a student of theology at Leiden on 18 September 1629.[87] He was installed in his first congregation, Hoek in States-Flanders, on 23 October 1633 and later left Hoek for Ritthem, where he was welcomed as the minister on 21 September 1642 and where he died on 21 February 1646.[88] He must have been instructed by Gataker in 1633.

> Johannes Thilenus

Johannes Thilenus, born in London in 1627, was the son of Willem Thilenus, of whom more anon. His mother enrolled him in the Latin school at Middelburg in 1639 and he remained there until going up to university in Utrecht in 1647.[89] His first congregation was Koudekerke on Walcheren, where he preached from 1652 until his installation at Goes on Zuid-Beveland on 24 October 1655 before moving on to Middelburg, where he

---

84 *Album Studiosorum Academiae Lugduno Batavae*, 242.
85 Van Lieburg [1996], 1:213.
86 Hessels, 3:1933.
87 *Album Studiosorum Academiae Lugduno Batavae*, 220.
88 Van Lieburg [1996], 1:245.
89 Vogler, 12b; *Album Studiosorum Academiae Rheno-Traiectinae*, 15.

was installed on 18 June 1666. He died as minister of that city on 1 June 1692.[90] In 1657, he married Susanna van Baerle, daughter of David van Baerle, the Amsterdam trustee of the Dutch West India Company. In his Koudekerke and Goes years, he corresponded with Caesar Calandrinus, the minister of the Dutch Church in London.[91]

In his final incumbency in the provincial capital of Zeeland, Thilenus was called to account several times by the city council for the pugnacious manner of his criticism of the civil authorities in his sermons. His fulminations include such matters as the city fathers' toleration of actors, tightrope walkers and jugglers; he also inveighed against women's elaborate hairstyles. On 23 September 1668, he preached at Middelburg in the audience of Prince Willem III, on the occasion of the latter's elevation to the title of First Lord of the States of Zeeland. This sermon was later printed under the title *Schat der princen* [Princes' Treasure]. Although Thilenus had initially had no thought whatsoever of having it published, he felt obliged to do so by the mistaken interpretations that a number of people had drawn from his words. It is probable that these critics' accusation was that Thilenus had behaved too theocratically and presumptuously towards the Prince. The matter of the sermon revolved around the fact that a prince's treasure consisted of his fear of the Lord, understood in the sense of experimental religion coupled with theocratic rule, with the Bible serving as the only standard there ought to be. A prince also had a duty to set a good example and it was incumbent upon him, for example, to promote no persons other than the godly to high office. In this last regard, Thilenus makes mention of the magnum opus of Willem Teellinck, a writer to whom he refers a further three times.[92] It should be no surprise that Thilenus also cites numerous English authors.

In 1671, Thilenus and a colleague provided a report on the state of the Province of Zeeland to the Prince, on behalf of Walcheren presbytery. After the death of his first wife, his eye had fallen upon the daughter of the well-to-do Mayor of Middelburg, Jacob Veth, but another local minister, Johannes vander Waeyen (1639-1701), beat him to the prize.[93] Thilenus uttered the dying wish that Bernardus Smijtegelt[94] (1665–1739), the renowned Further Reformer, should succeed him in office. This did in fact occur.

---

90 Lieburg [1996], 1:250.
91 London, Metropolitan Archives, Guildhall Library, MS 7424.
92 Thilenus [1668], 13, 17 (twice), 19.
93 Van Sluis, 443a.
94 De Vrijer; Post.

Thilenus' library went under the hammer at Middelburg on 7 August 1692.[95] The title page of the auction catalogue announces that the books were in two categories: theology—including very many English titles—and a category of all other subjects. There were 1,490 and 810 lots respectively sold in these two categories. Of the 1,490 theological lots, 412 were Puritan in character, the overwhelming majority of which were in English and a small fraction in Latin. No fewer than sixty of the theological book lots auctioned consisted of Dutch translations of Puritan works. The total number of Puritan titles, then, was 472 book lots. The original Dutch works on piety in his collection pale in comparison with these: there were only 120 such lots, eleven of which were works by Willem Teellinck.

All the indications are that Johannes Thilenus may with propriety be regarded as a man of the Further Reformation. It appears that he was at Gataker's household seminary in 1651.

> WILLEM THILENUS
Willem Thilenus[96] grew up in Middelburg, where he was born in 1596 to Joachim van Thielen and Josina Haack. He must have had a particularly close bond with the Middelburg preacher and lecturer of the *Illustre School*, Franciscus Gomarus[97] (1563–1641), for when the latter departed the city to teach at the University of Saumur in France, Thilenus went with him. It is beyond doubt that he had before that time been schooled in theology in Middelburg by the same professor. When Gomarus received a new appointment at Groningen, their ways parted. Thilenus went to Geneva, where he arrived with a letter of recommendation from Gomarus dated 26 March 1618. From 1 May to 25 September of that year, Thilenus studied under Professor Théodore Tronchin (1582–1657), who that autumn left to attend the Synod of Dordrecht (1618–1619) as a Genevan delegate. It is quite possible that Thilenus went back to his native land in the company of Tronchin. Whether or not he did, we find him in the Oxford matriculation register in 1619. It must have been for some or all of the period 1620–1622 that he was with Gataker.

In 1623, Thilenus moved to Walcheren to take up his first preaching ministry, at Grijpskerke. While there, he described the Dutch Church in London as "a true mother church, to which each of us is particularly indebted". The following year, he received a call from that church and accepted it, to the consternation of his parents. His installation at London

---

95 *Catalogus librorum, viri celeberrimi Joh. Thieleni* [1692].
96 Nagtglas [1888], 2:761; Priem, 222–224.
97 Van Itterzon [1930].

took place on 11 July 1624. While still at Middelburg, he had married Maria de Fraeye (1605–1661), a daughter of the merchant Jan de Fraye (d. 1616) and Maria Radermacher (1572-1612). On her mother's side, she was a granddaughter of the learned Humanist and renowned merchant Johan Radermacher[98] (1538–1617), who had held church offices both at the Dutch Church in London and in Middelburg. Willem and Maria's first child was born in 1626. When another of the Dutch clergymen in London, Johannes Regius, died in 1627, it fell to Thilenus and the third preacher, Ambrosius Regemortius, to apportion the late man's books between his sons Johannes and Samuel. Regius had also directed that his two brother ministers may each take two books of their own choosing from his library.[99] Finally, it is known that towards the end of his London period, he recommended Johann Heinrich Hummel (1611–1674), the later dean of Bern, to biblical scholar Jeremy Leech (1580–1644).[100]

Thilenus' health obliged him to retire from preaching in 1630. He returned with his family to the city of his birth in 1634 and died there in December 1638.[101] Thilenus' impressive library was auctioned off at Middelburg in 1640. Shortly before his family made the crossing to the Netherlands, he and his wife had their portraits done by Cornelis Jonson van Ceulen (1593–1661), who had been born in London to religious exiles from Antwerp. Van Ceulen played a significant role in the development of English portraiture. Whether the painter was a member of the Dutch Church has not been proven, but it is certainly not impossible. At any rate, he and Thilenus will have been acquaintances. On Thilenus' portrait, van Ceulen wrote the motto *In Christi ruste ick mij verluste* [I rest satisfied in Christ]; for his wife, the motto is *Fraij in deucht in Godt verheucht* [Attractive in virtue, delighted in God].

> TRESCHOVIUS

Nothing can be said with certainty about this man. Clarke believes him to have taken a doctorate, but even this detail does not help us pin down his identity.

---

98  Bostoen.
99  Birken, 284–285.
100  Larminie, 5.
101  Van Lieburg [1996], 1:250; Hessels, 2:1477.

Willem Thilenus

*Maria de Fraeye*

> Petrus Wittewrongel

Petrus Wittewrongel[102] was born in Middelburg in 1609 and was noted in the register of the University of Leiden as a student of philosophy on 13 September 1628.[103] His preaching ministry began at 1633 in Renesse on Schouwen-Duiveland; he moved to Zierikzee, on the same island, in 1636, and he was installed at Amsterdam on 23 July 1638, where he was buried on 22 December 1662.[104] Wittewrongel came into a fortune by his marriage to Apollonia van der Welle. At Amsterdam, he was one of the preachers who decried the theatre. They had some measure of success: a performance of *Lucifer* by leading Dutch dramatist Joost van den Vondel (1587–1679) was cancelled.

More has come to light regarding the background and dates of Wittewrongel's stay in England. He wrote to Walcheren presbytery on 13 October 1631 to request permission to sit the ministerial preparation examination. Those who passed this test were made candidate ministers and thus possessed a preaching licence. Wittewrongel will have been blissfully unaware of the arguments that his request would precipitate. The problem was that on 12 July 1629, the presbytery had resolved that students must have studied at least four full years at university before seeking admission to the preparatory examination. As Wittewrongel had been a student for only three years, he did not meet that requirement and was accordingly not allowed to take the examination. When the presbytery discussed this matter, it became evident that the operative decision had never been written up in their minutes. This was remedied on 13 October 1631. Not until 5 August 1632 was Wittewrongel accepted as a candidate by Walcheren presbytery.[105] His stay at Gataker's household seminary may thus be placed in the period between late 1631 and summer 1632. The above also implies that he would not have made his journey to England if he had not in the first instance been rejected by the presbytery. Therefore, his time learning from Gataker was in a certain sense a makeshift remedy.

---

102 Nagtglas [1888], 2:998–1000; Op 't Hof [2013-4].
103 *Album Studiosorum Academiae Lugduno Batavae*, 212.
104 Van Lieburg [1996], 1:282.
105 Middelburg, Zeeuws Archief [Zeeland Archives], Archief classis Walcheren [Archive of the Walcheren Presbytery], inv. no. 2, 13 October 1631 and 5 August 1632.

PETRUS WITTEWRONGEL,
Ecclesiastes Amstelodamensis.

## William Whately

A fascinating claim by Webster is that Willem Teellinck, whom he wrongly calls Walter,[106] was once a student at William Whately's household seminary at Banbury. After all, this represents an entirely new interpretation of the stay of about nine months[107] in this Oxfordshire market town, which was then a hub of Puritanism, by the father of the Dutch Pietist and theocratic movement of the Further Reformation. Not one of the many Dutch church historians who have concerned themselves intensely with Teellinck have placed such an interpretation on his time in Banbury.

It is true that in his extensive oeuvre, Teellinck wrote—and not just once, as Webster has it, but actually twice[108] in book dedications—an enthusiastic account of the exemplary practice of family devotions and of

---

106   Webster [1997], 27.
107   Op 't Hof [2008-1], 75.
108   Not only is Banbury religion mentioned in the dedication of the first volume of his *Huys-boecxken* [Little house-book] of 1618, but it is also described far earlier, in the preface to Teellinck's translation of a manuscript by his friend Whately, which was published in 1609 under the title *Corte verhandelinghe van de voornaemste christelicke oeffeninghen* [A brief treatment of the chief Christian exercises]: this study, 26.

the simple preaching style and earnest pastoral visitations that were maintained at Banbury. The fact that he dedicated his first report to Dutch candidate ministers and Christian congregations might seem to confirm Webster's interpretation. A counter-argument, however, is the fact that the second of his reports was dedicated to a different body of readers, namely Christian heads of households in Middelburg.

If that were not enough to decide the matter, the body of the text includes matters that tip the scales incontrovertibly towards a rebuttal of Webster's thesis. In the first place, there is no detail whatsoever in the text of either account that would in any way tend towards describing a household seminary—and it is precisely in the account dedicated to candidate ministers that one would expect such details. In the second place, Teellinck expressly states that he spent all those months in England in a citizen's family, and thus not in a preacher's household. Besides these considerations, there is an historical fact that puts an end to any uncertainty on the matter. Webster's interpretation assumes that Teellinck was already a student of theology at the time. Yet this is patently wrong, for he only perceived his call to the ministry at the end of his stay in Banbury and thereupon left England very rapidly in order to pursue theological studies in his homeland. These details are known from the first biography of Willem Teellinck, which was presented to the reader at his direction by his eldest son Maximiliaan in his posthumously-published commentary on Romans 7. What we read there about Teellinck's stay at Banbury, then, is:

> Where it also began to dawn upon him that he should change his course of study, a thought which he disclosed to several of the foremost of England's divines and sought advice from them as to whether he would be at liberty to do so, seeing as he had already graduated in another faculty; which [divines] tested him searchingly on the matter and, having held a day of fasting and prayer together before revealing their feelings, judged thereafter that he was indeed free to do so, and did not doubt that the Lord would bless this special yearning that He Himself had imparted to him and [would] cause it to fall out to the glory of God, the saving of many souls, and his own comforting.
> Shortly whereafter, he left England (having travelled abroad for seven years, in France, England and Scotland), and came to the Netherlands, staying for some time at Leiden to prepare himself to the service of the Gospel; where he exercised himself in the fundaments of religion under the most learned Lucas Trelcatius, Professor of Sacred Theology,

as well as in propounding, and then in German, and then in French, in the year 1606.[109]

It is clear enough that the revisionist interpretation of Teellinck's stay at Banbury is best immediately put aside and forgotten about. The father of the Further Reformation was never a student at an English household seminary.[110]

*John White*
The literature to date has described four Germans as having stayed at John White's household seminary: Fisher, Haak, Hopf and Sleer.

John White

---

109 Teellinck [1631], *3v.
110 This consideration also removes any grounds for regarding Teellinck's account as a report on the day-to-day schedule of Whately's household seminary, as Webster would have it: Webster [2006].

> FISHER

Unfortunately, nothing can be established regarding Fisher.

> THEODORE HAAK

The outbreak of the Thirty Years' War made it impossible for Theodore Haak[111] (1605–1690), who was born in the Palatinate, to go to university in Heidelberg. Instead, he left for England, where from summer 1625 until summer 1626 he attended lectures first at Oxford[112] and then at Cambridge. Rather than returning to his homeland immediately, he spent some time with White at Dorchester, together with Fisher, Hopf and Sleer. He departed for Germany later in 1626 and spent a year or two at Cologne, during which time he translated *The mystery of selfe-deceiving* (1614) by Daniel Dyke (d. 1614) into German.[113] From 1628–1631, he was again at Oxford, attending not just theology but also mathematics lectures. He was then ordained a deacon by the Bishop of Exeter, Joseph Hall (1574–1656). The following year, Haak was minded to return to the Continent, but his plans were disturbed by a request to organise collections for Reformed preachers from the Palatinate who had been forced to flee to England. Only once he had seen to these duties in late 1633 was he able to return home. The next year, however, the military situation compelled him to leave his native land again, this time forever. It is probable that he fled to the Netherlands at this juncture. At any rate, he was enrolled at the University of Leiden on 1 April 1638.[114] In the second half of that year, he again crossed the North Sea. His engagements in England included a number of diplomatic assignments on behalf of the English Parliament and helping to found the Royal Society. In addition, he rendered the annotations of the Dutch Bible translation, the Statenvertaling, into English. He began this enormous task in 1645 or 1646 and saw the fruits of his labours published in 1657 as *The Dutch annotations upon the whole Bible*.

---

111 For him and the following names, see Barnett.
112 À Wood, 4:278.
113 This translation was not published until 1638 and was given the title *Nosce Teipsum, das grosse Geheimnuß deß Selb-Betrugs* [Know Thyself: the great mystery of self-deceit]. Its eighteen reprints testify to its great popularity: McKenzie, 168–73, nos. 698–716.
114 *Album Studiosorum Academiae Lugduno Batavae*, 294.

*Theodore Haak*

The question is whether it was only in 1626 that Haak was at White's household seminary. In a letter dated January 1632, he as good as says that he is writing from Dorchester.[115] It is hardly conceivable that he was staying at any other house there than the one where he had lodged in 1626.

> Hopf

Since no data are available for Hopf (just as for Fisher), it is impossible to say anything more about him.

> Sleer

Matters are different with Sleer. There are two candidates for who he might have been. In the literature, there has been a proposal that we ought to understand this name as a reference to Friedrich Schloer,[116] a nephew of Haak's who studied at Heidelberg from 1617 onwards. The conquest of the city in 1621 obliged him to study elsewhere; he matriculated at the University of Geneva in 1621. After studying in England for some time, he obtained English citizenship on 8 May 1630. He then served as minister of the German Reformed Church at The Hague. In this capacity, he

---

115 Hessels, 3:1538; cf. van de Kamp [2012-2], 255.
116 Van de Kamp [2012-2], 200–201 footnote 84.

delivered a sermon in 1632 on the occasion of the deaths of two kings, Frederick V of the Palatinate (the 'Winter King') and Gustavus Adolphus of Sweden. Haak translated the sermon into English. He obtained his master's degree at Oxford in 1636; a year later, he became a clergyman in England.[117]

Another possible candidate is one Mr Sclaer, who had been in England and was licensed to preach by the Bishop of Bristol while there. In the early 1630s, he was chaplain of an English regiment stationed in the Netherlands and performed the same duties for the English garrison at Tiel. His nonconformist views prompted the English ambassador to the Netherlands, Sir William Boswell (d. 1649), to order him to England— which Sclaer refused to do, since his stipend came from the States-General of the Netherlands.[118] Although either of these men could in theory be the aforementioned Sleer, the fact that Schloer was a nephew of Haak's strongly suggests that it was he who together with Haak was trained by White. This supposition is bolstered by the fact that Haak translated Schloer's aforementioned sermon.

*Seminary?*
It is Grell who connects the stay of the four aforementioned Palatine men with White's household seminary. In support of his claim that such a household seminary existed, he refers to the entry for White in the ODNB.[119] Yet, oddly enough, the author of that ODNB entry writes nary a word about a seminary. All the available data on White and the four men from the Palatinate permit us to go no further in our interpretation than that the former took pity on the latter as religious refugees and put them up for some time. The sources do not speak of a household seminary. Pending the discovery of any further data that might serve to confirm White's having trained men for the ministry (whether English or foreign), researchers would be well advised not to assume that there was a household seminary led by White.

**Seminary students from the Palatinate, Hungary and Transylvania**
That there nevertheless were Palatine students trained in the homes of English preachers is unmistakably evident from what Clarke reports in his biography of Palmer. The problem, however, is that no concrete details have thus far come to light about them. This is equally true of the Hun-

---

117 Barnett, index.
118 Stearns, index; Sprunger [1982], index, under 'Sclaer'.
119 Grell [1989], 181.

garian and Transylvanian students who, according to that same source, were also educated at several household seminaries. The historicity of Clarke's claims need not be doubted but he unfortunately does not include actual names. Besides, it remains unclear whether the numbers of Central European ministerial trainees in England were substantial. In his study on the relation between international Calvinism and the Reformed Church in Hungary and Transylvania, Graeme Murdock names many students who spent time in England but remains entirely silent over the possibility of any of them having stayed at a Puritan household seminary.[120]

**Effects on the Continent**
The following section will seek to trace the outworkings that the Puritan household seminary training of Continental students had in their home countries. As no Hungarian or Transylvanian student is known to us by name, we can say nothing specific about the Hungarian Reformed territories. Research has, however, at least proven that it by no means automatically followed that having studied in England would open a man to Puritan influences. Puritanism gained no purchase on some of the visiting students; others indeed became implacably opposed to the practice of piety and battled against Puritan theology and practices on their return home.[121]

For Denmark, we can likewise say nothing of substance: while we have two surnames of students who evidently hailed from that country, they cannot be identified. Even Germany must be excluded from our scope: for all that Gribius, Grim and Rulice were Germans, they ministered largely in the Netherlands. The two brief periods in which Rulice filled a pulpit in Heidelberg have bequeathed no data of significance. The same obtains of Grim's time at Wesel, although we may note that he is categorised as a Church of England man in his ecclesiology.

For the Netherlands, the situation is different. Nothing associated with the ministries of Demetrius, de Rijcke, Proost, van de Sweerde or Willem Thilenus could be said to indicate Puritan influence. On the other hand, the lives of Bisschop, Gribius, Hoornbeeck, de Mey, Rulice, Maximiliaan Teellinck, Johannes Thilenus and Wittewrongel do reveal elements that have to do with Puritan influence.

It is incontrovertible that the education that Bisschop and Maximiliaan Teellinck had from Cotton left its mark on them: once back in the

---

120   Murdock [2000], 64–76.
121   Murdock [2000], 75.

Netherlands, they told Timotheus van Vleteren[122] (d. 1641) in glowing terms about Cotton's edifying conversation and let him read a copy of several of Cotton's works, referred to as "Catechisme, on the Canticles, of predestination".[123] The second of these manuscripts was also lent by Teellinck to his father Willem and his uncle Eeuwout[124] (1573–1629). At their behest, it was translated by the Middelburg schoolmaster Johannes de Swaef[125] (1594–1653).[126] From the manner of van Vleteren's description of the whole circumstance, and of Cotton's reply, the present author is of the opinion that Bisschop and Maximiliaan Teellinck were both at Cotton's household seminary at the same time.

Bisschop's stay in England left its mark on his descendants. His eldest son and namesake, born at Zoutelande, was confirmed in the Christian faith at Vlissingen in 1651, went to study theology at the University of Utrecht that same year, and held a disputation there under Voetius in 1655. He then left for England, returning to Vlissingen at the end of 1656. He became the minister of nearby Nieuw- en Sint-Joosland on 18 August 1657. His second congregation, also on Walcheren, was at the port of Veere; he was installed there in 1671 and died there in 1695.[127] What did Isaac Bisschop junior do in England in 1656? Might it not be stretching matters to infer that he followed in his father's footsteps by rounding off his ministerial training with a practical placement at a Puritan household seminary?

A younger son of Isaac Bisschop senior, Samuel, was born at Vlissingen, arrived at Utrecht in 1652 as a student, and became minister of the Dutch Church in London in 1668, remaining there until his death in 1700.[128]

Maximiliaan Teellinck and Gribius had matriculated in the same year at the University of Franeker. They must have struck up a friendship, for their lives thereafter were intertwined in two ways. The known facts allow for the conclusion that they travelled together to Boston, Lincolnshire, in 1626 after graduating from Franeker. On the basis of what we have seen in the foregoing paragraph, Teellinck, Gribius and Bisschop apparently

---

122  Op 't Hof [2016-20].
123  Bush, 39, 133–134.
124  Op 't Hof [1989, 1999-1].
125  Groenendijk [1990]; Op 't Hof [2016-13].
126  This study, 78.
127  Van Lieburg [1996], 1:23; *Album Studiosorum Academiae Rheno-Traiectinae*, 29; Vrolikhert [1758], 115.
128  *Album Studiosorum Academiae Rheno-Traiectinae*, 31; Vrolikhert [1758], 115; Moens [1884], 208.

all overlapped for a period—albeit briefly—at Cotton's household seminary. They may quite possibly have formed a quartet of students together with Grim, since the latter enrolled as a student at Franeker only a few months after Gribius and Teellinck had matriculated. As far as is currently known, the two Dutchmen returned home in 1627 and the two Germans remained longer with Cotton. Gribius even remained at Boston until early 1630. He and Teellinck must have remained in regular contact after their time together in England, since he married Teellinck's sister Johanna in 1633.

After the time he spent with Cotton, Maximiliaan followed his father's example by maintaining quite close connections with the Dutch Church in London. In September 1627, he succeeded in his efforts to persuade the civil magistrate at Vlissingen to grant van Vleteren permission to leave his Zoutelande congregation to take up the call from England.[129] When the Dutch pulpit in London fell vacant anew in 1631, Teellinck himself was the first candidate to be sought after.[130] This must be the same Teellinck as we find in London in late 1644 or early 1645 informing the Dutch Church officers that he would undertake to fill the vacancies at Canvey Island and at Maidstone with a student from his Walcheren presbytery. His brother Johannes Teellinck[131] (1623–1674) thereupon served as minister of the Dutch Church at Maidstone for one year, from May 1645 to May 1646.[132]

It is very possible that Teellinck and Bisschop became acquainted with the German Rulice in Cotton's household. The same applies to Rulice's acquaintance with Grim. In the case of Gribius, it is a certainty: Rulice and Gribius worked intensively together on Cotton's manuscript archive after he had left it behind when emigrating to Massachusetts. In late 1634, Gribius appears to have been in the possession of a large number of confidential manuscripts in shorthand that he had acquired from Rulice out of that archive. At that time, Rulice gave Gribius two further shorthand manuscripts. In a letter likely dated 11 February 1635, Gribius informed Hartlib that he was currently occupied with the tasks that Rulice had left undone and that he was looking for a number of theological treatises. We may suppose that these were mostly written by Cotton.[133] It appears that Rulice and Gribius never lost contact, for the latter succeeded the former as minister of the German Church in Amsterdam in 1652.

---

129   Hessels, 3:1346–1347.
130   Hessels, 3:1502.
131   Brienen [1990]; Op 't Hof [2016-15].
132   Hessels, 3:1941, 1975–1976, 2008.
133   Van de Kamp [2010], 42–43.

The rest of Hoornbeeck's life does not evince any particular influence by Puritanism. More generally, however, it may be said that his written defences of Lord's Day observance[134] have a Puritan background to them. All those in the seventeenth-century Netherlands who went into print to urge a strict observance of the Sabbath were inspired—indeed, in many cases decisively inspired—by Puritanism. The names Willem Teellinck, Voetius and Jacobus Koelman[135] (1631-1695) speak volumes (both figuratively and literally) in that regard.[136]

The Puritan John Quick (1636-1706), who ministered to the English Church in Middelburg from 1680-1681, had a spiritual bond with six of the total of twelve of his Dutch brother ministers in the city. These six were strict Puritans and his particular friends. The closest of all his ministerial friends was Johannes Thilenus, to whom he gave the honour of being the only foreigner—albeit one who had been born in England—to feature in his *Icones Sacrae Anglicanae* [Notable Anglican divines].[137]

Beels loved his older fellow Gouda minister, de Mey, as a father in Christ. It is thanks to de Mey that Beels refers occasionally to Gataker in his works.[138]

The man in whom Puritan influence found its most extensive expression was Wittewrongel. It must have been thanks to his English study trip that he never lost contact with the country again. We see him, for instance, exchanging letters in summer 1641 with his brother minister of the Dutch Church in London, van Vleteren, regarding the appointment of a Dutch and French schoolmaster in London. When a vacancy arose for the third ministerial position in the London church, he was one of the potential successors considered in 1643-1644. One of the contacts of the church officers informed them that he was told Wittewrongel inclined to the Independents.[139]

Far more significant than those contacts was Wittewrongel's own written work. After an initial concept was published—and reprinted—in 1655, his exhaustive compendium on the Christian family came out in 1661, entitled *Oeconomia christiana ofte christelicke huys-houdinghe* [The Christian economy or the Christian household]. It appeared in two substantial quarto volumes, running to a total of more than two thousand

---

134 Hoornbeeck [1655, 1659].
135 Krull; Van Lieburg [1990]; Meeuse [1990, 2008]; Op 't Hof [2013-1], 237-268; Groenendijk [2017].
136 H.B. Visser.
137 Sprunger [1982], 194, 362.
138 Verwijs, 77b.
139 Hessels, 3:1859-1860, 1911-1912, 1930-1931, 1933.

pages. Leendert F. Groenendijk, who has conducted penetrating research into the sources used by Wittewrongel, has convincingly demonstrated that Wittewrongel used Puritan sources for the most part.[140] It is reasonable to posit it was the deep impression left on him by the family worship in Gataker's household that inspired him to treat of this subject comprehensively in his own country and to propagate those thoughts. This assumption is corroborated when we see that he drew upon no other Puritan's writings more than those of Gataker, who is the author of four of the fifteen works that Wittewrongel cited.[141] Put another way, then, more than a quarter of the publications that Wittewrongel had recourse to were by the Englishman who inducted him into ministerial practice. When we consider that his stay with Gataker was a stopgap solution at the time, we may well wonder at the remarkable turns that history sometimes takes.

**Conclusions**

The first conclusion of this chapter must be there is a great deal we do not (yet) know about the Puritan household seminaries. Even though academic researchers have never written dedicated pieces on the subject, the little that they have gleaned does contain a fair amount of detail about these practical study courses. Sadly, we are bound to point out that researchers have not avoided misinterpretations of the sources and rash conclusions. They have not only been befuddled on details of the masters and students of individual household seminaries but have made at least equally serious errors regarding the nature of the institution. Future thorough academic research might enable us to be able to distinguish different types of household seminaries.

The literature to date has spoken of five distinct household seminaries at which Continental students are supposed to have been enrolled. We have seen from the above that in light of the current state of knowledge, these five must be reduced to three. As for Whately's household seminary, if indeed that is anything more than a figment, it is at least evident that Willem Teellinck did not obtain any practical preparation for the ministry there, for the very straightforward reason that he had not yet experienced his call to preach.[142] It is equally unproven from the foregoing data

---

140 Groenendijk [1978, 1979, 1983, 1984-1, 1986].
141 Groenendijk [1984-1], 50–52.
142 The fact—mentioned in the previous chapter—that a theology student named Coolman had lodged under Whately's roof in 1623 might possibly indicate the existence of a household academy there, but that detail is in itself insufficient to be conclusive.

that White ran a household seminary at which Haak and three other Palatinate Germans supposedly studied.

Willem Thilenus is chronologically the first foreigner known to have been at a household seminary, namely Gataker's. How, then, did he come to study there? As a boy in Middelburg, he sat under Willem Teellinck's ministry for years. Teellinck had become personally acquainted with Gataker in summer 1620, when the latter briefly stopped in Middelburg during his month-long tour of the Netherlands from 13 July to 14 August. The two men conceived a high regard for each other. Given this relationship, it is nigh unthinkable that Teellinck will not have had a hand in the placement of a member of his congregation at Gataker's household seminary in the period 1620–1622. Even in the unlikely eventuality that Thilenus' stay in England was uninterrupted since 1619, Teellinck could still very well have recommended Gataker as a teacher to him by letter.

Chronologically, the next overseas students whom we know to have stayed at a household seminary were Maximiliaan Teellinck, Bisschop, Gribius and Grim; the first two were Dutchmen, the latter a pair of German exiles forced to flee the Palatinate. All four arrived at one and the same household seminary—namely Cotton's—and probably all in the same year, 1626. For Teellinck, Gribius and Grim, staying with Cotton represented a postgraduate course after their theology studies at Franeker under another Englishman, Ames. This makes one suspect that it was at Ames' suggestion that the men went to Cotton. Unfortunately, nothing more can be said about the relationship between the Puritan professor at Franeker and the Boston Puritan preacher than that the latter wrote in 1646—that is, in his American years—to his renowned Puritan colleague Thomas Shepard on his moral conception of the Fourth Commandment and backed up his opinion with a reference to Ames' *Medvlla ss. theologiæ* [The marrow of sacred divinity] (1627) and that he accompanied that letter, among other remarks, with the note "Mr Ames le*tte*re of Cards & Dice iustifying his sermon (w*h*ich I heard him Preach at Cambridge) about *them*".[143] In any event, these few details do not in any way clash with the supposition that Ames was referring Franeker students to Cotton for their practical training.

One of the quartet of 1626 trainees, Bisschop, was in fact not a student at Franeker but only at Leiden; in his case, it cannot have been Ames who suggested a study trip across the North Sea. How, then, did Bisschop decide to study in England? It cannot be coincidental in this regard that he and Maximiliaan Teellinck both came up to university from Middelburg

---

143 Bush, 391.

and that they had both sat under Teellinck senior's ministry for years. As matters are revealed to us in the current state of research, it seems that Bisschop and Teellinck junior set out jointly to learn from Cotton.

We have a final problem to deal with on this score. Why, given that Willem Teellinck had sent his congregant Willem Thilenus to Gataker in 1622, was to Cotton that his own son went four years later? In all probability, the latter decision was largely the result of Ames' influence, who felt that he had more in common with Cotton than with Gataker. If so, then Teellinck senior did not oppose his son's tutor's choice.

Jonas Proost junior must have been sent to Blackerby's household seminary by his father, who at that time was serving the Dutch Church in Colchester. This implies that Jonas Proost senior harboured Puritan sympathies.

John Rulice's case is unique in that he, a German, was referred to Cotton by Preston, a Puritan college master at Cambridge.

It is evident from a letter written by Cotton to Goodyear in 1630, delivered to the preacher at Leiden by Gribius, that Goodyear was another Puritan who was referring Dutch students to Cotton.[144] It is a great pity for research that Cotton does not give the name of the student who had arrived under his roof through Goodyear's mediation. Was this student a Dutchman, or of another Continental nationality—or an Englishman?

It is striking that both Wittewrongel and van de Sweerde were trained in England not by Cotton but by Gataker, even though Cotton had not yet emigrated. This conundrum, too, becomes readily explicable upon close inspection. Both of these Dutch students were from Middelburg and had spent practically their whole childhood (in Wittewrongel's case) or their entire childhood (in the case of van de Sweerde) under the preaching of Willem Teellinck; most likely, they had also had direct dealings with him. It seems that Teellinck chose Gataker above Cotton on every occasion that he had a student to send to England. One detail known regarding the relationship between the Middelburg minister and Cotton may well provide the key to our understanding of this remarkably consistent bent. Teellinck had an outstandingly good relationship with fully-fledged English nonconformists residing in his own country, such as Ames; the minister of the English Church at Leiden, John Robinson (d.1625); the financier of the Pilgrim Fathers' Press, Thomas Brewer; the English army chaplain Samuel Bachiler;[145] and his local English colleague in Middelburg, John

---

144 Bush, 139–40.
145 Op 't Hof [1988-2].

Drake.¹⁴⁶ If he had such a friendship with all these, then why not with Cotton? Their coolness was surely no mere matter of physical distance.

It has already been mentioned that Teellinck's own son Maximiliaan prepared for the ministry not at Gataker's seminary but at Cotton's, and that this was in all likelihood at Ames' recommendation. There is reason to believe that Teellinck, who did not object to the choice of Cotton then, was in the end not entirely content with having the Boston minister as his son's instructor. It is not as if Teellinck senior failed to see any virtue in Cotton. After all, Maximiliaan had brought Cotton's exposition of the Song of Solomon back with him from England and had let his father and others read it. Teellinck senior was so impressed by the work that he expressed the wish that it ought to be translated. This indeed happened, even if the translation was not published until four years after Teellinck senior's death—and most likely then only at the instance of and thanks to the mediation of Maximiliaan. Nevertheless, Willem Teellinck's attitude towards Cotton was ambivalent. What, then, was the scruple that Teellinck senior, and doubtless also Maximiliaan, had regarding him?

One sentence from Cotton's 16 December 1629 letter to van Vleteren gives us an indication: "Let me also desire you to enquire of Mʳ Teelinck whether his father receiued a little discourse fro*m* me (shewing how farre *the* strongest endaeuours of me*n*, and Commo*n* Graces fall short of Conuersio*n*) w*h*ich his father desired me to write to him".¹⁴⁷ This passage has already been expounded upon once before in the literature. Jan van de Kamp interprets these words in light of the fact that William Twisse (1577/8- 1646) accused Cotton in 1618 of having Arminian sympathies. Since Willem Teellinck was the butt of the same accusations in the same period of time, he might have had an especial interest in Cotton's view of common grace.¹⁴⁸ In the present writer's opinion, however, the passage in question must be understood in terms of the ongoing development of Cotton's theological opinions during the 1620s. This was the decade in which he began increasingly to gravitate towards antinomian notions. Ultimately, in his new American environment, this stance caused him great trouble in the form of the Antinomian Controversy. It will not have eluded Maximiliaan that his instructor was tending in that direction, and this is something that he will have mentioned to his father upon returning from England. In turn, Teellinck senior will have wanted to know the

---

146  Op 't Hof [2008-1], index, under all the names mentioned.
147  Bush, 135.
148  Van de Kamp [2010], 38–39.

finer points of the matter and will very probably have sought clarification from Cotton through his eldest son.

It is unclear whether Willem Teellinck did actually read the requested explanatory reply. If so, we may assume that it failed to assuage his qualms, for he was anything but an antinomian.[149] Nor will his son Maximiliaan have been persuaded by the text. The consequence of all this was that the Middelburg circles to which Wittewrongel and van de Sweerde appertained did not regard the Boston preacher with unalloyed enthusiasm. With this in mind, we ought not to wonder that both of the Dutchmen preferred to train for the ministry under Gataker rather than under Cotton.

As far as is currently known, there was only one Dutchman at Blackerby's household seminary, and even this was a Dutchman who had lived and worked in England his whole life apart from his grammar school years. Accordingly, the international quotient of Blackerby's household seminary must be rated as very low. Cotton's was a far more internationally-oriented seminary, with evidence of two Dutchmen (both from Zeeland) and two from the Palatine. Two Puritans labouring in the Netherlands, Ames and Goodyear, were responsible for the international student intake. That they referred young men to Cotton—rather than to Gataker, who was also running a household seminary in that period— had to do with their ecclesiological views: Gataker alone among the seminary masters was a Church of England man, unlike Ames, Goodyear and Cotton, all outspoken nonconformists who could not bear to minister in the Church of England.

Once Cotton had left for the New World in 1633, however, Gataker's appears to have been the only household seminary whose doors were still open to overseas students. At least, it is remarkable that thus far, no details have come to light of any Continental student being trained for the ministry from that year onwards at any household seminary other than his. Gataker's household seminary is striking in three aspects. The first is the high number of foreign students there, who numbered more than those at Blackerby's and Cotton's seminaries combined. In the second place, the absence of any German students is notable. The third unusual aspect is the presence of another nationality, namely the Danes. Although no biographical details at all are forthcoming for the two Danish students who are known by name, we can nevertheless be certain about one aspect of the preliminaries to their stay with Gataker. Their state church adherence would not have permitted them to undergo practical formation in the

---

149 Op 't Hof [2011-1].

house of any kind of nonconformist, let alone an Independent. Gataker's ecclesiology was so conformist, on the other hand, that the Danish Lutherans had no real objection to his tutorship.

Given our reconstruction of the timing of their training under Gataker, it is possible that de Rijcke and Hoornbeeck were contemporaneous students of his in 1637. The same may also apply to de Mey and Johannes Thilenus in 1651.

Of all the seminary masters, only Cotton's and Gataker's work was published in Dutch. As far as is known, none of the translators of their works was a former household seminary student. It has, however, been seen in an earlier chapter that Maximiliaan Teellinck, having previously studied at Cotton's academy, became the intermediary between the author and the translator of the only work of Cotton's to be published in Dutch.

We opened this chapter by quoting Leydecker on the large number of theology students who crossed the North Sea to learn English and to become acquainted with Puritan homiletics and pastoral practice. That it should have been a Middelburg clergyman who wrote this is only to be expected, given the findings of the research presented in the present chapter, since most of the students heading to England came from Middelburg! The question thus remains unanswered whether there were many students at Puritan household seminaries who came from the rest of Zeeland, and certainly from the other United Provinces. A second unresolved matter is to what extent the students learned English. It might seem self-evident that mastering the language was a concomitant gain of studying in England; yet, remarkably, the sources are altogether silent on that aspect. The explanation might be that becoming fluent in English was so taken for granted that it did not need to be mentioned.

The foregoing might give rise to the impression that every student departing for England after graduating in theology did so with a set goal of experiencing Puritanism first-hand and gaining practical experience of preaching and pastoral work at a Puritan household seminary; yet a recently-discovered case disproves that notion.[150] Remarkably, it concerns one of those very men whom one might have expected to have cherished a desire to learn practical Puritanism. The man in question was Johannes Baers[151] (1580/1–1653). A son of the Pietist clergyman Paschasius Baers,[152] he was himself not entirely devoid of Pietist tendencies. As his father was serving the Reformed congregation of the Frisian capital,

---

150 For the following, see: Breuker and op 't Hof.
151 Breuker and op 't Hof, 21–30.
152 Op 't Hof [1991], 13–58; Breuker and op 't Hof, 30–34.

Leeuwarden, when he came of age, it was no surprise that he matriculated as a theology student at Friesland's own university, Franeker: he enrolled there on 24 March 1599.[153]

Baers senior had cordial relations with the stadholder of Friesland, Willem Lodewijk of Nassau,[154] (1560–1620) and, through him, was personally acquainted with the stadholder of Holland, Maurice of Nassau[155] (1567–1625), a cousin of Willem Lodewijk's. In consideration of services rendered, he managed to arrange with the two stadholders that his son Johannes could travel to England. Johannes reports on his journey in one of his writings.[156] Thanks to letters of recommendation, he enjoyed access while there to numerous movers and shakers in English politics, academia and the church. Tellingly, however, he describes not one encounter with a Puritan.

The only possible indication of a Pietist contact is found in Johannes' description of his brief stay at Cambridge. At Trinity College, he made the acquaintance of Wolfgang Meyer (1577–1653) of Basel. As Johannes himself reports, Meyer would go on to take up the chair of theology at Basel University, and it was on behalf of Basel that he was deputed to the Synod of Dort (1618–1619), during which occasion Baers once again sought him out and spoke to him. What makes this acquaintanceship with Meyer so intriguing is that the latter was permanently influenced by Puritanism in general, and William Perkins (1558–1602) in particular, by while studying theology in England. His translations—mostly into Latin—of Perkins' works achieved recognition for Perkins' theology across Europe.[157] This notwithstanding, Baers is quite silent as to any meetings with English Puritan divines.

De Mey's example serves to illustrate that Baers was probably an exception to the general pattern, since de Mey—even though sent to England on diplomatic business—seized the opportunity to spend nearly a whole year at Gataker's household seminary.

Researchers have been quick to assume that Puritan ministers' training of overseas students was due merely to the students' desire to be introduced to the practice of preaching and pastoral work. However, we do have one source to indicate that English preachers purposefully made use of the presence of foreign students in their households in order to export English practical divinity to the Continent. One of the best ways to do so—as

---

153 Fockema Andreae and Meijer, 27.
154 Wagenaar; Emmius.
155 Van Deursen [2000].
156 Baers [1648], 5–14.
157 Op 't Hof [2001-1], 357–358.

Thomas Ball writes to Hartlib—"is to traine up young divines in our Countrey ... and therfore I wil doe my endeavour that not only this yong Man, but many others of like quality may be maintained in Ministers-houses".[158]

The same resolution is evident in Durie's intended translation project, although it must be borne in mind that he was acting more as an intermediary between Germany and England and the initiative was not so much his own.[159] In 1633, a number of Reformed theologians and preachers from Wetteravia and the Palatinate addressed a request, approved by Frederick V of the Palatinate shortly before his death, to the Church of England and Church of Ireland. The request was that theologians in both realms compile a handbook of practical theology, arising from the beneficial effects that they had already seen Dutch and German translations of English devotional literature exert. The petition was signed by Joannes Daniel Wildius, Theodorus Leurelius, Conradus Ammodius, Paulus Tossanus (1572–1634), Clemens Boesius, Isaacus Boots (d. 1634)[160], Matthaeus Rowyer, Philippus Paraeus, Petrus Streithagen[161] (1591–1653), Johannes Moriae, Philippus Snabelius, Johannes Conradus Hopsius, Henricus Meerbottius, Johannes Irlin, Casparus Stippius (d. 1659)[162], Johannes Arcularius and Thomas Dern. It was not published until 1654, when it was given the title *An earnest plea for gospel-communion in the way of godliness, which is sued for by the Protestant churches of Germanie, unto the churches of Great Brittaine and Ireland*. According to Durie, the envisaged handbook was to be made up of three sections: the fundamentals of Christian doctrine; the principles of the pious life proper to the covenant of grace; and a detailed ethics of family, politics and the church. The petition had appended to it a letter from London Puritan ministers, promising Durie their assistance in putting together this compendium. The work itself was intended to be printed in English first before being translated into Latin. The preachers who assured Durie of their willingness to cooperate were William Gouge (1575-1653, John Stoughton (1593-1639), John Downham (1571-1652), Henry Burton (1578-1647/8), George Walker (d. 1651), Nicholas Morton, Sidrach Simpson (d. 1655), Adoniram Byfield, Richard Culverwell (1581/2-1644), Obadiah Sedgwick (1599/1600-1658), George Hughes (1603/4-1667) and Joseph Symonds (d. 1652). The planned compendium never saw the light of day.

---

158 Sheffield, University Library, Hartlib MS 29/3 fol. 55v., quoted by Webster [1997], 26, and Milton, 119.
159 For this paragraph, see Van de Kamp [2012-2], 201–204.
160 Rosenkranz, 52.
161 Goeters, 242–244.
162 Rosenkranz, 502.

In academic terms, it is a crucial question whether these two details were incidental or whether there were more Puritans besides Ball and Durie who felt called to offer the finest fruits of their English piety movement to enrich Continental theology. The quest for an answer to this question poses one of the greatest challenges that future researchers of Puritanism will face.

# 5. DUTCH CHURCHES IN ENGLAND AS CHANNELS BETWEEN PURITANISM AND DUTCH PIETY

## The significance of Dutch churches in England for Dutch translators of Puritan works

*That the Dutch churches in England were of major importance to the Reformed Church in the Netherlands, in the periods both before and after 1572, is a position that will not meet with disagreement from anyone. It is with good reason that these congregations—particularly the Dutch Church in London—have been the subject of considerable interest to church historians.[1] Their importance has thus already been demonstrated in many ways, but, as often happens in historical and even church history research, one aspect has escaped attention: piety.[2] The present chapter will demonstrate that this gap cannot be explained away as the result of any paucity of data. Rather, what has caused this lacuna is a lack of interest in the history of piety and perhaps a denial, subconscious or otherwise, of the importance in its own right of this branch of the history of religion.[3] This chapter seeks to bridge that gap.*

*The following chapter will consider not only Dutchmen who made themselves useful by rendering Puritan writings for a Dutch readership but also*

---

1 Van Schelven [1909], Lindeboom, Backhouse [1981, 1982, 1985], Pettegree, Grell [1986, 1989], Boersma, Eßer.
2 Cf. Op 't Hof [1996-1], 251. Symptomatic of the problem outlined above is Graeme Murdock's book on the intellectual, political and cultural world of Europe's Reformed churches from 1540 to 1620. In his first chapter, on Reformed ideas, he mentions the Puritan zeal to live by precise standards of moral behaviour and notes that this was also influential in Scotland, Hungary and the Netherlands, paying particular attention to supporters of further reformation in the Netherlands: Murdock [2004], 27-28. However, he pays no attention to the fact that piety (which was of Puritan character) was one of the most unifying aspects of international Reformed Protestantism in the era. It is remarkable that the first chapter has not one mention of piety!
3 In this regard, it holds promise for future researchers that a recent guide to the Dutch Golden Age book trade devotes a whole chapter to "The Marketplace of Devotion": Pettegree and der Weduwen, 121-148.

*Dutchmen who contributed in other ways to promote the introduction of Puritanism to the Dutch Republic in the seventeenth century. Relatively speaking, however, this latter group was very thin on the ground as a proportion of those who Puritanised Dutch spiritual life. It is for that practical reason that the subtitle of this chapter mentions only the translators.*

*It is generally known that the English Puritans regarded the Dutch congregations in East Anglia, with their Reformed liturgy and structure of church offices, as model churches. They saw them as shining examples of the reforms that they wished to introduce into the Church of England.[4] Some of them even took to joining the Dutch churches.[5] In this regard, Patrick Collinson even writes in terms of "the contribution of the foreign congregations to the developing puritan movement" and of an "obligation which the puritans of the Long Parliament would acknowledge in 1641".[6] Moreover, as a consequence of the closed nature of the strict faith community of the Dutch congregations, they compared favourably with Church of England parishes in terms of lived testimony; this was certainly something that the Puritans highly valued. A typical expression of this respect is the report of three English ministers in Colchester to Sir Francis Walsingham (d. 1590), Secretary of State, regarding the Dutch churches. They wrote of the good examples "both for liefe and religion generallie geeuen bie the straungers durynge their abode in Colchester" that "haue ben comfortable to all those that be godlie minded".[7] What is hardly known, however, is that Puritan piety in turn affected and even left an impression on various members of the Dutch congregations in England, and that this was not without its effect upon the spiritual climate in the Netherlands. We shall now endeavour to make good this lacuna in the knowledge of church history.*

*This chapter will look at Dutchmen who were born in England and/or spent part or all of their youth there; Dutchmen who studied in England or served a Dutch congregation in the country; and Dutchmen who for one reason or another spent considerable time in England as adults. Obviously, it is all but certain, if not certain, that they were all members of a Dutch congregation.*

---

4   Collinson [1958]; Grell [1989], 239; [1996], 54–56, 64; Dunthorne, 138.
5   Grell [1989], 227.
6   Collinson [1958], 540 and 555 respectively.
7   Moens [1905], vi.

## Dutch congregations in England[8]

Henry VIII (1491-1547) was succeeded as King of England by his son, Edward VI (1537-1553). Edward was still a minor in 1547. During his brief reign, the Church of England was rapidly Protestantised, particularly through the efforts of Thomas Cranmer (1489-1556), Archbishop of Canterbury. One of the means used to accomplish this reformation was the recruiting to England of leading Continental Protestant theologians. One of these was Johannes à Lasco *alias* Jan Łaski[9] (1499-1560), a Pole who had been Superintendent of the church in East Frisia (Ostfriesland). The local introduction to that territory on 16 July 1549 of the previous year's Augsburg Interim led to à Lasco being forced to give up his post, and he moved to England in early 1550. From 1549 onwards, Dutch-speaking refugees in London met as a congregation at Austin Friars, whose friary had been dissolved less than a decade earlier. As the congregation was finding its feet, Marten Micron[10] (1523-1559) led the services, but members hoped for something more official to be arranged. This was made possible with the arrival of à Lasco, who was appointed Superintendent of the Dutch Church. Edward VI officially recognised the émigrés' church in London on 24 July 1550; it was thus accorded autonomy. Edward's early death on 6 July 1553 and the succession of the Roman Catholic queen Mary (1516-1558) brought an early end to the existence of the Dutch Church in London. À Lasco and Micron fled England at the earliest opportunity and the final batch of Dutch families was gone by the following spring.

After the Protestants had undergone five years of the reign whose martyrdoms gave 'Bloody' Mary the name by which she is remembered, the pro-Protestant Elizabeth I (1533-1603) succeeded her as the last monarch before the Union of Crowns with Scotland. Elizabethan England became a land of refuge for persecuted Continental Protestants even more than Edwardian England had been. The Dutch immediately availed themselves of the opportunity to come back to England, settling particularly in London. Adriaan van Haemstede[11] (d. 1562) crossed the North Sea in spring 1559 on his own initiative to serve the returned Dutch as preacher. Late that year, or early in 1560, the Dutch received official permission to found a church and to resume services at their old venue of

---

8 For this survey, see Schelven [1909], 57-113, 131-208; Roker; Grell [1996], 54, 66-67, 69, 124-128.
9 Rodgers.
10 Dankbaar.
11 Jelsma.

Austin Friars. However, there was to be no resumption of the previous autonomy; the congregation was made subject to the episcopacy of the Bishop of London. The church's supervisor was now Edmund Grindal (1519–1583), whose Puritan sympathies brought him into sharp conflict with the Queen. Of all the Dutch congregations in England, that of London was by far the largest, counting between a thousand and two thousand members at any time during Elizabeth's reign (over 1% of the entire population of the capital). In its first decade, the restored congregation was plagued by many schisms, but a considerable improvement took place in that regard from 1572 onwards. From the late 1580s onwards, the flow of new Dutch immigrants all but dried up. Consequently, a gradual 'Anglicisation' took place in the church.

The Dutch Church in London planted a daughter congregation in the Kent port of Sandwich in 1561. It began with around 400 men, women and children but burgeoned under the ministry of its first preacher, Jacobus Bucerus *alias* Jacques de Bezère (d. 1572). Written testimony survives from the Archbishop of Canterbury, Matthew Parker (1504–1575), that the congregation stood out for its pious Lord's Day observance.

Around 1562, there were so many Dutch arriving at Sandwich that the congregation asked Grindal to arrange the founding of a third congregation; this came into existence around 1566, at Colchester in Essex. In 1569, the original Colchester congregation was reinforced by a follow-up group of around fifty newcomers. Thereafter, the congregation grew mightily, numbering 1,293 persons in 1586, at a time when the town's population was in the low tens of thousands. The Dutch Church in Colchester in turn planted around 200 Dutch settlers at Halstead, only ten miles away, in 1576. Hostility from the locals prompted the return to Colchester of half of the Dutch in 1580. The remaining hundred held out and continued independent church services until 1589.

In 1565, Dutch emigres received permission to settle in Norwich. They were able to found their congregation there at the end of the year. The high total number of Dutch in the city—no fewer than 2,866 in 1569—means that the Dutch Church will also have been a very large one. Norwich's "Elizabethan Strangers", a term encompassing all Continental arrivals, ultimately numbered one third of the city's population. However, this zenith of the Dutch presence in East Anglia was to prove short-lived, as from 1572 onwards some cities and districts in the Netherlands became welcoming of the open practice of the Reformed creed.

Such Dutch refugee congregations as continued to appear in England were the consequence of the arrival in the Netherlands of the Duke of Alva (1507–1582) to crush Protestantism. After Norfolk and Essex, a third county, Kent, received Dutch arrivals in 1567. Although the numbers in their congregation at Maidstone were never very high, they soldiered on as a church until 1655. The Norwich congregation calved in 1568, founding an outpost at the western end of Norfolk in King's Lynn. The county between Norfolk and Essex, Suffolk, also received a Dutch presence: they had their own congregation at Ipswich from 1568–1576. The Norfolk port of Great Yarmouth saw a Dutch congregation founded in 1569. It was already struggling to survive by 1575, owing to the departure of most of its members. However, it continued holding services until 1680, with just 36 members left when it closed its doors. The English Midlands also hosted Dutch arrivals. Coventry in Warwickshire had a Dutch congregation whose existence covered at a minimum the years 1570–1576. A Dutch church was founded at Dover in Kent in 1571. The following year, one was founded at Stamford in Lincolnshire, and the Dutch Church in Norwich planted a second daughter congregation in 1573, this time in Thetford on the southern edge of Norfolk, which lasted until 1578. The congregations at Ipswich, King's Lynn and Thetford did not manage to stretch out their existence beyond the 1580s. The trades brought by the immigrants also allowed them to stretch out along the Thames, with a group of tapestry weavers founding a congregation at Mortlake in Surrey in 1621 (which lasted until 1664) and a congregation in the estuary on Canvey Island founded in 1627, its presence being due to the sea defence works being carried out by the Dutch there. Canvey Island Dutch Chapel retained Dutch ministry until 1704, although its decline began in the 1680s.

In fact, by the 1690s there were only two significant Dutch churches left outside London: those of Colchester and Norwich. The former had around 700 heads of families in membership in 1635; the latter, around 360. Both of them maintained two ministerial positions each. In 1644, the pull of ecclesiastical separatism was strong in England in the wake of the First Civil War. The Dutch churches responded by taking a strong disciplinary hand. The congregations of Norwich and Colchester were still active communities in 1688, but they were pale shadows of their former selves.

**The Puritan nature of the Dutch congregations in England**
It has already been noted that the Puritan nature of the Dutch churches in England has almost entirely escaped the attention of researchers. The only exception is Ole Peter Grell, who in his book on Austin Friars states that in the period he covers (1603–1642), the four new appointments of men from outwith England to pastor the London congregation were not

spread evenly through the Netherlands; rather, they came from the province of Zeeland, and even more narrowly, from the presbytery of the island of Walcheren.[12] The reason for this was that Zeeland preachers were regarded as the most godly among the Dutch. This emphasis on the value of piety is characteristic of Puritanism. In light of this Puritan trait of the London congregation, Grell also mentions that two of its later ministers, Jonas Proost[13] (d. 1667) and Willem Thilenus[14] (1596-1638) had been trained at the household seminaries of Richard Blackerby and Thomas Gataker respectively.[15]

Nor was the London congregation the only Dutch church in England whose spiritual character was congruent with that of the English piety movement of Puritanism. The fact that Jonas Proost senior, as minister of the Dutch Church in Colchester, sent his namesake son to Blackerby's household seminary in 1627 or 1628 indicates that he was of Puritan sympathies. Considering that Jonas junior was trained both by his father and by Blackerby in a Puritan spirit, it is highly likely that he shared his father's Puritan-mindedness. Jonas senior came to minister to the Dutch Church in Colchester in 1599; his son succeeded him in the pulpit and later moved to the London congregation in 1644. This would mean, then, that the Colchester congregation was led by ministers of Puritan sympathies from 1599 to 1644.

Thus far, the Puritan nature of the Dutch congregations has only been seen to be connected with their preachers. Parker's aforementioned testimony of the exemplary Sabbatarianism of the Dutch Church at Sandwich, however, indicates that Puritan ideas and practices had established deep roots in the life of the wider congregation, too.

The members of the Dutch congregations in England were interwoven with English society not only economically but also socially. Hence, they were amenable to various kinds of English influence, particularly if these chimed with their own fields of interest. The large majority of the members of these Dutch churches were Flemish in family origin.[16] Past research has indicated that Pietism in the Dutch Republic largely originated in Flanders and that it owed its first growth to that impact.[17] The religious conviction of many Reformed Flemish emigrants had pronounced

---

12  Grell [1989], 70.
13  This study, 142-143.
14  This study, 156-157.
15  Cf. this study, 141 and 149.
16  Boersma, 56; Backhouse [1981, 1982]; *Revolt and Emigration*.
17  Op 't Hof [1987], 81-82, 613-619; [1996-1], 249.

leanings to, and perhaps even strong incitements to, Pietism. This holds also good for those in England: when they came into contact in that country with the Puritans, who had a much more highly-developed structure than they did of issues, models, standards and values around piety, it stood to reason that they were won over to the movement and fell in with Puritan insights and practices. Their acquaintance with Puritanism, in other words, led to the amplification of piety tendencies already incipient among them.

Sometimes, there are also grounds for positing that the Flemish emigres were so thoroughly influenced by Puritanism that one can speak of the Puritanisation of their spiritual life. A striking example is that of John la Motte,[18] born at Colchester on 1 May 1577. A successful merchant, he came to London in the 1610s. At first, he adhered to his local parish church, but in 1626 he was ordained an elder of the Dutch Church, where he remained until after 1642. He remarried in 1626, taking for his wife the wealthy widow Elisabeth van Poele. These steps earned him a prime position in the London merchant élite. That his abilities were highly thought of can be seen from the fact that he was elected Upper Bailiff of the Weavers' Company in 1629. Moreover, he became the first member of Austin Friars to be elected an alderman of the City of London in 1648. His daughter Elisabeth was given in marriage to the Puritan merchant Maurice Abbot. Another daughter, Hester, was wedded by an Essex Puritan, Sir Thomas Honeywood of Marks Hall (near Coggeshall). She was often joined for days of humiliation (a spiritual exercise), and for dinners, by the Puritan Ralph Josselin of Earls Colne, and occasionally by her father John. While the above details already prompt us to assume that la Motte was taken with Puritanism, the best expression of these sympathies is the fact that he was the only Dutchman included by the Puritan writer Samuel Clarke in his biographies of eminent Puritans. One of the ways in which Clarke describes him is as follows:

> For the nourishment and increase of Piety in his Soul, and maintaining Communion with God, he was constant and diligent in attendance upon the publick Ordinance and means of Grace, not only in the Dutch Church, whereof he was made a member, but also in the Parish Church wherein his habitation was, and wherein were several Lectures, which he frequented, as I myself observed, who was his near Neighbour for many years.[19]

---

18  Grell [1989,] index; [1996], index.
19  Clarke [1683 ], 104.

La Motte's funeral oration was given by Fulk Bellers, who drew out the practical aspects of his piety and praised him for his munificence, expressed especially towards co-religionists abroad, and for his zealous incitement of others to join him in this charity. During the first two royal collections for the refugees, administered by the consistory of Austin Friars, he was co-operating closely with leading Puritan ministers such as John Stoughton, William Gouge, John Goodwin, John White, Samuel Ward and Samuel Collins. All this considered, it is small wonder that Goodwin dedicated his *Christ's Approbation of Marie's Choice* to la Motte in 1641.

Although they were exceptions rather than the rule, some Austin Friars congregants were actually Englishmen with Puritan sympathies, such as the alderman and later Lord Mayor, Sir Thomas Middleton, and Sir Henry Marten, Dean of the Arches.[20] A resolution indicative of the practical effect of Puritan influence is the congregation's abolition in 1626 of the traditional practice of having the sexton announce the forthcoming market days immediately after the sermon.

However, we do have opposing data to mitigate our impression of the degree of Puritan influence exerted upon Austin Friars as a church overall. In 1614, the consistory, unlike its counterpart at the French Reformed Church in London, took the un-Puritan decision to celebrate holy days which fell on Tuesdays, Wednesdays and Fridays. This decision was reconfirmed in 1644, indicating that it was the settled will of the church officers. In 1614, long and sumptuous banquets on Sundays, organised by members of Austin Friars, offended both the French Reformed and the English Puritans. A couple of years later, these communities again had cause to complain about the Dutch, this time at the practice of the wealthy, merchant members of Austin Friars of attending business on the Exchange after Sunday service.[21]

### Vincentius Meusevoet

The chronologically first translator who put Puritan works into Dutch in order to promote the entry of Puritan views and practices into the Netherlands was Vincentius Meusevoet[22] (d. 1624). Since a whole chapter will be devoted to this translator in Volume II, we shall here consider only the data that will feature in the conclusion to the present chapter.

---

20  Grell [1996], 76.
21  Grell [1996], 40–41.
22  Op 't Hof [1987], 441–455; Frijhoff, 84–92; Op 't Hof [2016-5].

Meusevoet, the son of cobbler Reinier Meusevoet, was born *circa* 1560 in the Flemish town of Eeklo and spent his childhood in Norwich. He was in Norwich for roughly eighteen years: from 1568, when his father took the family out of the reach of the Spanish Inquisition, until 1586, when we see him matriculate at Leiden as a theology student. Meusevoet's first congregation after ordination was Zevenhoven, a Noord-Holland village (1590–1598). His second and final congregation was the town of Schagen in the same province, where he ministered the Gospel from 1598 until his death in 1614.

It is evident that during his upbringing in England, Meusevoet was strongly influenced by Puritanism, for as a clergyman in the Netherlands he enthusiastically delivered a redoubtable contribution to the Puritanisation of Dutch piety, translating no fewer than 31 Puritan works. Even more significantly, these works went through the impressive total of 91 editions. Most of these editions were in octavo format; eight of them were in quarto, and one was a folio edition.

**Michiel Panneel**

The chronologically second translator considered in this chapter is Michiel Panneel[23] (d. 1604).

*Biography*

The current assumptions that Michiel Panneel probably came from a family of high standing or even of nobility, and that he served as preacher to Flemish congregations during the Duke of Alva's persecutions, seem not unreasonable but cannot be verified. Historically, Panneel first comes to light as minister of the Dutch refugee congregation at Ipswich. This congregation consisted of just ten to twelve families. Panneel is documented as having been there between 21 September 1571 and 14 May 1572.[24] He then left Ipswich for Norwich, where he was ministering for at least the period 8 October 1573 to 2 September 1577.[25] As delegate of that congregation, he participated in a meeting of the Dutch churches in England held at London in March 1575.[26] What is intriguing in light of the subject of this chapter is that Meusevoet sat under his ministry for years and was probably also catechised by him.

---

23   Op 't Hof [1987], 466–468.
24   Hessels, 2:388–390, 408–409.
25   Hessels, 2:237; Van Toorenenbergen [1872], 54.
26   Van Toorenenbergen [1872], 3.

Around the time of his transfer from Ipswich to Norwich, Panneel had joined himself to the congregation of Eeklo; it is uncertain, however, whether he ever laboured there. The connection itself is proven beyond all doubt: at the Ghent presbytery session of 29 July 1578, the congregation of Eeklo asked for assistance in bringing to them their minister Panneel, duly promised to them five years previously.[27] This was unsuccessful, as it turned out. The Eeklo congregation repeated its request at the National Synod in Middelburg of 1581. Once again, they were thwarted, although now it was clear that their claim had merit in ecclesiastical law, because Panneel was "to be censured for his disorder".[28] The connection with Eeklo forms a second piece of evidence that links Panneel with Meusevoet.

On 13 April 1577, Panneel was called by the congregation of Middelburg,[29] after the Middelburg minister Gaspar van der Heyden[30] (1530–1586) had departed to England in January of that year, equipped with many documents including a letter of recommendation from the Netherlands' leading man of letters, Philips of Marnix, Lord of Mont-Saint-Aldegonde[31] (1540–1598).[32] After repeated requests from Prince Willem of Orange[33] (1533–1584), the Norwich church agreed to release Panneel. He was installed at Middelburg on 3 November 1577[34] and laboured in the city until his death in late 1604.

When Panneel had not been preaching in the provincial capital of Zeeland for long, he was lent out to the Reformed congregation of Bruges. This will not have been unrelated to the outstanding claim on him held by the nearby town of Eeklo. On 26 February, during his Bruges period, he signed the letter written to the States-General of the United Provinces by an assembly of divines met at Ghent in which they complained of what they regarded as the prince's weak and tolerant rule.[35] Panneel's role in wider ecclesiastical assemblies was slight. Only twice did he attend a provincial synod of Zeeland: February 1581 and April 1597,

---

27 Janssen, 1:123.
28 Van 't Spijker [1981], 77. This concurs with Panneel's change of pulpit from Norwich to Middelburg in 1577.
29 Nagtglas [1860], 40.
30 Van Lennep; Van Itterzon [1983-2].
31 Van Schelven [1939].
32 Van Toorenenbergen [1871], 1:42–43.
33 Klink.
34 Nagtglas [1860], 41.
35 Borsius.

both times in the capacity of assessor.³⁶ The zenith of his church career was his clerkship of the National Synod at Middelburg in 1581.³⁷ In preparation for that synod, he was tasked by the Zeeland Synod of February 1581 to draft a new template for the examination of candidate ministers, together with Johannes van Miggrode³⁸ (1531–1627).

Panneel married twice. Three children are known from his first marriage: Josintgen, Johannes and Gerson. The sons (the latter two of the three) were born in Norwich and both followed their father into the gospel ministry. The daughter was born at Ysegem (Izegem) near Bruges³⁹ and became the mother of Johannes de Swaef⁴⁰ (1594–1653), who has already been mentioned earlier in this book.

*Writings*
Two writings by Panneel are known. Both are translations from English and are from near the end of his life. In 1600, the first was published: *Een dudelijcke verclaringhe vande gantse Openbaringe Ioannis des apostels* [*A plaine discouery of the whole Revelation of saint John*] by the Scot John Napier (1550–1617). The translator dedicated his work to the civil government of Middelburg. In this dedication, he remarks that the obscure prophecies in Revelation are daily being fulfilled and that he is producing this translation at the insistent request of some who have a zeal for the glory of God and the edification of the church. By dedicating the work to the city fathers, Panneel explained, he wished not only to express his gratitude for the reception that he and his children had enjoyed in Middelburg for 22 years but above all to exhort the city government in these last and depraved days to battle manfully against the kingdom of Antichrist and to defend and extend the kingdom of Christ. The translation must have made headway, for it was twice reprinted.

Panneel's second translation was *Eene vuchtbare overdenckinghe, inhoudende eene clare ende duydelijcke uytlegginghe vande 7.8.9. ende 10. veersen, des 20. Capittels der Openbaringhe Joannis, in forme ofte maniere van een sermoen* [A fruitful meditation, containing a clear and evident exposition of the 7th, 8th, 9th and 10th verses of the 20th chapter of the Revelation of John, in the form or manner of a sermon] by King James VI/I.⁴¹

---

36  Reitsma and van Veen, 5:4, 37.
37  Van 't Spijker [1981], 71.
38  Flinterman.
39  Briels [1972], 274.
40  Groenendijk [1990]; Op 't Hof [2016-13].
41  For the background and content of the original work, see Stilma, 238–252; for the various aspects of the translation by Panneel, see Stilma, 254–267.

This translation was part of the project undertaken by Amsterdam publishers Cornelis Claeszoon[42] (d. 1609) and Laurens Jacobszoon[43] (d. 1603) to make the whole of King James' oeuvre available in Dutch. Most likely, Meusevoet had had no time to translate this writing along with all the others by the publishers' deadline and so he outsourced it to Panneel, whom he knew to be suitable for the job. Panneel added to the sermon an exposition of Gog and Magog translated from the Latin original of an author described only as a learned and godly minister at Zurich. All the indications are that this little work came out in 1603.

It is not without significance for our knowledge of Panneel that both his translations concerned the last book of the Bible. He was a man who very much viewed his own day as the fulfilment of the prophecies in Revelation and who in his life consciously expected the historic fall of the kingdom of Antichrist. It is quite possible, therefore, that motivating his translation of King James' work were apocalyptic expectations of his reign, as was the case for Meusevoet.

Panneel had an affinity with the book of Revelation earlier in life too, as is seen from his letter of 16 November 1576 to the officers of the Dutch Church in London:

> You are not unaware how miserably the Spanish bloodhounds dealt not only with Maastricht but also with the famous city of Antwerp. And it is to be feared that they will continue in this vein, since it appears that God has given the seven angels command to pour out the seven vials (Rev. 16) of His wrath upon the earth at this time.[44]

*Significance*
Panneel was among the abler ministers in the infancy of the Dutch Reformed Church. As such, he spent his efforts not only for his own parish but also for his presbytery and a couple of times for the provincial synod. The culmination of his labours for the church came when he was appointed clerk to the National Synod at Middelburg in 1581.

Panneel's spiritual significance lies in his keenness to arouse apocalyptic expectations in the Netherlands by translating two English books on Revelation. The reprints of his translation of Napier would indicate that he achieved his goal in this regard. Equally, his translation of this work

---

42  Stilma, 31–36.
43  Stilma, 36–39.
44  Hessels, 3:403.

fostered the growing movement of Pietism. In particular, Napier's dedication to King James VI/I reveals his Pietist inclination: the Reformation has now come but it must now be carried through to full implementation. All forms of popery, and even of neutralism, must now be removed. Napier unabashedly takes the king to task on this score and even dares to call him to make a start in his own family, wider relations and court. The author also remarks that he who would purify his own house ought first to be purified by meditations.

For the present chapter, it is significant that Panneel's life and work intersected with Meusevoet's in three ways: Panneel was the pastor of his later colleague for nearly a decade (1568–1577), he came to minister in the latter's birthplace around 1572, and it will have been at Meusevoet's instigation that he came to translate a work by James VI/I in 1604.

**Willem Teellinck**
The chronologically third Dutch translator of Puritan writings was Willem Teellinck[45] (1579–1629). Because his life and work will be treated in

---

45   Beeke [2003]; Op 't Hof [2008-1, 2011-1, 2015-1].

Volume II, here we shall only consider his connections with Dutch congregations in England.

*Teellinck's connections with Dutch congregations in England*
Teellinck was in England from the end of 1603 until early 1606. As well as staying among English Puritans, he forged links with Dutchmen in the country while there. In 1604, he wrote an inscription—unfortunately since lost—in the friendship album of the London-resident well-known merchant and historian Emanuel van Meteren[46] (1535–1612).[47] Also in his English years, Teellinck became a close friend of another Dutch merchant in the English capital, Jacob Cole Orteliaan *alias* Cool[48] (1563–1628).[49] They carried on a correspondence, with Cool expressing his appreciation of Teellinck's writings. In 1623, Cool sent Teellinck, now a minister at Middelburg, a manuscript of his thoughts on death. Teellinck was so taken with the work that he urged Cool to have it published. This did occur in 1624, under the title *Van de doot, een ware beschryvinge end tegen de doot een goede bereydinge* [Of death a true description of death: and against it a good preparation]. Given that it was published at Middelburg, it is reasonable to suppose that Teellinck had a role in seeing the book come out. Meanwhile, Teellinck had dedicated one of his major works, *Sleutel der devotie* [Key to devotion], to Cool on 1 November 1623. In the dedication, he praises the contents of a number of devotional tractates which, while anonymously published, are known to him to have been written by Cool. He adds that in his character of Apollos, one of the characters in the dialogue in *Sleutel der devotie*, he was thinking of Cool. He further remarks of Apollos that his contribution was the occasion for his writing the dialogue of which *Sleutel der devotie* consists. This might actually indicate that Cool in some way was, or at the least provided, the means of Teellinck's conversion. Might Teellinck have ended up among the Puritans through Cool's mediation?

In the Acts of the Apostles, of course, Apollos is described as a man who taught others fervently while not yet himself possessing much knowledge of the Christian faith. There is therefore a dual sense in Teellinck's identification of Apollos with Cool: on the one hand, he evidently wishes to honour Cool's role in his life, but on the other, his choice of characterisation indicates that Cool still has things to learn. What was the

---

46   Brummel, 81–185.
47   Rogge [1897], 206.
48   Van Dorsten; Van Dorsten and Schaap.
49   For the following, see Op 't Hof [2008-1], 284–286.

message that Teellinck wished to convey to Cool in *Sleutel der devotie*? After analysing the role and personal statements of Apollos in the dialogue, we obtain an impression of one who is resolved to live a holy life, who has spiritual acquaintances and who himself is not wholly lacking in godly opinions and practices. It would seem, then, that in dedicating *Sleutel der devotie* to Cool, Teellinck wished both to stiffen his resolve for sanctification and to warn him against the mystical sect that surrounds, menaces and perhaps even bewitches him. On the grounds of what is known of Cool's relatives and acquaintances in London, it may be concluded that what Teellinck primarily meant by this was to keep him away from, or to persuade him to forsake, the heretical influences of the Family of Love. This conclusion would imply that the penetration of the spiritual notions of the Family of Love among the Flemish élite in London was actually greater than an expert on that sect would have us believe.[50]

No decline came in the good relations between Cool and Teellinck as a result of the dedication. When Thilenus wrote to Cool on 14 December 1625, he conveyed most cordial greetings from Teellinck.[51] Both van Meteren and Cool were members of the Dutch Church in London; Cool even served as an elder from 1624 to 1628.[52]

It seems reasonable to infer, then, that Teellinck had followed the fortunes of that congregation for some time, however short or long, and had retained a bond with them. That he cherished an affection for them is proven by multiple facts. Firstly, there is the consideration that Simeon Ruytinck senior[53] (d. 1621), who ministered to the London church from 1601 until his death, twice in his history of the Dutch congregations in England approvingly cites a writing of Teellinck's as authoritative.[54] There is no doubt that he personally knew and admired Teellinck.

Willem Thilenus[55] (d. 1638), born in Middelburg, ministered in London from 1624–1630. Having grown up in that Zeeland city, he will have heard Teellinck's preaching on many occasions. That he was also a friend of the Father of the Further Reformation is evident in the fact that Teellinck, in the letter to Cool just mentioned, asks for his warm greetings to be passed to Thilenus.[56]

---

50  Hamilton, 113. Grell's description of Cool as a staunch Calvinist does not entirely do justice to the data at hand: Grell [1996], 111.
51  Hessels: 1:871.
52  Grell [1989], 38, 92 footnote 161, 134, 259, 269, 272, 295.
53  Van der Woude [1978-1].
54  Ruytinck *et al.*, 249, 308.
55  This study, 156-157.
56  Op 't Hof [2008-1], 284–286.

One of Thilenus' brother ministers at the Dutch Church in London was Timotheus van Vleteren[57] (d. 1641), whom we consider in his own right later in this chapter. He was born at Sandwich and served the London congregation from 1628 to 1641. In 1627, Teellinck not only recommended him to the church officers in London as a suitable man to call, but went on to make several efforts to effectuate this call. This testifies of a spiritual concord between the two men.

The best proof, however, of good relations between the Further Reformer of Middelburg and the Dutch Church in London is the dedication in Teellinck's *Christi waerschouwinge, om voor te komen het weeren van onsen candelaer uyt zyne plaetse* [Christ's warning to avoid the removal of our candlestick out of its place] (1626): the dedication is to that church. Teellinck mentions the following reasons for his dedicating the work to them. He preached the substance of this publication, Revelation 2:4-5, to the London congregation a few years previously. Also, the London congregation is a remarkable one because most of its members are the descendants of those who gave up all their worldly goods and even their lives for the truth of the gospel, and because the Lord has evidently been pleased to bless this church. Moreover, Teellinck has been given to understand that a positive trend is discernible in the church's development. This gives him reason to expect that the example set by this congregation will be followed elsewhere. In other words, he saw it as a model church.

Reciprocally, Teellinck was held by the London church, or at the least by its church officers, in high regard. When the consistory was seeking a successor for deceased minister Johannes Regius[58] (1574-1627), who in 1602 had taken over the pulpit from his deceased father Jacobus Regius[59] (1545-1601), it wrote a letter seeking the advice of three theologians in the Netherlands on 2 March 1627: Amsterdam preacher Roelof Pieterszoon[60] (1585-1649), Teellinck, and Leiden professor Antonius Walaeus[61] (1573-1639). In his answer of 5 April, Teellinck wrote that he rejoiced to see the church officers' good disposition towards him, as had been demonstrated by the response given to Teellinck's dedication of the previous year's book to them and now again by their request for his

---

57 Op 't Hof [2016-20].
58 Van Schelven [1918-2].
59 Van Schelven [1918-1].
60 Exalto [1974-1]; Op 't Hof [2016-9].
61 De Lind van Wijngaarden; Op 't Hof [2016-21].

advice. He recommended three candidates: Carolus de Maets[62] (1597–1651), minister of Scherpenisse in Zeeland; van Vleteren, minister of Zoutelande, also in Zeeland; and Nicolaas van der Deliën[63] (1600–1630), minister of Stad aan 't Haringvliet on the Zuid-Holland island of Overflakkee. We may safely conclude that Teellinck saw in these three men likeminded ministers who supported his reforming efforts.

It is evident from Walaeus' answer of 8 May that the London church officers had written to him that they had been thinking of asking Teellinck himself to be Regius' successor. His response on that point is as follows:

> As for the person of Rev. Teellinck, I maintain that he is above any censure and that he could render great services to your church there. I also know that he has been treated rather harshly by some, whereby he might be obliged to give ear to other callings [...], yet I would not gladly do the congregation of Middelburg the disservice of advising him so.

From the entire list of potential candidates submitted by the aforementioned three together with a further three advisors, the first choice of the London church officers was de Maets and the second van Vleteren. It is very remarkable that these two men, in the same order, had been recommended by Teellinck. Evidently, the London church had a great deal of confidence in his advice.

Once the London calling committee had negotiated for five weeks with de Maets and Middelburg city council (which had funded his theology studies) about his vocation, it became clear that the move could not go ahead. On 5 September, the committee therefore handed a written call to van Vleteren, accompanied by a letter of recommendation by Teellinck. Teellinck was also one of those who mediated to have van Vleteren's presbytery release him. His services were required once again to persuade van Vleteren's four patrons (presumably sponsors of his studies), one of whom was his own brother Eeuwout Teellinck[64] (1573–1629), to endorse the move. Finally, his son, Maximiliaan Teellinck[65] (1605–1653), did his utmost on behalf of the calling committee to persuade the civil government of Vlissingen (Flushing), which had jurisdiction over the village of

---

62   Broeyer [2016-1].
63   Op 't Hof [2015-13].
64   Op 't Hof [1989, 1999-1].
65   Brienen [1993]; Op 't Hof [2016-16].

Zoutelande. The upshot was that van Vleteren was permitted to accept the call. When the committee reported this final success to the London church officers by letter from the Netherlands on 20 September, they also passed on Teellinck's greetings.[66]

From the foregoing, we learn that the significance that the Dutch Church in London had for the initiator of the Further Reformation is not to be underrated, even if its role for him was a lesser one than for other Dutchmen discussed in this chapter. It was probably via a friend from that London congregation, Cool, that Teellinck landed in Puritan circles in the first place. Moreover, he regarded it highly as a model congregation for others to learn from. Conversely, too, Teellinck sought to conserve and foster the Pietist character of this congregation by advising on the filling of a ministerial vacancy.

*Puritan influence*
The influence that Puritanism, including by means of the Dutch Church in London, exerted upon Teellinck was immense. Once he had been won over to Puritanism, he gave all his skills and strength to achieve the Puritanisation of the Netherlands. Many of his efforts attest to this. In his own family circle, he managed to enthuse his brother Eeuwout and his cousin Adrianus Hofferus[67] (1589-1644) for this piety movement from overseas, and among fellow ministers, he won over Godefridus Udemans[68] (1581/2-1649), Josias van den Houte[69] (1582-1623) and Gisbertus Voetius[70] (1589-1676). He retained his connections to Puritans in both England and the Netherlands his whole life long; these connections account for a total of nine book editions. Three of his sixty writings were translations of Puritan works. Moreover, numerous of his writings address key themes of Puritanism, and even the rest of his oeuvre is teeming with Puritan topics. Finally, Teellinck brought about a more or less coherent piety movement, in the form of the Further Reformation, that was a match for Puritanism in England. He was also the unwitting means for the commencement of a Further Reformation in Germany.[71] Among the principal movers and shakers of the Further Reformation, he was, together with

---

66 Hessels, 3:1333-1350, 1358-1360. The quotation appears on 1338-1339.
67 Op 't Hof *et al.* [1993].
68 Meertens; Fieret; Exalto [1989]; Schutte [1989], 301-302, 310-311; Uil [2016-2].
69 Op 't Hof [2015-19].
70 Duker; Van Oort *et al.*; Andreas J. Beck.
71 Op 't Hof [2008-1], 571-572; Van de Kamp [2012-1], 155-156.

Jacobus Koelman[72] (1631–1695),[73] the most thoroughly seeped in Puritanism in his own life.

**Johannes Lamotius**
The chronologically fourth translator of Puritan writings was Johannes Lamotius[74] (d. 1627). As there will be a dedicated chapter on this translator in Volume II, here we shall consider only the data that concern England and that are germane to the conclusion of the present chapter.

Lamotius' father, likewise named Johannes, was minister to the Dutch refugee congregation in London. 'Lamotius' is a Latinisation of *la Motte*, a surname which makes it certain that this family came from the Southern Netherlands. Johannes junior was sent to the Latin school at Ghent from 1582 to 1584, at the expense of the Dutch Church in London. There, in 1584 at the least, his roommate was the man whom we shall consider directly below as our fifth translator. From 1588 to 1591, Lamotius studied theology at Heidelberg University, again funded by the Dutch Church in London. Not long after his arrival in Heidelberg, he wrote a letter to Cool, the Dutch merchant in London, which indicates a close friendship.

Once in the Netherlands, Lamotius served four congregations in turn: Giessen-Nieuwkerk (1592–1593), 's-Gravenzande (1593–1595), Kampen (1595–1604) and The Hague (1604–1627). All of these except Kampen are in Zuid-Holland; the call to Kampen came thanks to his ex-roommate from Ghent, who was already preaching in Kampen. In his Kampen years, Lamotius turned down a call from the Dutch Church in Colchester.

Like Meusevoet, Lamotius was so shaped by Puritanism in his English childhood that he later spent his leisure time translating Puritan writings. However, there was a difference between the two: whereas Meusevoet restricted himself to translating English Puritans, Lamotius concentrated on Scots Puritans, all of whom were in fact Episcopalian bishops. In total, Lamotius brought out 23 translations, and he published one other Puritan translation that set out the Puritan view of Sabbath-keeping. By dedicating that latter work to Eeuwout Teellinck, Lamotius—although based in Zuid-Holland—acknowledged the Zeeland origins of the Further Reformation, in which the brothers Willem and Eeuwout Teellinck were leading lights.

---

72  Krull; Van Lieburg [1990]; Meeuse [1990, 2008]; Op 't Hof [2013-1], 237–268; Groenendijk [2017].
73  Graafland *et al.*, 171.
74  Op 't Hof [1987-1], 423–437.

By one measure, Lamotius was a more acclaimed translator than Meusevoet: Lamotius achieved around ninety editions, sixteen of which were in quarto format and four in folio.

**Wilhelmus Baudartius**

The fifth translator in chronological terms was Wilhelmus Baudartius[75] (1565–1640).

*Biography*

Wilhelmus Baudartius was born at Deinze in Flanders on 13 February 1565 to glovemaker Willem Baudaert and Maria Zachmortel. His parents took the family out of Flanders at an unknown date and settled at Sandwich. They lived there from at least late 1573 until 1576, the period for which there is documentary evidence. Baudartius was educated at Canterbury as a young man and was in England for so long that he was able later in life to translate an English work into Dutch.

Before going up to university, Baudartius was at the Latin school in Ghent. He was a roommate of Johannes Lamotius'[76] (d. 1627) in 1584 during the siege of the city, and while lessons were suspended, the two of them together committed Terence's comedies to memory. He matriculated at Leiden on 20 June 1586 as a student of theology, and on 2 March 1588 entered Franeker University in the same subject. Having worked as vice-principal of the Latin school in Sneek, Friesland, for a year, he resumed his studies at Franeker in 1590. The following year, he matriculated at Heidelberg. Both in Leiden and in Franeker, he dedicated his efforts to studying Hebrew. In Heidelberg, where he assisted with the preparation of an index to the Bible edition of Franciscus Junius[77] (1545–1602) and Jacob Kimedoncius[78] (d. 1596), he declined the offer of a chair in Hebrew.

Baudartius' first congregation was in the city of Kampen in the eastern Dutch province of Overijssel, where he was installed in office in 1593. Remarkably, his old roommate from school in Ghent, Lamotius, was called to the same city two years into Baudartius' ministry at Kampen. It would seem that the men had remained close and that Baudartius had put in a good word for Lamotius when the vacancy arose. It will not be coincidental either that Lamotius conducted Baudartius' wedding service

---

75  Broel Roelofs; Op 't Hof [2015-4].
76  Op 't Hof [1987-1], 423–437.
77  Cuno; Venemans.
78  De Bie and Loosjes, 4:749–752.

on 3 October 1595. Baudartius' wife was a daughter of the mayor of Kampen, Marten Alberts.

While at Kampen, in 1596, Baudartius declined a call to the city of Zutphen in the neighbouring province of Guelders. The same year, however, he did accept a call to the town of Lisse in Zuid-Holland. While at Lisse, he was again called to Zutphen in 1598, and this time accepted. Here, he made efforts to build up the congregation and also did a great deal for the Zutphen presbytery. He was often a delegate to the provincial synod of Guelders, being elected chairman several times. He spent much effort over time to ensure the existence and consolidation of a properly-functioning church life across the province.

Theologically, Baudartius stood resolutely with Franciscus Gomarus[79] (1563–1641) from the beginning of the latter's conflict with Jacobus Arminius. In 1612, he and Johannes Fontanus[80] (1545–1615) were deputed to The Hague for a meeting to call for a national synod. There, he met the delegate from Zeeland, Willem Teellinck. In 1615 and 1616, with the same aim in mind, he took part in the Contra-Remonstrant sessions of correspondence held at Amsterdam. He chaired the Guelders Synod of 1618, held at the provincial capital of Arnhem, where the matter of the Remonstrants in the province was dealt with.

Baudartius was long occupied with the need for a new Bible translation.[81] In 1596, the provincial synods of both Guelders and Overijssel named him as the man in their midst most suited to see to a new Bible translation. The Guelders Synod of 1605 gave him the green light to translate Johannes Piscator's (1546–1625) Bible translation into Dutch. However, since another provincial synod, that of Noord-Holland, expressed the opinion that it was better to await the gathering of a national synod, the 1607 Guelders Synod decided to release him from this commission. The request by Noord-Holland to the Guelders Synod to suppress the dissemination of Baudartius' book calling for a fresh Bible translation did not go down well in Guelders: the provincial synod resolved to ask its Noord-Holland sister assembly to produce a signed declaration absolving Baudartius of any suspicion of improper life or doctrine. The 1618–1619 Synod of Dort was for Baudartius the long-awaited fulfilment of his desire to see a new Bible translation come about: he was awarded one of the three translator positions for the Old Testament,

---

79   Van Itterzon [1930].
80   Janssen and van Manen.
81   For the following, see Reitsma and van Veen, 4: index.

together with the translation committee chairman Johannes Bogerman[82] (1576–1637) and Gerson Bucerus[83] (d. 1631). Having made the first drafts of their apportioned sections individually at home, the translators all moved to Leiden to continue and refine the Bible translation. Baudartius was in that city with his family from April 1626 until early 1637. His full-time Bible translation left him no time to carry on with his parish ministry in Zutphen.

Baudartius' second marriage, to Josina Morn in the Guelders village of Brakel, was solemnised in September 1617. His personal motto was *Labor mihi quies* (Work is my leisure). He died at Zutphen on 15 December 1640 and was buried in the city's Walburgkerk, where the epitaph on his gravestone can still be read.

*Writings*
Baudartius' first work was connected with his childhood in England, and as such indicates to us that that period of his life left a deep impression on him: *Af-beeldinge der coninghinne Elyzabeth* [A portrait of Queen Elizabeth] (1604). The queen's death the previous year had inspired him to compose a grateful retrospective of her life.

A year later, his collection of proverbs was published: *Apophtegmata christiana. Ofte ghedenck-weerdighe, leersaeme, ende aerdighe spreucken* [Christian apophthegms, or memorable, instructive and pleasant proverbs]. Another year later, a work of his came out on a subject dear to his heart: *Wech-bereyder op de verbeteringhe van den Nederlantschen Bybel* [Preparing the way for the improvement of the Dutch Bible]. In this work, he signalled the urgency of the need for a new translation and made the case that Piscator's German version should be rendered into Dutch.

In 1610, Baudartius brought out a popular history of the felonious acts of the Habsburg party during the Dutch Revolt: *Morghen-wecker der vrye Nederlantsche provintien. Ofte, een cort verhael van de bloedighe vervolginghen ende wreetheden door de Spanjaerden ende hare adherenten inde Nederlanden [...] begaan* [An alarm for the free Dutch provinces, or a brief account of the bloody persecutions and cruelties perpetrated [...] in the Netherlands by the Spaniards and their adherents]. The following year, another product of his anti-Roman Catholic zeal became available to the reader, but now on a timelier topic: *Jaer-clachte over den schreckelijcken moort begaen aen Henricum III* [Lament of the year over the terrible murder perpetrated on Henry III (of Navarre and IV of France)]. In 1615,

---

82  Van Itterzon [1983-1].
83  Op 't Hof [2015-8].

Baudartius returned to the theme of the Dutch Revolt, giving indications of his love for the cause of the House of Orange, with the work *Afbeeldinge, ende beschrijvinghe van alle de veld-slagen, [...] ghevallen in de Nederlanden, geduerende d'oorloghe teghens den coningh van Spaengien* [Illustration and description of all the battles [...] waged in the Netherlands during the war against the King of Spain]. His major Dutch historiographical work appeared in 1618, entitled *Historie der Nederlandscher gheschiedenissen, van den jaere 1566. tot den jaere 1618* [History of events in the Netherlands from the year 1566 to the year 1618]. This publication was his sequel to *Belgische ofte Nederlantsche historie van onsen tijden* (1599), the well-known work of Emanuel van Meteren[84] (1535-1612). Two years later, Baudartius' history was published again, now under the amended title *Memorien, ofte kort verhael der ghedenckweerdighste gheschiedenissen van Nederlandt* [Memoirs, or a short account of the most memorable histories of the Netherlands].

In 1625, Baudartius proffered a description, Pietist in tone, of a contemporary military movement that posed a great threat to the district where he himself resided: *Velaus vastel-avond-spel, ofte cort verhael van den alarm die op vastel-avond in de Veelau gheweest is* [A Shrovetide evening play of the Veluwe, or brief account of the alarm that there was upon Shrove Tuesday evening in the Veluwe].

A posthumously published work of Baudartius' was a Latin chrestomathy of extracts of the New Testament from the Statenvertaling.

The Guelders Synod of 1611 asked Baudartius to write a work on the right use of ecclesiastical goods. As Baudartius told the following year's synod that he did not feel he could manage this commission on his own, it was resolved that he would write it together with the Harderwijk professor Anthonius Thysius[85] (1565-1640). However, since no results of these labours are known, we must assume that nothing came of the project.

Also never published, but at least completed by Baudartius in 1615, as he himself reports in his autobiography, was a translation of a mystical dialogue penned by the Scots bishop William Cowper (1568-1619). A new translation of this dialogue by Lamotius would be published three years later. Given that Lamotius was engaged from 1612 onwards on the translation of the complete works of that Scots Puritan, it may be assumed that Baudartius was put on to that work by his Hague colleague and friend, and may also have been given a copy of it by him.

---

84 Brummel, 81-185.
85 Lamping [2001].

*Significance*
Generally, Fontanus is regarded as the pre-eminent reformer of Guelders. Alongside and after him, however, Baudartius devoted much of his strength to the building and consolidation of the Reformed Church in the province. As a resolute Contra-Remonstrant, he left his mark on the development of that provincial church.

From his student days onwards, Baudartius cherished and propagated the ideal of a new Dutch Bible translation. With his own contribution to the Statenvertaling, his ideal was attained, albeit in a different way than he had originally proposed by calquing the Piscator Bible from the German. It must have been an unforgettable, even emotional, day for him when the first copies of the newly-completed Statenvertaling were presented in 1637.

In third place after his reformational and Bible translation efforts, Baudartius made his name as an historian. He continued van Meteren's work expertly, furnishing new material. Historical works on the Dutch Revolt and more recent events also flowed from his pen; in these, it is the fierceness of his anti-popery that comes to the fore.

In fourth place, this Zutphen minister delivered a valuable and highly influential contribution to the genre of proverb collection so beloved of the seventeenth century.

A further and final dimension of Baudartius may now be brought to light that hitherto has remained entirely obscure in scholarship of his life. The fact that he translated a work by Cowper shows in and of itself that he tended towards an openness to Pietism. What makes this translation even more compelling is that it was not just any of Cowper's works but the most mystical in his whole oeuvre![86] Clearly, Baudartius had not only a feel for mystical texts but an actual preference for them.

There is a second facet to the Pietist aspect of Baudartius. In his *Velaus vastel-avond-spel*, he links the calamitous encroachments of the enemy to the fact that the Dutch were persisting in holding such a Roman Catholic feast as Shrove Tuesday. By raising this issue of outward observance, Baudartius approaches the Further Reformation agenda. It is not surprising, then, that Willem Teellinck, in his *Gesonde bitterheyt voor den weelderighen christen die geerne kermisse houdt* [A salutary bitterness for the carnal Christian who is a keen fair-goer] (1624), expresses the wish that Baudartius' recently published *Velaus vastel-avond-spel* will cause many to think again about the life they lead.[87] Thus, we may discern in Baudartius both the inward and the outward aspects of Pietism to some degree.

---

86  Op 't Hof [1987-1], 210–211.
87  Op 't Hof [2008-1], 298.

*Influence*
As a translator on the Statenvertaling committee, Baudartius exerted an influence felt in the Dutch-speaking world down to the present day. More easily defined is the extent of the success he had with Dutch readers in his copious collection of proverbs. The third edition of 1616 was augmented with a second part, and some of the further reprints were further augmented. In total, the book went through eleven editions. In his popular account of the cruelties of the Spaniards, Baudartius achieved his aim: it had to be reprinted no fewer than four times in the year of its initial appearance, and in 1620 a further three editions came out.

Baudartius' *Memorien* was republished in 1624, but now in two parts, much extended and with a greater degree of independence: Baudartius now sought to separate church history from secular history. In his account of the ecclesiological struggle between Remonstrants and Contra-Remonstrants, he drew upon a germane pamphlet by the mayor and advocate of the Further Reformation, Frederick de Vrij[88] (1579–1646). In 1786, an extract of this work was brought into circulation as a publication in its own right: the passage dealing with the prosecution and condemnation of Johan van Oldenbarnevelt. *Afbeeldinge, ende beschrijvinghe van alle de veld-slagen* had a second edition in 1616.

Illustrative of the considerable scope of influence of Baudartius' work is the fact that *Afbeeldinge* was also published in French (1616) and Latin (1622) translations.

## Gerson Bucerus

Although Gerson Bucerus[89] (d. 1631) made no translations of his own, he earns a place in this chapter by his having urged the translation of a Puritan work.

*Biography*
Gerson Bucerus' entry in the Leiden student album states that he was born in Flanders. We have every cause to doubt the veracity of this, however. His parents, Jacobus Bucerus (or de Buzère) and Catharina de Raedt, were married at Sandwich on 24 August 1561. Jacobus, who had been a monk in an Ypres cloister until 1560, was minister of the Dutch Church in the Kentish town at the time of the birth.[90] Accordingly, Gerson was in all probability born at Sandwich.

---

88   Op 't Hof [1987-2].
89   Op 't Hof [2015-8].
90   Crew, index, under De Buzère.

Gerson Bucerus matriculated as a theology student at the University of Leiden on 28 April 1583.[91] After graduating, he became curate of the Dutch Church at Sandwich. His first independent cure of souls, which turned out to be the only parish he ever had, was another port: Veere on the island of Walcheren.

Bucerus was a talented man for whom there was much admiration in Veere, across Zeeland and even in the church nationwide. He was called to Leiden in 1615 and to Flushing in 1618, but turned down both requests. He was often a deputy to the provincial synod of Zeeland. He had much to do with the 1620 synod.[92] In the time leading up to the synod, the States of Zeeland had arbitrarily meddled with the complaints submitted in the register for consideration at the synod. Some cases were summarily struck out, others abridged, and some even had preordained decisions by the States entered against them in the margin. The Walcheren presbytery protested against this unlawful interference in internal church affairs. The protest was presented to the States of Zeeland by the delegation of Hermannus Faukelius[93] (d. 1625), Bucerus and Willem Teellinck, which led to a response that the presbytery could live with. At the synod itself, Bucerus was elected chairman. This synod's resolutions were more imbued with Further Reformation fire than were those of any other Zeeland synod ever. The resolutions concerned missions, discipline, education, Sabbatarianism and feast days inherited from Roman Catholicism. Bucerus, together with Teellinck, was given the task of making the synod's requests known to the States of Zeeland. They had the satisfaction of seeing the States agree to almost all their requests and promise them co-operation.

Bucerus was even renowned abroad. Dutch congregations in England, especially that of London, continually asked him for advice when considering which minister to call.

His academic proficiency in Hebrew and ancient history also saw Bucerus appointed a translator of the Old Testament in the Statenvertaling committee, alongside Bogerman and Baudartius. However, he could not join his comrades in Leiden for that work until November 1626, his appointment having been resisted by his church officers and by the civil government in Veere. His two fellow translators showed the height of their esteem for him by leaving the most challenging verses in the Old Testament for him to tackle. When death overtook him on 7 August 1631,

---

91 *Album Studiosorum Academiae Lugduno Batavae*, 13.
92 For the following, see Op 't Hof [2008-1], 202–208.
93 Op 't Hof [2015-16].

he was still translating at Leiden and had reached the middle of Ezekiel. The name of his first wife is unknown; his second wife was Willemijntje Bezar.

*Writings*
Bucerus has just one original work to his name. This was a tractate in Latin in which he contested the episcopal form of church government that had been defended by George Downham (1560–1634). It appeared in 1618, bearing the approbation of the Walcheren presbytery.

*Significance*
Bucerus was a leading theologian of his day. His work on the Statenvertaling gave him a significance that has lasted until the present time. His only original writing caused great ructions across the North Sea: it so incensed King James VI/I that he demanded—in vain—that the States-General force Bucerus to go and apologise to him in person. Perhaps precisely due to all this uproar, the tractate was in such demand that it had to be reprinted three times.

There are many reasons to suspect that Bucerus strongly sympathised with the aims of the Further Reformation. In the first place, there are the notable facts that Teellinck played a major role at the provincial synod that Bucerus chaired, and that many of the decisions taken by that assembly were expressly pro-Further Reformation in tone. Secondly, there are the joint efforts—theocratic in tone—of Bucerus and Teellinck in preparation for that synod, and their collaboration in presenting the synodal resolutions to the States afterwards. Thirdly, we have Bucerus' own report on these duties, contained in a letter to the Walcheren presbytery dated August 1621. In the letter, he also bemoaned the fact that Zeeland congregations were being slandered for their views on the keeping of the Lord's Day (views which were Puritan). Later, as recorded in the presbytery minutes, Bucerus said that he found Teellinck's book on the day of rest a fitting rejoinder to such accusations.[94] Fourthly and lastly, we have the facts concerning the little book *Miles christianus* [The Christian soldier] by Samuel Bachiler[95], chaplain of the English troops at Gorinchem. The Further Reformation advocate Johannes Spiljardus[96] (1593–1658), a fellow Gorinchem minister and friend of Bachiler's, sent copies of the 1625 English original of *Miles christianus* to Bucerus and Teellinck.

---

94  Op 't Hof [2008-1], 245–246.
95  Op 't Hof [1988-2].
96  Huisman [2010]; Op 't Hof [2016-12].

Evidently, then, Bucerus was part of that network. He wrote a letter of thanks back, containing the suggestion that the book ought to be translated into Dutch. The result, translated by Spiljardus and bearing the same Latin title as the original, came out in 1628, with an extract from Bucerus' letter of thanks included in the edition.

**Timotheus van Vleteren**
In early 1629, as minister of the Dutch Church in London, Timotheus van Vleteren[97] (d. 1641) sent copies of Arthur Hildersham's (1563–1632) exposition of John 4 to colleagues in the Netherlands. The Dutch preach-

> In a private Letter of his from *Boston* February 3. 1629. to him, he mentioneth a Letter he received from a *Dutch* Minister in *London*, (one *Timotheus Van Vleeren*) who telleth him, he had sent sundry of the books on *John* 4. to Ministers beyond the Seas, who do read them with such great satisfaction, that the said *Dutch* Minister did in the name of many others intreat Master *Cotton* to beseech Master *Hildersam* to put forth his Sermons on *Psal.* 51. and other his lucubrations.

ers were so enraptured by their reading of them that van Vleteren was obliged to urge Hildersham—through the person of John Cotton (1585–1652), a Puritan friend of the author's—to write more books.[98] In the present writer's research, the following have been borne in mind as likely Dutch ministers to have sent this encouragement: Daniel van Laren[99] (b. 1585), Willem Teellinck, Maximiliaan Teellinck, Isaac Bisschop[100] (1598/9–1661), Isaac Hoornbeeck (1587–1648), Godefridus Udemans, Martinus Bruynvisch[101] (1591–1661) and Joos van Laren[102] (1586–1653).[103] Whomever the request may have come from, van Vleteren (whom we have already seen in this book corresponding with Cotton) served as a conduit for the transmission of Puritan writing to brother ministers in the Netherlands who admired Puritanism. It is significant, therefore,

---

97  Op 't Hof [2016-20].
98  Grell [1989], 60.
99  Op 't Hof [2016-3].
100  This study, 144.
101  De Bie and Loosjes, 1:678; Van Lieburg [1996], 1:41; [2011], index.
102  Op 't Hof [2016-4].
103  Op 't Hof [2005-2], 110; Van de Kamp [2010], 40.

that his widow married a Puritan preacher in 1643: William Sedgwick (b. 1610).[104]

**Samuel van Haringhouk**
The chronologically sixth translator was Samuel van Haringhouk[105] (1621-1675). He is the first of our subjects who was not a preacher.

*Biography*
Both parents of Samuel van Haringhouk, the merchant Matheus van Haringhouk and Hester Carnier or Cunira, were born in the Dutch community in Sandwich. His grandfather Anthony van Haringhouk, who came from Steenvoorde in French Flanders, had become a freeman of Amsterdam in 1594. Samuel was born in Amersfoort in the province of Utrecht and was christened there on 14 June 1621.

His parents took him to London before he was even two years old, joining the Dutch Church there. After his father Matheus died, the family had moved to Bolsward in Friesland by 1633, leaving debts behind them. His mother Hester was a surgeon and continued practising the profession for many years. She was remarried to a Bolsward clerk Gellius Brunga (1598/9-1637) in 1634, and by 1639 at the latest made her last marriage, to the bookseller Abbe Ruurds.

Her son Samuel took over Ruurds' book trade after his death in 1647. A year later, he began publishing. 1656 was a crucial year for him. In the first place, he married Lamcke Gysberts Sierxma at Bolsward on 24 April. He had already had a long-term relationship with the woman, since children were born to them in 1651 and 1654. It will have been in connection with this illegitimacy of his children that he did not become an adult member of the church by confirmation until 1662. Secondly, 1656 was the year that he purchased his own printing press; previously, he had had his publications printed by others, first by Ids Alberts in Franeker. After Albert's Bolsward business associate Johannes Arcerius had bought his own press, van Haringhouk transferred his printing commissions to him until 1656. Even after 1656, van Haringhouk did not always do his own printing; another Bolsward man, Philippus Sioerts Boenja, sometimes undertook it for him.

From odes, we know that van Haringhouk's friends included the Fri-

---

104   Grell [1996], 96 footnote 59.
105   Bierma; Breuker [1989], 2: 231, 253-254, 256, 542-543 footnotes 338-346; [2015-4].

sian poet Gysbert Japicx[106] (1603–1666); preachers Sixtus Brunsvelt[107] (1632–1683) and Nollius Hajonides[108] (1634–1671), who had first been rector of the Latin school in Bolsward from 1654–1658; and a Bolsward man Hero Galama, who was employed as printer by the Leeuwarden publishers Claude Fonteyne (d. 1654) and Hendrik Rintjes (1630–1698) before starting his own business in Harlingen. Van Haringhouk was not a successful publisher. His debts were the subject of a civil procedure in 1673. After his death at Bolsward in late 1675, his widow carried on the business until it was auctioned off in 1677.

*Catalogue*
Van Haringhouk's first publication[109] was a joint edition with Alberts, the initiative being Alberts': the work in question was *Proef-praedicatien* [Sermons of preparation (for participation in the Lord's Supper)] (1648) by the retired Franeker preacher Focco Johannes[110] (1587–1650). His second publication, *Werelt-spiegel* [Mirror of the world] (1649), was by the freethinker Sebastiaan Franck[111] (1499–1542). The editor, the Franeker professor Johannes Phocylides Holwarda (1618–1651), was a son of Focco Johannes'. It seems that the publisher owed his gaining of the commission for this edition to the mediation of one of the mayors of Bolsward, Jan Gerbens, a brother-in-law of Focco Johannes'. Other editions of his also had to do with his own town. In 1652, he published an almanac: *Bolswarder almanach* [A Bolsward almanac]. He was funded by a relative of the deceased Bolsward schoolmaster Japicx to bring out Japicx' poetry collection *Friesche rijmlerije* [Frisian rhyme] (1668). The following year, he was responsible for the publication of a courtly novel translated by a Bolsward woman Catharina van Mellinga (b. 1644) from French, *Faramond of historie van Frankryk* [Faramond, or a Frankish history] (1669). For the sake of completeness, we mention here also his publication in 1669 of a death elegy written by an Oosthem schoolmaster Elconius Elcoma.

Van Haringhouk's first publication of a Puritan work in translation appeared in 1650: Thomas Taylor's (1576–1633), *Christi strijdt ende overwinninge* [*Christs combate and conquest* (1618)]. Two years later, his own first translation came out: a brief work by the French theologian Pierre du

---

106  Breuker [1989].
107  Exalto [1974-2]; Breuker [2015-2].
108  De Bie and Loosjes, 3:455.
109  For his output, see Eggermont.
110  Breuker [2015-5].
111  Jan-Dirk Müller.

Moulin[112] (1568–1658). After the reprint of a little work by Dionysius Spranckhuysen[113] (1587–1650) in 1653, there followed from 1656 onwards a long succession of translations of Puritan works. He had translated many of these himself, and for the rest of the works he was the instigator who had set the translator to work. It seems he had just these types of

112  Rimbault.
113  Leurdijk [1987].

translations in mind when buying his printing press. In sequence, he brought out translations of Taylor in 1656, Hildersham in 1659, Samuel Smith (1584–1665) in 1658, and Edward Reynolds (1599–1676) in 1660. He also submitted to the Dutch reading public some compendia of Puritan sermons: four volumes of sermons of repentance (1657–1668), a collection of funeral sermons (1662) and a collection of communion sermons (1671). In the midst of these publications, he brought out a further devotional work by Wilhelmus Schotanus Rinckema (1570–1666) in 1668, and the last of his publications was the three-volume (1672 and 1676) dogmatics of Simon Oomius[114] (1630–1706).

The output of this Bolsward publisher was not much in demand. There were just five reprints in his whole career, all of which are of the translated sermons of repentance from England. Van Haringhouk might have been able to boost the meagre sales of his books if he had had a better network of agents in other Dutch provinces.

*Significance*
Van Haringhouk was one of the few publishers of his time who allowed his own spiritual leaning, Pietism, to determine the composition of his output. Other than two works upon emergent occasions, only two of his editions do not qualify as Pietist, namely *Bolswarder almanach* and *Faramond*. His Pietism was strongly Puritan in tone. Seen this way, it will not have been a coincidence that he grew up in the Dutch Church in London. He used his knowledge of English to translate several of his publications himself. No other seventeenth-century Dutch publisher did so much to acquaint the reading public with Puritan books. Not only did he encourage others to translate Puritan works; he himself bought a printing press with the dissemination of that genre in mind, and turned out what was an impressive number of editions when we bear in mind his financial resources and Friesland's status as an outlying province. He evidently felt a calling of some sort to do this work. It is all the more surprising, then, to see him flouting Puritan standards up until 1656 by cohabiting, and procreating outside wedlock, with the woman whom he then did marry. Might his edition of Franck's writing provide the key for this facet of his behaviour? If so, then it seems he harboured a number of free-thinking convictions and then left them behind him for good in 1656, not only by entering into matrimony but also by buying a press in order to disseminate Puritan material. Towards the end of his publishing career, the Puritans in his catalogue made way for works by Oomius, but given the latter's

---

114  Van der Pol [1999, 2002, 2019].

love for Puritanism, this cannot be seen as a radical change of course. While his Pietist endeavours were of a high calibre, the quantity of his output rather less than its quality.

That van Haringhouk was the publisher of the first and most significant work of poetry ever published in the Frisian language cannot be credited to his initiative, as he did not incur the costs of the edition himself.

**Simeon Ruytinck**
The chronologically seventh translator we shall consider is Simeon Ruytinck[115] (1606–1666).

*Biography*
Simeon Ruytinck was born in London in 1606 as the namesake son of Simeon Ruytinck[116] (d. 1621), minister of the Dutch Church there. His grandfather, Jan Ruytinck, had been the city clerk of Ghent before fleeing to Norwich in 1573. On 23 March 1623, Simeon was awarded an annual bursary of £25 by his congregation to study theology at Leiden. The following year, he requested a raise of £5. This was turned down, but as he had outgrown his clothes, he was given a one-off gift to buy new ones. On 16 February 1624, he was officially registered as a theology student at the University of Leiden.[117] He returned to London in 1625 to exhibit the fruits of his study. His church officers found that his knowledge left something to be desired, and sent him back to Leiden. When he repeated his request in January 1626 to raise his allowance due to the high cost of living, the London consistory acceded on the 26th of that month and approved a £30 bursary. In May 1628, he indicated a desire to return to London, to remain there a year and then to pursue further studies at another university, either Saumur in France or Geneva in Switzerland. His church officers did not approve and told him to remain—and study—at Leiden. When he protested at this decision, the church officers responded by insisting that he submit to their decisions and pointing out that he was spending far too much. Before even receiving this letter, he was warned by an uncle that the church officers were not well disposed towards him. He immediately wrote a letter of apology and seized this opportunity to recommend his brother Johannes Ruytinck (1608–1663), an alumnus of the London congregation, for a bursary for theological study; this recommendation was successful.

---

115   For the following, see Grell [1989], index; [1996], index.
116   Van der Woude [1978-1].
117   *Album Studiosorum Academiae Lugduno Batavae*, 174.

Ruytinck's church officers then sought to send him on to Franeker for further study. To this end, they wrote a request to the Franeker professor Sixtinus Amama[118] (1593–1629), who had spent a year in London and Oxford from 1615 to 1616, where he must have become acquainted with at least some of the members of the Dutch Church in London. They asked whether Amama was willing to have Ruytinck stay in his house or otherwise recommend him to his academic colleague William Ames[119] (1576–1633). Simeon was not minded to go along with this. He wrote back that some of his professors had urged him not to go to Franeker, and that he had calculated that board and lodging with Ames would cost around 400 guilders a year. Although his church officers initially stuck to their plans, nothing came of them. Instead, Ruytinck pulled off his original scheme of travelling to France. He is documented as being in Paris in late December 1629. In May 1630, he reached Saumur, where he studied for only four months. By this time, he had already burned through almost the whole sum that he had been given for his study tour. The consistory forbade him from carrying out his plan to go on to Geneva. In 1630, he travelled west to Nantes, intending to carry on down to La Rochelle. Instead, the church officers ordered him to return to nearby Saumur. Owing to a famine in the Loire valley, however, he headed for Paris instead.

Ruytinck was in the French capital from March to July 1631. He then finally obtained permission to go on to Geneva, where he lodged with the Italian Bible translator Giovanni (Jean) Diodati[120] (1576–1649), a brother-in-law to one of the most prominent members of the French church in London, Philip Burlamachi (d. 1644) and a delegate to the Synod of Dort. From Geneva, he proceeded to Strasbourg. In Switzerland, he was asked to fill the vacancy left by Volckerus van Oosterwijck[121] (1602–1675) as Dutch embassy chaplain in Venice. Suspecting that this would not go down well with his church officers in London, however, he declined. Then, after having done a tour of Switzerland for nearly a month, he set off back to Leiden in early November 1631, where he resumed his studies of theology. The London church officers told him that he should try to obtain a parish in one of the western Dutch provinces, either Holland or Zeeland, but he replied that these prime posts were as rare as hen's teeth. He also indicated in his letter that he was minded to start preaching to the English refugees in Leiden. This was strictly forbidden by his church

---

118  Nauta [1983-1]; Platt.
119  Visscher; Sprunger [1972]; Van Vliet; Van 't Spijker [2015].
120  Budé.
121  Op 't Hof [2016-7].

officers, who charged him on the contrary that he must join a Dutch presbytery and must not start preaching in any language other than Dutch. This news went down so badly with him that he had a mental breakdown, which prompted a letter of consolation from the London consistory on 15 November 1632. Ruytinck, however, responded defiantly: not only had his church officers repeatedly accused him of wasting money during his Grand Tour, but while he had been back in London, some of them had even accused him of pride and conceit. As far as he was concerned, the chief culprit was the church's minister, Willem Thilenus. He added the defence that he had found himself obliged to seek a connection with the Englishmen in the Netherlands because the aforementioned accusations had prevented him from returning to London, and insisted that he had thought better of it afterwards anyway. His bursary was stopped in 1633. The considerable length of his studies is understandable, however, because his preparatory teaching in London will not have amounted to much.

The wealth of our knowledge of Ruytinck's student years is in contrast to the little that we know about the years of ministry that followed, which amounts to this: he was installed at Maastricht in 1633, later going to Nijmegen, where he preached from May 1639 until his death in 1666.

*Writings*
As far as is known, Ruytinck is to be credited with only two works, both translations from the English. The first consisted of a pair of texts, the first of which was a long one: Archbishop James Ussher (1581-1656), *'t Lichaem der goddelycke leere, of 't begrijp ende het wezen der christelijcke religie* [*A body of divinitie, or the summe and substance of christian religion* (1645)] (1656), to which was appended the same author's *Immanuel ofte de verborgentheydt der menschwerdinghe des soons Godts* [*Immanuel, or the mystery of the incarnation of the son of God* (1645)] (1655). Ruytinck dedicated the first work, with a date of 15 November[122] 1655, to the trustees of the Amsterdam chamber of the Dutch East India Company. The reason for this was as follows. Robertus Junius (1606-1655) had previously been sent out by the trustees to Formosa (now Taiwan) as chaplain. He laboured fourteen years on the island and had urged Ruytinck to translate the work, as he believed it could be very useful to the Reformed church in the East Indies. Junius had promised that he would have the trustees disseminate the completed Dutch translation to the mission field, but had since died, leaving Ruytinck to request this himself in the dedication.

---

122  De Bie and Loosjes, 4:622-624.

The work is catechetical and dogmatic in nature, not entirely devoid of Pietist emphases. The same is true of the second work in the pair.

In 1666, a Nijmegen printer and publisher brought out a combination of two more of Ruytinck's translations: Samuel Smith's (1584–1665) *Davids gesegende man* [*Davids blessed man* (1638)], translated by the dismissed Utrecht professor and Further Reformation advocate Matthias Nethenus[123] (1618–1686), and Nathaniel Pownall's (1583/4–1610) *Gulden cleynoot, ver-vattende een heylighe voor-bereydinghe van een jongh godts-geleerde voor sijnen inganck tot den dienst van den kercke* [*The young divines apologie for his continuance in the universitie* (1612)]. The first of the pair is a devotional exposition of the First Psalm. The second, only a quarter of the length of the first, is divided into four sections, the first of which is a theology student's explanation to his parents of why he is taking so long about his studies. We do not need much imagination to work out why Ruytinck felt drawn to this work, then. The rest of this latter work has an unmistakably Pietist dimension.

Given the place of publication, Ruytinck must have undertaken the publication of this combined work himself. This implies that he was an acquaintance, if not a friend, of Nethenus, the translator of Smith's work. The fact that publication occurred four years after Nethenus' dismissal from his professorship could be interpreted as an intended rehabilitation of the latter by Ruytinck. The sequence and the scope of both these works indicate that Ruytinck regarded his own translation as a handmaid to that of Nethenus.

*Significance*
Ruytinck is towered over by the figure of his father. Although he was a city preacher all his career, this was never a springboard for him to assume prominence in national church life. He lives on in his two translations. It needs to be clarified on this front, however, that he was more receptive than active as a translator: his first translation bears the character of absolving him of his debt of honour to his deceased friend and brother minister Junius, and his second could be seen as an effort to restore the reputation of another friend. Yet, significantly, it cannot be denied that both works have a Pietist accentuation.

---

123 Broeyer [2016-2].

### Johan Vermuyden

While all but one of those whom we have considered thus far were preachers, the last two men we shall look at now were not ministers of the gospel. The first was Johan Vermuyden[124] (1595–1669).

*Biography*
Johan Vermuyden was born at Sint-Maartensdijk on the Zeeland island of Tholen in 1595 to the later mayor Bartel Vermuyden[125] (1528–1609). He was christened in the town of Tholen. Around 1618, in London, he married Maria Liens[126] (d. 1635), daughter of Johan Liens[127] (1549–1594), a lawyer and the steward of the Nassau estates of Sint-Maartensdijk and the adjoining village of Scherpenisse. The reason for his being in England was to accompany Joachim Liens[128] (d. 1625) during his ambassadorship. In 1621, he once again crossed over to Britain, this time with Cornelis Vermuyden[129] (d. 1656), and now with the purpose of assisting the latter in his land reclamation in Yorkshire, a commission obtained from James VI/I. Johan remained in England for many years.

Johan will doubtless have belonged to Dutch churches in England during those years. At least, this is confirmed to have been the case for his uncle and uncle's family during the years that Johan was in England.[130]

Once back on his native island, Vermuyden settled in Tholen town, where he fairly quickly rose to local government: in May 1630, he became town bursar. He was reappointed to that office in 1640. He was alderman in the years 1634–1636, 1638, 1639–1644, 1650 and 1653–1655. He served as mayor in 1648, 1649, 1651 and 1652. He also held office a few times in the local Reformed congregation: he was elected deacon in 1622 and elder in 1632 and 1638. He steered a neutral course in Tholen politics between the pro-House of Orange and pro-States-General factions. He was also deputed to the States of Zeeland. In 1651, he was a deputy to the Great Assembly of the United Provinces at The Hague, where the decision was ratified not to appoint a new stadtholder and where it was also resolved not to establish the Reformed Church by law as the state church. After the Orange faction gained the upper hand in Tholen in 1655 and Vermuyden's mayoralty was proclaimed unlawful, it was probably at his

---

124 De la Rue [1741], 460–461; Romeijn, 605b–606b.
125 Romeijn, 604a–605a.
126 Romeijn, 486b.
127 Romeijn, 486a–b.
128 Romeijn, 488a–489a.
129 Korthals Altes; Harris; Romeijn, 606b–607b.
130 Korthals Altes, 61.

own initiative that he gave up politics the following year. Remaining on the island, he retreated to his homestead beside Schakerloo (later known as Kettinghoeve) to devote himself to pious writing. On 28 May 1636, in Tholen, he married again: his wife was Clasina Dallens (1611-1675), daughter of the mayor, Jaques Dallens (d. 1623).[131] He died on 17 October 1669 and was buried at Tholen on 25 October 1669. He was churchwarden of the town at the time of his death.

*Writings*
Vermuyden's writings prove that he was not spiritually unaffected by his time in England. In 1658, a version improved by him of Lamotius' translation *Een spieghel der barmhertigheydt* [*A mirrour of mercy* (1614)] by Cowper was published, augmented with a free reworking by Vermuyden of Dod's first sermon printed in Lamotius' translation of Dod's ten communion preparation sermons. The work cannot have been rapturously received, for the publisher found it necessary to resort to a title edition in 1670. Also published in 1658 was a compilation by Vermuyden of Puritan writers, chiefly Dyke, on the theme of the temptations of Christ: *Worstelende Christus* [Christ wrestling]. Clearly, this theme was one of existential significance for him personally, because in 1663 he brought out another writing on the same subject, probably also by Cowper.

*Significance*
While other statesmen of Vermuyden's time whiled away their spare hours in the writing of poetry, this Tholen politician devoted his years of retirement from public life to new translations and additions to devotional works by English Puritans. His long stay in England had given him an outstanding familiarity with the language. His choice for these writings betrays his personal theological preference, which he probably owed to the acquaintance he made with those works while living in England. The fact that two of his three translations concerned the temptations of Christ would imply that he himself struggled with many temptations.

**Mattheus du Bois**
The next translator whom we ought to consider in this chapter is Mattheus du Bois[132] (1630-1695).

---

131   Romeijn, 406a-408a.
132   Alblas, 64-69; Op 't Hof [2011-2], 70-92; [2013-5].

*Biography*
On his father's side, du Bois' ancestors came from Roeselare in Flanders. The oldest known of these is his grandfather, Vincent du Bois,[133] who was obliged because of his pro-Reformation views to quit Roeselare with forfeiture of his possessions in 1575, barely made it through the following years of oppression with his life, and after much grave persecution came to rest in Haarlem in 1584.[134] He enrolled as a member of the Reformed congregation of Haarlem on 17 April 1585, upon settling in the city.[135] He was elected a deacon of that church in 1587;[136] he was a merchant by trade.[137] Eight children proceeding from his marriage to Mayken Vereecke or Vereycke were christened at Haarlem between 27 January 1585 and 13 May 1601.[138] He buried his wife Mayken on 15 June 1614.[139]

Mattheus' father was named Zeger,[140] the youngest child of Vincent and Mayken, christened on 13 May 1601 at Haarlem.[141] Some time between 1614 and 1626, Vincent and Zeger crossed the North Sea and established themselves as London merchants. Vincent had died before 1628. We find Zeger still in England in 1635, but now in Great Yarmouth as deacon of the local Dutch church.[142] Zeger married Maria de Jonge.[143] Two children are known from their marriage: Mattheus and Vincent[144]. Zeger must have returned with his family to his native city in the latter half of the 1630s, for he was buried there on 30 March 1641.[145] He will have had to show an attestation from the Great Yarmouth church when

---

133   Haarlem, Noord-Hollands Archief [North Holland Provincial Archive] (NHA), Doopregisters [Baptismal Registers] (D), 17 January 1591 and 13 May 1601; NHA, *Archief van de kerkenraad van de hervormde gemeente Haarlem* 1578-1935 [Archive of the Church Officers of the Reformed Parish of Harlem] (AKHGH), inv. no. 98, 17 April 1585.
134   Mattheus du Bois [1681], 4.
135   NHA, AKHGH, inv. no. 98, 17 April 1585.
136   Du Bois [1681], 4. His enrolment as a member and his ordination to the diaconate are both also reported by: Spaans, 283.
137   NHA, Notariële archieven Haarlem [Notarial Archives of Haarlem] (NAH), inv. nos. 8, 247r.; 78, 105v.–106v.
138   NHA, D, 27 January 1585, 13 May 1587, 17 January 1591, 26 December 1591, 11 July 1593, 7 September 1595, 25 February 1599, 13 May 1601.
139   NHA, Begraafboeken [Burial Registers] (B), 15 June 1614.
140   NHA, NAH, inv. nos. 241, 496v., 516v.–517r.; 243, 34r.–35r.; 322, 307r.–308v.
141   NHA, D, 13 May 1601.
142   Hessels, 2:1318, 1362, 1678–1679; Du Bois [1681], 4.
143   NHA, NAH, inv. no. 242, 268r.–277v. She twice acted as witness at the christening of a grandchild: NHA, D, 18 June 1655 and 6 March 1657.
144   NHA, NAH, inv. nos. 241, 496v., 516v.–517r.; 243, 34r.–5r.; 322, 307r.–308v.
145   NHA, B, 30 March 1641.

enrolling in the Reformed congregation in Haarlem, but that arrival is not recorded in the membership roll.

Mattheus du Bois, the subject of the present section, was born in London.[146] It is not known when precisely he was born, but under the next heading we shall see that it must have been around 1630. Du Bois married Agatha (diminutively, Aagje) Dirksdochter (van Wijngaarden) on 26 May 1652 at Haarlem.[147] By his own account in his spiritual autobiography, he was confirmed as a Christian believer aged twenty. No trace of this is found in the Haarlem church registers. This does not necessarily imply that he did not join the Reformed congregation at Haarlem; the previous paragraph has already discussed that membership records there were not perfect, and other sources also inform us that this type of church registration was far from completely kept in the seventeenth century.[148] In total, eleven of Mattheus' children were christened in the years 1653-1672.[149]

On 28 July 1673, Mattheus, a merchant and shopkeeper, made a last will and testament together with his wife Agatha, as she was on her sickbed.[150] She was granted a new lease of life after that illness and survived a further twenty years, for her date of burial is registered as 17 March 1693. She was buried in the Janskerk in Haarlem.[151] Du Bois dictated his own will on 10 December 1694, giving his address as Groenmarkt in Haarlem.[152] This will makes it apparent that nine children—Hermanus, Susanna, Jacomina, Maria, Agatha, Geertruyt, Vincent, Jacob and Dirk—were still alive; that he had already acceded to giving Dirk,[153] who wished to seek his fortune abroad, his share of the inheritance the previous year; and that he had sold his shop and yarn to Hermanus and Susanna. According to the inventory made of his effects, he died on 3 April 1695.[154] Like his wife, he was buried in the Janskerk; the funeral was held on 7 April 1695.[155]

---

146 NHA, Trouwboeken [Wedding Registers] (T), 12 May 1652; D, 20 May 1653, 18 June 1655, 6 March 1657, 1 September 1658, 4 August 1660, 15 March 1662, 1 July 1664, 26 December 1665, 17 April 1668, 21 November 1669, 13 July 1672. In the first baptismal entry only, it is not London but merely England that is stated as Mattheus' birthplace.
147 NHA, T, 12 May 1652.
148 Op 't Hof [2004-1], 85, 101, 111.
149 NHA, D, 20 May 1653, 18 June 1655, 6 March 1657, 1 September 1658, 4 August 1660, 15 March 1662, 1 July 1664, 26 December 1665, 17 April 1668, 21 November 1669, 13 July 1672.
150 NHA, NAH, inv. no. 329, 140v.-142r.
151 NHA, B, 17 March 1693.
152 NHA, NAH, inv. no. 457, 462r.-465r.
153 NHA, NAH, inv. no. 444, 798r.-v.
154 NHA, NAH, inv. no. 501, 59.
155 NHA, B, 7 April 1695.

The inventory of du Bois' effects also contains a description, though deficient, of his books. Given the course of his life, it is no surprise that many of these were written by Puritans. Of the nearly 100 titles that can be identified, 38 are by a Puritan author, and 23—or a quarter of the total—are in Dutch translation. In addition, many of the original Dutch titles on the list are by Further Reformation and Pietist authors.[156]

*Writings*
The first of du Bois' own works to appear was *Godts wonder-werck, voor en in de weder-geboorte, met een korte alleen-spraeck over 't selve. Door eygen bevindinge beschreven, en nu tot nut van anderen in 't licht gebracht* [God's miraculous work prior to and during the new birth, with a brief monologue on the same; described through [the author's] own experience and now brought to light for the benefit of others] (1665). The author hid behind the initials "M.D.B." As the title makes plain, this work is an account of the author's conversion; therefore, it belongs to the genre of spiritual autobiography.

*Godts wonder-werck* has a preface by Edward Richardson[157] (d. 1677), the Puritan minister of the English Church in Haarlem. Richardson is an intriguing figure. He ministered to the English Church in Delft from 1643–1645. He subscribed to the three formularies that make up the confession of faith of the Dutch Reformed Church, but did not join the Reformed presbytery. In 1645, he returned to England to minister. He fled back to the Netherlands in 1663 because of his anti-Royalist activities. The following year, he became the minister of the English Church in Haarlem—the only man ever known to have fulfilled that role—and also obtained the citizenship of that city. In 1664, he obtained a doctorate in medicine from the University in Leiden. In 1670, he left the Haarlem congregation for another English church, that of Leiden. He became so deeply influenced by the millenarian Johannes Rothe[158] (1628–1702) that he renounced his office and moved to Amsterdam, dying there three years later. In 1676 appeared his translation of a mystical little work by Thomas Bromley (1629–1691) that had originally come out in English in 1655 and that had now been supplied with an introduction by Richardson that took up almost as many pages as the text itself: *De wegh tot den sabbath der ruste: ofte der zielen voortgang in 't werk der wedergeboorte,* [*The way to the sabbath of rest, or the progress of souls in the work of regen-*

---

156 Op 't Hof [2013-5].
157 Sprunger [1982], index.
158 Evenhuis [1978].

*eration*] . In the year of Richardson's death, his grammar of Dutch for English speakers was published;[159] it was reprinted numerous times.

In his preface to *Godts wonder-werck*, Richardson entirely endorses the content of du Bois' text and praises both it and its author. What the author describes is God's usual way of leading His people to heaven. Richardson also writes that it has been twenty years since the Spirit of God began to work in the author. Here, he is probably referring to the resolution in life that du Bois took as a fifteen-year-old. If so, then the implication of Richardson's words is that du Bois was born in 1630. Given that Richardson did not come to Haarlem until 1664, he had not been on hand during du Bois' conversion. The fact that he nevertheless has precise information about the timing of it shows unmistakably that Richardson and du Bois were close spiritual friends during the former's Haarlem years. It is even reasonable to suppose that the Englishman had a major hand in the appearance of du Bois' first publication—in the role of instigator, for instance. In light of the course of du Bois' life, it is no wonder that he became connected with Richardson.

Before the actual text of the work, there is a preface by du Bois, dated 30 March 1665, in which he writes that he aims particularly to strengthen the weak in faith with this little work. In the text itself, we find the following biographical and bibliographical reference points.

Du Bois resolved as a fifteen-year-old to live a virtuous life, in the legalistic sense.[160] At that period of his life, he was lapping up *De guldene annotatien* [The golden annotations] of Franciscus Heermans, a collection of largely worldly proverbs of classical antiquity. Later in his youth, du Bois began to find this unsatisfying reading matter and began to acquire godly books, such as *Hoemen leven sal, ende dat wel*[161] [*How to liue, and that well* (1601)] by Perkins, the father of Puritanism.[162] He was confirmed in church membership at the age of twenty.[163] As a 21-year-old, he heard a voice telling him one night that he could never be saved.[164] In this extremity, one factor in which was that he feared he might have committed the unpardonable sin against the Holy Ghost, he resorted to local minister Theodorus Wyckenburgius[165] (d. 1655), who supported him spiritually. Wyckenburgius had already translated three short Puritan

---

159 Loonen, 226–248.
160 Du Bois [1665], 11–12.
161 Op 't Hof [1987-1], 298–299.
162 Du Bois [1665], 13 and 16 respectively.
163 Du Bois [1665], 16–17.
164 Du Bois [1665], 18–19.
165 Op 't Hof [2016-23].

works into Dutch and would go on to bring out four devotional works of his own. When du Bois was 22, the fear of reprobation returned, stronger than ever. At that time, he was often reading *Disputaty van geestelicke verlatingen* [Disputation on spiritual abandonments] by Voetius and Johannes Hoornbeeck[166] (1617–1666), and went back to Wyckenburgius for consolation.[167] In his description of this period of his life, he quotes Perkins' *Salve voor een sieck mensche*[168] [*A salue for a sicke man* (1595)][169] As the anguish continued, he still sought consolation in Voetius and Hoornbeeck's book.[170] He plunged into the works of the father of the Further Reformation, Willem Teellinck, and of the Puritan Dyke, although he had been warned by an unnamed person that these authors were "too pernickety".[171] The *Book of martyrs* by John Foxe (1516/7–1587) was also among the books he consulted. Later on, he greatly appreciated the works of Robert Bolton (1572–1631).

Once he was finally able to believe that he possessed true saving faith, he developed a taste for sermons that called men to believe in Christ; for all sincere Christians (even though the world regarded them as the least attractive of people); for the Word of God; and for other good books, as well as for conversations with experienced Christians. In a later phase of his life, he was again assaulted by the thought that he might have committed the unpardonable sin. His worries on this front were assuaged by reading *Een christelick ende goddelick tractaet, inhoudende de medicine der ziele* [*A christian and heavenly treatise containing physicke for the soule* (1615)] by the Scots Puritan John Abernethy (d. 1639).[172] He also went to see Voetius personally in this period in order to resolve a particular spiritual problem that had troubled him for a year. This visit was a success;[173] he was unmolested spiritually for the following three or four years. During that time, he enthusiastically reached for all the means of grace available to him, such as hearing and reading the Word, taking communion—something he was often uneasy about—and speaking with mature believers. He was also an eager reader of books by Perkins, Willem Teel-

---

166  Hofmeyr; Op 't Hof [2015-17].
167  Du Bois [1665], 25 and 26 respectively.
168  Op 't Hof [1987-1], 283–285.
169  Du Bois [1665], 26.
170  Du Bois [1665], 28, 33, 34.
171  Du Bois [1665], 30.
172  Du Bois [1665], 46.
173  Du Bois [1667], 48. From this point on, we shall refer to the 1667 second edition, since quire C is missing in the sole copy known to survive from the 1665 edition.

linck, Udemans, Zacharias Ursinus[174] (1534–1583), Dyke, Bolton, Abernethy, John Downham (1571–1652), Cowper, Baynes, John Preston (1587–1628) and Jean Taffin[175] (1529–1602). He was also lent Foxe's *Book of martyrs* and was particularly struck by its third part.[176] Also in this period, he was assailed by temptations, including once more the troubling thought that he might have blasphemed against the Holy Ghost.

The conversion account is followed by a number of prayers of the individual to God.[177] In these, the sensible aspect of the inner experience of faith comes to the fore, with the accent primarily on the sequence in which sins are felt and redemption known. As a page-filler, a poem covers two sides, signed "Matth. Silvius". This is a Latinisation of the author's own name and therefore must certainly have been written by him. This conclusion is very much reinforced by du Bois' hymnbook, which came out later: the fourth song in it is identical with this page-filling poem.

Within two years, the first impression of *Godts wonder-werck* had sold out. The second edition appeared in 1667, in which du Bois had amended and extended the original text. He had also furnished it with a new preface, dated 9 February 1667. In this preface, he makes it clear that in this book he is seeking to describe the way that leads to Christ. He bewails the countless numbers of those who pass themselves off as Christians while actually being enemies of the cross of Christ. Richardson, too, had updated his approving foreword for this edition. New information provided by du Bois in the text itself is that he was able to believe that he was a partaker in genuine faith when he was 23 or 24 years old.[178] The spiritual song is missing from the end of this edition.

The second little work, *Annotatien van veelderley christelyke sin en geestryke spreuken, en sententien* [Annotations of many Christian proverbs rich in meaning and spirit, and statements], appeared in 1680 and constitutes a reader's selection curated mostly from English and Scots Puritans, and translated by du Bois himself. In his preface, du Bois justifies his choice of source-material by citing Eeuwout Teellinck, who said he knew no better reading besides the Bible than Puritan devotional books.[179] Following the preface is a poem by Amsterdam devotional book publisher Johannes Boekholt[180] (1656–1693).

---

174 Dirk Visser.
175 Boer; Van der Linde; Op 't Hof [2016-14].
176 Du Bois [1667], 70.
177 Du Bois [1667], 58[=78]–120.
178 Du Bois [1667], 47.
179 Du Bois [1680], A2v.
180 Alblas.

The second, greatly augmented, version of the work appeared in 1684 under the amended title *Christelijke sin- en geest-rijke annotatien, mitsgaders de stralen van den Geest, tot levendig-makinge, verligtinge en verblijdinge van de ziele* [Christian annotations rich in meaning and spirit, together with the beams of the Spirit unto quickening, enlightenment and rejoicing]. The work had now grown from 48 pages to 272. It had also now acquired a frontispiece, a dedication and a foreword. The dedication by the compiler and translator is to the mayor of Haarlem, Gillis Bouchellion, and is dated 18 April 1684. In it, du Bois reports that the unusually severe winter just past served to withhold him from his regular labours for a considerable time. He put the time so gained to good use in the reading not only of Scripture but also of many works by English and other authors. He noted down various passages and the result was now being published in book form. His reasons given for dedicating the work to Bouchellion are his mayoral rank and more particularly the fact that he has often served as elder and obtained great praise in that office.

The first part of the book is *Stralen van den Geest*, describing the Holy Spirit's beams in 68 sayings.[181] Du Bois explains in the preface that the English Puritan Joseph Caryl (1602–1673) is the author, that the original was made available to him by a friend "as a particularly rare gem", and that he has read through it several times over the past winter and translated it. He has added to this little work some "useful and instructive histories, and meaningful proverbs".[182] This latter collection consists of three parts, each arranged alphabetically by key word.[183] The twin facts that the preface refers specifically to Caryl's work and that the original title page has been cut away indicate that the collection had originally been intended as a separate publication. Du Bois' *Annotatien* will have been added to it at a later stage. Both parts of the publication have the same, continuous, collation; the second and third parts of the *Annotatien* each have their own collation.

The third impression came out in 1691, entitled *Christelyke annotatien, zijnde een versamelinge van vele uytgelesene christelijcke ondervindingen, spreuken, sententien, historien en exempelen; dienende tot levendigh-makinge, verlichtinge en verblijdinge van de ziele* [Christian annotations, being a collection of many choice Christian experiences, proverbs, statements, histories and examples, serving to quicken, enlighten and rejoice the soul]. Not only had du Bois filled out his work with brief his-

---

181  Du Bois [1684], 5–24.
182  Du Bois [1684], 3.
183  Du Bois [1684], 25–96, 97–196 and 197–264 respectively.

tories and exemplary lives and deaths; he also twice in this edition emerged from the shadow of his relative obscurity. Firstly, he dedicated the work, with a date of 10 March 1691, to none other than the Dutch stadtholder and now king of Great Britain, William III.[184] He praises the Prince of Orange as the man raised up by God to deliver the oppressed people of God in that land. Here, the reference to Eeuwout Teellinck recurs. By dedicating the work to William III, du Bois is following in the footsteps of both Heermans, who dedicated his collection of proverbs to Willem II, and Petrus de Lange[185] (1631/2–1716), who did likewise in 1660, in this instance to William III. Secondly, du Bois had asked an impressive number of poets to deliver a contribution to the book. The dedication is followed by the work of six poets, one of whom is the renowned poet-preacher Johannes Vollenhove[186] (1631–1708). Du Bois had evidently succeeded in transcending the bounds of his own conventicle society and penetrating the world of high-art poetry.

One letter by du Bois is known to survive: his request to Vollenhove to write an ode for *Christelyke annotatien*. It is dated 9 March 1688.[187] Were we to go on the fact that *Christelyke annotatien* contains a foreword by Richardson, we might well conclude that he was closely involved in the publication of the work or even that he was the instigator of its publishing. Nevertheless, du Bois outlines a very different backstory in this letter. He had submitted the manuscript to the Dutch preacher Salomon van Echten (1609–1675) for evaluation. Van Echten ministered in Haarlem from 1643 until his death in 1675.[188] The latter judged that the conversion story was worthy publishing, and also devised the title of the book. It seems, then, that of all the Reformed ministers in Haarlem at that time, it was with van Echten that du Bois felt the closest bond.

How, then, did it come about that the work was furnished with a foreword by Richardson, the minister of the city's English congregation? On this point, du Bois reveals in the letter that Richardson had written it of his own accord, unbidden. Faced with this fait accompli, he acquiesced in the inclusion of the foreword. While we have no cause to doubt the veracity of the statement that Richardson proffered his contribution unasked, we do have reason to suspect that the friendship between him and du Bois was more intimate than the latter reveals in his letter to Vollenhove.

---

184   Troost.
185   Op 't Hof [2013-1], 275–283.
186   Dibbets.
187   Amsterdam, University Library, H. 43.
188   Van Lieburg [1996], 55.

In truth, du Bois will have found it an unalloyed pleasure in 1665 that the English preacher was prepared to endorse his first book. Why, then, does he present the case in a different light in 1688? The answer lies in the change of position that Richardson made in the 1670s: enamoured of Rothe, he not only forsook his ministry but in 1676 even turned against Willem III. Du Bois must have sensed that these acts irked Vollenhove, who was the stadtholder's parish minister in The Hague. Hence it was that he played down in his account the significance of Richardson's input.

One might think that du Bois himself was also embarrassed in hindsight to have Richardson's name associated with his own conversion testimony. That this is nevertheless not the case is evident from the fact that he retained Richardson's foreword to the augmented 1680 edition of *Godts wonder-werck*, which will be mentioned below. Presumably, the memory of the spiritual concourse that he had had with Richardson remained sweet enough to him that he was unwilling to repudiate him publicly, for all that he presented the matter to Vollenhove as if that were his inclination.

A final detail intriguing to the modern researcher is that in his letter to Vollenhove, du Bois remarks that he never intended for his authorship of *Godts wonder-werck* to become public knowledge. This might mean one of two things: either the Haarlem printer of his own accord and against the author's own wishes placed du Bois' initials on the title page and at the foot of the preface, or alternatively what upset du Bois was that the Amsterdam printer of the second edition of 1667 amplified the initials into "M. du Bois" and that in the instance of the signature at the end of the preface, this printer even added that he lived at Haarlem. The latter possibility seems the more likely.

The third work written by du Bois contained no prose as the first two had done, but exclusively poetry. Du Bois' biographer and bibliographer Jacob Baltus Huibert Alblas writes of a publication by du Bois that he came to know of only through its being mentioned in an advertisement in the 26 March 1680 edition of a newspaper, and which is said to be called *Gezangen [Hyms]* and to be duodecimo in format.[189] There can be no doubt at all that the work that popped up in a private book collection in 1995, entitled *Geestelijck lusthofje, beplant met verscheyde christelijcke gezangen* [A spiritual pleasure-garden planted with various Christian hymns] (Amsterdam 1681), is this long-sought *Gezangen*.[190] It is immediately striking that neither the publication year nor the format of the book agree with what

---

189   Alblas, 274.
190   Kwekkeboom.

Alblas states. However, a glance at the title page of the copy that has recently emerged is sufficient to reassure us that Alblas need not be suspected of an error of fact or interpretation, for the title page announces: "Desen Druck vermeerdert" [Enlarged for this edition]. The first edition hence did indeed come out in 1680. Evidently, it sold so well that a reprint was necessitated just the following year. What is more, the augmentation of this edition was clearly so substantial that it called for a larger format.

As is so often seen in old works, the author's dedication—to his children, in this case—is full of instruction. Du Bois declares a good deal in it about his spiritual life, and also provides important information about his forefathers; this is what has enabled the account of his genealogy given above. The author's intention in dedicating the work to all his children was to inspire them, as an addition to his spoken incitements and his other writings, to a continual practice of piety. He emphasises that a pious life is a pleasant life, and accordingly urges them to rejoice in the Lord and to sing from the heart. They should always seek to have a lively feeling and experience of the things that they sing. Du Bois also intended this work to be a spiritual testament.

His hymns are without exception expressions of a personal life of faith in which the poet unfailingly senses his dependence upon the Holy Spirit's guidance. He expresses his thankfulness for natural and spiritual favours of which he is sensible, and begs for an increase and deepening of his faith and his spiritual experiences. He also sings of the state of spiritual abandonment.[191] Expressions such as "Dear *Jesus*"[192], "*Sweet Jesus*"[193], "sweetly enjoy" and "God's well-disposed countenance"[194] [Lieve *Jesus*; *Soete Jesus*; soet'lijck genieten; Godes vriendelijck aenschijn] indicate a mystical dimension. At times, a yearning for heaven is apparent.[195] After all, many of his hymns can also be construed as Pietist songs of the soul.

Yet it is not all about the inner life. The hymn that du Bois writes after a summer walk through the countryside around Haarlem,[196] and his putting into words of the feelings that beholding nature in general awakes in him,[197] demonstrate that for him, experimental description of the life of the soul need not exclude one's experiences of the natural world. His complaints at the unspiritualness and cloying wealth of his day are likewise expressions of the same concern for outward circumstances.[198] This is also applicable to the poem in which he upbraids his contemporaries for the widespread unease that was felt in December 1680 and January 1681 at the appearance of a comet in the heavens.[199]

---

191  Du Bois [1681], 18–19.
192  Du Bois [1681], 6; see also 21, 37.
193  Du Bois [1681], 7; see also 21.
194  Du Bois [1681], 10; cf. 24.
195  Du Bois [1681], 8; see also 27.
196  Du Bois [1681], 28–30.
197  Du Bois [1681], 46–48.
198  Du Bois [1681], 33–e4. Further references to wealth are found at: 49.
199  Du Bois [1681], 58.

Finally, two noteworthy aspects of du Bois' poetry as a whole are his concentration upon Jesus and the role of the emotions of excitement and joy. For this poet, Christ is all in all. He emphasises the wondrousness of the life spiritual and how it rejoices the soul.

The literary qualities of du Bois' poetry are decent enough that it might without undue dismissiveness be typified as pious doggerel; clearly, a poet such as du Bois does not write to achieve staggering literary heights. His aim was nothing more than to encounter his readers in the spiritual states that they felt themselves to be in, and to reinforce and consolidate their faith. Nor could one reasonably expect more of the raw gifts of an amateur poet.

*Geestelijck lusthofje* contains at the back of the volume an index of first lines and an index of tunes. The latter index refers to the Further Reformation poet-preachers Bernard Busschof[200] (1593–1639) and Jodocus van Lodensteyn[201] (1620–1677).

*Significance*
Of all the men considered in this chapter, du Bois was the least highly-placed in ecclesiastical terms. While it is true that Vermuyden too was not a preacher, he did serve as an elder, unlike du Bois, who never advanced further than the position of a confirmed member. This might also be the reason why he was shy of being identified as the author of his first work. It is all the more remarkable, then, that he felt called to write and disseminate piety literature.

All the indications are that du Bois wished his works especially to be of use to those Christians who met in conventicles. After all, it was at conventicles that those people came together out of a shared interest in spiritual edification and in order to discuss all manner of Biblical, catechetical and experimental matters under the guidance of a spiritual authority figure. These conventicles also included prayers and hymns. That du Bois wrote a spiritual autobiography in the true sense of the term and had it printed was completely congruent with the interests of conventicle-attending folk. In international terms, the first context in which the description of one's own spiritual life emerged as a genre was within Puritanism in England.[202]

Du Bois' English background, his evident preference for Puritan works, the role of the Puritan Richardson in bringing about the first edition

---

200  Op 't Hof [2015-10].
201  Trimp [1987].
202  Watkins, 25–28.

of his autobiography, and the addition of that autobiography to a number of Puritan spiritual biographies are all indications that the genre of the Reformed spiritual autobiography must be seen as a cross-fertilisation arising from the embedding of Puritanism in seventeenth-century Dutch spiritual life. Having spent his childhood in England, he was ideally suited to acting as a broker to bring Puritan thinking to the attention of his Dutch co-religionists.

In assembling his own devotional collection of sayings, du Bois was seeking to offer a judicious alternative to the secular book by Heermans that had so occupied him as a teenager. From the third impression onwards, in which spiritual biographies were afforded a place in the book, this was a work that perfectly followed up his first publication.

As a poet, du Bois' sole aim was to meet people where they were in their felt spiritual state and to reinforce and consolidate their faith. Many of his hymns were Pietist songs of the soul, even if there were a few that took as their themes nature and the unspiritual character of his times. His soul's experiences were characterised by a focus upon Jesus and by the role of emotional excitement and joy. In the conventicle circles in which he moved, then, folk were anything but stolid or sombre in their demeanour.

The foregoing has thrown up the fact that du Bois placed himself in the tradition of Busschof and van Lodensteyn with his hymnbook. This categorisation indicates which tradition du Bois wished to be part of in his production of this genre, not only with regard to the secular tunes he set his words to but very much also with regard to the content of his verses. Van Lodensteyn was incontrovertibly one of the key representatives of the Further Reformation, which was a Reformed piety movement, and Els Stronks has demonstrated in her doctorate that Busschof was the initiator of Further Reformation hymnology.[203] It cannot escape our attention that these poets served as inspiring examples and figures of imitation for du Bois.

A pointer must be given in this regard, however, to a fundamental distinction between du Bois and his fellows. Busschof and van Lodensteyn were both ministers of the gospel and thus by definition academically trained and culturally refined. The same cannot be said of du Bois, who was very much a lay hymnologist. Even in that capacity, however, he still stands in a line of sorts, for his publisher Boekholt had gone before him in writing and publishing a collection of spiritual songs: *Zielsklachten, lof-zangen, en aendachtige meditatien op verscheyde stoffen uyt*

---

203 Stronks, index.

*Gods h. Woord* [Soul-complaints, songs of praise, and thoughtful meditations upon various subjects from God's sacred Word].[204] Given that Boekholt brought out his own edition just one year before du Bois', we cannot really speak of a fully-fledged tradition, but rather of two near-simultaneous expressions of the same phenomenon: a hymnbook flowing from the pen of a poetic non-theologian. Even before these two writers, another man had set the precedent: Hendrik Uilenbroek[205] (d. 1681), an Amsterdam visitor of the sick, with his book *Christelycke gesangen* [Christian hymns]. The oldest editions are unfortunately not known to us. The earliest that is presently known dates from 1666 and this was already the fifth edition. There were dozens of editions in all of this collection of Christian songs. Although neither Boekholt nor du Bois name Uilenbroek as their trailblazer, they clearly must be seen as following in his line. All three had the same target audience in mind: conventicle attenders. While it was exclusively the psalter and a dozen songs from Scripture that were sung in Dutch Reformed church services, at conventicles one could sing freely-written spiritual songs. Boekholt as publisher provided the Amsterdam conventicles, which were sometimes led by Koelman, with material to sing, coming from both his own pen and du Bois' as the case might be. Uilenbroek had gone before him in this path in the same city: besides being a visitor of the sick, he had also been a leader of conventicles. In fact, he also allowed Koelman to lead meetings held in his own house.[206]

As a lay writer and poet, du Bois' significance is not to be underestimated, particularly in conventicle circles. It will become evident under the next heading that this significance was not confined to his own era but continued through the following century. The 1691 dedication of his *Christelyke annotatien* to William III, the poems in that edition, and his request written to Vollenhove show that he was not the kind of conventicle figure to cut himself off from the world and wider society as drastically as possible, but one who on the contrary sought to build bridges between the Christian fellowship subculture and the political and élite culture of his day.

*Influence*
Du Bois' work enjoyed considerable success. His premiere was reprinted at least a further three times after its second edition. The third edition appeared in 1680, published by Boekholt, *inter alia*. We also know that

---
204  Alblas, 229–234.
205  Op 't Hof [2016-19].
206  Evenhuis [1965], 3:index.

the fourth edition was printed in 1733 and marketed by the Rotterdam publisher Hermanus Kentlink. A photomechanical reprint of this 1733 edition recently appeared in a limited print run.[207] Finally, one copy is extant of an edition whose year of publication is unknown. as it lacks its title page.[208] The difference between this unidentified edition and all other known editions is that it alone bears the addition of a letter from one E.M. (not further identifiable) to his sister offering rules of living.

Du Bois' autobiography exerted influence in other ways beyond its numerous reprints. It was also incorporated into a larger volume. An abridged version of the first edition—where, again, the initials "M.D.B." are all that is given of the author's name—figures in *De blijcken van godtzaligheydt* [*The evidences of godliness*], which appears as the second appendix, edited by Koelman, to the 1672 second edition of *Des christens groot interest* [*The christians great interest* (1659)] by William Guthrie (1620-1665).[209] This appendix presents the biographies of twelve pious persons, mostly Englishmen. M.D.B.'s narrative has been shortened in several places, including by the omission of the conversation between himself and Voetius. In this form, as part of the aforementioned larger work, du Bois' autobiography was printed no fewer than eighteen times prior to 1800. All in all, his conversion history had a considerable effect upon that part of the Dutch reading public which was crying out for pastoral guidance.

While du Bois' proverbs went through three editions in the seventeenth century, the work was even more popular in the eighteenth century, when four reprints were made. The first came out in 1728, published by a Rotterdam man, Kentlink. In this edition, the publisher retained the dedication to William III and two odes, one of which is Vollenhove's. In all other respects, this fourth edition was textually identical with the third edition.

Kentlink was clever enough to ask a Rotterdam Pietist preacher, Wilhelmus Eversdijk[210] (1653-1729), to write a foreword for the edition. Having initially asked to be spared this duty owing to his advanced age and struggling health, Eversdijk gave in after repeated requests. The reasons he gave for deciding to write the foreword after all were the following. In the first place, he wished to support Kentlink as he found his feet in the world of publishing. In the second place, this undertaking was an

---

207  This is a 1980s edition but undated and with no place of publication given.
208  This copy is in a private collection.
209  Koelman [1672], 269–290.
210  Florijn [2015-3].

expression of his affection for Kentlink's virtuous parents, who were good friends of his. In the third place, it was the piety-related content that spoke to him. Eversdijk remarks that most professed Christians of his day are not actually saints at all. He recommends that everyone buy and read this little book and suggests it might even play a role in the upbringing of children, for he advises readers to teach their children proverbs and personal histories by heart. This foreword of recommendation stretches to the impressive length of 52 pages.[211] It will be thanks especially to this recommendation by Eversdijk, a minister beloved in pious circles, that there was the demand for reprints to appear from the same publisher in 1735, 1745 and 1773.

The Haarlem merchant's hymnbook had the least impact of any of his works. However, a reprint was necessary the year after its first publication. The conclusion is thus merited that du Bois' spiritual songs were sung in many conventicles and at family worship in many Noord-Holland homes.

**Johannes Ubelman**
Our penultimate translator is Johannes Ubelman[212] (d. 1715).

*Biography*
The first glimpse we have of Ubelman is as a student at the Athenæum in Amsterdam, where he held two disputations in 1657.[213] As we shall shortly see, he probably went up to the University of Utrecht after this. Since student registrations at that university were full of omissions in this period, we ought not to attach any significance to the fact that his name is not found in the Utrecht *album studiosorum*.

In summer 1661, Ubelman, now a candidate minister from the Amsterdam presbytery, is noted at the Dutch Church in Great Yarmouth. He had sailed over to England with Johannes Pythius (1632–1676), who had occupied the pulpit there since 1659, to learn English. In the 1661 record, the church officers testify that he was exemplary in conduct. Ubelman ministered to the congregation for three months, both before and after Pythius' departure. This ministry was received so well that the congregation called him in September 1661, which Ubelman accepted. The congregation was small and poor. Ubelman returned to his own country in October 1663. He had to wait for a call to come once back in

---

211   Du Bois [1728], *5r.–3*6v.
212   Op 't Hof [2016-18].
213   Van Miert, index.

the Netherlands, but come it did, and in September 1664 he began preaching at Nieuwpoort in Zuid-Holland.[214]

As the years progressed, Ubelman must have built up a solid reputation as a preacher, because he was called to the nearby city of Gorinchem in 1670, remaining there until his death on 24 January 1715. One F.G. Westhovius, otherwise unknown to history, wrote a commemorative poem on Ubelman's death: *Ter gedachtenis van den eerwaardigen, godzaligen en nu zaligen heere Joannes Ubelman, getrou opziender der gemeinte van Gorinchem, ontslapen den 24 van loumaand, M. D. CC. XV* [In memory of the honourable and gentleman Joannes Ubelman, now at blessed [rest], the faithful shepherd of the congregation at Gorinchem, who fell asleep on 24 Tanning-month 1715].[215]

The fact that Ubelman remained 45 years at Gorinchem is sufficient grounds for us to conclude that he became the embodiment of the church in that city. The three works he left in plano format indicate that he enjoyed good relations with the city fathers. His wife's maiden name was Gruterus. She died at Gorinchem, prior to 1698.

Ubelman bestowed his gifts not only on his local congregations but also at provincial level: he was a deputy to the Synod of Zuid-Holland in 1667, 1675, 1683, 1692 and 1697. He was also elected the provincial correspondent with Overijssel in 1675 and correspondent with Guelders in 1697.[216]

*Writings*
Ubelman produced no works of his own apart from two poetic ones; otherwise, he was purely a translator from English. A single-volume Dutch translation was published in 1670 of the works of the Puritan Jeremiah Dyke (1584–1639), entitled *Opera omnia, of alle de God-geleerde wercken* [Opera omnia, or all the theological works]. This compendium was the work of Ubelman, who had also produced new translations especially for this edition.

Ubelman dedicated his efforts to his uncle, Jacob Lieftinck, a councillor and ex-alderman of the city of Utrecht and a governor of the Admiralty at Amsterdam appointed by the province of Utrecht. Both during his years of academic study and after his return from England, he was favoured by Lieftinck. As Ubelman himself puts it, he translated four writings and four sermons of Dyke's; in reality, the four writings were likewise sermons.

---

214  Hessels, 3:index.
215  Stamkot, 177 no. 24.13.
216  Knuttel, 4:408; 5:index; 6:index.

Ubelman's second translation was *Origines sacrae, heilige oorsprongkelykheden, of een redelijk bewijs van de gronden des christelijken geloofs, tot bevestiginge vande waarheid, en goddelijke authoriteit der h. Schriftuur* [*Origines sacrae, or a rational account of the grounds of christian faith* (1662)] (1690) by Edward Stillingfleet (1635–1699). This time, the translator dedicated his work to his brother-in-law Samuel Gruterus (1635–1705), preacher at Haarlem. In his dedication, dated 1 December 1689, he states that several persons before him had set out to translate the work but never managed to finish it.[217] Gruterus urged him to translate the book and facilitated the work by making available some of the books in his famed and copious library in order to confirm the definitions of some difficult words. Ubelman writes that he married a sister of Gruterus.[218] The transition from the dedication to the work is ornamented with verses, the first of which is by Gruterus and the second by the noted preacher-poet Vollenhove.

There are three known sheets in which Ubelman celebrates in verse his friendship with members of the civil government of his home city, Gorinchem.[219] The first, dated 1699, is entitled *Geluk aan de stad Gorinchem, met het burgermeesterschap van den heer en mr. Henrik van Barneveld, enz. In die waardigheid beëdigd op den 11den february 1699* [A health to the city of Gorinchem upon the mayoralty of the gentleman and master Henrik van Barneveld, etc.; avowed upon the 11 February 1699]. The death two years later of Hendrik van Barneveld (1664–1701) prompted Ubelman to write *Zerk-schrift voor den heer, en mr. Henrik van Barneveld, waardig raad en vroedschap, outburgermeester der stad Gorinchem, president schepen, weesheer, enz. ontslapen den 11. van slagtmaand 1701* [Epitaph for the gentleman and master Henrik van Barneveld, worthy councillor and city father, ex-mayor of the city of Gorinchem, chairman of the aldermen, guardian of orphans, etc., who fell asleep on 11 Slaughter-month [November] 1701]. A decade later, in 1711, the Gorinchem minister wrote an epithalamion for another city father with whom he was befriended: *Ter bruiloft van den heer Adriaan Raap, regerend schepen der stad Gorinchem; en mevrouw Margarete van Byland; vereenigd den 14den van hooymaand, in 't jaar 1711* [Upon the wedding of the gentleman Adriaan Raap, governing alderman of the city of Gorinchem, and the lady Margarete van Byland, united upon 14 Hay-month [July] 1711].

Thirdly, Ubelman translated a work by Charles Wolseley (d. 1714): *De*

---

217  Stillingfleet [1690], *4v.
218  Stillingfleet [1690], 2*1r.
219  Stamkot, 176–177 nos. 24.03, 24.06, 24.08.

*redelykheid van't Schriftuur-geloof, of een redenering over de redelijke gronden op welke wy den Bijbel als Gods Woord aannemen* [*The reasonablenes of Scripture-belief, or a reasoning upon the reasonable grounds upon which we accept the Bible as God's Word*] (1695). Appended to this work, and also translated by Ubelman, was *Vertoog tegen de hedendaagsche atheïsten* [An invective against present-day atheists] by John Tillotson (1630–1694). In his dedication to his congregation of Gorinchem, Ubelman provides the significant information that while he was in Great Yarmouth, he had the opportunity to acquaint himself with English books. He had come to highly value many of them.[220] The success of his translation of Stillingfleet's book induced him to translate Wolseley's work, too.[221] On a personal note, he informs the reader that he was so ill in late 1694 that he thought he was going to die.[222] The translation is ornamented with poems between dedication and text, written, *inter alia*, by Ubelman's brother-in-law Daniel Gruterus, by the translator himself, and by Vollenhove.

Ubelman's fourth translation was published in 1704: Matthew Poole's (1624–1679) *De geloofs-belydenis der roomsche kerke wedersproken* [*The nullity of the Romish faith*]. This edition is prefaced by remarks by the Utrecht professor of theology Melchior Leydecker[223] (1642–1721). There are also dedicatory poems in it from men including Vollenhove, the Deventer preacher-poet Arnold Moonen (1644–1711), and Ubelman himself.

In his final translation, published posthumously in 1717, Ubelman returned to the genre of his first efforts, that of Puritan piety: Joseph Alleine's (1634–1668), *Een alarm voor onbekeerde zondaren* [*An alarme to unconverted sinners* (1671)]. It is noteworthy that, as Ubelman himself writes in his preface, he undertook the translation at the request of the Rotterdam printer Reinier van Doesburg[224] (d. 1731).[225] Regarding the author, he remarks that he was a master letter-writer, hardly inferior to the correspondence of Samuel Rutherford (d. 1661). To prove this, Ubelman refers to "several letters [of Alleine's] translated into Dutch by Johannes Hofman". Ubelman believes works like Alleine's to be needful in a day when libertinism is in the ascendancy and "atheism boasts the name

---

220 Wolseley [1695], *3v.
221 Wolseley [1695], 3v.–4r.
222 Wolseley [1695], *6r.
223 Hoek.
224 Heijting [2015].
225 Alleine [1717], (a)4r.

# EEN
# ALARM
## VOOR ONBEKEERDE
# ZONDAREN

In een ernstige Verhandeling van deze
gewightige Hooftzaken/

I. Wat de Bekeering niet is, en verbeterende
eenige Misslagen daar ontrent.
II. Van de Bekeering, en de Nature der zelve.
III. Van de Nootzakelykheit der Bekeeringe.
IV. Van de Merkteekenen der Onbekeerden.
V. Van de Ellenden der Onbekeerden.
VI. Van de Bestieringen ontrent de Bekeering.
VII. Van de Beweegredenen tot Bekeering.

Benevens een
## AANHANGSEL
Van verscheide Nuttige Stoffen, in 't Engels
beschreven door
## JOZEF ALLEINE,
In zyn leven Leeraar te TAUNTON
in SOMMERSET:

En nu in 't Nederduitsch gebragt door
## JOANNES UBELMAN,
In zyn Leven Bedienaar des H. Euangeliums
te GORINCHEM.
Hier is by gevoegt het leven en sterven van
JOZEF ALLEINE.

Te ROTTERDAM,
By REINIER VAN DOESBURG, 1717.

of religion".[226] Finally, he remarks that while translating the book, he came across some wordings and expressions that might offend some, and which he might have toned down a little if he himself had been the author.[227] Following the preface is a letter by Richard Baxter (1615–1691). Also preceding the actual text is a long biography of Alleine, translated into Dutch by the aforementioned contemporary translator of Puritan works, Johannes Hofman[228] (1666–1735). Hofman was won over entirely by Puritan preaching during stays in London, as a result of which he translated dozens of sermon collections for a Dutch readership. As such, Hofman would be a perfect candidate for inclusion in the present chapter; however, since his first translation was not published until 1700, he does not qualify under our terms of reference.

Before the actual text of the work, the reader encounters a transitional verse by one J. van Tol, an otherwise unknown figure.

*Significance*
As a city preacher, Ubelman enjoyed greater prominence than many of his brother ministers, but his renown is nevertheless entirely due to his translations. Given his years in England, in which he mastered the language, it is hardly surprising that he translated exclusively English works for his countrymen. He began with Dyke's Puritan works in 1670. After a twenty years' silence, he brought out Stillingfleet in Dutch in 1690, an oeuvre of an entirely different nature: Stillingfleet was an Arminian scholar who based his theological opinions on reason and natural theology. Within the Church of England, he was a leader of the Latitudinarian party. After a few poems in plano format relating to local politicians, Ubelman proceeded to translate the works of two further Latitudinarians, namely Wolseley and Tillotson. The titles and contents of the three Latitudinarian works demonstrate that Ubelman restricted himself among Latitudinarian books to those that were defences of the authority of the Bible and of the Christian faith. This was his way of helping combat the radical Enlightenment thinking that refused to countenance the authority of revealed Scripture. In no way did this Dutch translator share common ground with the Latitudinarians' Arminianism or their rationalism.

As the eighteenth century dawned, Ubelman left his Latitudinarian sources behind. He made a further two translations, which appeared in

---

226 Alleine [1717], (a)5r.
227 Alleine [1717], (a)6v.
228 Groenendijk [1984-2]; Op 't Hof [2015-17].

1704 and 1707 respectively. The first was an anti-Roman Catholic tractate by the nonconformist theologian Poole; the second was a revivalist work, a genuinely Puritan one, by Alleine. The fact that van Doesburg as publisher had to propose the idea of this translation to Ubelman is an indication that while he did have much affinity with Puritan writing, he would if left to his own devices have preferred to translate more academic books into Dutch.

The three broadsheets show that Ubelman was a productive poet. That all his translations except that of Dyke's works are enriched by at least one prefatory poem further shows that he was a friend of several poets. Moonen wrote one poem for Ubelman; Vollenhove, no fewer than three.

*Influence*
Ubelman's translation of the works of Stillingfleet made considerable headway in the Netherlands, being reprinted in 1694 and 1704. The last reprint was augmented with another of Stillingfleet's works: *Vervolg tegen de ongodisten en godisten* [A continuation against the atheists and deists]. The combined translation of Wolseley and Tillotson was also successful, with a second edition required in 1724.

Ubelman made a still greater impression with his posthumously-published translation of Alleine. Initially, this did not seem at all likely: after the first edition came out in 1717, a title edition appeared in 1735— the run of the first edition had not fully sold after nearly twenty years. The publisher of the title edition had more success. A second edition of it came as soon as 1738, for which the Zevenhuizen preacher Georgius Sohnius (1702–1740) had written a foreword of recommendation. Remarkably enough, interest in the work revived in the nineteenth century, with two reprints: 1855 and *circa* 1889.

**Aemilius van Cuilemborgh**
The last translator we shall consider is Aemilius van Cuilemborgh[229] (d. 1704), minister of the Dutch Church in London.

*Biography*
Aemilius van Cuilemborgh was born at Wageningen in the eastern Netherlands. A son of the medical doctor Hermannus van Cuilemborgh, who

---

229   Van Wijk [2019], 131–133.

graduated from Harderwijk in 1648,[230] Aemilius matriculated at the University of Utrecht in 1667. He married Hillegond van Essen, a daughter of his teacher Andreas Essenius[231] (1618–1677), on 12 November 1672. His first parish was Batenburg in his home province of Guelders, where he was installed in 1673. Five years later, he moved south to Heusden. His second marriage, on 12 June 1678, was to Anna Catharina Rentsen. In 1688 and 1689, when his brother-in-law Cornelius de Kranckel[232] (1643–1708), a clergyman in nearby Veen, was holding daily prayer meetings for the success of Willem III's campaign while the stadholder was crossing the sea and campaigning for the English throne, van Cuilemborgh encouraged him in the undertaking and imitated it in his own parish. In 1692, he exchanged his Heusden pulpit for that of the Dutch Church in London. Van Cuilemborgh was in written correspondence with Ubelman in November 1691 concerning his call to London.[233]

By the end of his time in London, a gulf had opened up between van Cuilemborgh on the one side and his congregation and church officers on the other. He was accused of having dealings with people of ill conduct, of slandering congregants and of trying to introduce the Book of Common Prayer. Moreover, he was not a hale man, either physically or mentally. Following his suspension from office in November 1702, a committee had to be formed to seek a resolution. Van Cuilemborgh was asked to consider his position. If he gave up his post, the church officers would allot him £50 a year and, if he predeceased his wife, she would receive an annual pension of £20. He rejected this offer, whereupon the church officers resolved in late January 1703 to expel him. This was prevented in the first instance by the intervention of Henry Compton (1632–1713), Bishop of London. Despite having been deposed, van Cuilemborgh managed somehow to lead a church service on 22 August. This led to the bishop deciding to act personally as arbiter. On 28 September 1703, he decided that the previously-proposed agreement must come into force, that all papers in this case must be destroyed, and that all the entries in the church minutes about the affair must be struck out. The final outcome was that van Cuilemborgh voluntarily (!) resigned his preaching office in London on 28 October 1703.[234]

---

230 His name does not appear in the published, incomplete list of Harderwijk graduates, Schutte [1980], but is sourced here from Van Cuilemborgh [1683], *8v.
231 Broeyer [2015].
232 Van Wijk [2004].
233 Hessels, 3:2695.
234 Hessels, 3:2727–2765, 2933–2934.

After this tumultuous period in his life, van Cuilemborgh went to live on Canvey Island, where he breathed his last in 1704 and was buried in nearby South Benfleet—evidently, the recent vicissitudes in his ministry had sapped his strength.

*Writings*
The first of van Cuilemborgh's works were two disputations: the first held under his future father-in-law Essenius and published in 1670, and the second defended under Voetius' chairmanship and published in 1671. The first work that he wrote as a preacher, published in 1676, reflects his poetic interests: *Gheoorlofde tijt-kortinghe of geestelicke mengel-dichten* [A permissible pastime, or a spiritual medley of poems]. Although the contents of this first volume of poetry were as mixed as the title suggests, his second poetic work, which came out in 1683, was entirely devoted to matters of the spirit: *Godtvruchtige, sangh- en rym-stoffe* [Godly song and rhyme]. He had a particular love of writing poetry, for his third publication too, published in 1686 (the year after Louis XIV's revocation of the Edict of Nantes), was rhymed: *Zions klaegh-liedt, over de bloedige en wreede vervolgingen, tegens haar in Vranckryk aengericht* [Zion's lament over the bloody and savage persecutions visited upon her in France]. His fourth book, published in 1687, was likewise poetic in nature: *Eerbiedige en vrymoedige aenspraeck, aen den grooten Louis, koninck van Vranckrijck en Navarre* [A respectful yet bold address to the great Louis, King of France and Navarre]. For his fifth, in 1691, he continued in poetic vein: *Oratie of reden tot lof van het doorluchtige huis van Orangien* [An oration or speech of praise to the illustrious House of Orange]. His next writing, also in verse, was a continuation of a sort of the subject matter of the previous book: *Oratie of reden, behelsende de roemwaardigste daden van [...] Willem den derden [...] coning van Engeland* [An oration or speech containing the most fame-worthy deeds of [...] William the Third [...], King of England]. It was published in 1695, by which time he, like the king before him, had crossed over from the Netherlands to London. Accordingly, it was in London that this book of Dutch verse was published. Between those editions, he had written a lament, published in plano format, for the drowning of all four of the children of Arnoud van Citters (1633–1696), Dutch ambassador in England. His final book, published in 1698, was a translation of a prayer book by John Meriton (d. 1704), published at Oxford under the title *Voor-schriften der gebeden voor elcken dagh in de weeck, 'smorgens en 'savonds. T'samen gestelt voor het gebruick van by-sondere huys-gezinnen* [*Forms of prayer for every day in the week, morning and evening. Composed for the use of private families* (1682)].

Two years after its publication, Hofman added it to the reformational sermon *Vrede-basuyne* [A trumpet of peace], collated by him from extracts of Puritan writings. Also dating from 1698 is van Cuylemborgh's catechism guide *'t Beginsel der leere Christ* [The fundamentals of the doctrine of Christ].

One more written work of van Cuilemborgh's is known from his London years. One of his predecessors in the Dutch Church pulpit, Simeon Ruytinck, had written the history of the Dutch presence and congregations in England, and in particular that of the London church, as far as 1620. Another London minister, Caesar Calandrinus, continued this project as far as 1625, and van Cuilemborgh added a history of the years 1626 and 1627.

*Significance*

In print, van Cuilemborgh largely profiled himself as an enthusiastic poet, including on devotional topics. It is striking that he was called to the Dutch Church in London after publishing his *Oratie of reden tot lof van het doorluchtige huis van Orangien*, at a time when Willem III of Orange had already become William III of England and II of Scotland. Any suspicion of a possible connection is only reinforced by his next poetic publication, which concerns William himself. His continuation of the history of the Dutch congregation in London and associated themes is so narrow in temporal scope that it is almost insignificant. It is his translation of Meriton's prayer book that adds him to the long list of Dutch translators of British devotional literature. The fact that none of his publications achieved a single reprint is a clear indication that he enjoyed little success with his writings. That is understandable enough in the case of his last two writings, because they were printed in England and therefore evidently intended for the small number of Dutch readers in that country.

Van Cuilemborgh's conflict with his London congregation is difficult to evaluate. On the one hand, his previous conduct had never been problematic; on the other, the sources strongly suggest that he was hardly a spotless character. It is intriguing that he was accused of seeking to introduce the Book of Common Prayer into his church. The Bishop of London's intervention to ensure a reasonably tolerable outcome for van Cuilemborgh may indicate that the latter did in fact harbour Anglican sympathies. Whatever the truth of this, his last translation indicates that this Dutchman was also interested in devotional prayer culture and its propagation.

**Conclusions**

The Dutch congregations in England played some role in the lives of twelve Dutchmen who were largely enthusiastic propagandists for English and Scots Puritanism by bringing them under the influence of Puritan views and practices: Meusevoet, Panneel, Willem Teellinck, Lamotius, Bucerus, van Vleteren, van Haringhouk, Ruytinck, Vermuyden, du Bois, Ubelman and van Cuilemborgh. This number might not be impressive enough on its own, but what is impressive is the means that they used to import Puritanism into Dutch spiritual life and to anchor it in the soil. The most redoubtable feat that they have to their name—considering here the seventeenth century only—is the high number of book editions that were translations of Puritan writings, translated compilations, translated reworkings or the provision of a translation. As there are only five editions that belong to the latter three of those categories, all the editions are hereafter regarded as translations. Meusevoet translated a full 31 Puritan works, Panneel one, Willem Teellinck three, Lamotius 28, van Haringhouk nine, Ruytinck two, Vermuyden three, du Bois, Ubelman and van Cuilemborgh one each; a total of 114 book editions. While this is a very respectable figure in itself, the number of editions is a yet better indication of the penetration that Puritanism had in the seventeenth-century Netherlands: these 114 translations achieved no fewer than 244 editions. Most of these were small books but six of them were of the largest format, folio. In addition, we must consider the fact that Bucerus, by his instigations to have Bachiler's work translated, must perhaps be viewed as the man ultimately responsible for that translation. The foregoing proves that our twelve men connected to the Dutch congregations in England had a disproportionately large role in the propagation of Puritan thought in the Netherlands.

Van Vleteren, the Sandwich-born minister of the Dutch Church in London, is the only one of the twelve on our list who produced no translations. His contribution to the Dutch Puritan project was limited to sending Puritan reading material in English to colleagues in the Netherlands. His contact with the renowned Puritan, Cotton, is a further proof of the hypothesis that the London Dutch congregation was Puritan in its leanings.

It is striking that five of the twelve—Lamotius, Bucerus, van Vleteren, Ruytinck and du Bois—were born and brought up in England. Two of them, Meusevoet and van Haringhouk, although not English-born, spent their childhood in London. Two of our men, Lamotius and Ruytinck, were sons of preachers of the London congregation, and another of them, Bucerus, had the preacher of another Dutch congregation in England as a father, namely of the church at Sandwich. Van Vleteren preached the Word in the London church for thirteen years; van Cuilemborgh, for eleven years. Ubelman preached for more than two years at the Dutch

Church in Great Yarmouth. It is an even more eloquent fact that just two of the six English-born men—Meusevoet and Lamotius—accounted for fully 59 of the 114 translations and for 155 of the 244 editions. Other ways of being associated with the Dutch congregations in England were evidently less productive of Puritan impact. Panneel ministered to two of these congregations for seven years; Vermuyden lived and worked in England for many years and must have been a member of one or more of the congregations in question; Willem Teellinck spent over two years there as a student and was apparently never a member of a Dutch church in England but maintained many contacts with the Dutch Church in London for the rest of his life, including with ministers there.

The chronologically earliest six of our twelve men were interrelated. Meusevoet attended services, and perhaps catechism classes, led by Panneel at Norwich from 1573-1577. Since he is in all probability the man responsible for having involved Panneel, then minister at Middelburg, in the Amsterdam publishers Claeszoon and Jacobszoon's project to translate James VI/I's writings in 1603, he must have remained in contact with his former pastor and now brother minister. Lamotius dedicated his translation of John Sprint (d. 1623) in 1625 to Eeuwout Teellinck, brother of Willem Teellinck, whose efforts he implicitly blesses at the end of the dedication. Willem Teellinck urged the officers of the Dutch Church in London to issue a call to van Vleteren when a vacancy arose, and once this call was actually issued and van Vleteren had accepted it, Teellinck did all in his power to help him on his way to London.[235] In addition, van Vleteren was a close friend of Willem's eldest son, Maximiliaan.[236]

The fact that Vermuyden and du Bois were not preachers or theologians may indicate that as the seventeenth century progressed, non-professionals were increasingly active in the Puritanising of a section of Dutch society. We say 'a section' in consideration of du Bois, a pillar of Dutch conventicle society, which was a subculture in itself, even if du Bois himself was quite open to the wider society and culture around him.

Van Cuilemborgh is unique among our twelve in that his translation alone was published in England and thus must have been predominantly intended for Dutch readers in England.

Finally, the geographical origins of the twelve men considered in this chapter calls for attention. Vermuyden and Teellinck were not only both from Zeeland themselves but were scions of deep-rooted Zeeland lineages. Conversely, Meusevoet and Panneel had been born in the Spanish

---

235 This study, 198-199.
236 This study, 78-79, 170.

Netherlands. Ruytinck's, Bucerus' and du Bois' forefathers also hailed from that southern region. The surnames of Lamotius and van Vleteren are indicators that the same was also true of their ancestors. This means that as many as eight of our twelve men were of Southern Netherlands blood. Add to this the consideration that Zeeland was oriented towards the Southern Netherlands province of Flanders in this age, and we are left with only two fully-fledged Northern Netherlands men in the list: Ubelman and van Cuilemborgh. The twelve subjects of this research, then, provide ample evidence in support of the thesis that Pietism, and the receptiveness for Puritanism found in the Dutch Republic, owes very much indeed to a Southern Netherlands background.[237]

It would be an anticlimax, though, to end this chapter with an open-ended observation. Better to pursue the matter and seek an explanation for the overwhelming strength of the Southern Netherlands contingent. We must seek our explanation in the following. Although most of the Southern Netherlands immigrants in England left their homeland for economic reasons, it may be assumed that the forefathers of the eight men named in the previous paragraph did so for religious reasons. Religious exiles are always, by definition, highly serious people as regards their spiritual convictions. Their flight not only radically severed their connections with their pasts but also meant that they were giving up any kind of certainty; for many, emigration also caused financial haemorrhaging. So greatly did they value their belief! In addition to this deep religious conviction, the refugees had to cope with great deprivations during and after their flight, with their sense of general displacement and the many uncertainties of their new situation. Each of these factors is in general very conducive indeed to the development or maintenance of Pietism. The combination of all of them in one experience makes it quite understandable that many religious exiles had little understanding for others who were not so concerned with their manner of life and that they continually found fault with lackadaisical attitudes, and that as a reaction they increasingly emphasised the experimental aspects of Reformed doctrine and a correspondingly pious lifestyle.[238]

---

237   Op 't Hof [1987-1], 81–82, 613–619; Op 't Hof [1996-1], 249–253; Van de Kamp [2012-1], 141.

238   A doctoral thesis appeared on exile memories and the Dutch Revolt in 2014, whose author devotes a whole chapter to the relationship between exile and Pietism: Johannes Martin Müller, 179–208.

Yet the foregoing is just as applicable to those who left the Northern Netherlands for religious reasons as it is to those who left the Southern Netherlands. Why, then, this evident Southern Netherlands majority? There are two explanations. First and foremost, religious refugees from the Southern Netherlands greatly outnumbered those from the Northern Netherlands. The predominance of the former reflects, therefore, the relative strength of both groups in the composition of the Dutch congregations in England. As a second and supplementary consideration, the grief suffered by Southern Netherlands religious refugees was a permanent sore. They were never again able to return home, whereas the Northern Netherlands religious exiles increasingly did find ways and means to return to their country of origin from 1572 onwards. For them, at least, the worst was over.

# 6. LATENT CITATIONS

## Hidden Puritan content in Dutch Pietist works

*One of the many ways in which Puritan influence on the Netherlands becomes apparent is when Dutch Pietist, and especially Further Reformation, authors refer to Puritan writings and when they actually cite short or longer passages from them. In most cases, this is done overtly, with the names of both work and author quoted. More often than one might expect, however, a Dutch promoter of piety cites a Puritan writer without giving the title or author. In some such cases, the reader is still able to discern that there is a borrowing taking place: these are the instances where either the text states that an author says something or the quotation is given in a different type. Yet there are many other cases where there is no indication at all that the material has been borrowed. The discovery of such latent borrowings depends in such cases on the knowledge and alertness of the reader.*

*Research has indicated that two Dutch piety manuals, as well as one preface to and the additional matter in two translations of Puritan works, are substantially citations of Puritan works, with no citation given to the reader. Paradoxically, those details are not referred to in the present chapter, because the borrowings in those piety manuals are so copious that they would require a book-length treatment in their own right, and also because the present work considers exclusively the main body of text in books. Nevertheless, the gist of these additional borrowings will be presented before the conclusion at the close of this chapter, so that the conclusion can take account of them.*

*A key point of attention with such loans is whether they constitute publications of existing translations of the original or whether they rather indicate a Dutch author's home-made translation of the English text. Even more intriguing and compelling an avenue of research is that which concerns the Dutch authors' reasons for concealing their sources. It may well be that these motives will shed light on the role of Puritan influence upon the ecclesiastical and wider culture of the Low Countries, particularly as regards the resistance that that influence encountered. We can also expect that our discoveries regarding their motives for concealment will teach us more about the Puritan inclinations (including the substance thereof) of the Dutch authors in question.*

*The chapter that follows will provide a chronological overview of the data, arranged by Puritan author. Where a Puritan was cited from again at a later date, that later citation or those later citations are placed with the oldest one. The second part of this chapter is a chronological list of the Dutch authors involved in citations, whose motives are considered. One field of research has deliberately been excluded here: that of sermons. Latent citations in homiletic writings are treated separately in the next chapter, which is dedicated to preaching.*

**William Whately**
We saw in Chapter 1 that *Corte verhandelinghe van de voornaemste christelicke oeffeninghen* [A brief treatment of the chief Christian exercises] (1609) by William Whately (1583-1639) exerted a huge influence, extending internationally.[1] The importance of this role is underscored by the fact that unacknowledged citations of it have to date been discovered in no fewer than four Dutch works of the Further Reformation. These are by Eeuwout Teellinck[2] (1573-1629), his younger brother (and the translator of the work) Willem Teellinck[3] (1579-1629), and the Utrecht theology professor whom the brothers strongly influenced, Gisbertus Voetius[4] (1589-1676).[5]

*Eeuwout Teellinck*
The year 1618 saw publication of Eeuwout Teellinck's devotional work *Christelicke clachte van eenige godsalige luyden over hare onvruchtbaerheydt in het ware christelicke leven* [The Christian lament of some godly people at their unfruitfulness in the true Christian life]. As well as identifying six chief causes of spiritual unfruitfulness, he offers six remedies against them in this work. The description of the third remedy is substantially identical verbatim with a form of words found in *Corte verhandelinghe*. That this is not a chance similarity becomes evident when the reader proceeds to the treatment of the fourth remedy, namely meditation, and to a later passage that again touches upon meditation. In both of these places, there is—with no indication of source—more than a whole page in all that is lifted almost word-for-word from that translation. The first borrowing, moreover, returns—in a more extensive form, and in a different context—and unsourced again, in his magnum opus, a complete ethics: *Vyer ende wolck-calomne, lichtende nacht ende dach, om het Israel Godes, by eenige algemeene regels, nae een gesette ordre ende mate, in elck*

---

1 This study, 30-34.
2 Op 't Hof [1989, 1999-1].
3 Beeke [2003]; Op 't Hof [2008-1, 2011-1, 2015-1].
4 Duker; Van Oort *et al.*; Andreas J. Beck.
5 Op 't Hof [1989].

# 6. LATENT CITATIONS

*deel des daeghs, ende daed des levens, van stap tot stap door de grousame woestenie deses werelts, tot in het hemelsche Canaan te leyden* [The pillar of fire and cloud, shining night and day to lead the Israel of God step by step through the dismal desert of this world into the heavenly Canaan by certain general rules, after a set order and measure, in each part of the day and each deed in life] (1622).[6]

*Willem Teellinck*
Middelburg preacher Willem Teellinck brought out the first part of his piety manual *Sleutel der devotie* [Key to devotion] in 1624. When in this work he turns to the power of prayer to enhance many spiritual gifts in the believer, he avails himself unannounced of four pages 'worth of his own translation of Whately's manuscript.[7]

*Gisbertus Voetius*
It is evident how lasting the impression was that Whately's work made upon Voetius, and how it shaped the piety and piety education that he practised, when we compare Voetius 'academic manual *TA ΑΣΚΗΤΙΚΑ sive exercitia pietatis* [Ascetics, or the exercise of piety] (1664) with Whately's text. Cornelis Adrianus de Niet undertook that comparison for his doctoral thesis. He summarizes his findings as follows:

> This writing [Whately's work] has a much narrower scope than TA ΑΣΚΗΤΙΚΑ, yet their thematic relatedness is clear. However, that is not the only commonality. There is also a striking agreement between the structure of the two works: in both cases, Chapter 1 addresses the structuring of spiritual exercises, Chapter 3 meditation, and Chapter 4 prayer; both works consider the preaching of the Word and how one ought to behave under it, and sacraments, Sabbath-keeping, and special exercises such as fasting and vows—and in the same sequence in both cases![8]

**Lewis Bayly**
The piety manual *The practise of pietie* (1612) by Lewis Bayly (d. 1631) is another work that was surreptitiously worked into the writing of more than one Dutch Pietist author. Three Dutchmen in all did so: Willem Teellinck, Johannes Beeltsnyder[9] (1603–1683) and Voetius.

---
6   Op 't Hof [1999-1], 105–111.
7   Op 't Hof [2011-1], 277.
8   De Niet, 1:xli.
9   Op 't Hof [2015-5].

*Willem Teellinck*
In his aforementioned *Sleutel der devotie* (1624), Willem Teellinck incorporated not only part of his own translation of Whately's manuscript but also four longer extracts from Bayly's guide. The first three quotations concern, in this sequence, the following hindrances to the practice of piety: 1. a misconceived trusting to divine mercy alone; 2. the fancy that one still has plenty of time left to live; 3. the impression that practising piety will turn people melancholic, especially the young. The final quotation is one combating the foregoing three objections with the contention that one must strive in all earnestness for the life of grace.[10]

*Johannes Beeltsnyder*
Johannes Beeltsnyder was born at Epe near Zwolle in 1603. He matriculated as a theology student at Franeker on 9 December 1624 and was ordained a minister at Beilen, Drenthe, on 1 January 1630. He preached the Gospel there for a full 48 years. Beeltsnyder also had a leading role in ecclesiastical affairs at a provincial level, twice serving as chairman and clerk of the Synod of Drenthe. He retired in April 1678 and was succeeded as parish minister of Beilen by his son-in-law Willem Hofstede (1652-1717). The prominent eighteenth-century preacher Petrus Hofstede[11] (1716-1803) was a great-grandson of Beeltsnyder's.

In his student years, Beeltsnyder was in the same intake as several men who would later become Pietist and Further Reformation proponents, such as Petrus Gribius[12] (1602/3-1666), Maximiliaan Teellinck[13] (1605-1653) and Justus Teellinck[14] (b. 1607/8). Beeltsnyder's works also saw publication. A collection of his sermons on the *ars moriendi* came out in 1654/5, entitled *Euthanasia. Dat is, de salighe sterf-konst der kinderen Gods* [A good death, or the skill of the children of God in dying blessedly]. In this work, Beeltsnyder goes further than calling for a pious manner of life: he laments the backsliding that church and society has seen in this regard since the sixteenth-century Reformation.[15] Characteristic of his spiritual stance is that he twice refers to works by the Further Reformation preacher Godefridus Udemans[16] (1581-1649) and once to the

---

10  Op 't Hof [2008-1], 292.
11  De Bie and Loosjes, 2:138-152.
12  Van de Kamp [2015].
13  Brienen [1993]; Op 't Hof [2016-16].
14  Op 't Hof [2001-4].
15  Beeltsnyder [1654/5], 124-125.
16  Meertens; Fieret; Exalto [1989]; Schutte [1989], 301-302, 310-311; Uil [2016-2].

Puritan theology professor of Franeker, William Ames[17] (1576–1633).[18] In his description of the joy that will spring up when body and soul are reunited on the day of resurrection after so many centuries of parting, he provides a one-and-a-half-page quotation[19] whose source he omits to mention. Research has shown that the citation is from Bayly's work.[20]

*Gisbertus Voetius*
If Whately's writing left a lifelong impression on Voetius, so much the more did Bayly's piety handbook. In all, more than twenty pages of his manual for the practice of piety, *TA AΣKHTIKA sive Exercitia pietatis* (1664), are lifted from Bayly. The themes covered in these borrowings are hindrances to repentance, four requirements for spiritual fruit to be produced from one's baptism, the right way to sanctify the Lord's Day, and five manners of fasting. In none of these instances does Voetius name the author from whom he is borrowing.[21]

**William Perkins**
Although William Perkins (1559–1602) was one of the most influential, if not the most influential, Puritan to the seventeenth-century Dutch church,[22] research has so far thrown up only one latent citation of his work. That said, it is a borrowing that in extent is many times greater than all others.

*Eeuwout Teellinck*
Of the 22 works in all by Eeuwout Teellinck that were published, one was posthumous: *Voorbereydinge tot de doodt* [Preparing for death], published in 1649, twenty years after his decease. At the end of the twentieth century, a researcher made the discovery that this work is in fact an adaptation and reworking of Perkins' work on the same subject. Teellinck not only follows the flow and divisions of the English work but also lifts dozens of pages verbatim, without so much as a word of acknowledgement.[23]

---

17 Visscher; Sprunger [1972]; Van Vliet; Van 't Spijker [2015].
18 Beeltsnyder, [1654/5], 58, 266 and 74 respectively.
19 Beeltsnyder, [1654/5], 288–289.
20 Op 't Hof [2011-4].
21 De Niet, 1:lxv–lxvii.
22 Op 't Hof [1987-1], [2001-1], 379–380.
23 Op 't Hof [1999-1], 78, 115–149.

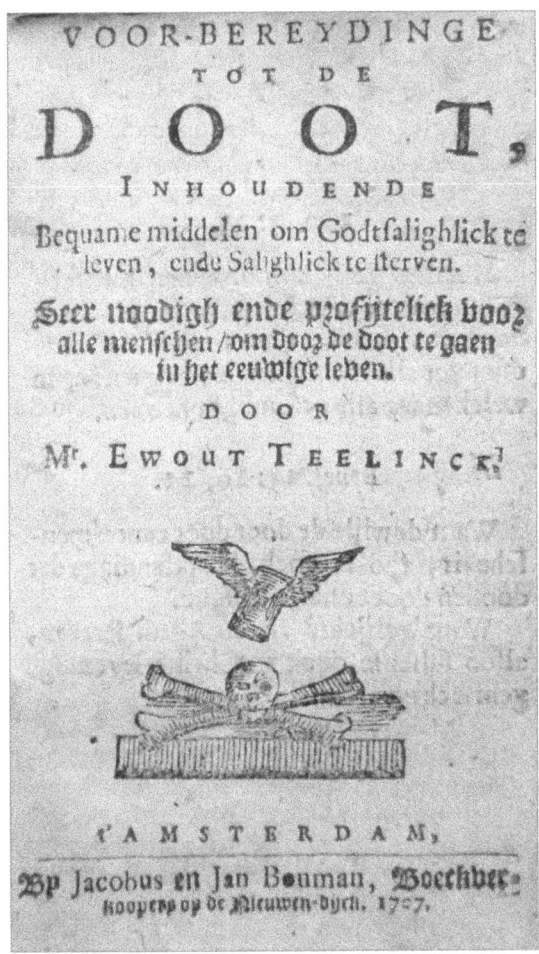

## Christopher Love
Another Puritan whose works met with a considerable reception in the Low Countries was the Presbyterian Christopher Love[24] (1618–1651). As with Perkins, there is only one known passage of his that was borrowed in a Dutch work without explicit accreditation.

*Johannes Quintius*
The minister of Herwijnen in Guelders, Johannes Quintius[25] (d. 1701), had a work of his published at Utrecht in 1659: *Wraack-toneel handelende*

---

24   Huisman [2013].
25   Op 't Hof [2016-10].

*van de sonden van Neder-landt* [A scene of vengeance, concerning the sins of the Netherlands]. At the opening of his dedication, which is to the congregation of Herwijnen, he recalls having read in a renowned Englishman's work that the Holy Spirit is compared with a dove and that just as a dove will always stay in her cote as long as it is kept clean, so the Spirit will always remain in a person's heart as long as he keeps it pure.[26] Quintius does not name the author, but it was in the collection of Love's sermons on spiritual warfare, *The combat between the flesh and Spirit*, that he had read this remark.[27]

**Matthew Mead**
Chronologically, the last known silent borrowing of a Puritan is from the work of Matthew Mead (1629–1699). A Dutch translation of his *The almost christian discovered* (1662) was reprinted many times. There is one known occasion of a Frisian minister having copied his words without acknowledgement.

*Sixtus Brunsvelt*
A Further Reformation promoter in Friesland, Sixtus Brunsvelt[28] (1635–1683), produced many Pietist works. One of these was published under the title *Het naukeurige christendom* [Exact Christianity] in 1680. Research has proven that a substantial proportion of this work is highly similar to Mead's aforementioned work.[29]

**How and why unacknowledged borrowings were made**
The following will consider how the Dutch authors availed themselves of Puritan sources without crediting them, and the reasons that they may have had for doing so. Nothing in this section can be asserted with total certainty, since none of the authors in question provided an explanation for their conduct. Nevertheless, quite a few of the particulars can be propounded with a reasonable degree of likelihood, drawing on existing knowledge of how the authors in question typically worked.

*Eeuwout Teellinck*
In two of his works, Eeuwout Teellinck, a lay theologian, incorporates a passage from the aforementioned work by Whately. The incorporations

---

26 Quintius [1659], *6r.–v.
27 Love [1656], 29.
28 Exalto [1974-2]; Breuker [2015-2].
29 Groenendijk [1977].

are lifted almost verbatim from his brother Willem's translation. In the third known occasion on which he borrowed from a Puritan book, it was a writing by Perkins that was the source, whose Dutch translation had come out in 1599 entitled *Salve voor een sieck mensche* [*A salue for a sicke man* (1595)]. Its translator was Vincentius Meusevoet[30] (d. 1624), preacher at Schagen in Noord-Holland. Significantly, Teellinck praises that clergyman in his first published work, *Philometor* [He who loves his mother], where he also informs the reader that besides the Bible, he has never read anything with more delight or profit than Puritan books. Since he became acquainted with them, he explains, he has developed a distaste for all other kinds of books. Oftentimes, he expresses his heartfelt good wishes to Meusevoet, despite not knowing him personally.[31] Given this background, it is hardly surprising that his posthumously-published work was Puritan in nature. Although it is a reworking of Meusevoet's translation of Perkins' writing, there are dozens of passages which are substantially in word-for-word agreement with the source. In all three known cases, then, Eeuwout Teellinck used Dutch translations for his unacknowledged borrowings.

Nor is there a single indication in any of the three cases that the reader is being fed quotations. Why this clandestineness? In the case of the first two writings in which Willem's translation of Whately's manuscript had served as source, that does not appear at first sight to be a hard question to answer. The 21 pamphlets by Eeuwout that rolled off the press during his lifetime were all published either anonymously or under a pseudonym. The reason why he was not keen to be publicly credited as their author will doubtless have had to do with the high civil office he held as Comptroller of the States of Zeeland. It is quite possible that he was also seeking thus to avoid harsh and rash attacks on his character. Such kneejerk responses were all too common in the period, particularly in the heat of the struggle between the Remonstrants and Contra-Remonstrants. In light of the sharp criticisms and accusations that were indeed levelled at the unknown person responsible for his pamphlets,[32] it was a wise precaution that Teellinck had taken. He entirely succeeded, in fact, in keeping the public guessing. For instance, the leader of the Remonstrant party, Johannes Wtenbogaert[33] (1557–1644), took the author to be one or other

---

30 Op 't Hof [1987-1], 441–455; Frijhoff, 84–92; Op 't Hof [2016-5].
31 Op 't Hof [1999-1], 70.
32 These can be found in the pamphlets directed against him: Op 't Hof [1999-1], 81.
33 Hoenderdaal.

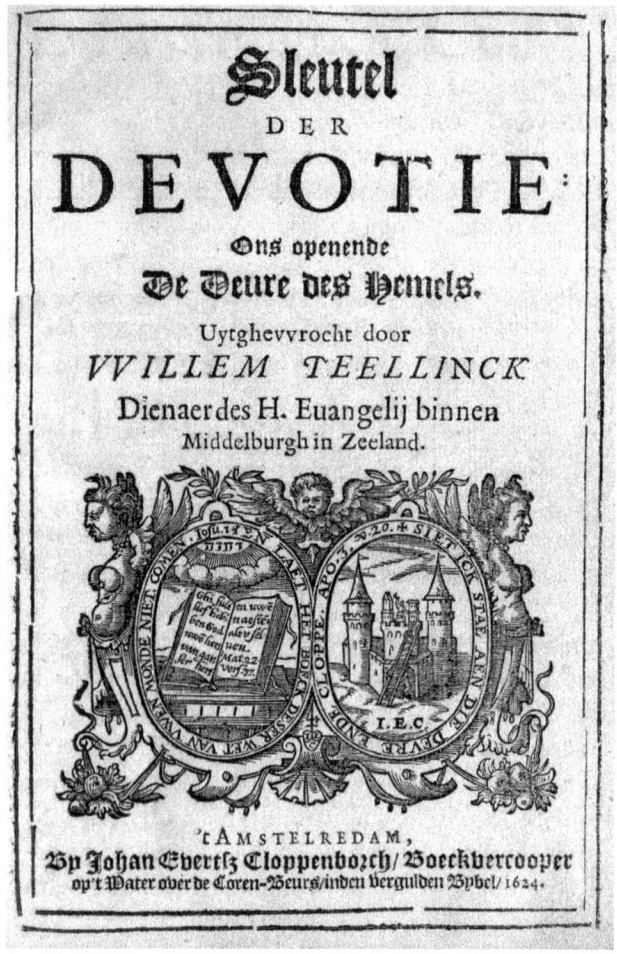

of the foremost Amsterdam clergymen of the day.[34] Even within Zeeland, the Tholen preacher Jacobus Bursius[35] (1589–1650), the first man to go into print to attack the Further Reformation as a movement,[36] failed to recognise Eeuwout Teellinck's authorship, although his father Gillis Bursius (d. 1634) sat alongside Teellinck as a fellow Reformed church officer of the Middelburg congregation![37]

The explanation that might leap out at the researcher, namely that Eeuwout wished to throw the curious reader off his trail by not explicitly

---

34  Wtenbogaert [1621], 60.
35  Op 't Hof [2015-9].
36  Op 't Hof [1991], 61–155.
37  Op 't Hof [1991], 88.

citing his own brother, is nevertheless not certain. After all, he often does, in so many words, praise his brother—without calling him his brother—and his brother's works. Moreover, he also openly quotes from Willem's oeuvre on other occasions.[38] The only reason one can think of to explain why he did so is that where translations were concerned, he did not consider it so important to state his source clearly.

Now we have formulated this explanation, it can also be said to be applicable to Eeuwout's posthumous publication. Nevertheless, in that latter case, caution is called for in judging his motives, since *Voorbereydinge tot de doodt* was printed and brought into circulation without any shadow of authorial involvement. It is quite possible, in fact, that he himself never had publication in mind and might not even have wished it. If that was indeed the case, then the work would not even be eligible for inclusion in the present deliberations.

*Willem Teellinck*
In his *Sleutel der devotie* (1624), Willem Teellinck incorporates extracts from both Whately and Bayly. What is striking is that he is not consistent on the two occasions: he conceals the provenance of the Whately passage that he uses, but reveals his borrowing from Bayly's piety manual. The first of the Bayly quotations is introduced with the sentence: "I have recently been faithfully instructed on this matter by a man of God who treats of the practice of piety."[39] The last of the citations is announced with the following sentence: "For this cause, the aforementioned man of God closes his address to the yet unconverted thus".[40]

> Priscilla. Daer over is my onlanckx van een man Gods/ handelende van de practijcke der Godtsalichepdt / trouwe bescheet gedaen / tot desen propooste.

*The first quoted passage in the original*

---

38  Op 't Hof [1991], 71–72.
39  Teellinck [1624], 318a.
40  Teellinck [1624], 339b.

Although Teellinck does not go so far as to identify Bayly or his work in explicit terms, he does intimate enough of its title that the informed reader would readily understand whom and which book Teellinck was referring to.

Fortuitously, all the references and quotations in Willem Teellinck's oeuvre have already been systematically indexed, with a dedicated category maintained for his uncredited sources. That overview leads us to the following conclusions. In his life's work overall, Teellinck is not a prolific user of references or citations, but he does sprinkle them through his books with a measure of regularity. He names a select number of Puritans a modest number of times, one of whom is Whately, whom he speaks of with high regard no fewer than six times in the dedication of his own translation of Whately's manuscript.[41] So why did he not name his esteemed source in *Sleutel der devotie*? The most logical explanation is that he did not wish to bang the drum about a translation he had written himself; leaving an impression of arrogance upon the reader was the last thing he would wish.

It seems that Teellinck walked a *via media* in the case of Bayly's work. How is this to be accounted for? The fact that he tipped the book a nod for the discerning reader to pick up on shows us that he did on the one hand want to speak well of the work, being entirely in agreement with its contents and describing as he did its author with the lofty title of a man of God. On the other hand, he was clearly not prepared to praise the author openly. What could have held him back from doing so? There is *prima facie* evidence that the following was his concern.[42] The first published assault on the Further Reformation, a book whose especial target Teellinck was,[43] was written by Jacobus Bursius in 1627 and takes a number of pot-shots at Bayly's book. Significantly, Bursius does not shrink from identifying Bayly and his book by name several times, even though he does not explicitly refer to his main target, Teellinck. Evidently, Bayly's book was a hot potato in the Dutch church scene of the 1620s and some very harsh criticism was being levelled at it. It is very possible that this circumstance was what prevented Teellinck from being too fulsome in his praise of that Puritan work. He was not the sort to heap coals needlessly upon the polemical fire.[44]

---

41  Op 't Hof [2011-1], 241–283.
42  For the following, see Op 't Hof [2009-2], 246–249.
43  Op 't Hof [1991], 98–102.
44  Op 't Hof [2008-1], 558.

*Gisbertus Voetius*
It has been established that Whately's work was decisive in shaping the academic approach taken to the practice of piety in his own day, as set out by Voetius in his *TA ΑΣΚΗΤΙΚΑ sive exercitia pietatis*. Given that this Puritan work was only ever published in Dutch translation, there is no question but that Voetius worked from that translation, particularly in light of his own remarks about the impact that that translation had on himself and others. Yet in no way does he acknowledge in writing that Whately's work was the key motivation for him to write his own piety handbook.

The foregoing applies equally to the dozens of pages that Voetius cites from Bayly's piety manual. The translation by Everhardus Schuttenius[45] (d. 1655) is his source for that borrowing, albeit in a corrected form. It was he himself who had, with a view to his intention of producing a new edition of *De practycke ofte oeffeninghe der godtzaligheydt* (which would eventually come out in 1642), commissioned that corrected version.[46] The passages from Bayly are likewise inserted tacitly into his book.

What, then, prompted Voetius to withhold his sources? In the case of Bayly's work, previous research has already proposed an answer. De Niet asserts that this most likely has to do with the reservations that Voetius himself voiced, in his edition of Bayly's book, regarding some of the Bishop of Bangor's standpoints and arguments.[47] Discoveries that have been made since de Niet's study on Voetius' academic piety manual bring something else to light, something that constitutes a much more intriguing explanation of our problem. Without notifying the reader, Voetius made *Het geestelijck cieraet* [The spiritual jewel] (1620) by Willem Teellinck the template for the thirteenth chapter of his book, a chapter dedicated to the right use of the Lord's Supper. The very chapter title is enough to drop a heavy hint that the subtitle of that work by Teellinck was the model. However, what clinches the matter is that the structure of Voetius' handbook exactly follows in many respects that of Teellinck's sermon collection, and that Voetius borrows much from the Teellinck compendium in his elaborating material.[48] What is more, chapter fifteen of Voetius' work, which concerns itself with how to spend one's day piously and profitably, is actually in large measure a series of extracts from *Vyer ende wolck-calomne* [The pillar of fire and cloud] (1622) by Eeuwout Teellinck, again uncredited by Voetius. These extracts are nothing less than crucial to the

---

45  Op 't Hof [2009-1].
46  Van de Kamp [2009], 225–234.
47  De Niet, 1:lxvii.
48  Op 't Hof [2008-1], 467–468.

GISBERTI VOETII
*Theol. in Acad. Ultraj. Prof.*

# ΤΑ ΑΣΚΗΤΙΚΑ
## SIVE
# EXERCITIA PIETATIS
*In usum Juventutis Academicæ*
nunc edita.

*Addita est, ob materiæ affinitatem,*
Oratio de Pietate cum scientiâ
conjungendâ,

Habita Anno 1634

GORICHEMI,
Officinâ Pauli Vink, Bibliopolæ.
Anno cIɔ Iɔc Lxiv.

overall structure of Voetius' chapter, and many parts of the chapter are taken from that source.[49] As we have already seen, Voetius does not explicitly admit that he is so dependent on the Teellinck brothers' material. What he does, however, is to name authors in the first paragraph of his thirteenth chapter who have previously written on his subject matter, and only in Willem Teellinck's case does he give the name of a work, namely the sermon collection.[50] This could be taken as an acknowledgement that this was the work above all that had been of significance to the chapter at hand; however, it is not stated unambiguously. The first sentence of chapter fifteen lists more authors, seven in all, one of whom is Eeuwout Teellinck. In this case, Voetius gives a few titles of works, not just one. Thus, the distinctive place accorded to Teellinck as a source in the thirteenth chapter is not repeated two chapters later. In contrast, Voetius does reveal the identity of Irenaeus Philalethius ['Peaceful lover of the truth'] here.[51]

So, although Voetius identifies the author and work from which he is borrowing on both occasions, among the other sources that he names, he does not expressly announce that this particular work and the particular men responsible for it were largely to thank for his writing the chapter in question. Honesty compelled him to state his sources, but on the other hand he evidently did not feel in a position to set out the matter fully and frankly. The question arises, then, whether this might not have been how he went about matters in the instances of Whately's and Bayly's books. A close examination reveals that it was indeed. In the second paragraph of his preface, he refers to writings that constitute a school of the practice of piety. Alongside a French and a German work, he includes the books of Bayly and Whately in this list.[52] Even more significantly, he remarks in his first chapter that the practices discussed in his work are treated summarily in Bayly. Bayly's is the only book to which he calls the reader's attention.[53] Later on in his piety manual, he refers a few more times to Bayly's work. There is not the slightest indication that he had any qualms about the book such as to make him in any way unwilling to draw attention to it. How, then, to explain that he drew upon it often without naming the name of Bayly? What we have seen with regard to *Het geestelijck cieraet* by Willem Teellinck and *Vyer ende wolck-calomne* by his brother Eeuwout also applies to Bayly's work. Voetius first makes clear at the start of his

---

49  Op 't Hof [1999-1], 82, 106.
50  De Niet, 1:[342]; 2:275.
51  De Niet, 1:[363–364]; 2:291.
52  De Niet, 1:[3]; 2:16.
53  De Niet, 1:[20]; 2:31.

book what great worth he attaches to the work in question and then cites liberally from it without necessarily always attributing the quotations.

There could perhaps be an even deeper aspect to be sounded out as regards why Voetius behaved in this way. The Graeco-Latin title of *TA ΑΣΚΗΤΙΚΑ sive exercitia pietatis* announces loud and clear that it is a book for academics. It is entirely possible that the reason Voetius was not minded to provide his readership with details of his sources was that he thought academically-trained readers ought to track down for themselves where he was indebted to others. Seen this way, his behaviour would be part of what Jeroen Jansen has called the learned game.[54]

*Johannes Beeltsnyder*
The quotation[55] from Bayly's piety manual that Beeltsnyder incorporated in his *Euthanasia* runs to three paragraphs. The first paragraph is set in the same Gothic typeface as the body of the work; the second and third are typeset in Roman. This presentation serves to pass off the first paragraph as part of Beeltsnyder's own text and gives the impression that only the latter two are the citation. In fact, all three paragraphs are nothing but citation, apart from part of the third. Although the reader is alerted by the customary switch to Antiqua that he is reading a quotation, there is no indication to him of its source. This too, then, is a latent citation.

Given that the work appeared in 1654/5, Beeltsnyder could have used either Schuttenius' translation or Voetius' revision thereof as his source-text for Bayly. Close comparison indicates that it was Schuttenius' original translation that he used, albeit that he allowed himself the liberties of minor transmutations and other amendments to the text in his edition.

How to interpret the printing of the first paragraph of the quotation in Gothic script is a difficult matter, since we must address the question of whether this was done accidentally or on purpose. If it was a mere printing error, no motive can be sought behind it. However, if the typesetting was not at fault, then we have another item to add to our stock of evidence that Beeltsnyder played fast and loose with his source-texts.

Finally, we have the intriguing fact that the author conceals the source of the citation, against his normal practice. Here, too, there is the theoretical possibility of an error having crept in during the text production and the proofreading (if, indeed, there was any). That aside, however, we must give serious thought to the possibility that Beeltsnyder was deliberately hiding his source at this point. But what reason might he have had for

---

54  Jansen, 270–273.
55  For the following, see: Op 't Hof [2011-4].

doing such a thing? It is quite possible that the same consideration motivated Beeltsnyder that seems to have been in Willem Teellinck's mind, as set out above. If so, then this would indicate that *De practycke* was a book which had not only generated a hostile reception in the Zeeland of the first quarter of the seventeenth century but that this even lingered at the other end of the country in the third quarter of the century.

*Johannes Quintius*
At the opening of his dedication to his own congregation, Quintius relates in his *Wraack-toneel* that he has read something of a renowned Englishman. He intimates as much as to make clear that he is citing a work, but does not disclose the Englishman's identity. Although the wording in the dedication does not amount to a literal quotation, it agrees so closely with a passage in a collection of Love's sermons translated by Jacobus Koelman[56] (1631-1695) that the conclusion is justified that Quintius was using that translation as his source.

Did Quintius have a particular reason not to admit to having read Love? There is no indication that he had any such reason. Now and again in the work, he does name some authors, but with equal readiness he conceals others. For instance, in one paragraph, he cites Augustine by name in one sentence and accredits the next sentence merely to "a distinguished minister".[57] It does not appear that he had any special motive for having left Love unacknowledged.

*Sixtus Brunsvelt*
In his *Het naukeurige christendom*, of 1680, Brunsvelt gives no indication whatsoever of being substantially beholden to a work by a Puritan, namely Mead. Yet he demonstrates in the same book that he is not shy of reeling off many other authors' names. The most rational explanation for his total quiescence about Mead is that he was unwilling to acknowledge that he was heavily leaning upon another man's work for his actual content. Brunsvelt could rest easy in the confident assumption that it would take a long while for any reader to cry "Alas, master, for it was borrowed", since no Dutch translation of Mead was on the market in 1680.[58] This must mean that he availed himself of an English copy, which in turn prompts the conclusion that Brunsvelt had good English.

---

56 Krull; Van Lieburg [1990]; Meeuse [1990, 2008]; Op 't Hof [2013-1], 237–268; Groenendijk [2017].
57 Quintius [1659], 42.
58 The oldest dates from 1682.

## Comparable borrowings in other European countries

The phenomenon of latent Puritan citations is not restricted to the Low Countries; far from it. It was a regular occurrence in other parts of the Continent, too. A range of data from other European countries follows in order to place the Dutch data in a broader context.

*Switzerland*
Under Edward VI (1547–1553), the Protestant-minded Archbishop of Canterbury, Thomas Cranmer (1489–1556), took the opportunity to introduce the Reformation in England. To do so, he brought over some of the foremost Continental Protestant theologians. Among these was Martin Bucer[59] (1491–1551), who had been obliged by political circumstance to leave his ministry at Strasbourg in 1548. He was offered a professorship at Cambridge and gave direction in many ways to the process of reformation in England, although his efforts were cut short by his death in 1551. It is no exaggeration to see in his theology one of the roots of Puritanism.

Edward VI had founded a bursary to permit relatives of Bucer's to study in England. In 1597, a step-grandson of Bucer's from Basel, Wolfgang Meyer (1577–1653),[60] drew on these funds to come and study theology, which he did for four years at both Oxford and Cambridge. It was in the latter city that he completed his studies with a doctorate in 1601. His encounter with Puritanism, and particularly with Perkins, was an impression that never left him. When, nearly two decades later, he represented Switzerland at the Synod of Dort, he took the opportunity to cross the North Sea again to look up his old friends and acquaintances. While back in England, he was asked by James VI/I (1566–1625) whether he thought the pro-Arminian works of Conradus Vorstius[61] (1569–1622) worth translating, and replied unabashedly that they ought rather to be burnt than disseminated!

After his initial visit to England and once ordained as a Reformed preacher, Meyer translated many of Perkins' works and some of other Puritans. He chose not to render them into German but into the language of international scholarship, Latin, since his intent was to propagate the Puritan theology of Perkins in particular across Europe, not merely in the German-speaking lands. On occasion, however, he did translate into his native language.[62] One example of a German translation of his, published at Basel in 1648 and reprinted the following year in the same city, is *Die*

---

59 Greschat.
60 Welti, index.
61 Van der Woude [1978-2].
62 For the following, see Schmidt [1969].

*geistliche Bad-Cur, oder Tractat von der Wiedergeburt* [The spiritual water-cure, or a tractate on regeneration]. Although the publication is accredited to Meyer, it is really a translation of a work by Thomas Taylor (1576–1633), very copiously augmented by Meyer.

*Germany*
Peter Streithagen[63] (1591–1653) of the Palatinate was first court chaplain to Frederick V[64] (1596–1632), the 'Winter King' of Bohemia, in 1631–1632 and then performed the same duties for his son Charles Louis[65] (1617–1680). Both father and son resided in exile at The Hague until 1650. During that period, Streithagen accompanied Charles Louis to England for three lengthy stays (1635–1637, 1641–1642 and 1645–1649), which acquainted him with Puritanism. Posthumously, his anthology of choice Puritan passages on the new birth was published as *Homo novus das ist: ein neu, gelehrt und Gottseliges Tractätlein, von deß Menschen Wieder-geburt, aus unterschiedtlichen der berümbsten Englischen Theologen* [The new man; that is, a new, learned and godly little tractate on the regeneration of man, taken from several of the most noted English theologians] (1658). The contents of this collection had first been presented by him as spoken sermons in The Hague. The odd thing is that this publication—which constitutes the first Reformed monograph on regeneration in the German-speaking world—contains not one English author's name within its covers.[66] As the publication is posthumous, the question arises of whether this obscurity really had been the compiler's intention.

The foregoing proves the Puritan influence upon a German Reformed preacher; far more intriguing a matter is the great impact which the Father of the Further Reformation, Willem Teellinck of the Netherlands, had upon the German Lutheran clergyman Theophil Großgebauer[67] (1627–1661), a figure well known for his authorship of the first reformational agenda written in German Protestantism, *Wächterstimme auß dem verwüsteten Zion* [A watchman's voice from the ruins of Zion] (1661). In his call for reformation, Großgebauer refers five times to an excellent teacher, each time citing from his work. Martin Schmidt (1909–1982) assumed that this teacher must have been an Englishman; Jonathan Strom thought he was a Reformed theologian; but it is Jan van de Kamp who managed to

---

63   Rotscheidt.
64   Groenveld.
65   Hauck.
66   For this section, see Goeters, 242–244.
67   Strom, 195–221.

pin down his identity:[68] it was Teellinck whom Großgebauer was citing. Close inspection reveals that the structure of Großgebauer's reformation programme is all but identical to Teellinck's own model of the genre, *Noodwendigh vertoogh* [Necessary exposition] (1627), and that there is plenty of material common to both works. Moreover, the aforementioned five quotations are just the tip of the iceberg of Großgebauer's borrowings. His book is in fact rife with citations and paraphrases of Teellinck's *Noodwendigh vertoogh* and also from the Dutchman's tractate on the Lord's Day, *Rust-tydt* [The time of rest] (1622). As one might expect, Großgebauer filtered Reformed peculiarities repugnant to Lutheran feelings out of the citations and paraphrases that he included. Doubtless, then, the reason why he concealed the identity of the writer and works from which he was citing was that he was keen not to be accused of heresy, for then his call to reformation would have been doomed to failure. That this call was, however, in no sense a failure is proof of the effect that his reformational agenda had. To take just two indicators of its success, the work was published no fewer than five times and it served as the key source for what is generally acknowledged to be the doyen of all German Lutheran Pietist reformation programmes: *Pia desideria* [Pious desires] (1675) by Philipp Jakob Spener[69] (1635–1705).[70]

The third instance chronologically comes from 1674,[71] when *Das grosse Interesse eines gewissenhafften Kauffmans. Dat ist: eine christliche Unterrichtung, wie man sich um Kauffen und Verkauffen verhalten müsse* [A conscientious merchant's great interest; that is, a Christian instruction in how to conduct oneself in buying and selling] was published. The material following on from the title page makes clear that one J.D. collated the material for this book from English sources. Van de Kamp has deduced that J.D. was Johann Deusing[72] and has gone on, moreover, to identify the source-texts of each of the seven chapters of this compendium. Its first chapter is a reworking of a work by Perkins; the fourth borrowed from another of Perkins' writings. Chapters two, three and six are translations of sermons by Love. For the fifth chapter, Deusing consulted Ames 'ethics and a work by Joseph Hall (1574–1656). Parts of the seventh chapter are taken from works by Robert Bolton (1572–1635) and Richard Sibbes (1577–1635).

---

68  Schmidt [1951], 98 footnote 2; Strom, 202 footnote 41; Van de Kamp [2016], 267–277.
69  Grünberg; Wallmann [1986].
70  Van de Kamp [2016], 276–277.
71  Van de Kamp [2012–1], 51.
72  Van de Kamp [2007], 21–31; [2012–1], 45–68.

What is interesting with this book is to trace the variations in Deusing's presentation of the material. While some chapters are straight translations of their source, others are made up of a reworked writing and others still are compounded from a plurality of sources. *Das grosse Interesse eines gewissenhafften Kauffmans* becomes an even more intriguing publication when van de Kamp's findings regarding the sources used by Deusing are considered.[73] For the first and the fourth chapters, the compiler used the Dutch translations of the Perkins works concerned to present the material in German. The second, third and sixth chapters of the German work are also derived from Dutch translations of three of Love's sermons. For chapter five, Deusing's source-text was the original Latin of the Ames material and the Dutch translation for Hall. Deusing's borrowings from Bolton and Sibbes were also made from their Dutch translations. In the case of Sibbes, admittedly the translation itself contains insufficient evidence to identify its source language, but there is a concomitant fact that establishes beyond doubt that it was once again the Dutch version that Deusing was consulting. The year after the publication of *Das grosse Interesse eines gewissenhafften Kauffmans*, Deusing's German translation came out of the entire work by Sibbes that had featured in the compendium, and the same was done the following year with the relevant work by Bolton. In these full books, it is unmistakably the Dutch translations that were used to produce the German. It is thus established that Deusing did all his own translations for his compendium.

Why did Deusing conceal his sources? In this instance, we cannot fall back on the argument that Puritan authors were a bone of contention among the Lutherans. Nor is it plausible that the reason was that Deusing, as a Reformed German, was overly concerned with unduly offending his Lutheran countrymen. For if either of these had been his thinking, he would not have gone on to present the German reading public with a work by Sibbes, and two (no less) by Bolton, under their original authors' names. So did Deusing consider it too much of a bother to himself, or too confusing to his readers, to list his plethora of Puritan sources? That is not impossible, but it is perhaps likelier that the reason is to be sought in the then-current theory of translation. In Early Modern Europe, and particularly when a translator had gone about his work creatively (and Deusing had done so by producing a compilation), a translation was regarded as a fresh product. Naturally, one does not identify one's sources when presenting a work as original.[74]

---

73  Van de Kamp [2012-1], 64.
74  Jansen, 315–318.

## Two Dutch piety manuals and translations

In 1661, the Amsterdam Further Reformer Petrus Wittewrongel[75] (1609–1662) published his *Oeconomia christiana ofte christelicke huys-houdinghe* [Christian economy or the Christian household], a family handbook running to two volumes and over two thousand pages; in 1679, Koelman brought out his own pedagogical work, *De pligten der ouders* [The duties of parents]. Thanks to the exemplary research findings of L.F. Groenendijk, we know that Wittewrongel borrowed from at least fifteen Puritan works without citing his sources: Ames, *De conscientia et eius iure, vel casibus* [*Conscience with the power and cases thereof* (1639)] (1630); Bolton, *Some generall directions for a comfortable walking* (1626); John Dod (1549–1645) and Robert Cleaver (d. 1613), *A godlie forme of householde government* (1598); John Downham (1571–1652), *A treatise against fornication and adulterie* (in *Foure treatises*, 1613); Thomas Gataker (1574–1654), *A good wife Gods gift* (1620); Gataker, *Marriage duties* (1620); Gataker, *A wife in deed* (1623); Gataker, *Davids instructer* (1620; Gataker, *The benefit of a good name* (1620); William Gouge (1575–1653), *Of domesticall duties* (1622); Arthur Hildersham (1563–1632), *CLII lectures upon Psalme LI* (1635); Perkins, *The government of the tongue* (1593); Perkins, *Christian oeconomie* (1609); Henry Smith (d. 1591), *A preparative to marriage* (1591); and Whately, *Corte verhandelinghe* [A brief treatment] (1609). Of all these works, it was Gouge's standard work from which Wittewrongel drew the most, by far. Only on one occasion, in the preface to Volume II, does he intimate that he wrote almost nothing "without attentively consulting the best authors, and in particular many of the English theologians, who have so often and rightly earned the greatest honour in the right practice of true godliness"[76].[77] At the time of writing of Groenendijk's study, it was not yet known that Wittewrongel had been at Gataker's household seminary in 1631–1632. That datum explains three things: the great quantity of his borrowings; the fact that five of his fifteen unacknowledged sources are writings of Gataker's; and that all but one of the works he cites pre-date Wittewrongel's stay in England. Accordingly, we have to do with books that he must have acquired while studying at Gataker's household seminary.

There may well be a practical reason why Wittewrongel, although acknowledging (be it only in the middle of his work) that he copied much from English writers, nonetheless never identified specific sources: namely, that there was such a wealth of material at his disposal that he would not

---

75  Nagtglas [1888], 2:998–1000; Op 't Hof [2013-4].
76  Wittewrongel [1661], 2:(* )4r.–v.
77  Groenendijk [1984], 49–52, 205–206.

have managed to cite it all. Added to this may have been the factor that—particularly in his own city of Amsterdam—there was widespread disdain for Puritans. By concealing his chiefly Puritan sources, Wittewrongel might have hoped to foster a positive reception of his compendium.

A few years ago, Groenendijk convincingly demonstrated that Koelman, too, in his Amsterdam-published handbook of child-rearing, tacitly borrowed from Englishmen and Scots. These included Thomas White (d. 1672), *A manual for parents* (1660); Richard Baxter (1615-1691), *The saints everlasting rest* (1650); Baxter, *A christian directory* (1673); Baxter, *The poor man's family book* (1674); Thomas Vincent (1634-1678), *An explicatory catechism* (1673); Henry Jessey (1603-1663), *A looking-glass for children* (1673); James Janeway (1636-1674), *A token for children* (1671-1672); Janeway, *Invisibles, realities, demonstrated in the holy life and triumphant death of mr. John Janeway* (1673); Janeway, *Death unstung* (1669); Baxter, *A call to the unconverted* (1658); William Guthrie (1620-1665), *The christians great interest* (1659); Thomas Brooks (1608-1680), *Apples of gold for young men and women* (1657); and Hildersham, *CLII lectures upon Psalme LI* (1635). Moreover, much of the catechetical section of Koelman's book is based on the Westminster Shorter Catechism.[78]

Both of the reasons given above for Wittewrongel's reticence to cite his sources may also have applied to Koelman, who in 1679 was resident in Amsterdam.

As far back as 1981, however, the same researcher discovered that the appendices added by Koelman to his translation of Guthrie's aforementioned work were likewise mostly translations of Puritan matter. Koelman added to the first edition of his translation (1669) a detailing of 32 examples of English Pietists who had attained assurance of salvation after much spiritual conflict. This he borrowed from Henry Walker's *Spiritual experience of sundry believers* (1652). Koelman amplified his second edition (1672) with spiritual sketches of the lives of twelve Englishmen and Englishwomen, seven of whom he had taken from works by Samuel Clarke (1599-1683): two came from Clarke's *The marrow of ecclesiastical historie* (1650), one from "The lives of sundry modern English Divines" appended to Clarke's *A generall martyrologie* (1651), and four came from Clarke's *A collection of the lives of ten eminent divines* (1662). The sources of two others of these biographies were *Comforts against the fear of death* (1649) by Anne Skelton (d. 1648) and 'Mris. Moores evidences for heaven' appended to *The godly mans ark* (1657) by Edmund Calamy (1600-1666). Finally, Koelman added to the fourth edition of his translation (1680) one

---

78 Groenendijk [2017], 61-69, 82-83 footnote 317, 153, 156, 159, 203 footnote 796; 215, 219.

extra appendix, consisting of four more spiritual biographies. One of these he took from Clarke's "The lives of sundry modern English Divines" and two more from Clarke's *A collection of the lives of ten eminent divines*.[79]

What reason should be sought to explain the concealment of the source-material in this case? Neither of the reasons valid for Wittewrongel is applicable in this case: the number of source citations in this case would have been manageable, and there was no point in disguising the Puritan origin of appendices bundled with a Puritan translation. The only readily conceivable reason for the decision is that Koelman was not keen to accentuate the extent of his reliance on Puritanism; that is, we might again have to do with practical considerations.

It is apparent that Koelman made a learned game of his latent citations, for he did so as early as the preface to his first publication, a translation of Christopher Love (1618–6151), *Den strijdt tusschen vleesch en geest* [*The combate between the flesh and Spirit* (1654)] (1656).[80] That preface was addressed to students preparing for church ministry, and in it, he urged them as follows: "We have to mount from earth to heaven, to the heavenly academy". In the margin, he cited a writing of 1655 whose authorship he apparently did not know, *Interiora regni Dei* [The inward things of the Kingdom of God]. Later in life, he did know the work's authorship, for when he went on to translate it himself in 1678, he gave its author as the English puritan Francis Rous (1579–1659). While the marginal reference might give rise to the impression that it was only the phrase in question that was borrowed from the second treatise in that book, in reality not less than half of Koelman's preface is lifted from Rous' treatise!

One-off citation of the source coupled with copious borrowing from it is a combination that suggests the aforementioned habit of playful scholarly allusion, particularly when it is borne in mind that both Koelman and his addressees were theology students at the time.

**Conclusions**

It is the very propensity under investigation in this chapter, that of hiddenness, that makes it the most difficult research area to elucidate. That so much data has nevertheless surfaced in this domain is an indication that latent citations were a widespread phenomenon. Our Swiss and German examples demonstrate that it was also an international phenomenon, and given that, it is even likelier that it was not just widespread but

---

79  Groenendijk [1981].
80  Op 't Hof [2001-3], 82–83.

ubiquitous. It should be borne in mind here that the discoveries made thus far were made by chance. Should it ever prove possible to conduct a targeted search of the entire field of Dutch devotional literature for latent citations, the harvest could well surpass all expectations. White as the fields may be unto harvest, the labourers still have to be seen!

The target readership of the publications we have reviewed was not always one and the same. In all but one of the cases – the Latin piety manual for Voetius' theology students – the publications were in Dutch. Moreover, with the exception of Koelman's first work the, the intended readership largely consisted of readers who had not had an academic education. Whether the distinction holds true overall is something that will have to be answered by future research, but it is striking within the scope of this chapter that in thoese two exceptional cases, the latency of the borrowings made was relative, whereas it was an absolute latency in the other works reviewed. There might be a correlation between this difference and the difference in intended readership, namely engagement in scholarly interplay.

The first part of this chapter has indicated that, generally speaking, authors based their borrowings on a published translation of the source-text. Only Brunsvelt did not do so, instead presenting the reader with his own translation of the original English. That both Willem Teellinck and Voetius cited from a home-made translation (in the case of Teellinck) and home-made revision of a translation (in Voetius' case) ought not to be so surprising. The authors discussed in the foregoing section, on the other hand, could not have recourse to any existing translation, which is why they supplied their own. Consequently, authors' selftranslated latent citations far exceed in volume latent citations of existing translations. The sole exception to this was Wittewrongel, who used the translation of the work by Whately as his source. Thereby, Wittewrongel's case constitutes a supplementary argument for the assertion that the translations of Whately was of major importance.[81]

As one might have expected, the Dutch authors' reasons for not disclosing a Puritan source differed considerably. For Eeuwout Teellinck, translations were probably a textual feature not even worthy of special mention. For his brother Willem, it was most likely modesty that prevented him from blowing his own trumpet, as he had translated the source, Whately, himself. That he did give an indication of the citation in the case of Bayly's book (but left it at that) can be explained by the dislike that his own opponents had of that Puritan work. The same general aversion will have been a factor in Wittewrongel's concealment of his sources,

---

81  This study, 30-34.

and to a lesser extent in Koelman's case too, although both of these authors will also have had a considerable practical objection to citing their source. Voetius appears to have found it sufficient to have made reference to the borrowing of material in the preliminaries to his work and in the chapters he wrote for students. For that cultivated and experienced readership, it seems, he thought it superfluous to flag up time and again which source he was borrowing from. There is, however, an even likelier explanation for his failure to accredit his sources: that he thought it as well when he had an academic readership to string them along in the customary learned game of hide-and-seek. The same must also apply to Koelman's preface. For Quintius, no satisfying explanation really suggests itself. It is very much open to question whether he even had a reason for hiding his sources. The most plausible scenario in his case is that he was too proud to let the reader know when his material was borrowed.

In not one of the cases in the present chapter is it reasonable to assume that commonplace books or florilegia were the authors' sources. This is in itself a remarkable finding, as they were so common in the literary world of the period.[82] As for Quintius, not even he will have ransacked a book of quotations; he must have reproduced from memory the borrowings that he made.

Previous research has already indicated the great measure of influence that the Teellinck brothers had on Voetius.[83] That all of them silently cited Whately's writing furnishes yet more proof of the spiritual unity that there was between them as a trio. This also applies to Wittewrongel, who in his youth had sat under Willem Teellinck's preaching.

Chronologically, comparison between the latter half beats the first half of the seventeenth century reveals that the first half beats the latter half statistically across the board. The cause of this is the overwhelming bulk of citations discussed in the foregoing section. Moreover, late seventeenth-century borrowings were much more varied than early seventeenth-century borrowings. In the current state of knowledge, is was just two authors who were responsible for that great preponderance: Wittewrongel and Koelman. At the least, this preponderance is a cogent argument for the hypothesis that Puritan influence on the Netherlands swelled rather than receded as the seventeenth century progressed.

---

82  Jansen, 127–134.
83  Op 't Hof [1989].

# 7. PURITAN PREACHING BY DUTCH MINISTERS
## Puritan content in Dutch sermons

*In 1671, the academically-trained reader could find, in a Dutch author's writing on the study of theology that was appended to a work of dogmatics, the following sentence about Puritan books:*

> Moreover, these writings and others of their genre, very many of which have been translated into our national language, are being heard more than enough from the pulpit; such that homilies of that kind are often being dished out verbosely to the people in place of fresh material and original meditation.[1]

*This statement contains several observations and implications that are worth looking at one by one in more detail and upheld or rejected for veracity. The dependent clause of the first half of the sentence argues that a great many Puritan works had been translated into Dutch by 1671. A cursory search in Pietas, which holds details of no fewer than at least 325 Puritan works and 275 reprints published in the language by that year, will confirm that this was an entirely accurate statement of historical reality. The main clause of the first half of the statement contains an observation and an evaluation. The observation is that the contents of Puritan works were resounding from Dutch pulpits. That is to say, Dutch preachers were drawing on English sermons in their own sermon delivery. The author of our passage voiced no objection to that in and of itself, but what cannot meet with his approval is—and this is where his evaluation comes in—that it is happening on such an intensive scale. To his mind, churchgoers are being fed a surfeit of Puritan homiletic material. This negative evaluation is elaborated upon in the second statement, where he argues that the borrowing of Puritan sermons is occurring at the expense of original effort by Dutch ministers. Consequently, the latter are no longer obliged to dig for their own preaching texts, which automatically obviates any meditating upon texts*

---

1 Burmannus [1671], 2:683.

*that they might otherwise have undertaken. What the author of our passage is in fact accusing those Dutch preachers of who avail themselves of Puritan texts is spiritual indolence and convenience preaching.*

*In 1672, readers of Dutch were able to read the assertion by Further Reformer Simon Oomius[2] (1630–1706) that there were clergymen around who were learning Puritan sermons by heart and delivering them from the pulpit, passing them off as their own work.[3]*

*The tendency of Dutch ministers to reproduce Puritan material parrot-fashion was known in the country of origin, too. A few years before such complaints as the foregoing started to be made by Dutchmen, Thomas Sprat, the later Bishop of Rochester, had already fulminated:*

> Our famous Divines have been innumerable, as the Dutch Men may witnes, who, in some of their Theological Treatises, have been as Bold with the English Sermons, as with our Fishing; and their Robberies have been so manifest, that our Church ought to have Reprizals against them, as well as our Merchants.[4]

*The major issue that this chapter will seek to address, then, is whether seventeenth-century Dutch preachers really did bootleg Puritan sermons on an industrial scale. The subordinate issues tackled will therefore be whether sermons made up a considerable proportion of the translated material available; whether (and, if so, to what extent) Puritan homiletics underpinned Dutch sermons (particularly published ones); and whether such dependence on homiletics was a dependence on published translations alone or whether unpublished translations were also made use of.*

**Joos van Laren**
The literature to date has already referred copiously to the influence of the Puritans upon the preaching of Dutch Pietists and Further Reformation men in general.[5] But have specific commonalities in the preaching been demonstrated? Jan van der Haar, in 1978, was the first researcher to present

---

2  Van de Pol [1999, 2002, 2019]
3  Oomius [1672], 375b–376a.
4  Schoneveld, 123; cf. Pettegree and der Weduwen, 138.
5  Although Brienen refused to accept in 1974 that there had been Puritan homiletic influence on the Further Reformation, later researchers have proven him wrong: Brienen [1974], 218–221; Graafland, 10–11; Op 't Hof [2001-1], 336; Westerink, 93–100.

a convincing case of formal, material borrowing in this domain,[6] when he demonstrated with documentary proofs that the Vlissingen preacher Joos van Laren[7] (1586–1653) preached to his congregation on II Timothy 4:17 on 27 March 1639 and that in treating the text, he followed in the footsteps of the Puritan Richard Sibbes (1577–1635). Not only in his

*Joos van Laren in the pulpit at Vlissingen*

---

6  Van der Haar [1978].
7  Op 't Hof [2016-4].

introduction and division of points but even in the exposition of the text could one detect Sibbes' precedents. Some passages of the sermon were translated almost verbatim by van Laren from the original. Moreover, since no Dutch translation of the Sibbes sermon in question had been published, van Laren must have used a home-made translation.

That van der Haar's discovery was not a one-off was shown by Pieter den Ouden in 2003,[8] when he demonstrated that in his 23 December 1632 sermon on I John 4:9, van Laren borrowed several passages from a sermon by Arthur Hildersham (1563–1632) on I John 4:10. Again, van Laren will have had to translate these himself, since there was not yet any published Dutch translation available; one did come out in 1634, written by van Laren's brother Daniel van Laren[9] (b. 1585). A comparison of the Dutch of the two translations indicates that the brothers translated the English text independently of each other.[10]

### Gerhardus van Velsen[11]

Born in 1627, Gerhardus van Velsen was the son of Lambertus van Velsen, co-rector of the Latin school in Sneek in southern Friesland. His mother was a sister of the preacher Tobias Tegnejus[12] (d. 1668).[13] He matriculated at the Academy of Franeker on 10 August 1644[14] and began his preaching career in 1649 when he was installed in the parishes of Goënga, Gauw and Offingawier. He moved to another group of parishes near Sneek, namely Oosthem, Abbega and Folsgara, in 1665 and died in that post on 28 December 1673. He was buried in Goënga parish church.[15]

Van Velsen and his brother minister Franciscus Elgersma[16] (1625–1712) struck a contract in 1662. Elgersma, born in the Frisian provincial capital of Leeuwarden in 1625, had his theology studies at Franeker funded by his native city. As he matriculated on 15 February 1644,[17] he was an exact contemporary of van Velsen's and they will therefore have

---

8 Den Ouden.
9 Op 't Hof [2016-3].
10 Den Ouden, 99.
11 The following is taken almost in its entirety from Op 't Hof [1996-3].
12 Op 't Hof [1998].
13 Leeuwarden, Tresoar, Gen. 535 (Reddingius). I am indebted to Prof. Dr. Philippus H. Breuker for this detail.
14 Fockema Andreae and Meijer, 131.
15 Romein, 339, 382.
16 Breuker [2015-3].
17 Fockema Andreae and Meijer, 129.

# 7. PURITAN PREACHING BY DUTCH MINISTERS - 281

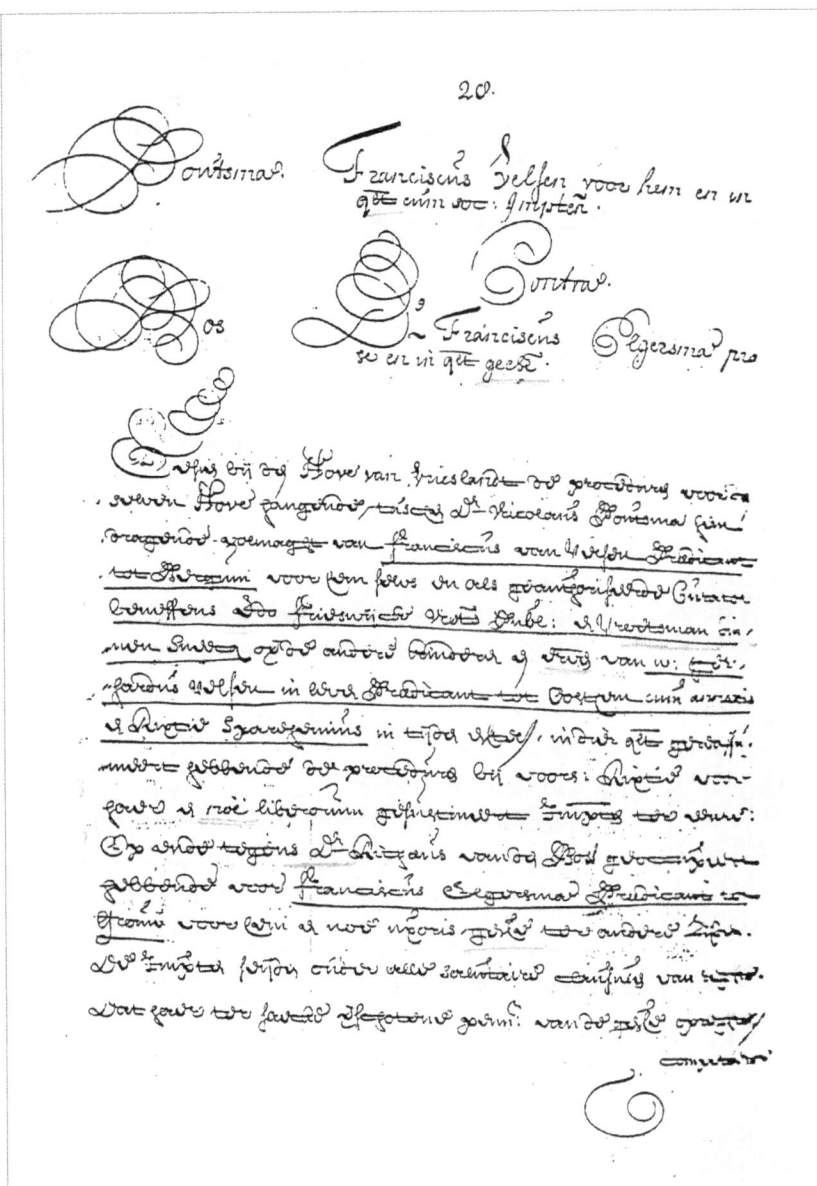

*The first page of the legal document*

sat together in lectures for five years. In 1650, Elgersma was installed in his first parishes, Oudkerk and Roodkerk, not far from Leeuwarden. He was called to his native city two years later but his independent bearing towards the city council necessitated his departure in 1667, when he accepted a call to Oudeschoot and Nieuweschoot, a pair of parishes near Sneek.[18] From 1669 until his death in 1712, he ministered to the congregation at Grouw. He married Aeltje Harmens in September 1650. He has a great many books to his name, chiefly Pietist in nature.[19] The contract between him and van Velsen is evidence that the two remained in contact after studying together.

The only source for our knowledge of the contract and its repercussions is a legal document[20] which records the final pronouncement of the Court of Friesland on 27 October 1692 at the end of the dispute between van Velsen's heirs and Elgersma. The lawsuit had dragged on for a very long time: the matters at dispute had occurred thirty years previously, and the provisional judicial verdict in the case had been given in 1679. Many details of the matter remain obscure, but the text of the document permits the below reconstruction of events.

In 1662, van Velsen and Elgersma struck a deal as follows. Van Velsen was to pay Elgersma a hundred guilders for the purchase of English tractates. Elgersma, who had English, would excerpt the contents of these pamphlets as Dutch gists which van Velsen would work up into ready sermons. This agreement was signed as a formal contract on 25 April 1662, drafted by van Velsen's father Lambertus and signed by Elgersma. Lambertus also handed Elgersma his son's hundred guilders on the spot at the signing of the contract. Elgersma was as good as his word and duly churned out more than two hundred sermon outlines for van Velsen's use.

After Gerhardus' death, Widow van Velsen brought—for reasons unclear—a suit against Elgersma in regard of his performance of the contract. The provincial court made its provisional finding on 25 February 1679, although its findings are not preserved for us, nor is it evident why it had to take another thirteen and a half years for the final verdict to be handed down. That judgement itself, however, was as clear as a bell when it came: Elgersma had breached contract and was ordered to pay a hundred guilders with interest and court costs.

---

18  Kalma, 61-63.
19  Van der Haar [1987], 121-122.
20  Leeuwarden, Tresoar, Hof WW (27-10-1692).

That van Velsen left the legalities and formalities of the agreement to his father will have had to do with Lambertus' profession of co-rector. A striking case detail is that it was Gerhardus' widow, Rixtie Sparehemius, who lodged the papers. Why had her late husband not done so in life? Had he perhaps resolved to hold out for an amicable solution right up to his deathbed? Did he find the prospect of a lawsuit unbecoming of his calling, choosing rather to suffer damage than to bring a dispute between preachers of the Gospel before a judge of worldly affairs? Whatever her reasons, Rixtie had little cheer from her writ: the 1679 provisional judgement did not achieve her aim, and it was only after her death that her son Franciscus, the minister of Bergum from 1679–1693,[21] reopened the suit and saw it successfully concluded.

The wording of the document is couched such that one would take Elgersma's knowledge of English to be a rare and remarkable skill; and so it was. Few Dutchmen knew English in his time: there were few opportunities to study the language at home, and indeed the literature[22] tells us that the only Dutchmen who had mastered English were those who had either spent time in England or who were close to Scots or Englishmen living in the Netherlands. We unfortunately have no indication of how Elgersma came by his English.

The existence of such a contract between van Velsen and Elgersma implies that both had a pronounced interest in English theology, or more precisely in English homiletics. After all, given the aim of the contract, namely to provide a boost to van Velsen's preaching career, it is extremely probable that the English tractates that Elgersma was to purchase were sermon collections. Clearly, both parties to the deal needed no convincing that English sermons had a certain something that made them surpass what was on offer on the Continent.

Now, it is known that the only kind of English preaching that had a considerable power of attraction to the seventeenth-century Dutch was Puritan preaching. The Puritan preaching method was characterised by a relatively brief exposition of the text, followed by an extensive application thereof to both the inner life and the sanctification of life. What is known as the classificatory method was a key tool for the first of those two branches of application.[23] The great quantity of translated Puritan sermons speaks volumes for the Dutch taste for this preaching style. Moreover, we

---

21  Romein, 118.
22  De Vooys, 12–14; Ossolton, 23–33; Schoneveld, 118; Frank-van Westrienen, 162; Loonen, 23.
23  Graafland, 10–11.

see a zenith of appreciation for this kind of sermon in the Friesland of the third quarter of the century. For instance, between 1648 and 1672, the Bolsward printer-publisher Samuel van Haringhouk[24] (1621–1675) alone produced hundreds of sermons of this type for an eager readership, translated by himself and by Frisian clergymen.[25] In fact, they were the staple of his publishing catalogue. There is no reason at all, then, to doubt that the English tractates envisaged in the contract were Puritan publications.

**Evaluating the evidence obtained**
The foregoing can be interpreted in one of two ways: either we take the matters described as being exceptional, or we posit that they were characteristic (or at least indicative) of the spiritual allegiances of a considerable proportion of seventeenth-century Dutch preachers. However, given the recorded outbursts with which this chapter began, we must discount the first possibility. The data unearthed on both van Laren and van Velsen bear out their observations as accurate. They might have over-egged the pudding a little, but their description of homiletic borrowing gets to the heart of the matter historically.

The data that form the backbone of this chapter relate to one preacher from Zeeland and two from Friesland. It might be tempting to regard Puritan homiletics as only having held sway in those outlying coastal provinces, both of which were indeed areas where Puritanism took deep roots.[26] Nevertheless, we can see from the productions of the Dutch translators with high outputs, Vincentius Meusevoet[27] (d. 1624) and Johannes Lamotius[28] (d. 1627), and from the Amsterdam publishing catalogue of Johannes Boekholt[29] (1656–1693), that Holland, the keystone province of the Netherlands, was also enthused by Puritanism. Catalogues from publishers in the centre and east of the country, Hendrik Versteeg[30] (1630–1673) in Utrecht and Jacob van Biesen[31] (d. 1677) in Arnhem, indicate that the provinces of Utrecht and Guelders were not left cold by Puritanism either. This is, then, another aspect in which Franciscus Burmannus[32] (1628-1679), Oomius and Sprat were accurate, as

---

24  This study, 211-215.
25  Eggermont.
26  Op 't Hof [2008-2], 52–53; Op 't Hof [2004-2], 62–63.
27  Op 't Hof [1987-1], 441–455; Frijhoff, 84–92; Op 't Hof [2016-5].
28  Op 't Hof [1987-1], 423–437.
29  Alblas.
30  Op 't Hof and Huisman [2016].
31  Op 't Hof [2013-3], 219–234.
32  Broeyer [2015-1].

they implicitly spoke of the entire Dutch Republic displaying the phenomenon.

The pronouncedly devotional nature, pastoral focus and everyday applicability of Puritan preaching were not only enormously appealing to Dutch clergymen but set an example that they wished to follow by taking on the Puritan preaching manner wholesale. On the one hand, these efforts will have been the consequence of preachers' personal preferences; on the other, they will also have been won over to this style by the proof of experience that the Puritan preaching method went down well with their congregations. In addition, congregants may have positively urged their ministers to preach the Word in the Puritan manner.[33]

The ablest preachers will have had no trouble working Puritan elements into original sermons of their own; van Laren was one such preacher. The less able and/or the more bone idle of the nation's preachers took refuge in the practice of lifting sermons lock, stock and barrel from an existing Puritan sermon, embellished with their own wording and adaptations. Presumably, given the scarce knowledge of English in the period, most such preachers based their borrowed efforts on a translation of the original. Yet the risk was not imaginary that the more serious listeners of such a preacher would already possess the published translation in question and that the pastor's jolly good sermon would be unmasked as second-hand material. Van Velsen, then, represents to us the clerical type who were too crafty to be caught out that way. This is why he hired his old fellow-student to extract the gist of sermons not yet available in Dutch translation, so as to be able to pass off his delivery as 'new material'. The number of sermon précis that Elgersma knocked out for him, over two hundred of them, is highly telling. In practice, that converts to more than four years' Puritan material for van Velsen to charm his congregation with; and they imagining all the while that the reverend was a master pulpiteer.

There is no doubt that Elgersma was reputed as one of the best men of the cloth. Not for nothing was his name proposed in 1664 for a theology lecturer's post at Franeker.[34] Might not he himself have succumbed likewise to the temptation to work Puritan sources into his exposition? It might yet prove that careful research will be able to demonstrate that he, too, was indebted to the Puritans for his renown.

---

33  This would probably serve to explain the tendency towards Puritanism that van der Haar detected in another Frisian preacher, Gellius Boëtius: Van der Haar [1988]; Breuker [2015-1].
34  Boeles, 2:245.

# 8. MILITARY AND PIETY
## English and Scots soldiers and their Puritan influence in the Dutch Republic

*At first sight, the title of this chapter might cause some puzzlement and could give rise to misconceptions. What have soldiers to do with Pietists?[1] Are these not generally two mutually exclusive categories of men? Besides his possible surprise, the reader of the above title might labour under the misapprehension that it refers to some sort of military brutality to snuff out instances of Puritan devotion in the Netherlands. But if that is not what is meant, then what is this chapter all about?*

*From 1585 onwards, some five or six thousand soldiers from the British realms were on active duty in the fledgling Dutch Republic. The numbers of these troops on duty in the country must have risen by degrees from then on, for in the final three decades of the Eighty Years' War, there were around 13,000 British fighting men in the country in all, serving in four English and two Scots regiments, each of which had its own chaplain.[2] The Scotsmen actually stayed in service to the United Provinces until 1782.[3] In fact, soldiers were the largest contingent of the British resident community in the Netherlands.*

*It is remarkable that before their ranks were purged by Archbishop William Laud and the English Ambassador William Boswell in 1633, the English and Scots army chaplains stationed in the Dutch Republic were almost unanimously nonconformist Puritans. Obviously, that composition of the chaplains could never have been possible were it not for the fact that most of the English, and indeed Scots, officers were of that same spiritual and ecclesiastical persuasion.[4] Armed with this knowledge, we can now take a second look at the chapter title and will now grasp its meaning better, although we*

---

1 That the two can overlap is clear enough from Carl Hinrichs' study on 'Preußentum' and Pietism, an entire chapter of which is devoted to the relationship between Pietism and the military: Hinrichs, 126–173. However, that study covers the eighteenth century, thus falling outwith the scope of this book.
2 Sprunger [1982], 5.
3 Sprunger [1982], 263. For the role played by Scots in Dutch military service, see Ferguson.
4 Sprunger [1982], 264–265; Trim, 243–258.

*have still not seen what the influence referred to in the sub-heading refers to. That is what the body of this chapter will do.*

*The chapter below will first review two Englishmen and a Scot who served as actual soldiers, then an English army chaplain, each of whom played a modest part in Puritanising Dutch spiritual life, and finally we shall direct our gaze towards two Dutchmen, Further Reformation preachers who were very significantly (in one case) and moderately (in the other) subjected to Puritan influence from military men from across the North Sea. The contacts that the latter had, and the activities arising from those contacts, even spurred him on to advocate the armed resistance that the militant Scots Presbyterians were mounting.*

**Henry Hexham**
Henry Hexham[5] (d. 1658) was born, probably in the 1580s, in Holland, south-eastern Lincolnshire. For religious reasons, he decided to enter the service of the English troops of the Army of the States-General. Being of gentle birth, he served as page to another English soldier in the States-General army, Sir Francis Vere (1560–1609), from 1600 to 1606. In that post, he witnessed the Siege of Ostend. Hexham probably owed this appointment to a relative, Sir Christopher Heydon (1561–1623), who had long been a comrade of Vere's. In the years after 1606, Hexham pursued his army career, achieving the rank of captain as quartermaster to Sir Horace Vere's Regiment, whose command was taken over in 1633 by Colonel George Goring (1608–1657). Hexham was on the scene during the key military events of the age.

Hexham spent the Twelve Years' Truce at Dordrecht, where he befriended the clergyman and later Leiden professor Johannes Polyander[6] (1568–1646), under whose preaching he often sat. In 1632, he returned to Delft, a city in which he had previously resided. Here, too, he maintained close contacts with not just English but also native preachers, especially Dionysius Spranckhuysen[7] (1587–1650). Although his efforts met with little success at first, he sought to leverage these connections to keep the English Church at Delft (newly founded in 1636) free of nonconformist and Independent influences. Also in 1636, he is documented as collaborating to that end with the English Ambassador to the Netherlands, Sir William Boswell (d. 1650). Not until 1645, under the ministry of Alexan-

---

5   Markham, 318, 447–50; Scheurweghs, 133–134, 145–146; Osselton, 35–42; Sprunger [1982], 158–61, 267; Op 't Hof [1987-1], 417–422; Hoftijzer.
6   Lamping [2001]; Op 't Hof [1983-2].
7   Leurdijk [1987].

der Petrie, did the church elect officers, among whom Hexham was numbered: first, in 1645, as deacon and clerk, and later, in 1648, as elder. He died in the first half of 1658.

Hexham was one who did battle with Rome not only with arms but also with that instrument mightier than the sword: the pen. He translated two of Polyander's anti-papist works from French to English and augmented the Dutch Book of Martyrs by Adriaan van Haemstede[8] (d. 1562) with several extracts from the French Book of Martyrs by Jean Crespin (d. 1572) and from its English equivalent by John Foxe (1517–1587). He also wrote five works to enthuse his fellow Englishmen for the Dutch struggle against the Spaniards, which he regarded as above all a war of religion. Four of the five were reports of military climaxes of his day, three of which went on to be translated into Dutch. He also wrote an influential military manual and translated a French book on the science of fortification.

A versatile character, Hexham deployed his skills in various cultural domains, for instance translating the world atlas of Gerardus Mercator (1512–1594) and Johannes Hondius. He gained a far greater reputation, however, in the new science of lexicography, compiling both an English-Dutch and a Dutch-English dictionary. The former was reprinted twice; the latter once.

Hexham's ecclesiastical convictions are indicated by his translation into Dutch of a speech by the Archbishop of Canterbury, William Laud (1573–1645), defending measures taken by the Church of England against its opponents. However, Hexham was not intolerant, militant or exclusivist in his churchmanship. When the chaplain of Sir Horace Vere's Regiment expressed his qualms about using the Book of Common Prayer, Hexham had no hesitation in copying into the chaplain's Bible his own translation of the formularies used in the Dutch Reformed Church. Most likely, the tie that bound the two men was a shared predilection for Pietism. It will have been the Puritan dimension of Hexham's character that mitigated his Church of England convictions and that rendered him amenable to those who, while Puritan in their Pietist tendencies, had different opinions to his own on matters of liturgy and church government.

Three translations by Hexham that gave vent to his Puritan sentiments went to press. The first, published in 1611, was of a work by Thomas Tuke (d. 1657), entitled *De conincklicke wech tot den hemel*, originally published two years previously as *The high-way to heaven*. It addresses election in eternity past, its application in time, and glory in eternity future.

---

8  Jelsma.

By making this translation, Hexham supplied the contribution of a foreigner in the Netherlands to the dogmatic strife between Remonstrants and Contra-Remonstrants. Given that he translated Tuke, there is no doubt that Hexham sided with the Contra-Remonstrants.

There is more, however, to be said about Tuke's work than that. It is a book that brings out the interplay between the doctrine of double predestination and the anthropological outworking of pneumatology. It is the latter pole of this interplay that has a Pietist character in Tuke: there is a focus on the offices of the Holy Spirit to—and, above all, in—man, with plenty of room accorded to experience and emotion. On the burning question of assurance, Tuke makes the latter pole the touchstone to determine one's status in the former.

1632 saw the publication of Hexham's second translation, *Een tractaet des gheloofs, waer in word verklaert hoe men door 't geloove kan leven, ende in alle benautheden troost vinden: den swacken christenen bysonderlick toe-ge-eygent*. Its author was Ezekiel Culverwell (1560–1631) and its original title was *A treatise of faith: vvherein is declared how a man may liue by faith, and finde releefe in all his necessities. Applied especially vnto the vse of the weakest Christians* (1623). The full title on its own is sufficient to indicate that this is a Pietist work through and through. The same is true, albeit to a slightly lesser extent, of the 1639 publication of Hexham's third translation, *Sekere on-weder-leggelijcke propositien [...] Aengaende eeden ende verbonden* [*Certaine irrefragable propositions worthy of serious consideration* (1639)] by Bishop Joseph Hall (1574–1656).

A remarkable character, Hexham thus wrote on a plethora of subjects. As such, he played a major role in Anglo-Dutch cultural exchange. Given his religious motivation early in life to enrol in the English forces fighting for the Dutch Republic, it is no surprise that he was concerned with theological matters. The three translations to his name introduce the Dutch reader to Puritan piety, although he did not achieve great influence with them: only his translation of Tuke was reprinted (twice, in 1614 and 1649).

**Sir Edward Harwood**

Sir Edward Harwood (1581–1632) was born in the parish of Thurlby, Lincolnshire. In about 1597, he went to the Netherlands to serve as a military page. In 1607, he was promoted to captain of a company of 150 foot soldiers. Around the same time, he came to the notice of Prince Maurice of Nassau[9] (1567–1625), who appointed him to his Privy Chamber. From

---

9  Van Deursen [2000].

1609–1610, he was back in England. In 1614, he was knighted by James I (1566–1625). In 1626, he was one of the four colonels whom the English army had put at the disposal of the States-General of the Netherlands. He was struck and died during the Siege of Maastricht in 1632. He left £100 in his will to be distributed for pious uses chosen by godly ministers.[10]

*Sir Edward Harwood*

---

10  Trim, 244.

The reason for his being featured in this chapter is that he exerted his good offices with Prince Maurice to have the Puritan William Ames[11] (1576–1633) appointed professor at Franeker. During his eleven-year tenure there, Ames won over countless young Dutchmen and a great number of Hungarian students for Puritanism, and in the longer term his influence was considerable.[12] Ultimately, all this was due to Harwood, himself an outspoken Puritan[13] and a military man who made it his business to help Puritan views and practices find acceptance in the Netherlands while he was serving there.

**John Fargharson**
The third military man whom we shall now consider for his part in Puritanising the spiritual scene in the seventeenth-century Netherlands was not an Englishman but a Scot: John Fargharson.[14] His name and his service in a Scots company are sufficient proof that he was not from south of the border. Besides nationality, there is another difference between Hexham and Fargharson. While Hexham is associated with the province of Holland (the cities of Dordrecht and Delft), Fargharson's influence was in the eastern province of Overijssel and particularly in the provincial capital, Zwolle, and in the northern province of Friesland. Every time that Fargharson is named in historical sources, he is identified as the ensign of Captain Archibald Bethune, also a Scot. The fact that Fargharson's wife's name was Margaretha Spruyt indicates that he married locally after his deployment. The source material on him covers only the years 1618–1627.

Fargharson's name is preserved for posterity as translator of two Puritan works. His first effort was *De alghemeyne verthooninghe der heyligher Schriftueren*, published in 1618, a Dutch translation of Welsh Puritan Hugh Broughton's book *A concent of Scripture* (1590). As a work, its aim is to promote understanding of the Bible. It cannot be ruled out altogether that translator and author were personally acquainted, since Broughton served as minister of the English Church at Middelburg from approximately 1605 to 1611. Be that as it may, Fargharson's total silence about any personal connection makes this a not very likely possibility.

---

11  Visscher; Sprunger [1972]; Van Vliet; Van 't Spijker [2015].
12  Cf. van Vliet.
13  Bush, 166–171.
14  Op 't Hof [1993-3].

Fargharson dedicated this first translation to the stadtholder of Friesland, Willem Lodewijk of Nassau[15] (1560–1620), and to the Provincial Executive of Friesland. The dedication itself states the following. Fargharson has made the translation with two purposes: first, to edify others, and second, so that the English church can build up her Dutch sister. He can perfectly well foresee that others—even comrades and fellow countrymen—will deride him for his pains: some will no doubt make it the butt of their jokes that a soldier should take up amateur theology, others will perhaps find it hilarious that such a slender volume should have been dedicated to such high and mighty statesmen. His rejoinder to the first group of anticipated mockers is that the knowledge of Holy Writ is even more essential for men-at-arms than it is for those in other callings. The second objection is parried with his contention that it is out of a profound sense of personal gratitude that he has made his dedication to these figures. He praises their zeal for the Word of God, for the church and for doctrine (by which he means the Contra-Remonstrant position). He adds that he also intends this translation as a rival to a book that had already been dedicated by a clergyman of the province of Utrecht to Prince Maurice and all army officers, a collection of dialogues by Desiderius Erasmus (d. 1536) and Lucianus, published in 1612–1613.[16] Fargharson objects to that clergyman's claim that the work is devotional: in reality, it contains idle and immoral matters inappropriate to a Christian. Fargharson goes on to make clear that his translation and its dedication came about at the instigation of some godly close friends of his. The address of this dedication to the rulers of Friesland will have reflected the fact that the unit in which Fargharson served had previously operated in that province.[17]

Fargharson's second translation was of *The doctrine and vse of repentance* (1608) by a London vicar, Richard Stock (d. 1626). The translation, which came out in 1627, was entitled *De stemme Iohannes des dopers, dat is: een uytnemend tractaet van de leere ende nutticheyt der waere-boetveerdicheyt*. This edition has three distinct sets of preliminaries, sold by two different Kampen booksellers. One of these booksellers was the printer of the work, Frans Jurissen; the other was the publisher, Jacob Roelofsen Steenbarch. One variant belongs to Jurissen, and two to Steenbarch. On all versions of the title page, the translation establishes his credentials as a Pietist in a most exceptional manner, by announcing that he translated

---

15 Wagenaar; Emmius.
16 Bijl, 285–293. The preacher in question was Andreas van Oosterbeeck, minister of the parish of Montfoort.
17 Ferguson, 1:232.

the work for the consolation of all pious hearts that are stricken and afflicted, for those who groan under the weight of their sins and who are penitent, and also for the upbraiding of all careless worldlings who relish their sins and revel in them. The work itself consists of typical Puritan matter.

All versions of Fargharson's translation carry an identical dedication, which is to Catharina van Eck, wife of the outspoken nonconformist[18] Thomas Holles, captain of an English company, and to Mechteld Ripperda,[19] wife of the clerk of Overijssel, Herman Roelinck[20]. The dedication lauds the knowledge of Christ that both ladies have, their true repentance and their eagerness to read the Word of God. The translator also intimates here that it was these ladies who urged him to translate the work. This is the first recorded instance in history of women's role in the translation of Puritan books.

In two variants, the dedication is followed by three poems recommending the work, written by (in sequence) the printer-publisher and man of letters Zacharias Heyns[21] (1566–1638); the Zwolle clergyman and co-translator of Puritan books Everhardus Schuttenius[22] (d. 1655); and Catharina Holles (*née* van Eck). One might take this series of poems to indicate the existence of a Puritan-minded group in Zwolle.

Yet did such a group actually exist; are there any other suggestions of it? There are indeed, and not a few. In the first place, Holles was one of the two addressees of Schuttenius' dedication of the 1628 edition of his translation of the Puritan Lewis Bayly's (d.1631) Puritan manual *De practycke ofte oeffeninghe der godtsaligheyt* [*The practise of pietie* (1612)], where Schuttenius calls Holles a fine example of real piety. From the 1620 first edition onwards, this translation was preceded by a sonnet by Heyns in praise of the work. The first volume of Schuttenius' magnum opus *Den christelicken ridder* [The Christian knight] (1628/9) contained not one but two such poems by Heyns. Conversely, a Latin ode by Schuttenius, together with its Dutch translation, appears in Heyns' *Weg-wyser ter salicheyt onder een sinnebeeld van des werelts beschryvinge den christen wandelaer voorgestelt* [Signpost to salvation described to the Christian wanderer in the analogy of a world guide] of 1629. Fargharson's translation furnishes a further proof besides these of the bond between Schutte-

---

18  Stearns, 44, 49; Sprunger [1982], 304.
19  The renowned poet-preacher Johannes Vollenhove penned a verse on the occasion of her death in 1661: Vollenhove [1686], 229–230.
20  Gevers and Mensema, 95.
21  Briels [1974], 317–319; Meeus.
22  Op 't Hof [2009-1].

nius and Heyns, since Schuttenius' poem in the Scotsman's work is in Latin and the translation is by Heyns; a close partnership indeed.

There is more besides. The first volume of Schuttenius' translation of Hall's *Contemplationes Sionis*, covering the New Testament, was published in 1634 and was dedicated by the translator to several persons including Catharina van Eck, the wife of Holles, who had evidently been promoted to Lieutenant-Colonel that year. Schuttenius describes Holles as a "dear godly man" and writes of the man's wife, whom he has known for years, that she is known to all God-fearing Christians for her godliness and her zeal for Reformed congregations and preachers. All the indications are, then, that there was an Overijssel Pietist circle around Schuttenius in Zwolle, comprising all the aforementioned figures. Two of these were Puritans from Britain, both of them military men.

One more aspect must still be considered. All the members of the Zwolle circle are known to have been Pietists or Puritans, with one exception: Heyns, who practised a dogmatically and ecclesiastically indifferent Christianity in the tradition of Erasmus. How did he fit into the group? His non-denominationalism must surely have made him somewhat of an oddity in this Reformed coterie. It will have been the other aspect of Erasmianism, namely its emphasis on Biblicist, individualist and moralist lay piety, that was the common ground on which Heyns, indifferent to church affiliation, could stand with the Pietists and Puritans, despite their exactitude on such matters.[23]

The inscription in Fargharson's own hand in the copy of his second translation that he presented to the English Puritan army chaplain Samuel Bachiler (our next subject below) establishes the intimacy of their friendship. It reads: "Johan fargharson dois giue this boock to his dear freend M$^r$ Samuel Batchiler, in signe of Loue".[24]

## Samuel Bachiler

The early decades of the life of our next Englishman, Samuel Bachiler,[25] are altogether obscure. From 1620–1633, he served as chaplain to the Regiment of Colonel Charles Morgan, a band of English soldiers in the south-central Netherlands that was stationed in Heusden from 1620–1622 and in Gorinchem from 1622–1633. In 1636, he ministered to the English Church in Pariba (now Paraíba), Dutch Brazil, and from 1641–1644 he was incumbent at nearby Mauritsstad (now Recife).

---

23  Op 't Hof [1995].
24  The copy in question is in the library of the late Dr C. Steenblok, Gouda.
25  Sprunger [1982], index; Op 't Hof [1988-2].

In his Heusden period, Bachiler was mentored by a local brother minister of note, Gisbertus Voetius[26] (1589–1676). A fervent Puritan, Bachiler was viscerally opposed to the ceremonies of the Church of England and refused, with a few minor exceptions, to use the Book of Common Prayer. He was one of the eleven at whose initiative the English Synod in the Netherlands was founded and gradually became one of its most influential and active members. From 1631 onwards, he was its clerk. When his fellow minister John Forbes[27] (d. 1634) turned the form of church government of the congregation of the Merchant Adventurers at Delft from Presbyterianism towards Congregationalism in the 1630s, he was supported in so doing by (*inter alia*) Bachiler, who also occasionally preached for that congregation.

In 1633, Morgan, under pressure from London, dismissed Bachiler from his post, and Bachiler was ordered to appear in court in England on account of his nonconformist views. However, he was able to ignore the summons, thanks to the Dutch political connections that the English Synod enjoyed.

It was after this turn of events that Bachiler engineered his dispatch to Dutch Brazil as an army chaplain. In Pariba, he relieved the minister of the local Dutch church of his duties for seven or eight months in 1640 to allow him a furlough back in the Netherlands. Evidently, then, Bachiler had fluent Dutch. He also took an active part in the presbytery meetings, serving as assessor a few times.

After the encroachments of dementia forced him to resign his office and return to Gorinchem, Bachiler was given assistance by the Synod of Zuid-Holland in the years 1647–1649 for the sake of his six or seven needy children. However, a request by that synod to the States of Holland to support him was declined. Thereupon, the Synod turned to the English churches in the province and to its own constituent congregations with the same request. The Synod particularly asked the English merchants in Rotterdam, via the Dutch church officers of that city, to contribute. In 1650, Bachiler left for Cromwellian England, well supplied financially by the Gorinchem congregation. He is last documented alive in 1653.

It is known that in addition to the work discussed in the next paragraph, Bachiler wrote a commentary on the Book of Joshua, which Willem Teellinck[28] (1579–1629) desired to have published,[29] although his

---

26  Duker; Van Oort *et al.*; Andreas J. Beck.
27  De Jong.
28  Beeke [2003]; Op 't Hof [2008-1, 2011-1, 2015-1].
29  Op 't Hof [1983-1], 64–65.

# MILES CHRISTIANUS
## ofte
# HET CONINGLIICK VELD-LEGER,

Voorgestelt in corte *Betrachtingen* over de woorden des Propheeten *Mosis*,

*Deuter. 23.*
*Wanneer ghy uyt den Leger gaet* &c.

*vers. 14.*
*Want de Heere uwen God wandelt* &c.

Wtgegeven int Engelsch/
Door SAMVEL BACHILER, Engelsch Predicant resideerende tot Gorinchem.

Ende nu ten dienste niet alleen van alle Nederlandsche Crijchs-Heeren ende Crijchs-knechten/ Maer oock van alle vroome Christenen ende Lief-hebberen des Vader-Lands vertaelt.

TOT GROENINGEN,
By Hans Sas, Boeck-drucker Ordinaris/ woonende in de Heere-straet/ Anno 1628.

wish was never granted. In addition to friends already named, Bachiler was close to another English minister in the Netherlands, Thomas Scott[30] (d. 1626), and to Fargharson, discussed above.

The only published work by Bachiler is *Miles christianus, or the campe royal in briefe meditations on Deut. 23,9,14*, which came out at Amsterdam in 1625. Some of the print run was published with the revised title *The campe royal*, which is also the title borne by the 1629 second edition published in London. Bachiler's local brother minister Johannes Spiljardus[31] (1593–1658) handed out copies to fellow preachers; these were well received, with the result that a Dutch translation was made and published in 1628 under the title *Miles christianus ofte het coninglijck veld-leger*. The translation, almost certainly by Spiljardus, was never reprinted. The purpose of Bachiler's book is to promote the sanctification of the English troops in the Netherlands and to drive out the sins prevailing among them. The translator dedicates his efforts to Prince Frederik Hendrik[32] (1584–1647) and changes the original target audience, the English troops in the country, to the national army itself. While this was hardly a substantive change, since the English soldiers were a unit subordinate to the Dutch army, it did constitute an intensification of the Puritan call for the reformation of the Dutch army. An even more powerful call to the army, however, was yet to come—and again at Puritan instigation.

**Everhardus Schuttenius**
We need not consider here the biography or achievements in general of Zwolle preacher Everhardus Schuttenius[33] (d. 1655) here, as these will be covered by a chapter in Volume II. Here, we shall look more narrowly at the role played by English and Scots military men in Schuttenius' work and in his two-volume magnum opus. It is likely that he was won over even in his youth to the thought-world of Puritanism through contacts with just such soldiers. If so, then his studies in England were nothing more than the logical follow-up, as also was his dedication of his first translation to (among others) a Scots cavalry lieutenant, Hugh Montgomery. Due to the latter's death, he replaced his name with that of Holles in the 1628 edition.

---

30  Sprunger [1982], index.
31  Huisman [2010]; Op 't Hof [2016-12].
32  Poelhekke.
33  Op 't Hof [2009-1].

1628 also saw publication of the first volume of what can be regarded as Schuttenius' key work: *Den christelicken ridder, seer nut ende profytelick voor alle staten ende standen der menschen* [The Christian knight, most useful and profitable for all states and conditions of men]. Its authorial dedication, dated 26 September 1628, is to the Prince of Orange, Frederik Hendrik, in his capacity as commander-in-chief of land and maritime forces. Schuttenius explains that the first reason for the dedication being to him is that it is a work which sets forth the state of the church and of the children of God in the imagery of warfare. The second reason is that he intends for this book to reprove the great and heinous sins that are rife among soldiers who would claim the name of a Christian, such as cursing, oaths, blasphemy, drunkenness, gluttony, whoring, adultery, theft and murder. The book will also demonstrate, he adds, how these sins can be nipped in the bud. Things have reached such a pitch, he complains, that any man in the ranks who is not willing to go along with this godless manner of living will not be taken to be a worthy, brave soldier and will be mocked and derided. The wrath of God cannot fail to respond to this state of affairs. Indeed, according to the author, the godlessness of the military is the reason why the Anabaptists refuse to serve in it. Schuttenius warns that he does not spare any layer of society from criticism, since these impieties are in evidence among people of all classes.

The dedication goes on to explain that the writing of this book was occasioned by a request by some godly captains and officers for a work that would pierce many soldiers to the heart such as to cause them to repent of their ungodly lives. At the insistence of a number of people, Schuttenius explains, he is dedicating the work to Frederik Hendrik with a plea to set about the sorely-needed reformation of his army. He holds out to the prince the prospect that such a reformation will be answered with the Lord's blessing, a blessing that will also take the form of victories in the field.

Some copies of the 1628 edition append a second dedication to this first. It is addressed to all the officers in the service of the States-General and particularly to the officers of the Zwolle garrison. It was a group of captains and officers from that city's garrison who had urged Schuttenius to write the book in the first place. His threefold intention in writing *Den christelicken ridder*, he writes in this dedication, is: 1. to praise the soldier's calling; 2. to cause men to understand that they have a warfare to wage not only against physical enemies but first and foremost against those spiritual foes of the world, the flesh and the devil; 3. to stir readers up to have done with the prevailing sins, which are many and atrocious, among the Christian soldiery. While martial laws have already been

enacted against sins, they are being weakly enforced, he writes. At the Last Judgement, officers will have to render account to God for the spiritual life of their troops as well as for themselves.

This second dedication gives rise to the suspicion that the publication costs of *Den christelicken ridder* were met by the officers who instigated its writing. This would mean that the book was in the first instance a provincial affair specific to Overijssel.

The second volume of *Den christelicken ridder* came onto the market in 1638. Its dedication, dated 20 August 1638, is to Hendrik Casimir of Nassau (1612-1640), stadtholder of the northern provinces of Friesland, Groningen, Ommelanden and Drenthe. In it, Schuttenius writes that this volume will set out how soldiers in the battle spiritual are to don their armour and how they should use it against their enemies. While discussing the distinction that there ought to be between Christian and unbelieving soldiers, he remarks:

> It could be wished that this would be rather better embraced and noted in our day by all officers, captains and regular soldiers in our Christian armies; whereby, without doubt, God's righteous anger and wrath at the horrible sins committed and perpetrated not only outside but especially within our armies would be appeased and removed, and God's gracious blessing and victory against her enemies would again be obtained.[34]

At the time of his dedicating the first volume to Frederik Hendrik, Schuttenius explains, he had been intending to dedicate the second to Count Ernest Casimir (1573-1632), but owing to the latter's death in the interim, he is now dedicating it to his son, Hendrik Casimir.

It is very evident that Schuttenius intended his two-volume magnum opus to achieve a reformation of the Dutch army. He himself writes that it was at the urging of some godly captains and officers stationed at Zwolle that he wrote it. So who were these men? Since all the military officers known to have been in close contact with Schuttenius were Englishmen or Scots serving the Netherlands, it cannot but be the case that it was British captains and officers who instigated the writing of his military reformation blueprint. Specifically, based on the foregoing data, one's thoughts turn here to the Puritan soldiers Holles, Montgomery and Fargharson. This implies that the most important and most extensive Dutch work aimed at the religious and moral reform of the army came

---

34  Schuttenius [1638], (\*\*\*)6r.–v.

into being due to the stimulus of Puritan army officers. The appearance of the two volumes of *Den christelicken ridder* marks the apogee of influence that military men had in the Puritanisation of the spiritual life of the Netherlands.

Early seventeenth-century Zwolle, then, saw piety fostered by the presence of an army garrison. Is it unique as a city in that respect? The question is not a straightforward one to answer, but what is beyond contention is that the capital of Overijssel was an outstanding example of how political and military circumstances can have a knock-on effect on spiritual developments. Military life and religious life need not always be mutually exclusive!

**Jacobus Koelman**

The Reformed preacher Jacobus Koelman[35] (1631–1695) is another of our subjects whose life and work will be described at length in a dedicated chapter in Volume II. Consequently, we shall restrict ourselves here to his contacts with Puritan soldiers. As far as is known, such contacts arose in his life only after his banishment from Sluis in 1675, although it would not be fanciful to suppose that these contacts actually stemmed from an earlier period of his life. In the first year after the banishment, when he was staying in Rotterdam, he found himself in the immediate vicinity of the Scots Covenanters who had settled in that city. This community was made up not only of exiled Presbyterian preachers but also of soldiers of militant anti-Stuart tendency such as Colonel James Wallace (d. 1678) and Archibald Campbell, the Earl of Argyll (d. 1685). Koelman preached a good many times in the Scots Church in Rotterdam. Later on in life, he would do the same for a group of Scots in the Frisian provincial capital, who were Covenanters affiliated to the United Societies, having taken up arms against the King out of religious conviction. Heading this group of Scots in Leeuwarden were two military men: Sir Robert Hamilton and another Hamilton, a former captain in the Earl of Dumbarton's Regiment.[36] It is above all Koelman's intimacy with the Scots in Friesland which demonstrates that he had no objection to armed insurrection against the powers that be in Scotland.

Previous researchers have not spotted that Koelman even translated a pamphlet into his native language that justified the militant revolt against the Crown. This diatribe was published in 1681, without mention of the

---

35 Krull; Van Lieburg [1990]; Meeuse [1990, 2008]; Op 't Hof [2013-1], 237–268; Groenendijk [2017].
36 Sprunger [1982], index, under 'Koelman'.

year or place of publication, under the title *Een waarachtige en volkomene copye van 't nieuw covenant, of verbondt, onlangs in Schotlandt gemaakt, 't welk genoomen is uit de papieren van Henry Hall, en mr. Donald Cargill, tot Queens-Ferry, den 3. juny 1680. Nevens de verklaaring, en 't getuigenis van mr. Richard Cameron, en van verscheydene, die met hem waren* [A true and exact copy of a treasonable and bloody paper called The fanaticks new covenant which was taken from Mr. Donald Cargill at Queens-Ferry, June 3, 1680 one of their field-preachers, a declared rebel and traytor; together with their execrable declaration, published at the Cross of Sanquhair, on the 22. of the said month of June, after a solemn procession and singing of Psalms by Cameron, the notorious ring-leader of, and preacher at their field-conventicles, accompanied with twenty of that wicked crew]. The preface is signed by the translator, using his initials J.K. There is no reason to doubt that these stand for Jacobus Koelman. Supplementary arguments for this identity are that the translator refers to Koelman's magnum opus; that he speaks of a "longed-for reformation of morals"[37]; and that he himself took part in the laying-on of hands in 1679 when Cameron was consecrated to preach in the Scots Church in Rotterdam.

In his preface to the pamphlet, Koelman provides an overview of Scots church history from the time of the National Covenant in 1638 onwards. He describes how Charles II (1630–1685), having once accepted the Covenant in 1651 while in exile, shamefully broke with it in 1660 when he was restored as monarch of Scotland, England and Ireland, hideously persecuting and even killing his opponents. When Charles offered his Indulgence in 1669 to Scots preachers to permit them pulpit freedom under certain conditions, a faction of clergymen did not accept the deal, as they found it contrary to the Covenant by which both parties were bound. These non-indulged Covenanters, Koelman continues, took to the highways and byways to preach, bearing arms as they went to protect themselves from soldiers of the Crown. Two years before the writing of the preface, he adds, a few courageous souls of this confession had even burned all the acts of Parliament and Royal decrees directed against them. In 1680, two of these preachers, namely Donald Cargill (1619–1681) and Richard Cameron (d. 1680), even abjured the King's authority and openly broke with their brother ministers who had been weak enough to accept the conditions laid upon them for their permission to preach. The texts referred to, Koelman adds, will follow in the actual text of the pamphlet. Concluding his historical review, although the translator writes, "I leave

---

37 *Een waarachtige en volkomene copye van 't nieuw covenant* [1680], 3 and 4 respectively.

Een Waarachtige en volkomene Copye van

# 't NIEUW COVENANT,

*Of*

# VERBONDT,

Onlangs in *Schotlandt* gemaakt,

't Welk genoomen is uit de Papieren van *Henry Hall*, en *Mr. Donald Cargill*, tot *Queens-Ferry*, den 3. Juny 1680.

Nevens

*De* Verklaaring, *en* 't Getuigenis *van* M<sup>r</sup>. Richard Cameron, *en van verscheydene, die met hem waren.*

Gedrukt, en uitgegeven door Order van den *Geheymen Raadt* van zijn Majesteit, in gehoorzaamheidt aan zijn *Majesteyts* bevel, in zijn Brief, geschreven tot *Windsor-Castle*, den 5. *July* 1680.

Getrouwelijk uit het Engels Vertaalt, na de *Copye*, gedrukt tot *Edinburg*, by de Erfgenaam van *Andrew Anderson*, Drukker van zijn Majesteyt, Anno 1680.

it to the impartial reader to judge what is right or wrong in this affair", the reader is in no doubt at all that his sympathies lie with Cargill and Cameron.

Koelman's having translated the pamphlet and written such a preface indicates that he not only condoned rebellion against Charles II across the sea but also advocated this notion in his own land and was keen to promote it by garnering support for armed insurrection. This aspect of Koelman's activities has been altogether too little studied by church historians heretofore. We have every reason to start looking more closely into this aspect of Koelman's life. While that is beyond the scope of the present chapter, I would emphasise this research need as strongly as I can. Such future research ought not to be limited to Koelman only but should also encompass other Further Reformation men. It is striking, for instance, that when Robert Hamilton was seeking some route to ordination for James Renwick (1662–1688), a United Societies adherent, it was to Koelman's friend and spiritual ally Wilhelmus à Brakel[38] (1635–1711) that he turned.[39] It would appear that a clutch of Further Reformation clergymen were involved in one way or another with the Scots Covenanters' armed resistance. Whereas the relations between British soldiers and Dutch promoters of piety had been largely law-abiding and devotional in nature during the Eighty Years' War, they took on an armed and subversive tone in the 1670s and 1680s. This being so, our chapter has ended with an unexpected twist.

---

38 Los; Op 't Hof [2015-7].
39 Howie, 530–531.

# 9. SHOPS OPENED ON EASTER MONDAY 1673
## An unique instance of further reformation at Sluis

*The fortified town of Sluis, which sits in the south-western corner of the Netherlands on the Belgian border and which has long served as the district centre of western Zeeland-Flanders, has always had a defiant attitude towards trading hours regulations. In the late twentieth century, Sluis shopkeepers were among the first in the whole country to throw their doors open on the Lord's Day. This chapter considers a comparably revolutionary act as far back as the seventeenth century in the same town. However, amongst all the superficial similarities between the two events, there is one great difference. Whereas opening the shops on the Lord's Day in the twentieth century was a testament to the total disappearance of Calvinist principles and practice from Sluis, opening for business on Easter Monday in 1673 was the deliberate opposite: the direct consequence of a remarkable form of Calvinism, or more properly of Puritanism. How times change!*

**Calvinisation**[1]
When, in 1604, Sluis was definitively wrested from the Spaniards by the Army of the States-General, one of the obvious ramifications was that the Dutch Reformed Church supplanted the Roman Catholic Church as the official confession. The congregation at Sluis then saw an unbroken succession of resolute Calvinists as incumbents, who at once made targeted and determined efforts to Calvinise local society.

Unlike the little town of Aardenburg (less than three miles distant), Sluis retained the overwhelming majority of its indigenous population after the victory of the Dutch Republic; most probably, around 90% of its citizens stayed put. Nevertheless, Sluis society was transformed relatively quickly from a Roman Catholic to a Reformed model. The reasons for this are to be found in a complex of arguments, at least five of them: the

---
1 For this section, see Op 't Hof [2004-1].

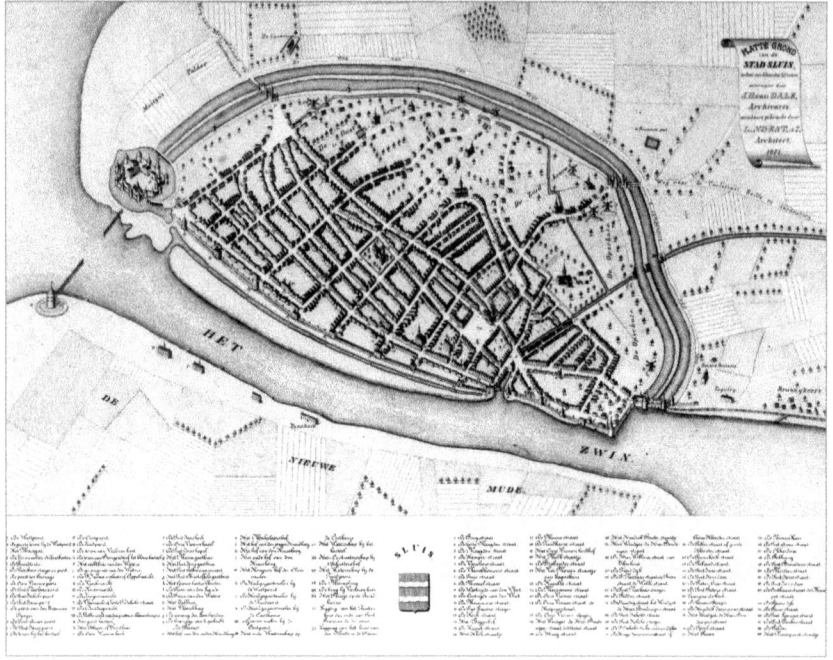

tactical, political, social, demographic and religious strands of motivation.

After the rout of the Habsburg forces, not all Roman Catholics were cleared out at once from the key political and social functions of the city's life. In the early years of Dutch rule, the policy followed was that of a tactical phased transition; consequently, the locals did not feel antagonised to the point of resenting the Reformed Church. The political factor blew plenty of wind into the sails of the Calvinisation agenda at Sluis. Those eager to attain the top rung of the social ladder in the city could not avoid dealing with the Reformed Church: most signally, a confessing membership of the Church was an absolute prerequisite to candidacy for the city council. The social strand was no less important in people's motivations for conversion: the strings of local education were now being pulled by Reformed hands. The Reformed church officers, together with the (likewise fully Reformed-membership) council, appointed the teachers, and the Religious Education curriculum at the schools was Calvinistic in tenor. Thus, the rising generation of Sluis was now steeped in Reformed views and codes of conduct. Other key local-level institutions of the era, such as the orphanage and the parish poor relief, were also under the management of the city's Reformed congregation.

A fourth important reason for the shift in affiliations is the considerable influx of refugees from religious persecution, largely a Calvinist-minded intake. The border of Spanish Flanders lay just to the south and west of Sluis, and in the first years especially after the States' conquest of the city, it received a stream of newcomers, particularly from Ostend, which the Spaniards took in 1604. A final factor in the explanation, and one not to be overlooked, has to do with the fact that Reformed preachers were typically highly-educated and always driven men. Without the skills, passion and massive commitment that these clergymen brought to bear, Sluis could never have been turned into a Reformed city—at least one ostensibly so—in such short order.

The first two arguments could not have held true if the many citizens who remained in Sluis after the transfer of military, political and ecclesiastical power had been staunch Roman Catholics. The fact that they remained *in situ* also indicates that other factors and motives were more pressing for them than loyalty to the Church of Rome. This situation brought about a remarkable ambiguity in the Calvinisation of Sluis: on the one hand, there were indifferent nominal Roman Catholics in the local population, forming a somewhat biddable and thus promising constituency for the Reformed conversion drive. On the other hand, the flip side of this malleability was that the new flock of the Reformed Church proved to be just as indifferent and unmotivated about their acquired faith than they had been about the one they had been born into. As it swelled its ranks with many ex-Roman Catholics, the Reformed Church of Sluis was also garnering what would become a persistent source of religious apathy and nominalism. What the city's Protestant congregation was actually doing was sacrificing quality for quantity, and the prevalence of a mixed multitude in this border city proved fertile soil for the rise and later flourishing of piety tendencies: Reformed Pietism[2] in general and the Pietistic and theocratic movement of the Further Reformation[3] in particular.

**Reformed variety**
For most practitioners and aficionados of history as a discipline, the concept of Calvinism in the Netherlands of the so-called Golden Age is all much of a muchness. Most will have read something of the struggle between the Remonstrants and the Contra-Remonstrants that came to a head during the Twelve Years' Truce and was officially resolved at the

---
2 Op 't Hof [2005-1].
3 Graafland *et al.*

Synod of Dort (1618–1619), and they will (correctly) regard the Remonstrants, whom the Reformed Church excluded during and excommunicated following that Synod, as not falling under the heading of Calvinism in the Dutch Republic. What many will not appreciate, however, is the extent and asperity of the struggle that ensued *within* the national Reformed Church.

Yet such struggles there very much were. The Dutch Reformed Church was anything but a body united and at peace with herself even after the sharpness of the Synod was past. She presented a united front to the outside world as far as she could, but in truth she was rent by divisions: real and sometimes profound ones. Political figures, having been given a rude awakening by the twists and turns of the Remonstrance controversy and now wise to the risks, kept a watchful eye on the internal tensions of the established denomination in order to avoid internal Reformed divisions becoming interwoven with tussles in civil government. They were so determined to keep order that they did not hesitate to involve themselves in local, provincial and even national ecclesiastical affairs, nor were they shy about using their temporal sway to tackle and defuse cases of *odium theologicum* within the Reformed Church.

So what were these substantial internal divisions within the established church of the United Provinces?[4] First and foremost, they had to do with the variety of interpretations that there were of the resolutions of the Synod of Dort. Many clergymen had, for the sake of peace in the church or merely to hold on to their living and their social status, assented to the Canons of Dort through clenched teeth, or genuinely submitted themselves to the official theology although not previously convicted of it. Although there was a wave of ejections from the Dutch Reformed Church with the promulgation of the Canons in 1619, the less doughty of the Remonstrant preachers and those not resolutely convinced of Arminianism stayed on board. We can, however, also consider the non-Remonstrant wing of the clergy and wonder how many even of them could say a hearty amen to all the formulations of the Synod of Dort. The doctrinal diversity that had so characterised the Dutch Reformed as a denomination before 1618 was by no means removed in 1619.

Besides this, opinions varied sharply on some matters within the strongly Contra-Remonstrant wing of the Church. One such point of contention was the relationship between church and state: while the majority of Contra-Remonstrants advocated the position that the Church was sovereign over her own affairs, some of their brethren had no particular

---

4   For this and the next paragraph, see Op 't Hof [1991], 84–86.

problem with government intervention. As it turned out, the whole Contra-Remonstrant party had to deal with the refusal of the national government and most of the provincial governments to ratify the Synod's new ecclesiastical law, the Dort Church Order. Nor were the Contra-Remonstrants united on all matters of dogma. Even at the Synod itself, a major division became painfully apparent regarding the doctrine of election, and the point in question was deliberately left unaddressed in the Canons: that of the supralapsarian versus infralapsarian chronology of salvation.

Another matter of controversy among Calvinists yawned open at Dort: the celebration of the Lord's Day.[5] This appeared at first sight containable to a lower synodal level, as the argument was openly raging only among the Zeeland delegates. When the delegates convened, however, it came to light that this contention was not unknown in other provinces. Accordingly, the theology professors in attendance were asked to discourse with the brethren from Zeeland to hammer out a compromise wording in a stay-behind meeting after the Synod's main business had been seen to and the foreign delegates dismissed. The idea was that both wings of the Sabbath dispute would then be expected to honour that text pending a definitive resolution of the matter at the next National Synod. However, the civil government of the Netherlands never again countenanced the convocation of a national synod after Dort!

In addition, the latter half of the seventeenth century saw a controversy break out between Johannes Coccejus[6] (1603–1669) and Gisbertus Voetius[7] (1589–1676) and their respective adherents, one which would hold the Reformed Church in its grip for some hundred years and which chiefly raged about the matters of forgiveness of sins and Sabbatarianism.[8]

There was one last serious division among the Contra-Remonstrants. One party was made up of partisan souls for whom dogmatic polemicism was the duty above all duties. The other consisted of those Calvinists whose focus was not so much on the refutation of erroneous doctrines themselves as it was on bringing about a reformation of the sins that lay at the root of such heresies. The former party was concerned above all with the orthodoxy of the Reformed faith; the latter with its orthopraxy.

---

5  For the following, see H.B. Visser, 62–67; Op 't Hof [1991], 124.
6  Van Asselt [1997, 2001].
7  Duker; *De onbekende Voetius*; Andreas J. Beck.
8  Broeyer and van der Wall.

**Reformed Pietism and the Further Reformation at Sluis**
The tendency within Dutch Calvinism that placed piety at the centre of its theology and practice is referred to as Reformed Pietism. These Reformed Pietists—a substantial proportion of whom were preachers—propagated their views from the pulpit, during pastoral visits and in personal exchanges, but above all via the printed word. Since (with a few exceptions) the first three of these means of dissemination leave no sources behind for us to consult, the present researcher has had recourse almost exclusively to the extant books of the movement in order to identify particular persons as Reformed Pietists and to characterise the peculiarities of their individual strands of Pietism.

Pietist books form not just an important[9] segment but also a segment in their own right[10] of book production in the seventeenth-century Netherlands in general. Since 1987, a bibliographical reference work has been available that brings together almost all the Pietist publications originating in the Netherlands.[11] If we lay the list of Reformed preachers who had the living of Sluis in the seventeenth century alongside that bibliography, we make the startling discovery that no fewer than seven of them are known Pietists. In the chronological order in which they served the congregation of Sluis, they are:[12] Johannes van Dorth[13] (1638–1654), Nicolaus Barenzonius[14] (1642–1644), Jodocus van Lodensteyn[15] (1649–1652), Adriaan Cocquius[16] (1653–1662), David Montanus[17] (1656–1687), Jacobus Koelman[18] (1662–1675) and Casparus Alardin[19] (1682–1684). Three of them even published Pietist works while incumbent at Sluis: one publication in the case of Cocquius, and several each in the cases of Montanus and Koelman.

The fact that there were seven Pietist preachers in the city during the period of 1638–1687, and that their years in post overlapped each other, gives us sufficient grounds for describing the Reformed congregation of

---

9   Van Lieburg [1989].
10  Op 't Hof [1993-2, 2013-3, 2014].
11  Van der Haar [1987].
12  Van der Haar [1987], 112, 19–20, 281–287, 86, 319–320, 244–250, 5–6 respectively.
13  Op 't Hof [2015-15].
14  Op 't Hof [2015-3].
15  Trimp, 46–50.
16  Op 't Hof [2015-12].
17  Ros [1995]; Op 't Hof [2016-6].
18  Krull; Van Lieburg [1990]; Meeuwse [1990, 2008]; Op 't Hof [2013-1], 237–268; Groenendijk [2017].
19  Exalto [1976], 86–92; Op 't Hof [1999-3]; Florijn [2015-1].

Sluis in that period as pronouncedly Pietist in character. Consistent with this is Koelman's positive appreciation of his immediate predecessors: Barenzonius, Balduinus Cousemaker (d. 1647), Cornelius van der Lingen (d. 1651), van Lodensteyn and Cornelius Hauchepied (1625–1657).[20] Their terms of preaching office in the city cover the years 1642–1656. Koelman signally omits to mention Cocquius in his appreciative remarks. The reason for this must be that the latter predecessor of Koelman's had left a negative impression on him when Cocquius visited the Reformed Church of Sluis in late April 1673 as part of a visitation committee from the district presbytery. The Pietist works written in the manses of Sluis demonstrate that the *floruit* of Reformed Pietism in the city was the years 1653–1687.

The Further Reformation went beyond Reformed Pietism by converting the latter's striving for piety into programmes and theocratically-minded actions. To what extent could Sluis be said to have been a locus of the Further Reformation? Of the city's seven Pietist preachers, four bear the label of being Further Reformation figures: van Dorth, van Lodensteyn, Montanus and Koelman. That is not to say that there were very few Further Reformation advocates in Sluis, but rather that these are only ones whose allegiance to the Further Reformation can to date be proven beyond doubt, and that there are no proofs or arguments regarding the adherence of the others, as yet. The years in which these four known Further Reformation men served Sluis were 1638–1687. We note that this corresponds exactly with the city's seven-Pietists period, and this therefore means that Pietism manifested itself in Sluis predominantly in its theocratic form, the Further Reformation. The greatest climax of the Further Reformation in Sluis was Koelman's ministry, who behind Willem Teellinck[21] (1579–1629) can justly be regarded as the most important proponent[22] of the Further Reformation. Teellinck drafted the movement's most wide-ranging programme of reform, published at Middelburg in 1627 under the title *Noodwendigh vertoogh* [Necessary exposition]. In 1678, Koelman's offering in the same genre was published in nearby Vlissingen, becoming the second most significant reformation blueprint: *De pointen van nodige reformatie, ontrent de kerk, en kerkelijke, en belijders der Gereformeerde Kerke van Nederlandt* [The points of needful reformation regarding the church and church affairs, and confessing members of the Reformed Church of the Netherlands]. While that is in

---

20  Theophilus Parresius [1677], 1.
21  Beeke [2003]; Op 't Hof [2008-1, 2011-1, 2015-1].
22  For this conception, see Graafland *et al.*, 171.

itself reason enough to regard Koelman as Teellinck's only serious contender for the title of most prominent Further Reformation leader, Koelman has another string to his bow: he was unrivalled in his drive at both parish and presbytery level to achieve substantial results in practice for the ideals and aims of the Further Reformation. As he was only able to serve one congregation in his clerical career, all his efforts were played out in States-Flanders, within the fortified walls of Sluis.

**Sluis**
To understand properly the incessant struggle in which Koelman engaged for a thoroughgoing reformation of ecclesiastical, social and political morals in Sluis, it is essential that we first outline the standing that Sluis as a city had in the regional and national frameworks of church and state and that we then look at the arrangements of political, social and church government locally.

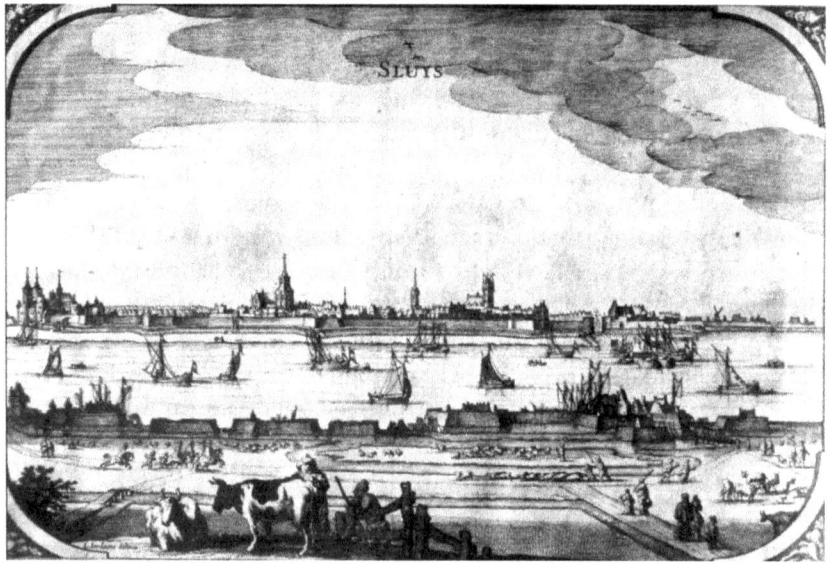

The Dutch Republic was a nation with two central organs of government: the States-General and the Council of State. However, as the name United Provinces indicates, the real fulcrum of national politics was not in The Hague at all: it was the resolutions of the States of the individual provinces that really counted. These were carried by provincial deputies to the States-General, which was obliged to translate them into the terms of reference of national government. Dutch politics in the Republican era was thus entirely devolved, its agenda riddled with the parochial concerns of each province. Sluis was, however, an exceptional case: it was situated in States-Flanders, which was not a province at all but a Generality. Due to their liminal status as territorial outliers, these Generalities had no home rule (so the writ of the States of Zeeland did not run in Sluis); they were directly governed from The Hague, more specifically by the Council of State. Consequently, Sluis had direct lines of contact to The Hague and the state councillors sitting there.

States-Flanders' ecclesiastical status, however, did not match the political lie of the land: it fell under Zeeland for synodal purposes. The western half of the territory was part of the Walcheren presbytery of the Zeeland provincial synod; the eastern half belonged to its Zuid-Beveland presbytery. However, as the wide Western Scheldt divides Zeeland-Flanders from the island of Walcheren, it was known to happen, especially in winter, that inclement weather prevented the States-Flemish delegates' attendance at presbytery sessions.

The Reformed Church in the Netherlands followed in the wake of the nation's particularist organisation of government by herself being not a single hierarchical body but rather an affiliation of the provincial churches. Many of these constituent churches even had their own ecclesiastical law, including Zeeland, whose Church Order was established in 1591. Because the provincial churches were forbidden by the civil government from gathering together in national synod after the upheavals of Dort, they developed a system of mutual consultation by correspondence, whereby each provincial synod maintained one or two correspondents in the others. The States of Zeeland, however, even forbade the Church of Zeeland from participating in that national church coordination.

Each provincial church consisted in turn of a number of district presbyteries. The Church of Zeeland had four of them, corresponding with the larger island groups: Walcheren, Schouwen with Duiveland, Zuid-Beveland, and Tholen with Bergen op Zoom. The latter name preserves for posterity that the south-western corner of what is now the province of Noord-Brabant was ecclesiastically part of Zeeland during the Republican era. There was one exception provided for in the geographical subdivision of the Reformed Church: the Huguenots, known to the Dutch as the Walloon (*Waals*) Church, were permitted to have their own synod. Consisting in practice of a single national presbytery, it had representation from every French Calvinist congregation in the United Provinces.

While one might speak loosely of the Reformed Church as having been the established church of the United Provinces, its status was derived solely from the fact that it had the unique privilege of political recognition. Even this role was an artefact of this church's having taken over the function of the Roman Catholic Church as the public confession at the Reformation. The training of students for the ministry in the Reformed Church was typically funded by the government, and in all cases it was the government that paid that church's stipends, as well as the wages of the Reformed visitors of the sick, churchwardens and lay readers. Building and maintenance costs of churches and manses were also drawn on the public purse. Other Protestant churches enjoyed none of these financial benefits.

On the other hand, privilege entails patronage. Dutch politicians had thoroughly learned their lesson from the Contra-Remonstrant controversies about the church being in the state's pocket, which had driven the country to the brink of civil war. The lesson they took from this was that from the local through to the national level, the Church was effectively muzzled. At the national level, this was achieved by preventing any repetition of the troubled Synod of Dort for the remaining two centuries of the Republic's existence. At the provincial level, Zeeland pursued a similar policy: after the 1638 Synod of Tholen, no provincial synod was ever allowed by the States of Zeeland. This was in complete contrast to the practice of the other provinces, all of which held an annual synod by provincial government licence. It is not hard to see why it was in Zeeland that the Reformed Church was uniquely more subjugated by politicians than she was in other parts of the country: it was only in Zeeland that the majority of the population belonged to that confession,[23] such that the Church was a far more significant player in the social power game there than in any other province. This was also the reason why it was in Zeeland alone that politicians, via the organ of the *collegium qualificatum*, insisted on filling the election of church office-bearers with more of its own place-men. Moreover, all over the Netherlands, a Reformed congregation's call of a preacher was only effective after being rubber-stamped by the civil authorities.

At Sluis, the city council was made up of two mayors and seven aldermen, who were appointed to each year's term of office by the Council of State at the recommendation of the local council and sworn in by deputies of that supreme national political forum (the ceremony being held in Sluis itself). The direct viceregent of the Council of State on the council was the bailiff, who had considerable powers, especially in the domains of court trials and of law and order. The city's social life was heavily influenced by

---

23 Kluiver, 35–38.

the boards of the professional guilds: these were each made up of a senior dean, a dean and a number of inspectors. The senior dean of each sat on the city council and formed the point of contact between that political body and his guild. The regular dean under him chaired the guild, and the inspectors performed quality inspections. All these guild offices were in the gift of the city council.

*Sluis Town Hall*

Being a frontier town, Sluis played host to a military contingent besides its civilian population. The soldiers garrisoned in the city took their orders from a fortress governor whose appointment was by the national government. The political and military vicissitudes of the seventeenth century caused fluctuations in the number of companies billeted on the city. Even at the low ebbs, however, day-to-day life in Sluis was considerably shaped by the presence of the troops in town.

The Reformed Church was governed by its church officers, who in Koelman's incumbency were two preachers, six elders and six deacons. The elders and deacons had a two-year term of office. Serving elders and deacons could not immediately be re-elected. Owing to the loss of the relevant sources, we cannot tell whether, and if so how, the city council arranged for itself to be represented in church officers' meetings, but we do know that in practice a third of the elders' and deacons' seats were reserved for councillors. As if this were not a substantial enough direct political influence upon the workings of the Reformed congregation, the pressure that the city council could exert (via the *collegium qualificatum*) upon the church officers at election times was enhanced further: the *collegium* contained deputies of the city council besides the actual church officers. In Sluis, the number of votes reserved for such city council deputies was two. The political manipulation that this could entail for the church officers almost without fail led to tensions on every hand, and in some places these spilled over into conflicts that were taken to high levels. Sluis did not escape that fate.

**Koelman's efforts for the further reformation of Sluis**
After having served as chaplain to the Dutch envoys in Copenhagen and then Brussels in 1657, Koelman was entrusted with his own parish in August 1662: Sluis.[24] No sooner had he arrived than he began to dominate the church officers' meetings and to take the lead in a plethora of activities aimed at accomplishing further reformation.

At Sluis, as laid down in the Zeeland Church Order, the calling of a preacher, like the appointment of a schoolmaster, was a matter for the *collegium qualificatum*. Very soon indeed after Koelman's installation in the parish, the Sluis church officers received a letter from the Council of State insisting that they must in future not proceed with the installation of a new incumbent without having obtained prior permission from that body in The Hague. At Koelman's instigation, the elders and deacons determined to resist fiercely this political attempt to nullify ecclesiastical law: their reply was a theocratic plea for the sovereignty of the Church. The resistance was in vain: the withholding of Koelman's stipend forced it to its knees.

More wide-ranging in its implications was the conflict that ensued between the church officers and city council of Sluis. In 1664, the councillors resolved that from now on, they would be sending not two but three of their number to sit on the panel electing elders and deacons.

---

24  For this section in general, see Theophilus Parresius [1677], 1–39; Krull, 12–45.

They erroneously cited the 1638 Synod of Tholen to justify their decision. In this case, with Walcheren presbytery involving itself, the council climbed down.

Interwoven with this was yet another ruction. As of May 1664, the Walloon Synod had a project to found a dedicated congregation at Sluis for the French speakers, with her own minister, elders and deacons. The city councillors strove with might and main to see this plan come to fruition. The Dutch Reformed church officers, however, whipped up by Koelman, opposed the Walloons' intent: the reasons that Koelman furnished to the elders and deacons included the arguent that any new congregation would become a meeting of malcontents and misfits from the regular Reformed congregation, and that there would be much scope for the Dutch and French deacons to argue over cases of need. Ultimately, the church officers won this struggle.[25]

In 1665, the city council, particularly Mayor Abraham Parent (1632–1670),[26] sought to exact vengeance. The mayor had taken umbrage at a speech made by Koelman's brother minister Henricus Berdenis (1628–1695) at a *collegium qualificatum* session that had been called to fill the vacancy left by Berdenis' acceptance of a call to Vollenhove in Overijssel. Reconciliation was only achieved after escalation through the presbytery to the Council of State. However, the truce did not last long: shortly thereafter, the councillors announced that they were prepared to carry on seeking a replacement preacher, but on the condition that the known Further Reformation advocate Hermannus Witsius[27] (1636–1708), then serving the parish of Wormer in Noord-Holland and recommended for the vacancy by Koelman, be struck from the shortlist. Unsurprisingly, the church officers were not impressed. After many twists and turns, Witsius himself lost heart and withdrew his own candidacy.[28]

In September 1666, a clash developed that pitted the councillors not only against Koelman but even against his wife Anna. A savage outbreak of the plague had cropped up in Sluis in mid-August that year. The city's clergymen, and also Anna Hus (d. 1675), started visiting and tending to those stricken with the disease. When the government issued an edict banning those residing under the same roof as a plague victim and those visiting them from attending church, to contain the epidemic, Koelman

---

25  De Hullu.
26  The life dates of the Sluis figures are taken from a list of Sluis genealogical data, chiefly from the seventeenth century, compiled by the author of this study.
27  Van Genderen.
28  Van Genderen, 27–28.

and his wife merely redoubled their efforts for the afflicted. In response, the council placed them both under house arrest on 29 September and sent a man round to nail a white bar across their window. The church officers were up in arms at once; this time with success. The bar was removed and the Koelmans were given a place apart to sit in church. Once the epidemic had died down, two councillors were even deputed to give the couple a vote of thanks on behalf of all citizens of Sluis for their errands of mercy during the outbreak!

*Sint-Janskerk, Sluis*

If the above has amply proven Koelman's theocratic attitude and that of his adherents towards the government, the following demonstrates his Further Reformation convictions in the matter of church discipline. From 1663 onwards, Koelman had the elders and deacons start taking a firm hand against open sin. Confirmed church members who had been spotted dancing at night in various hostelries were placed under censure. Members who had slipped across the border to enjoy themselves at Bruges Fair received a caution. On 3 January 1665, there was a fully-fledged incident. Exciseman Pieter Brienen (b. 1619), then serving on the council as an alderman, had a home visit by Koelman and an elder to inform him he was to be barred from the Lord's table for his drinking habit. Enraged, Brienen sprang on top of Koelman and pummelled the minister's chest.

As one might expect, the church officers demanded satisfaction of the matter from the councillors. Whether such was ever forthcoming is doubtful, as the sources are notably silent thereafter about this affair. Both in 1665 and in 1667, the council warned the church officers—obviously Koelman above all—that there was to be no invective against Lombards[29] from the pulpit. It was Philippus van der Mast whom Koelman had so condemned, insisting in a sermon that setting interest rates upwards of 22% was insufferable usury.

After a few years, Koelman's Further Reformation push was beginning to bear fruit even at presbytery level. By 1670, several of the congregations on Walcheren were expressing the desire to address numerous abuses prevalent in church and personal life and to strive for a thoroughgoing reformation of morals. That year, for instance, the presbytery resolved unanimously that all Sabbath-breakers, all who indulged in the game of cards or dice and all who skipped church services must be censured. This resolution was promptly abrogated by the States of Zeeland. Grumblingly, the presbytery gave way—but Koelman was not so readily defeated. He remained alert for his chance to pounce.

His resolve was stiffened by the success that crowned his ministry, which he began to savour in late 1671 and early 1672. As he himself put it, "a great number of people of every degree—civilians and soldiers, men and women, young and old—have been mightily converted to the living God".[30] He reported this revival in an account written to "domene n.b." [Reverend N.B.]. The church historian Albert Eekhof[31] (1884–1933), who published a transcript of the account, was unable to identify its addressee,[32] yet there need be no doubt that it was Koelman's predecessor as minister of Sluis, Barenzonius, whose translation of a Puritan work had been published at Utrecht in 1659 bound together with one by Koelman. Evidently, they had kept in touch with each other.

Koelman's opportunity to urge the entire presbytery to seek further reformation presented itself in 1672, the year of calamity for the Dutch Republic. As the enemy advanced, he wrote to the presbytery (in his capacity as clerk of the Sluis church officers) on 2 June 1672, outlining his old reformational aims and noting pointedly that other presbyteries, even some outside Zeeland, were taking a cue from the Walcheren presbytery

---

29 i.e., lending bankers.
30 Theophilus Parresius [1677], 1.
31 De Groot [1978].
32 Eekhof, 200.

and had started Further Reformation programmes of their own. This was a slightly premature statement but it does show that he had regular contact with brother ministers in those presbyteries (which as we shall shortly see were at the other end of the country), for after the date of Koelman's letter they did as he had anticipated and proceeded to reform themselves on the Walcheren model. In his preface to *Vier zamenspraaken, over ettelijke kerkelyke zaaken* [Four discourses on some ecclesiastical matters] (1677), which reproduces the reformation agendas of three Zeeland presbyteries whose names we shall encounter below, Koelman again made the point that Walcheren had become a trailblazer.³³ First, on the authority of a minister who had been present at the meeting, he cites the gathering of all Frisian clergymen in 1672, and then two Zeeland presbytery sessions, Zuid-Beveland and Schouwen-Duiveland, that same year. We therefore conclude that in his 2 June letter, the church bodies to which Koelman was alluding were the Church of Friesland and those two Zeeland presbyteries. In reality, however, the action that these bodies undertook followed 2 June rather than preceding it.³⁴ The convocation of all the preachers of Friesland took place on 22 and 23 July, and Koelman had had advance notice of it. It was on 15 August that the presbytery of Friesland's university town, Franeker, adopted a programme of ecclesiastical reforms and even asked those in attendance to put their signatures to it. Other Frisian presbyteries soon followed suit: Sneek on 13 September, Zevenwolde on 18 September and the provincial capital, Leeuwarden, on 17 April 1673. Bolsward had meanwhile done likewise, and Dokkum had on 12 September 1672 dusted off a presbyterial reform agenda that it had written independently some time previously. In *Vier zamenspraaken, over ettelijke kerkelyke zaaken*, Koelman reproduces the text of the articles of reformation as drawn up by Walcheren presbytery on 14 September 1672; as drawn up during 1672 by Zuid-Beveland presbytery; and as drawn up by Schouwen-Duiveland presbytery.³⁵

The letter of petition that the church officers of Sluis penned on 2 June 1672 brought about a resolution by the Walcheren presbytery to convert reforming propositions into action. Heartened by this success, the officers, obviously led by Koelman, submitted a formal complaint (*gravamen*) to the presbytery on 5 September regarding the administration of baptism. Their grievances were that they ought not to be obliged by law to christen the children of Roman Catholics; that the baptism of the chil-

---

33   Christianus Parresius [1677], *3v.
34   For the following, see Op 't Hof [2004-2], 57–59.
35   Christianus Parresius [1677], *4v.–3*1v.

dren of nominal Protestants who had no actual knowledge of Reformed doctrine ought to be withheld until those parents had been better instructed; that there should be mechanisms to restrict godless parents from proffering their offspring for christening; and that there generally needed to be better arrangements for scrutinising candidates for baptism. As the presbytery was rather listless in its reception of the letter, the Sluis church officers resolved to go straight to the civil government locally to prevent desecration of the Sabbath, taking God's Name in vain, games of chance, usurious lending, busking by vagrants, various excesses at the annual fete, and the use of the organ in the liturgy. This petition, dated 13 November, was followed by a request in the same vein, signed by 53 pious notables of the city. Two months later, the church officers sent a separate petition to the military governor of Sluis, Maurice Louis I van Nassau la Leck,[36] urging the reformation of sins rife in the army. The government responded with some fine words but did not make good on its promises. Koelman had a similar experience with the presbytery, to whom he resubmitted his *gravamen* in 1674. Now that the present dangers of 1672 had been seen off, it seemed there was no real willingness left to implement a reformation programme.

By this time, Koelman, who had had his fill of being stalled, was beginning to apply on his own initiative those of his desiderata which he felt he could implement single-handedly, namely dropping the observance of the ecclesiastical calendar and the reading of set liturgies. On these latter two points, he was more stringent than almost any other Further Reformation men. While the rest of this movement were not fond of feast days or formularies either, they regarded such matters as adiaphora: not good or bad enough in and of themselves to argue over. Koelman, however, was a staunch opponent of these alleged vestiges of Romanism. It was not by chance that the same extreme rejection of feast days and formularies was prevalent in Presbyterian and congregationalist Puritanism,[37] nor that when Koelman published his *Reformatie nodigh ontrent de feestdagen* [The necessity of reformation concerning festival days] in 1675 after his exile from Sluis, he appended to it a sixty-page extract from a work by a Scots Puritan, John Brown (1610–1679).

---

36  Ten Raa, 5: 526.
37  Cf. Theophilus Parresius [1677], 23–24.

# Reformatie
## Nodigh ontrent de
# FEEST-DAGEN,
Naaktelijk vertoont, ende bewezen,
Door
JACOBUS KOELMAN,
Dienaar des H. Euangeliums, tot
*Sluys* in *Vlaanderen*.

Tot ROTTERDAM,

Gedrukt bij Henricus Goddæus, Boekdrukker
in den Oppert / Anno 1675.

While he had never been one to hide his opinions on either of these matters under a bushel, the Further Reformer of Sluis made a dedicated assault on formulary prayers in a sermon on praying in the Holy Ghost on 24 July 1672, taking as his text the Epistle of Jude, verse 20. Hereby, Koelman, and his older brother minister Montanus, were casting themselves adrift from the prayer book. On 26 December (known in the Dutch tradition as Second Christmas Day) that year, Koelman preached on the weak and beggarly practices of observing times and seasons in the church (Galatians 4:9–11) and declared publicly that he would never again observe them.[38] As soon as the congregation filed out, several shopkeepers among his adherents went and opened up for business, nor did they encounter any reprimand from the city council. On 5 January of the following year, Koelman went as far as to dispense altogether with the formularies for baptism and marriage, and instead gave an extempore sermon along the same lines as the wording of the prayer book. The commotion that this stirred up prompted him to devote the following Sunday morning sermon, on 8 January, to a defence and further explanation of his decision, based on I Chronicles 21:24. Immediately after the service, his own church officers called him in to account for himself. The elders and deacons were annoyed that he had launched into these actions without giving his fellow parish preachers or themselves prior notice of his intent, although they assured him that they were with him on the point of principle.

This would have put an end to the matter, had it not been for the fact that Mayor Willem Sluymer (1627–1682), who had previously been openly reprimanded by the church for drunkenness in public and who had been called upon to confess his sin at a plenary session of the church officers (which he had refused to do), now seized his chance to cut his nemesis down to size. He had the city council send a formal accusation against Koelman to the presbytery on 17 January, one which demanded that Koelman must use the formularies in future. In its reply dated 27 January, the Walcheren presbytery referred the matter back—quite correctly under the Dort Church Order—to the local church officers, who on 4 February unanimously voted to tolerate Koelman's new policy. The presbytery took this as reason enough to order Koelman to appear on 25 February. In turn, this summons prompted 26 serving and former church officers to stand in the breach for Koelman, urging the presbytery not to make any overhasty judgements. It also prompted Koelman himself to

---

38 In an extensively augmented form, this sermon was published in 1675 as *Reformatie nodigh ontrent de feest-dagen*.

send to the publishers two augmented sermons that he had preached on this subject, entitled *Reformatie, noodig ontrent het gebruyk der formulieren* [The necessity of reformation concerning formularies] (1673). His aim in going into print was to make his position crystal clear to all parties, since many of his fellow ministers, especially in the environs of Sluis, were now demanding his deportation and one of them (whose identity remains unknown) had even published a lampoon of him. The 25 February presbytery meeting went ahead and made a resolution to depute four men to follow up the matter in more detail with Koelman. Koelman himself was directed to set out his arguments in writing for these four, which he duly did within a few days.

On 5 March, Koelman, writing on behalf of the Sluis church officers, insistently requested that the presbytery direct that the Lord's Supper be withheld from church members with insufficient doctrinal knowledge, that those who went about in worldly dress be censured, that Coccejus' too elastic view of the Fourth Commandment be withstood, and that the ecclesiastical feast days be abolished. The next day, a letter addressed by the church officers to the presbytery requested that the committee of inquiry should hold its interview with Koelman not in the presbytery's seat of Middelburg but on home territory in Sluis.

Before the interview could be held, events intervened. The presbytery became aware that Koelman was having his sermons against formularies disseminated by a printer-publisher within their own remit: Abraham van Laren[39] (1633–1679) of Vlissingen. They lost no time in dispatching missives to both the author and the publisher. Koelman's response was that, alas, the text was out of his hands and he had no copy. For his part, van Laren offered the presbytery the options of either covering all his losses if he were to pull the book from the press, or demonstrating that the contents of the book were heterodox or harmful to the Church, in which case he would absorb the losses himself. This ultimatum demonstrates that van Laren was spiritually a supporter of Koelman's. Two months later, he brought out his very own reformation programme very much in the spirit of Koelman: *Noodtsaeckelijcke reformatie, ontrent het ampt der ouderlingen, vertoondt in eenige vragen/ getrocken uyt het formulier van bevestiginge der ouderlinge* [The necessity of reformation concerning the office of eldership demonstrated by certain questions taken from the formulary for the ordination of elders]. Its preface bears the date of 31 May 1673.

---

39  Op 't Hof [2013-1], 268–272; [2013-2], 306–310; [2016-2].

The interview itself was a damp squib. Yet before the presbytery had a chance to issue its verdict on 13 April, Sluis witnessed a day to remember: one that further aggravated the already tense local relations.

**An Easter Monday like no other**
Many of the people of Sluis will have been looking forward to 3 April 1673 with a certain frisson of excitement.[40] That Monday morning, as was customary on what is known in the Netherlands as Second Easter Day, there would be a 9 a.m. church service. This, however, was destined to be a day with a difference: it had become common knowledge that Reverend Koelman would not be filling his preaching slot that morning because he had taken against festival days, and that he would not even be showing up in church, and even that the most avid of his adherents would be taking this view to its logical conclusion by opening their shops early that morning. To do so constituted a proclamation of revolt, because the days after Christmas, Easter and Whitsun were not just public holidays but were regarded by the civil government as Lord's days, on which businesses ought to be shut, above all while service was being held. Sluis had never before known the shops to open during a service on these festival days. The furthest that matters had come hitherto was that some Sluis shopkeepers, inspired by Koelman's sermon on 26 December 1672, had gone off and opened up their businesses—*after* having attended church, a much more moderate position than opening up *before* the service began.

Two events on the Easter Sunday must have greatly exacerbated the atmosphere. In the Sunday morning service, Koelman was on the rota to administer communion. He went ahead with the sacrament, but for the first time in his ministry he proceeded to the Lord's table without reading the relevant formulary of the prayer book. Instead, he read out I Corinthians 11:23-29 and transitioned into a lengthy meditation on those verses. Five or six members, two of whom were serving councillors,[41]

---

40  For this and the next section, see Theophilus Parresius [1677], 39–47.
41  It is clear from the signatures under the remonstrances against Koelman that, from among the bailiff, the mayoral duumvirate and the seven aldermen then serving, the following were confirmed opponents of Koelman's: Bailiff Nicolaes Swancke, Mayor Willem Sluymer and Aldermen Franciscus de Raet, Abraham van Dordt and Beerent Engels: Middelburg (hereinafter M), Zeeuws Archief [Zeeland Archives] (hereinafter ZA), Acta Classis Walcheren [Minutes of Walcheren Presbytery] (hereinafter ACW), inv.no. 25, no. 936 (12 September 1673). One of the two councillors who left the church will have been Mayor Sluymer, given that he was at the forefront of efforts to put a halt to Koelman's programme. The other of them will have been one of the four other of the above men. The reconstruction of the composition of the council at that

were so offended at this that they walked out of the service; a second group remained in church but stayed put in the pews when the call was issued to come up to the table; and a third group, having received advance intelligence of Koelman's intentions, had stayed away from church altogether. During his actual Sunday morning sermon, and again in his afternoon sermon, Koelman studiously avoided any mention of the resurrection of Christ. In all probability, it was after that service that a councillor who was not much taken with Koelman's churchmanship repaired to the manse with the express request that he baptise his child using the formulary. Koelman declined and referred the gentleman to another clergyman who was due to preach the following day. In a fit of pique, the councillor asked the Walloons to christen his child instead.

Those denizens of Sluis who had been hoping for a good dose of scandal will not have been disappointed that Easter Monday. Koelman ostentatiously stayed away from church, together with his household and the majority of his followers. Moreover, quite a number of those followers who were in trades had opened up shop before church (i.e., before 9 a.m.), so that they were making the day a regular working day. They even went so far as to call out to churchgoers that it would be better to stay away and to urge the rest of the shopkeepers to come out and open up too. When the service had just started, soldiers of Roman Catholic and other allegiances came out of the guardroom and plundered eight to ten (according to the council)[42] or three or four (according to Koelman)[43] of the open bakeries. They then fell to arguing among themselves about dividing up the booty, which resulted in fisticuffs and the wounding of several of them. Koelman and his party averred that the governor was behind this raid, but he insisted that he was innocent of any involvement.

**Repercussions of the incident**

Obviously, these events set the parties on even more of a collision course than they already had been on. The selfsame day, the city council wrote a letter to the presbytery in which it painted the scene in lurid colours and invoked this turn of events as a reason to urge haste in the ecclesiastical meeting that would deal with Koelman. On Tuesday 4 April, the bailiff,

---

moment was gleaned from the September 1672 renewal of the guild boards: Oostburg (hereinafter O), Gemeentearchief Sluis [Municipal Archive of Sluis] (hereinafter MAS), Oud archief Sluis [Sluis Old Archive] (hereinafter OAS), inv. no. 10, September 1672.

42  M, ZA, ACW, inv. no. 25, no. 918a (3 April 1673).
43  Theophilus Parresius [1677], 39.

mayors and aldermen passed a resolution pursuant to the previous day's events, which on 7 April they had nailed up as an official proclamation, taking cognisance of the fact that numerous citizens had been open for business during the Easter Monday service. The new information that this document adds for the historian is that it was not only tradesmen but other strata of Sluis society that had taken part by going to work as normal. Evidently, the action had not been restricted to shopkeepers alone but had included a broader cross-section of Koelman's supporters. The novelty of it all had given rise to disorder, and the council, apprehensive of further fracas, expressly forbade the opening of shops and the practice of trades or professions on future second-day church festivals at any time of the day. Any infringements would incur the fine of one pound Flemish. For Koelman, this merely served to reinforce his impression that more ado was made in his society about ecclesiastical feast days than about the Lord's day, given that the existing fine for breach of a Sabbath or a weekday of prayer and fasting was set at only half of that amount. What was more, the council by taking this decision had made itself just as guilty of introducing novelties as he had been, for up until that point it had been perfectly legal for anyone in Sluis who wished to open his store on a church festival day to do so.[44]

When Koelman got wind of the council's letter to the presbytery of 3 April, and the more so when he read the proclamation that Friday, it dawned on him that the councillors might have it in mind to charge him with insurrection. His precautionary response was as follows. On Saturday 8 April, at Koelman's clandestine instigation, a quartet of Sluis citizens and master bakers, all of whom had thrown open their shop doors bright and early that Monday morning, appeared before Sluis notary Thomas Mattheeusen (1643/4–1694), himself a Koelmanite,[45] to deposit an affidavit to the effect that (a) they had been persuaded by their minister's preaching that the observance of feast days was contrary to sound doctrine and (b) it had been entirely of their own volition that they had opened for business on Easter Monday, with Koelman never having publicly or privately instigated the action. They also declared that they were not aware of any law against this. Quite the opposite: the first signatory, Maerten Maertens (d. 1695), declared, together with his fellow Sluis citizen Pieter de Coninck, that he had heard Koelman assert that shopkeepers

---

44 Theophilus Parresius [1677], 330–331.
45 This is evident from his signature placed under two remonstrances written to plead Koelman's cause: M, ZA, ACW, inv. no. 25, nos. 914 (18 February 1673) and 930 (4 August 1673).

would need to ask licence from the council to open their shops on such occasions and that one of the city's mayors[46] had responded that it would not be necessary to make a special application. The two witnesses to the affidavit were Leendert van de Crane (b. 1651) and Geleyn Hemeryck.[47] It would be tempting to interpret their signatures as implying that both were on Koelman's side. The former is, indeed, known to have been pro-Koelman from the presence of his signature on a remonstrance pleading his cause;[48] the convictions of the latter are not known.

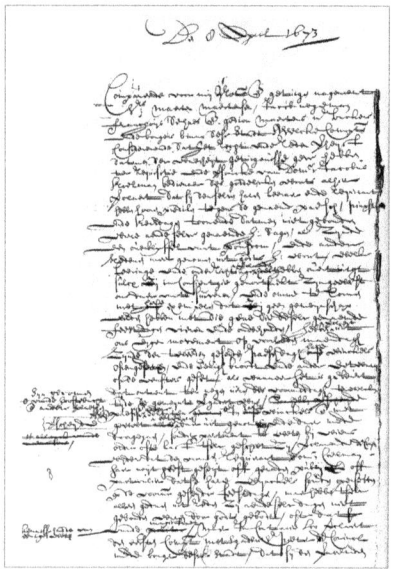 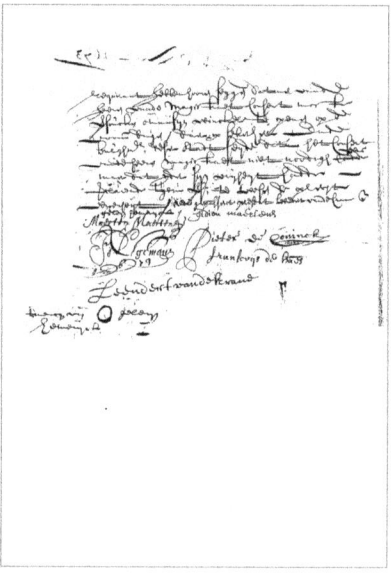

*The pro-Koelman affidavit of 8 April 1673*

On 11 April, 42 male and 60 female confirmed members of the Reformed Church of Sluis signed a petition to the presbytery on Koelman's behalf. It was never actually presented to the presbytery, because the organisers anticipated that it would not go down well with them that women had signed it.

---

46 Given that one of the two mayors, Sluymer, was a known opponent of Koelman's, the mayor meant here can only have referred to Maljard van den Bussche.
47 Middelburg (hereinafter M), Zeeuws Archief [Zeeland Archives] (hereinafter ZA), Archieven van de rechtbanken, weeskamers en notarissen in Zeeuwsch-Vlaanderen 1447–1796 [Archives of the Law Courts, Orphan Guardianships, and Notaries in Zeeland 1447–1796] (hereinafter ARWNZV), inv.no. 1935, 8 April 1673.
48 M, ZA, ACW, inv.no. 25, no. 930 (4 August 1673).

The Sluis council letter of 3 April was dealt with at the presbytery session ten days later. The Sluis church officers' meeting of 15 April heard an account by Koelman and one of the church's two presbytery delegates, Mayor Maljard van den Bussche, of what had gone on at that meeting. The two Sluis deputies—the other one besides van den Bussche was Reverend Montanus—had insisted as eyewitnesses to the event that Koelman had been quite correct to say that there had been only five or six walkouts during the service, not the "many" suggested in the council report, and that it was equally untrue for the city fathers to have written that "nearly half" of the congregation had refrained from the Lord's Supper. They added that Koelman, availing himself of the aforementioned affidavit, had demonstrated to the presbytery that he had not in any way incited the shopkeepers who had opened up early on Easter Monday morning to do so. Finally, they said, van den Bussche had declared to the presbytery that a small coterie within the council had actually penned the 3 April letter, exploiting the absence of himself and some others,[49] and moreover, that the Council of State commissioners who had attended the communion service in question had found Koelman's conduct of it most edifying. The presbytery's decision was to require a visitation committee, including the former incumbent of Sluis, Cocquius, to scope the situation there, bring the Koelman affair to the attention of the other presbyteries in Zeeland and continue the efforts to make Koelman change his mind.

It took fully two years for the Easter Monday 1673 incident to culminate in its unanticipated, highly significant and life-changing repercussions.[50] On 3 June 1675, a Whit Monday (the day after Pentecost), Sluis council decided to strike out the second part of the by-law it had enacted two years previously. The mood in that year's council was evidently that that clause had been going too far. It was resolved in as many words, and

---

49 The council counted five avowed opponents of Koelman's at that time. Among the remaining councillors, he had (as attested by their having signed remonstrances for his cause) two outspoken supporters: Nicolaes Duyst van Voorhoudt and Samuel Maertens. The neutral remainder of the council included, besides van den Bussche, Arnout Weyts and Ferdinand de Bacquere. Together with van den Bussche, it appears that Duyst van Voorhoudt, Maertens, Weyts and de Bacquere missed the 3 April session, or even if one or two of them did show up, they must have been insufficient to have formed a blocking minority. Although van den Bussche was never a party man, this statement of his at the presbytery session, and his declaration that shopkeepers did not need to ask any special permission to open their establishments on ecclesiastical festival days, indicate that he did not stand in the way of Koelman's agenda, and that he actually spoke up for him when he felt that the latter was being given short shrift.
50 For this and the following paragraphs, see Theophilus Parresius [1677], 329–338.

published through the city that very day, that all citizens and residents of Sluis were at liberty to open their shops after the morning church service on second-day church festivals and go about their lawful business. We know from the letter of the three aldermen (discussed below) how this council resolution was taken. At the initiative of the Chairman of the College of Aldermen, who that year was van den Bussche, a meeting was convened for 7 a.m. that Whit Monday. Six councillors turned up: besides van den Bussche, they were Bailiff Nicolaes Swancke (d. 1711) and four aldermen, Franciscus de Raet (1624–1681), Abraham Mattheeusen (1629/30–1688), Gillis van Kerrebroeck (1628–1681) and Jacob de Jonge (1635/6–1690). Proposed by van den Bussche, the resolution was passed by a majority of votes. The two to vote against were de Raet and Mattheeusen, who felt strongly enough about the change of policy to write to the States-General of the Netherlands about it. Through this letter, The Hague came to know of the whole affair and Koelman's implication therein. Their protest was sent on 7 June and co-signed by Alderman Martinus Gipson (d. 1681), who had not been present at the Whit Monday council session. The trio's aim was evidently to put pressure on national policymakers to hasten the expulsion of the Further Reformer, but equally to portray their fellow councillors in an unflattering light to central government.

Comparison of the voting records for the 3 June 1675 by-law amendment with the remonstrances earlier signed for and against Koelman yields surprising results. Van den Bussche is the only figure who had not declared for either of the warring factions. It is no great wonder that de Raet voted against the relaxation, nor that Gipson joined his party later: they were both among the men who had come out against Koelman in the earlier remonstrance. Since Kerrebroeck and de Jonge had signed the competing remonstrance, their votes in favour of the relaxation are equally understandable. What is striking, however, is the change of positions seen in Swancke and Mattheeusen. Swancke, who had put his name to the public protest against Koelman in 1673, nevertheless voted for the motion in 1675. According to Koelman himself, he had dissociated himself in the interim from the opposition to Koelman's programme.[51] The background to his change of heart is shrouded in mystery. On the other hand, Mattheeusen had twice in 1673 signed petitions in favour of the Further Reformation preacher, but two years later, we see him declaring his opposition to his theology. No other explanation is possible than that he had changed his views and switched camps. One can only guess at his reasons for doing so.

---

51 Theophilus Parresius [1677], 329.

The trio's letter of 7 June achieved the double effect intended. On 11 June, the States-General decided to assign Mayor Sluymer and the trio the charge of ensuring that Koelman leave Sluis, and besides, their excellencies were so indignant at how the majority of the councillors had acted that they temporarily suspended them from office. The unwonted severity of this answer from The Hague is an indication of just how sensitive a matter this was at that juncture.

**The bakers, the most fervent of Koelman's flock**
The affidavit with which Koelman disarmed at the presbytery meeting the council's implicit charge against him of civil disobedience and social agitation took the form of a declaration of his innocence by four master bakers. This calls for closer enquiry, as it throws up numerous research questions. The first of these must be: Were the bakers the only trade in town to open for business that morning? The relevant passages from the council's letter to the presbytery make it highly unlikely that that was the case: we read of Sluis citizens heading for work, "among whom were various who work at trades and crafts".[52] The relevant clause in the minutes of the church officers' meetings sheds more light on the matter: they narrate "that many of the citizens had had their shops open from early that morning, whereupon a looting was made by the soldiers of the bakers' shops."[53] This understanding of events is confirmed by Koelman's own account that "it occurred on Easter Monday morning that a few citizens had opened their shops, and some papist soldiers, instigated by their papist captain (and moreover, as folk believed, by a gentleman for whom this was conduct most unbecoming), had robbed three or four bakers' shops".[54]

These forms of words allow us to conclude that although it was only the bakers who were pillaged that Easter Monday morning, there were plenty of other kinds of shops open for business in the city. From that perspective, the affidavit served not only to exculpate Koelman but also to incriminate the scheming governor and council. The robbery was their fault, after all, and we have no indication that these authorities punished the guilty parties. It is very probable that in having the affidavit made up, Koelman neutralised some real threats that were emanating from that quarter.

---

52 M, ZA, ACW, inv. no. 25, no. 918a (3 April 1673).
53 M, ZA, Hervormde Gemeente te Sluis [Reformed Congregation of Sluis], inv. no. 4, 15 April 1673.
54 Theophilus Parresius [1677], 39.

The question that now becomes urgent is this: Did the soldiers decide of their own accord that it was the bakers whom they were going to target, or had a suggestion been whispered in their ear to that effect? There is, naturally, always the prosaic consideration that the garrison canteen will not have been serving gourmet meals and that they were feeling quite partial to some of Sluis' finest baking when they struck out into town. However, one can hardly imagine that soldiers on a spree would, if left to their own devices, think of nothing that took their fancy more than a nice bit of bread and cake. On the other hand, if we do posit that they had been given their plundering orders in advance, then it is quite reasonable that whoever was pulling the strings would have told them to stick to just one type of shop to maximise the impact. We would then still have to find a reason why the faceless masterminds had such a bone to pick with the bakers of Sluis. Normally, the historian would have to give up in perplexity at such an obscure question. Yet, happily for our research, the Bakers' Guild has the best-preserved records of any guild in Sluis, and its material from the 1670s has survived particularly well, and on top of that, the annual appointment of the guild boards in September 1672 permits us to evaluate the Bakers' Guild in comparison with other professional bodies in the city.

We derive our data on the pro- and contra-Koelman parties from remonstrances signed for and against him.[55] Holding up the aforementioned renewal of the guild boards (consisting of a senior dean, a dean and a number of inspectors) against the light of these lists, we find that of the six men on the board of the Tallowmen's Guild, two inspectors had come out for Koelman and that the dean was an opponent. Among the five board members of the Grocers' Guild, the dean and one of the inspectors were pro-Koelman while another of the inspectors was an adversary. Of the five board members of the Drapers' Guild, two inspectors were for Koelman and one against. Of the five board members of the Cobblers' Guild, the dean and two inspectors were on Koelman's side and the senior dean opposed him. Of the four board members of the Blacksmiths' Guild, only the dean was publicly for Koelman and the senior dean and one inspector were against him. The Bakers' Guild is thus seen to be the only professional body in town whose board was entirely made up of Koelman men.[56] In that exceptional aspect of the guild, we have the obvious reason why the city fathers of Sluis were determined to strike a blow against their trade.

---

55  In chronological order: M. ZA, ACW, inv. no. 25, nos. 914 (18 February 1673), 930 (4 August 1673), 936 (12 September 1673).
56  O, MAS, OAS, inv. no. 10, September 1672.

The board of the Sluis Bakers' Guild for the year 1672–73 was entirely favourably disposed to Koelman. Was this the result of chance, or did it reflect the spiritual affections of Sluis bakers in general? Fortunately, the membership roll of the Guild of Bakers for that very year has been preserved.[57] It contains seventeen enrolments. We can tell from their signatures on one or more remonstrances that eight of them were patent supporters of Koelman's: Philips du Rieu (1641–1677), Maerten Maertens, Jacob Negeman (1636/7–1680), François de Haes, Gidion Maertens, Jan Schieux (d. 1677), Pieter de la Croix and Erasmus Marinissoon (d. 1704). On the other hand, based on the signatures of more remonstrances for the other side, we know of only one Sluis baker who was a resolute opponent of Koelman's: Cornelis Boudry (b. 1650). These figures make it plain that the religious stance taken by the whole board of the guild was representative of a broad majority of its members. It is not exaggerating matters to state that of all the respected trades, it was the bakers who lent Koelman their most wholehearted support. That finding is supported by the composition of the Guild's board for the years around 1672–73, too. The previous year, all but one of the inspectors were avowed supporters of Koelman's; in 1673–74 and 1674–75, the whole board was pro-Koelman; and in 1675–76 and 1676–77, the senior dean was the only member whom we do not know for certain to have had that affiliation.[58]

A final problem is that of how many bakeries were robbed. The council spoke of eight to ten; Koelman of three or four. The affidavit is evidence that all four of the bakers who signed it had fallen victim to the plunder, so Koelman's number was the bare minimum. It is not hard to see why he understated the matter: the fewer shops were robbed, the less serious the incident would appear and the less the danger that he would be condemned as an insurrectionist. Conversely, the council had every reason to inflate the number of shops that had suffered damage. The true figure, then, will lie somewhere in between.

This finding makes us immediately wonder why only four of the zealous bakers had signed the affidavit when all of them could just as well have done so. The bakers who signed were Gidion Maertens, Maerten Maertens, Jacob Negeman and François de Haes. If we glance across to the list of board members of the Bakers' Guild at that period, we have a clue. The two lists are identical apart from one name, Philips du Rieu, who although a head of the guild did not come to the notary's office. He

---

57 O, MAS, OAS, inv. no. 338, 10 April 1673.
58 O, MAS, OAS, inv. no. 10, 4 September 1671, 23 November 1673, 13 September 1674, 15 September 1675, 24 September 1676.

was a known supporter of Koelman's but probably too timid or moderate to open his bakery while the service was in progress that Monday morning. More to the point, however, why was it only the guild high-ups who made the affidavit? Could they have been the sole targets of the soldiers' running amok? That cannot of course be ruled out, but it is rather implausible that the plunderers left all the humbler bakers' shops alone. Rather, an affidavit whose signatories were exclusively men on the board of their guild would be taken as official. Armed with this document, Koelman was even better defended against any charges that might be brought against him, and it also made the implicit condemnation of the government so much the more compelling.

**Conclusions**

The most recent scholarly definition of the Further Reformation contains the following intriguing passage: "One can even go further and raise the question of whether the movement ever had an historical identity. Might its defining characteristic actually be that it never progressed beyond a cherished utopia?"[59]

The unique events of 3 April 1673 at Sluis reveal to us that such a spiritual movement as the Further Reformation, and one with such towering and all-encompassing objectives, very much *was* a movement capable of rearranging the furniture of society. Through his preaching against the observance of the ecclesiastical calendar, Koelman had managed to persuade a good many local shopkeepers of his cause, even to the extent that they opened their doors during the service held that day. This was nothing less than a revolutionary act.

The affidavit that we have considered is evidence that Koelman had succeeded in winning over practically the whole board of the Bakers' Guild to the principle of ditching festival days. It cannot be coincidental that the soldiers made straight for the bakeries on their pillage, and it is highly unlikely that the governor had had nothing at all to do with the raid. If he did, then the city council will have been in league with him. Whatever the truth of the matter, it is most revealing that the city council laid all the blame for the breakdown of law and order at the feet of the Further Reformation clergyman in its midst.

The cooperation of civil government was an absolute prerequisite for the achievement of the Further Reformation at Sluis. However, Koelman found the majority of the 1672–73 council against him, making the failure of his project a foregone conclusion in such an age as his. He enjoyed

---

59   Graafland *et al.*, 110.

a greater following among the tradesmen. His ability to gather the signatures of almost the whole board of the Bakers' Guild in his favour prompts the conclusion that that middle-class socio-economic group was prepared to translate its displeasure at the religious tendencies of the council into social and even political action. The appointment of a city council more conducive to Koelman in 1675 profited him nothing, because by now national politicians were determined to deal with him.

It should also be borne in mind that the Easter Monday tumult of 1673 remained an isolated incident: we have no indication that the Koelman faction in Sluis ever repeated the demonstration of its point on other ecclesiastical feast days. That is, then, a datum which tends to answer in the affirmative the question raised at the beginning of this section. However, to write off the commotion as a one-off is an inadequate way of coming to terms with what happened that morning. It was the embodiment in deed of a view that remained a marginal one even within the Further Reformation. As a wider whole, that movement did eschew the Roman Catholic background of the feast days inherited from the pre-Reformation church and would have preferred to see them abolished, but the default position of the movement was that since this was a politically unattainable goal, it remained a lawful necessity that at least one service be conducted on these days, and that holding them would at least do something to lessen the riotous living all too customary on holidays. Koelman's utterly consistent stance made him more or less an *Athanasius contra mundum* within his piety movement. If he managed to leverage social capital so startlingly even on this extreme point, it stands to reason that his achievements on less extreme components of the Further Reformation agenda were even greater and more lasting. Sadly, the available historical sources are not sufficient to allow us even to trace the outworkings, let alone to detail them. Be that as it may, the source material used for this chapter serves to show that in exceptional cases, historians can find out more than they often imagine they could.

# 10. A SCOTS HANDMAID AT SLUIS
## The Sluis handmaid Barbara Jobs in light of her wills

*Barbara Jobs, or Barbel Jobs, who is the subject of this final chapter, was not a celebrated figure when she lived in Sluis. Besides, as a maid, her station was so lowly that in her own time almost everyone around her ignored her. After her passing, she delighted several institutions and individuals with bequests from her modest legacy. Thereafter, she was quite forgotten to posterity.*

During the years that Barbara lived at Sluis, there were others in that city who did attract the gaze of publicity. These included councillors, not only those of the city but also those residing within the city who were councillors of het Vrije van Sluis, *a territory that nowadays is the western portion of Zeeland-Flanders. One of this latter group of councillors, Pieter Manteau van Dalem*[1] *(1607–1688), a celebrated land surveyor and engineer, secured his name for posterity by writing a book on his professional expertise, and by his collection of Biblical poetry.*[2] *The Reformed preacher David Montanus*[3] *(d. 1687) published a whole series of poetry volumes while incumbent at Sluis.*[4] *However, among Barbara's contemporary fellow citizens, the best-known to this day, after whom three present-day primary schools in the Netherlands are named,*[5] *was Montanus' brother minister Jacobus Koelman*[6] *(1631–1695). His expulsion from Sluis in 1675 was national and even international news at the time, and he also produced several books while ministering in the city. In updated Dutch, these are sometimes still marketed and sold, and lithographic reprints are also still sold. In historical terms, he was incontestably the most important resident of Sluis in Barbara's day.*

---

1 Regt.
2 Ros [2010], 194–195.
3 Ros [1995]; Op 't Hof [2016-6].
4 Ros [1995].
5 These are located at Gorinchem and Krimpen aan den IJssel in the Province of Zuid-Holland and at Goes in the Province of Zeeland.
6 Krull; Van Lieburg [1990]; Meeuse [1990, 2008]; Op 't Hof [2013-1], 237–268; Groenendijk [2017].

A few sketches have been published of Manteau van Dalem and Montanus, and Koelman studies have generated a whole cottage industry of their own. Other prominent inhabitants of seventeenth-century Sluis have been profiled in scholarly literature.[7] One will look in vain for any mention of Barbara in them; she does not even warrant a mention in genealogies. No wonder, for maids were disregarded in their own time and even today's researchers—sometimes wrongly—regard them as insignificant. Moreover, it was a rare servant who left writings for posterity. This is another way in which Barbara is a remarkable personage: she left no fewer than four known wills.[8] The information that these provide prompted the present author to research her life. After all, Barbara was no less a part of Sluis society than anyone else who resided there, and the lack of information forthcoming on most of those of her station in life make what we know of her all the more compelling. Besides all this, and despite her humble status, she was evidently an interesting character, one who in all likelihood was closely involved with the development at the end of the third quarter of the seventeenth century that gave Sluis a lasting name in church history.

**Biographical sketch**

We know from Barbara Jobs' third and fourth wills that she was a Scotswoman. Consequently, it is no surprise that an English Bible was part of the inventory of her goods in her first will. As we learn from her last two wills, she was born near Aberdeen; most likely in one of the crowded villages of the Aberdeenshire countryside. It is anyone's guess how the course of her young life progressed. The will of Jacob Caulier (d. 1676),[9] dated 31 December 1669,[10] mentions Barbara's "encroaching old age", so she will not have been much under fifty years old then. We therefore conclude that she was born in the first quarter of the seventeenth century and grew up during the reign of James VI/I.

Information on Barbara's relations is scarce. Her 1668 first will indicates that her mother was still alive, together with brothers, sisters, nieces and nephews. In her third will, dated 1678, her mother's name emerges,

---

7   Apart from genealogical articles, there are also scholarly works on the graves within the church walls of Sluis and a published list of Sluis councillors: Dorrenboom [1886, 1893]; Juten; J.M. Bos.
8   M, ZA, ARWNZV, inv. nos. 1853, 3 November 1668; 1936, 5 October 1675; 1938, 15 October 1678; 1939, 1680.
9   The life dates of the Sluis residents in this chapter are derived from an overview of genealogical data of Sluis figures, chiefly from the seventeenth century, which the present author has maintained.
10  M, ZA, ARWNZV, inv. no. 1854, 31 December 1669.

Isabella Rob, and we discover that she had three surviving sisters and one brother, all of whom were still residing in the Aberdeen hinterland. This will also mentions the name of one of her nephews: Pieter Maes, a merchant at Middelburg.[11] Her fourth and final will, dated 1680, mentions only one brother and two sisters, so her mother will have died in the interim.

Barbara signed her wills with the then customary signature of the non-writer: by leaving her mark. We can learn more about her lack of development opportunities from the fact that the four marks are completely different from each other, which implies that she was a total stranger to holding a pen. This was not unusual: Scotswomen in the mid- to late seventeenth century were over 90% illiterate, and the rate was closer to 100% than to 90%.[12] Yet we must not take her for a non-*reader*, for the presence of an English Bible in her inventory, and the mention in her second will of a pew edition of the Bible (containing the psalter and formularies) with silver clasps, reveal that she was presumably able to read both English and Dutch. Consequently, she had probably had some schooling as a girl, and we ought not underestimate the intellectual milieu in which she was raised.

The sources document that Barbara never married and that she was a maid during her years at Sluis, at any rate until 1675 inclusive. It is thus quite reasonable to presume that she had been in domestic service from her youth onwards. She may very well have been one of the old maids of her day whose physical unattractiveness consigned her to a life of spinsterhood and thus of drudgery in other people's homes. The intriguing question here, of course, is how a Scots lass ended up working in the Netherlands.

As we set out in search of an answer, we have at least one datum to guide us: the known fact that she was in service at Sluis for at least the last fifteen years of her life. Therefore, our question can be reformulated: it is not a matter of how a Scots lass ended up in the Netherlands, but of how an established Scots maid came to Sluis. It is known to history that as a garrison town, Sluis was teeming with foreign men in the military service of the States. Very many of these mercenaries were Scotsmen, and complete companies of Scots soldiers were garrisoned in Sluis (being, as it

---

11 It has not been possible to unravel the exact familial relationship between them. This Pieter Maes will have been the same Pieter Maes who became an elder of the Reformed Church at Middelburg on 19 January 1687: Nagtglas [1860], 83b.

12 Houston [1985]; [1989], 134–136. Unfortunately, the latter article does not consider the social class of handmaids.

was, the key city of western States-Flanders) for shorter and longer periods.[13] It is quite plausible that Barbara crossed the North Sea—whether or not already hired by a Scots army officer—as an experienced maid, and that she stayed settled in Sluis for the rest of her days.

The above reasoning may require some unpacking. It depends on the correctness of the researcher's identification of our maid of Sluis with one Barbara Job(s) who crops up on the membership rolls of the English Church at Middelburg. Entered on 2 April 1659 is one *Barbara Job by profession* [of faith]*, gone to Ter Veer with attestation* (indicating a move from Middelburg to the port of Veere on the north side of the same island), and an entry for 8 October 1664 records *Barbara Job returned from Terveer* [Veere] *with attestation*.[14] Assuming that both Barbaras are one and the same, the following reconstruction is very reasonable. Middelburg merchant Pieter Maes was a nephew or cousin of Barbara's, so his mother was a sister or aunt of hers. If Pieter was a merchant, his father will also have been one. The wife of Maes senior will have offered her sister/niece, Barbara, an appointment in the home of a Zeeland merchant, an attractive enough prospect for her to emigrate. The fact that Barbara was working in Veere from 1659 to 1664 is entirely to be expected if this reconstruction is valid, since that port was home to a whole colony of Scots merchants who stocked transhipped goods. However, there are two facts that might plead against the identification of our Barbara with this Barbara. The first is that this Barbara became a confessing member of the church only in 1659, at Middelburg, when our Barbara would have been a mature woman unlikely to undergo confirmation for the first time in her life. The second is that the Middelburg membership rolls do not record that Barbara's departure to anywhere else after 1664.

How and when did our Barbara arrive in Sluis? The first time we encounter her in Sluis sources is in her first will, that of 1668. We see her here as the maid of the bachelor exciseman Jacob Caulier, who worked for the investigations department and who had arrived at Sluis in 1653 aged 22 or 23.[15] In his 1669 will, Caulier, mindful of what he called Bar-

---

13  For an overview of the marriages of Scots soldiers solemnised at Sluis, see Maclean, 273.

14  M, ZA, Archief van de Engelse gemeente te Middelburg [Archive of the English Church at Middelburg], inv. no. 27.

15  After all, he participated in the Lord's Supper at the Reformed Church at Sluis on 6 July 1653 with attestation of membership and good conduct from another congregation: M, ZA, Hervormde Gemeente te Sluis [Reformed Congregation of Sluis] (hereinafter HGS), inv. no. 146, 6 July 1653. For his age, see M, ZA, ARWNZV, inv. no. 1877, 10 May 1658.

bara's faithful service, her frailty and her encroaching old age, left her £125 0s. 0d. Flemish,[16] quite a fortune in that time. This generosity and the mention of her faithful labours will not least have had to do with the fact that a maid in the house of an unmarried man had more expected of her than a maid in the service of a lady of the house. A maid working for an unmarried man had to be far more independent-minded about what needed doing, and had more responsibilities resting on her shoulders, than one working for a housewife.[17] Yet Caulier's choice of words in his will rather indicates that the faithfulness he was meaning was that of long service. Yet if she was the Middelburg Barbara, then she cannot have been more than five years at most in Caulier's service as of 1669. This aspect, too, tends to imply that the two Barbaras were not the same person.

It is nigh certain that Barbara stayed with her employer to the end. The wording of her second will, dated 5 October 1675, throws up the fact that she was still at Caulier's house. Her master died less than a year later and was buried at Sluis on 3 October 1676.[18]

Barbara's last two wills, both of which postdate Caulier's death, fail to mention any new employer or hiring. It would appear that Barbara retired from domestic service in October 1676 and perhaps acquired a small dwelling for herself. That presumption is consistent with the following details about her health.

Caulier mentioned Barbara's frailty in his will. She must have been weak from at least November 1668 onwards, because the note beside her mark on her first will dated that month states that she was bedridden with illness. On both 5 October 1675 and 15 October 1678, the dates of her middle two wills, she was abed, and in 1680, while her last will and testament was being made up, she was not bedridden but was sick with a fever. She breathed her last in early February 1681 and was buried at Sluis on 6 February.

**Chattels**
Making a last will and testament is a sensible proposition only where there are valuable chattels to be passed on. Therefore, Barbara Jobs' having called

---

16 The pound Flemish, rather than the Dutch guilder, was the currency of States-Flanders.
17 The notarial archive of Sluis contains a second known case of a master bequeathing to a servant. In that case, it was the foreman and civilian marshal Abraham Rubbens, who left a third of all his worldly goods and effects to his maid Adriana Cornelis: M, ZA, ARWNZV, inv. no. 1856, 15 December 1671. We note that here, again, the employer was a bachelor.
18 M, ZA, Genealogische Afschriften [Genealogical Transcripts], no. 42. All further burial details also come from this source.

a notary and paid him to write her will indicates that she must have had some desirable goods in her possession. This makes her exceptional within the servant class. Maids' wills are very thin on the ground in the Sluis notarial archive for the seventeenth century.[19] A maid who made no fewer than four of them is an absolute one-off in that archive, as it no doubt would be in many an archive. So did she, as we are now given to expect, have a goodly estate to bequeath?

In her 1668 first will, we read that Barbara had amassed around two hundred guilders. This must have been her savings. She also had wages outstanding from her employer of £9 0s. 0d. Flemish, which she willed to the poor. Her overall capital value was therefore approximately $f$. 254.[20] Besides her well-stocked wardrobe, she had a handmade closet to keep it in, a bejewelled gold ring, a "silver iron" (a reference to the ladies' head-worn jewellery customary in the Netherlands), a silver needle and silver thimble, and her English Bible. This did not amount to a great legacy in absolute terms but was one that any woman of her social status would have been glad to have. As a lifelong spinster, she had been in a position to apply thrift for many years to accumulate these possessions. Something of her strength of character shines through in her stipulation that "her dead body be buried honourably". The Dutch adverb used here refers to a manner of burial which does not come cheap. Nevertheless, she had the means to pay.

In Barbara's second will of 1669, there is explicit mention of a bequest of $f$. 100 for diaconal assistance and $f$. 50 for certain of the local poor, and of a pew Bible with silver clasps. Barbara had most probably not long bought the latter. The rest of her estate was willed to her relatives in Scotland.

Barbara's third will was made in 1678 and in it she bequeathed Koelman $f$. 100 and the poor $f$. 50, and promised one piece each of her jewellery to Martina Maertens (1650–1726) and the little daughter[21] of Thomas Mattheeusen (1643/4–1694). The rest, as before, was for her family. There is thus no evident change in her financial standing compared with the second will, but in fact she had become wealthier: the death of her master in 1676 will have enriched her by £125 0s. 0d. Flemish, as per his will. At

---

19 Other than Barbara, we have only one known example of this: the will of Mayken de Poorter, maid of Samuel Maertens, whom she also appointed her executor: M, ZA, ARWNZV, inv. no. 1845, 27 August 1660.
20 The pound Flemish was equivalent to six guilders.
21 This can only be a reference to Maria Mattheeusen, who was carried to her grave in Sluis on 25 February 1681.

this stage, an unmistakable self-esteem does come through, as this time she stipulates that her "honourable" burial is to be *in* the church (whereas all others of her station in life were buried out in the churchyard).

Barbara's final will, dated 1680, does not make us much the wiser. Koelman was still to get his hundred guilders; the rest of her *f*. 250 was now to go to the deacons, the orphanage and Maria Nemegeer—fifty guilders each. Her non-cash assets were, as before, willed to the relatives in Scotland. What is remarkable is her determination that her furniture and clothes should be sold off at auction after her decease. Are we to see this as another self-conscious sign of risen status, with her presuming that her wardrobe was worth a pretty penny?

**Contacts**
Such was the relationship between Barbara Jobs and her employer Caulier that they trusted each other implicitly and held each other in high esteem. Given this excellent mutual understanding, which most probably was the fruit of long service, it is understandable that she entrusted the execution of her first will to him and that he in turn remembered her with a generous sum in his will. The clause "the good affection that he bears Barbara Jobs" is anything but an empty phrase. The genuineness of his concern for her is expressed in his description of her frailty and advancing years.

Caulier died within a year of the writing of Barbara's second will, and it will not have been without reason that he had drawn up his own will around five years previously. Therefore, Caulier's state of health will have been what impelled Barbara in her second will to divide the responsibilities. While she entrusted the execution of the least personal sections of the document to the notaries Adriaen Maertens (1636/6–1677) and Thomas Mattheeusen, there was no-one else but her master whom she trusted to see to the disbursement of *f*. 50 to certain local paupers and to send her relatives her physical goods.

Barbara's first will had been made up by Johan Cant senior (d. 1686), but Mattheeusen took care of the remaining three wills (the first of those three in partnership with Maertens), even though Cant was still alive and in practice. Evidently, she preferred Mattheeusen as a person. Her instruction of Cant for the first will must have been in consideration of the fact that he served as notary to her employer, Caulier.[22] Her relationship with

---

22 Both times that Caulier needed a legal document written, it was Cant whom he instructed: M, ZA, ARWNZV, inv. no. 1854, 21 December 1669; 1861, 26 September 1676.

Mattheeusen, especially later in life, was more personal: in 1678 and again in 1680, she appointed him one of her two executors, and in the earlier of those two latter wills she also left his young daughter a piece of jewellery.

The other executor was Cornelis Cambij, *alias* Camby. Barbara remembered his wife (the aforementioned Martina Maertens), too, bequeathing her the other piece of jewellery in 1678. Cambij was the bailiff of the States-General in Sluis. The sources have nothing to say directly about Barbara's relationship with Mattheeusen or Cambij, but by casting further out, we can endeavour to gain a view of it. It is notable that both of these notaries were elected deacons (for the customary two-year term of office) on 8 December 1678.[23] Barbara left a legacy to diaconal needs in all her wills, and her master, Caulier, had also been a deacon—although in the Walloon Church—from 1675 to 1677.[24] It seems that Barbara chose these two notaries because of their church office. That would also explain in one fell swoop why in 1675 she appointed Adriaen Maertens and Mattheeusen executors of her will: they were at that time deacons of the Dutch Reformed Church at Sluis, and thus brethren in office of Caulier's.[25] Two objections might be made to this explanation. Firstly, the wills make no mention of the office of deacon; secondly, Mattheeusen and Cambij were not appointed to that office until 8 December 1678, while Barbara had written her (third) will nearly two months earlier, on 15 October. The explanation is therefore not entirely satisfying or complete.

An alternative explanation would be that Barbara regarded Mattheeusen and Adriaen Maertens as the most trustworthy men apart from her master, and that after the latter's death (Maertens was buried at Sluis on 29 September 1677), she opted for Cambij because he had just (on 11 May 1678) married Maertens' daughter Martina[26]. This explanation, however, would leave unresolved the question of what virtues they were that Barbara saw in Mattheeusen and Maertens.

It is not customary in historical research to set much store by the names of witnesses appearing on legal documents. Historians are well aware that all too often, those writing their last will and testament have grabbed convenient people almost at random to sign as required, and that agreeing to be a witness is certainly not tantamount to having a par-

---

23  M, ZA, HGS, inv. no. 6, 8 December 1678.
24  It was not without cause, then, that in 1676 Caulier entrusted the execution of his will to two deacons, namely Thomas Mattheeusen and Adriaen Maertens: M, ZA, ARWNZV, inv. no. 1861, 26 September 1676.
25  M, ZA, HGS, inv. no. 4.
26  Dorrenboom [1886], 287a.

ticular relation to the testator. At first sight, we might assume the same randomness in the choice of witnesses to all four of Barbara's wills. There are eight different names in these slots; none was recalled to witness a subsequent will. However, what makes it worth considering their identities is the fact that at the signing of at least three, and probably all four, of Barbara's wills, the document had to be written under the roof where Barbara was housebound, and not at the more standard venue of the notary's office. Would a responsible notary really have chosen people willy-nilly to witness at the testator's home in cases of confinement? In my opinion, it is far more plausible that in such cases, the testator would name a couple of trusted local personages for him to go and fetch. The identities of those whom the testator named out of choice (where such was indeed the case) will tell us something of substance about the circle of contacts of the person who had called the notary to attend.

Serving as witnesses to Barbara's first will were Steven Hendricx and Isbrant Terwisca. Who were they? Hendricx had employment in the army and was married to Elisabeth Andries.[27] Terwisca was a provost and his wife was Sara de Haes (d. 1669). There is no evident connection between them and Barbara—or, at least, there would not be if one failed to think geographically. What leaps out at the peruser of a Sluis street map is that Hendricx lived directly opposite Caulier at the west side of Nieuwstraat.[28] Caulier himself, together with his maid Barbara, had an address on the corner of the east side of Nieuwstraat with the south side of Geweldigerstraat.[29] Provost Terwisca lived in Geweldigerstraat; where else, since the literal name of that road is 'Provost Street', using a native Dutch word for the same job title. So Hendricx and Terwisca knew Barbara as a neighbour. She was on excellent terms with at least the former of these neighbours, since in her second will she wished some of her clothes to go to one of Hendricx' daughters, Elsken Snijer, *alias* Snijder.[30] In 1675, Elsken was a widow of slender means with a daughter to care for.[31]

---

27  Wherever the derivation is not given in a footnote, all details are taken from the digital file mentioned in footnote 9.
28  M, ZA, ARWNZV, inv. no. 1749, 13 July 1662. The Steven Snyders mentioned there is identical with the Steven Hendricx mentioned here and later in this chapter.
29  M, ZA, ARWNZV, inv. no. 1750, 25 July 1679.
30  For this, see footnote 27.
31  M, ZA, ARWNZV, inv. no. 1802, 8 July 1669.

*The house on Nieuwstraat where Barbara Jobs and Jacob Caulier lived*

The two witnesses to Barbara's second will were the two notaries whom she had also appointed executors. As such, they had a direct involvement in the dispositions. Neither of them lived near Barbara.

Johannes Holsaert and Abraham van de Putte acted as witnesses for Barbara's third will. They, likewise, will have had to make a special visit to the house where Barbara lay abed to have witnessed the will, but it is not clear which Sluis address she was living at in 1678, so our opportunity is lost to perform a geographical triangulation to narrow the search. Holsaert was married to Adriana Verbeke; van de Putte was a coppersmith by trade, and his wife was named Maria de Coninck (d. 1690). Holsaert and van de Putte probably both had a special bond with Barbara; van de Putte undoubtedly did, since we see strikingly that in her second will, Barbara had wanted her silver-clasped psalter to go to van de Putte's eldest daughter, Egidia (b. 1678).

The names of the witnesses to Barbara's final will are Jan Façon and Pieter Rooseboom. Façon, a tailor, was married to Susanna van Ytegem. We know nothing of van Rooseboom save that he served as a deacon in the Walloon Church from 23 December 1685 to 1 February 1688.[32]

The wife and daughter of Jan Kanu mentioned in Barbara's second will cannot have been very comfortably off, given that clothes were bequeathed to them. It is unclear whether they lived in her immediate vicinity or whether Barbara had struck up a bond with them in some other way.

---

32  M, ZA, GHS, inv. no. 7.

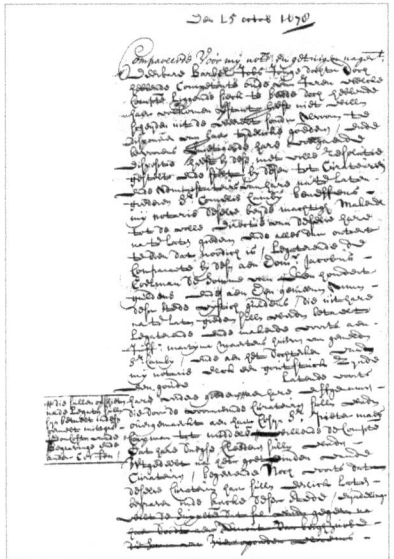 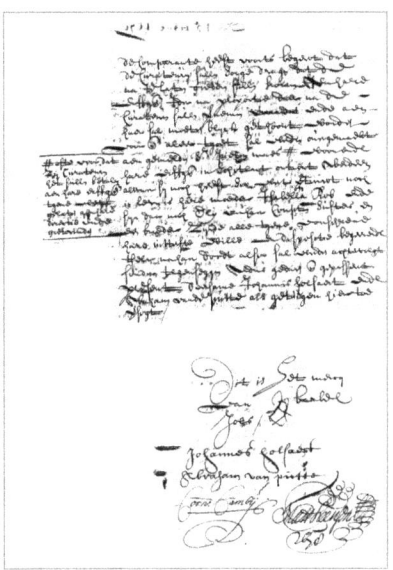

*Barbara's third will, dated 15 October 1678*

There was a withdrawal of bequest: in her third will, Barbara left £4 0s. 0d. Flemish to Aernout van Berghuyzen, of whom unfortunately no further civil details are known, and she subsequently reversed that decision. We do not know why.

In her final will, the maid of Sluis left ƒ. 15 to Maria Nemegeer for services rendered. Maria was a daughter of the stadtholder of *het Vrije van Sluis*, Laurens Nemegeer (d. 1681). She must have tended to Barbara in the latter's declining years.

**Religious conviction**
If we compare Barbara Jobs' four wills, we see a striking difference between the earlier two and the last two: Koelman is not named in the first pair but is in the latter. At least as importantly, Koelman is the greatest beneficiary among the individual legatees, inheriting a hundred guilders, and in both wills he heads the list of named heirs.

Koelman had served the Reformed Church at Sluis as preacher from 1662 to 1675, the year in which he was banned from the city for refusing to use the formularies in worship or to observe ecclesiastical festival days not falling on a Sunday. This position of his was relatively extreme within the Reformed piety movement covered by the name of the Further Reformation[33]. At the root of his objections was the decisive influence that Scots Puritanism[34] exerted on Koelman. While these stated views and practices were the occasion that was seized upon to have Koelman expelled, in reality it was his fiery and unapologetic contention for Further Reformation ideals—a zeal in which he did not always act as wisely as he might have done—that made his name mud with local, provincial and even national politicians. That he exerted his exacting church discipline upon city councillors in exactly the same manner as he would treat a case of sin among the lower orders was an extremely risky policy, given the relationship that obtained in the Dutch Republic and especially in Zeeland between government and the established church. It made all that he stood for such a stench in the nostrils of councillors that some of them became his sworn enemies, resolved not to rest until they had put paid to this troubler of Sluis.

Getting rid of a man of Koelman's calibre was easier said than done. After all, he had drummed up very considerable ranks of appreciators within the Reformed congregation of Sluis for his obvious personal authenticity and his sensitive pastoral touch. To what extent political and social tensions may have played a role, including the possibility of a factional war behind the scenes, is something that we cannot know in the current state of research and that will probably always remain an open question owing to lack of appropriate sources. At any rate, we do know that from February 1673 onwards, a varying group of Koelmanites from all the social classes of Sluis stepped into the ring to defend Koelman. These advocates of the Further Reformation took up the fight for him by penning remonstrances and petitions to political and ecclesiastical governing bodies, doing their utmost to prevent him being expelled.

The fact that the petitions in Koelman's favour were preceded by a petition of 53 congregants of the Reformed Church at Sluis and citizens of the city calling for urgent reformation of a whole range of abuses in the religious, ethical, societal and social spheres, and the actual content of those later petitions, reveal to us that the impulse to defend Koelman in writing was driven more by an appreciation of what he was striving for than of him personally.[35] The precursor petition mentioned above dates from November 1672. After clergymen in Sluis and Zeeland had begun putting it about that by shunning the liturgy Koelman would be bringing

---

33  Graafland *et al.*
34  Coffey and Lim; this study, 15-16.
35  For the following, see Theophilus Parresius [1677], 17–238.

suspension or even expulsion down upon his own head, 26 serving and former elders and deacons of the congregation wrote to Walcheren presbytery on 18 February 1673 with a remonstrance standing foursquare behind Koelman and his reforming aims. Hot on the heels of the Easter Monday events described in the previous chapter, a similar petition was sent to the presbytery on 11 April 1673, this time with over a hundred church members' signatures on it: to be precise, sixty women and 42 men.

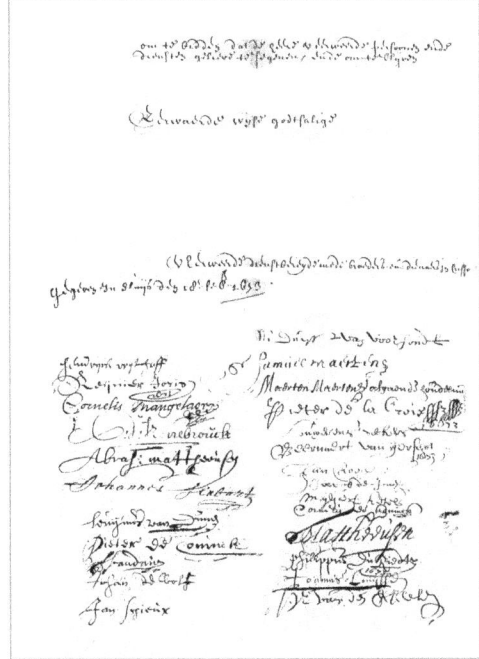

*Signatures appended to the pro-Koelman petition of 18 February 1673 by current and former Sluis church officers*

However, when it actually came to submitting the petition, the organisers had second thoughts, as they (not unreasonably) feared that the presbytery would not take kindly to women publicly involving themselves in affairs of church. Sixteen days later, having learned by their trial and error, the organisers gathered 72 male congregants' names for a petition of identical nature to the previous one, which this time was submitted to the presbytery. Another petition landed on the presbytery's table that August, this time signed by 52 male church members. When a deputation of the church officers was dispatched in February 1674 to speak up for Koelman at the States-General, they had two further pro-Koelman petitions sent on to The Hague to sway their minds: one had the names of serving and former elders and deacons under it, the other the names of 69 male confirmed members. In October 1674, a second petition of male congregants to the States-General boasted 84 signatories. On 29 November, six councillors composed a remonstrance declaring their opposition to any suspension of Koelman.

After Koelman's expulsion from Sluis on 17 June 1675, he was officially the subject of a nationwide pulpit ban and spent the rest of his life leading private fellowship meetings and translating Puritan (largely Scots) reading matter.

In making Koelman the first heir whom she mentioned in her two last wills of 1678 and 1680, Barbara will have been mindful of this turn of events in his earthly fortunes. She was evidently so moved at her old preacher's plight, left bereft as he was of any chance of financial support from any public body, that she resolved to let him partake largely of her legacy. There cannot be any other conclusion than that she was a fervent supporter of him and of his ideals.

It is therefore not stretching matters to assume that Barbara's was one of the sixty women's names adorning the undelivered (and sadly unpreserved) petition to the Walcheren presbytery of 11 April 1673.

Two facts would appear to make the conclusion less likely that Barbara was a supporter of Koelman's and that she was one of the petition signatories for him. We shall consider them at length. The first is that her name is not encountered in the membership rolls of the Reformed Church at Sluis, even though it is a chronological and completely-preserved list. She cannot therefore have signed that particular petition, as it was reserved to confirmed members of the congregation. If she was not a member, then it is very much open to question whether she attended the Reformed Church in her years in that city. Might she not just as well have belonged to another denomination represented there, or even perhaps have chosen not to join any church exclusively? In other words, might her appreciation for Koelman have been something very personal rather than determined by affiliation; might it have been his steadfastness and the injury done him that aroused in her the feelings of fondness, love and care that she had earlier in life channelled towards her employer(s), without her necessarily having been associated with his congregation or denomination?

Barbara's is one of those cases where such thoughtful and involved historical questions as these are actually very easily answered, thanks to the existence of a list that preserves as a snapshot the membership of the Reformed Church at Sluis as of March 1672. Under the address of the fourth house on Beestenmarkt, the entry in this list reads "Jacob Cauwlier,

Berbel Jobs".[36] So, although her name is not on the regular rolls, Barbara appears to have been very much a member of the Reformed Church at Sluis after all!

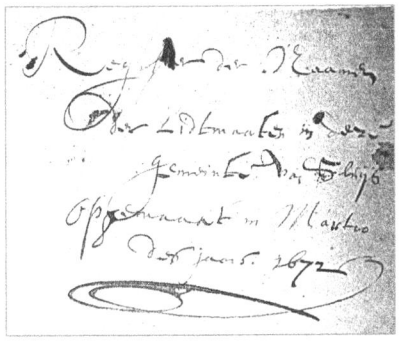

March 1672 membership roll of Sluis Reformed Church

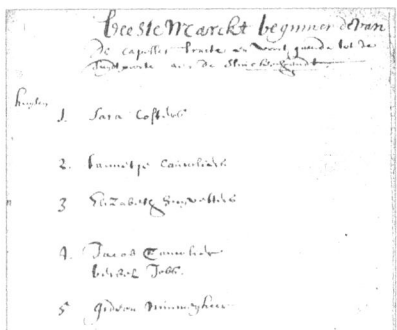

Item no. 4 is the entry concerning Jacob Caulier and 'Berbel' (Barbara) Jobs

Yet this discovery merely presents a further problem, and a serious one at that: how could Barbara's name have been left off the membership roll, which as preserved contains no hiatus in time? Is it an incidental omission or does it imply that there were more members of the Reformed Church at Sluis in the seventeenth century whose names were never enrolled? Thoroughgoing research allows us to state here that Barbara was certainly not the only member whose name is sought in vain on the rolls. Although these give the appearance of being an exhaustive register, that is not the truth of the matter. Besides, experience teaches that seventeenth-century registers are seldom complete, at least not those from Sluis. Many a modern researcher would be quick to dismiss Barbara's omission as an indication of prejudice against her class, but in fact people from all walks of life have been found to have been omitted from the Sluis membership rolls.[37]

Now, on the grounds that she actually was a church member, we can safely posit that Barbara regularly heard Koelman preach, and probably preferred his sermons to those of other clergymen. Another hypothesis

---

36  M, ZA, HGS, inv. no. 148.
37  For examples of this incompleteness, even regarding persons of the higher classes, see Op 't Hof [2004-1], 85, 101, 111. This phenomenon can also be seen elsewhere: Op 't Hof [2011-2], 71.

that has now become highly probable is that she was one of the sixty women to sign their names to the petition of 11 April 1673.

The second of the facts appearing to militate against taking Barbara for a Koelmanite or as a signatory of the petition for him is that Koelman does not feature in Barbara's second will, that of 5 October 1675, even though he had already (and very recently) been banished from Sluis at that date. For this detail, which admittedly is puzzling at first sight, two possible explanations can be proposed. Barbara had her second will drawn up at her employer Caulier's house, and he was given a substantial role in its execution. Most probably, Caulier, who as we shall see below was also an adherent of Koelman's, had principled objections to leaving money to a preacher, even one as deserving as Koelman, and Barbara did not at this stage have the courage to contradict her master's opinion. Not only was such a legacy unheard-of on the Continent, but it was probably even repugnant to Caulier's mind. There might have been a moral and social aspect to what we are presuming was his disapproval. That a woman, and an unmarried woman at that, should leave money to a man of the cloth might provoke some salacious gossip about the relationship they had enjoyed. Besides, in the pronounced class thinking of the seventeenth century, it would be hard to swallow that a mere maid should put on the airs and graces of leaving money to a preacher—a man very much her social superior.

A secondary explanation for Barbara's hesitancy may have been that less than four months after Koelman's expulsion, the dust had not yet settled on the matter and it remained to be seen whether he would ever be able to mount a pulpit again, perhaps even the very pulpit he had been forced out of. Put otherwise, Koelman's need for financial support was not as clear-cut in October 1675 as it was by 1678 and 1680.

Now that we have established that Barbara was a zealous advocate of Koelman and the Further Reformation ideals that he espoused, it is worthwhile that we at least experiment with reviewing all her social contacts through that prism in the expectation that some of them will thus become more transparent to our gaze, adding to our stock of knowledge.

On the grounds of his signature on the 4 August 1673 petition to Walcheren presbytery, it is known that Barbara's employer Caulier was also a believer in Koelman and his Further Reformation.[38] We thus see that the closeness between maid and master was enhanced by a spiritual dimension, one which makes their concern for each other the more readily

---

38 M, ZA, Acta Classis Walcheren [Minutes of Walcheren Presbytery] (hereinafter ACW), inv. no. 25, no. 930 (4 August 1673).

understood. This religious congeniality is, in fact, most likely the reason why Barbara had entered Caulier's service.

The first time that Barbara made her last will and testament, it was Cant who undertook the notarial duties. He was a declared opponent of Koelman's: he twice signed documents condemning the preacher.[39] The foregoing has already made clear that Barbara chose Cant because he was her master's notary. Yet when Cant openly put his name to the efforts to remove Koelman from Sluis, Barbara wanted nothing more to do with him and looked for other notaries. For the next will, her second, of 1675, she opted for Mattheeusen and Adriaen Maertens. That this choice really was motivated by her religious convictions, or more accurately by her approval of the religious convictions that Koelman was putting into action, is confirmed by the fact that both Mattheeusen and Maertens were among the Further Reformation preacher's convinced adherents and were prepared to state so publicly: Mattheeusen signed two pro-Koelman petitions[40] and Maertens one[41]. Her instruction of Mattheeusen on his own for the third and fourth wills was simply due to the fact that Maertens had since died, and had nothing to do with Mattheeusen being preferred above Maertens. We see this clearly from the fact that in the fourth and final will, Cornelis Cambij takes Maertens' place as beneficiary, being his son-in-law. It is notable that Cambij himself was not an outspoken Koelmanite, although he was not a declared opponent of the preacher either. Barbara evidently had enough trust in him arising from his marriage to Maertens' daughter that she was prepared to appoint him executor even though she did not entirely see eye to eye with him religiously.[42]

It has already been seen that the witnesses to Barbara's first will were people whom she knew from the neighbourhood. Hendricx probably died before the Koelman controversy came to a head; it is known for sure that he had become a member of the Reformed Church at Sluis on 2 January 1661.[43] Terwisca did live to see the whole Koelman affair play out, but no surviving documents state that he was a church member.

Research into the witnesses of Barbara's will does not throw up anything more concrete than this, either. Façon did not produce an attestation to

---

39  M, ZA, ACW, inv.no. 25, no. 936 (12 September 1673)
40  M, ZA, ACW, inv.no. 25, nos. 914 (18 February 1673) and 930 (4 August 1673).
41  M, ZA, ACW, inv.no. 25, no. 930 (4 August 1673).
42  Between the years 1679 and 1694, Cambij twice served the Reformed congregation of Sluis as a deacon and twice as an elder: M, ZA, HGS, inv. nos. 6–8.
43  M, ZA, HGS, inv. no. 147, 2 January 1661.

join the Lord's Supper until 6 April 1681, and Rooseboom became a communicating member on 7 April 1675, having undergone confirmation.[44] Rooseboom thus took this step in his church life only once Koelman's number appeared to be up, which can responsibly be interpreted as meaning that he was far from being a supporter of Koelman's. These considerations rather fortify our impression, formed earlier, that there was no particularly close bond between the testatrix and her witnesses.

Matters were clearly different with Barbara's third will, since the witnesses' names are appended with the special phrase "asked to be witnesses hereof". There is no other way to interpret these words than that the testatrix had herself asked these two people to be witnesses, or that the notary had done so on her behalf. We were not able in the previous section to determine the nature of the relationship of Barbara to her witnesses. Perhaps her love of Koelman will now fill in the gaps for us? Indeed it will. Both Holsaert and van de Putte had declared themselves to be among Koelman's sympathisers by their signatures of the 4 August 1673 petition.[45]

The poor whom Barbara remembered in her second will with her clothes may have been needy people whom she knew only socially, but there is equally the possibility that there was a likemindedness at play. At least Jacomina van Ixem, the wife of Jan Kanu, is known for certain to have been a confessing member of the Reformed Church.[46] The same spiritual agreement may have been at work between Barbara and Martina Maertens, the daughter of Adriaen Maertens and wife of Cornelis Cambij. In the cases of Aernout van Berghuyzen and Maria Nemegeer, that appears a less well-founded proposition.[47]

There is a passage in Barbara's second will (1675) that fuels the idea that her social concerns were most especially for the poor of her own religious convictions. Besides willing $f.$ 100 to diaconal work at Sluis[48], she left $f.$ 50 to certain paupers, leaving it to her master Caulier to apportion the latter sum. What was the reason for her making that exception to

---

44  M, ZA, HGS, inv. no. 147, 7 April 1675.
45  M, ZA, ACW, inv. no. 25, no. 930 (4 August 1673).
46  M, ZA, HGS, inv. no. 147, 6 April 1664.
47  The first occasions that they presented themselves for communion as confirmed members were on 3 January 1672 and 5 January 1670 respectively: M, ZA, HGS, inv. no. 147, 5 January 1670, 3 January 1672.
48  Besides, her wording *de diaconie van Sluis* is theologically significant: it reveals that the deacons of the city's Reformed Church were collectively regarded by the public as a municipal institution, as indeed they were in actual practice. The Reformed Church was the *public* church, even in the eyes of a Further Reformation adherent!

her testamentary arrangements? The fact that she directed Caulier, a fervent follower of Koelman's, to choose the beneficiaries of the ƒ. 50 may indicate that Barbara knew he would understand her wishes to be that the recipients should be those local poor who, together with both him and her, had had a special place in their hearts for the Further Reformation preacher. Taken together with the foregoing facts, this datum could indicate the existence of a fully-fledged grouping of the pious within the Reformed Church at Sluis.

**Puritan background?**
We can, then, state that even though seventeenth-century Sluis did not take much notice of Barbara Jobs, her last two wills made her all but unique in the degree of loyalty she showed Koelman. In the ocean of ink spilt over the Further Reformation in particular and Reformed Pietism[49] in the Netherlands more generally, never before has an example surfaced of ordinary congregants loving their preacher enough to remember him in their will. Barbara is therefore a truly exceptional woman. Had not the present author pored over the whole archives of every notary in Sluis in the relevant period, he would have confidently written that Barbara is unique in her testamentary disposition to Koelman. However, she turns out not to be: his quest has thrown up a total of three other wills in which the same preacher was named as an heir.

The earliest of those wills to be made was (like Barbara's) that of a woman, Maria Moerman (1635/36–1682), a daughter of the city doctor Johannes Moerman, who died in 1662. Maria was confirmed into full church membership in 1652.[50] The first of her wills, which is the one that is one of those three that made Koelman a beneficiary, is dated 10 November 1663.[51] Of all the sums of money that Maria mentions, the highest, £50 0s. 0d. Flemish, is for Anna Hus (d. 1675), Koelman's wife, to whom she also bequeaths a set of silver-handled knives, a silver goblet and two silver spoons. Should Anna predecease Maria, the 1663 will provides that Koelman himself will inherit that silverware. Besides, the testatrix appoints both of the Koelmans as executors of her will. On 3 May 1666, Maria Moerman replaced her first will with a second[52] that left the dispositions to the Koelmans intact. What is very remarkable is that when Maria married Cornelis Mangelaer in 1672, she was very particular in her

---

49  Op 't Hof [2005-1].
50  M, ZA, HGS, inv. no. 146, 7 July 1652.
51  M, ZA, ARWNZV., inv. no. 1848, 10 November 1663.
52  M, ZA, ARWNZV., inv. no. 1866, 3 May 1666.

prenuptial contract[53] that should she predecease her husband, £25 0s. 0d. Flemish should be disbursed to Anna Hus, and if Anna had already died by then, that the money not be made over to Koelman if he survived her but instead be bequeathed to the poor.

The stipulations of her prenuptial contract allow us to see that it was not so much Reverend Koelman himself whom Maria Moerman wished to remember with her goods but rather the vicar's wife, especially if we bear in mind that Mangelaer himself was a resolute defender of their Further Reformation preacher. In addition, the bequests to Koelman in this will are of a different nature than Barbara's final disposition: not only would he only receive money if his wife had died, but more tellingly, Maria made him an inheritor three years prior to his exile.

In what light, then, should we see these bequests? A 1666 list of Sluis householders records that Koelman was at that time renting a dwelling from Maria Moerman.[54] So did the Koelmans move into her property as soon as they arrived at Sluis in 1662, and did the friendship emerge from a landlady-tenant relationship?

The third will to feature Koelman as a legatee is that of Maerten Maertens (d. 1695), dated 10 June 1690.[55] He was a baker and merchant by trade. He was elected deacon once and elder six times in his life, holding his first church office in 1663.[56] From 1676 onwards, with breaks, he was on the College of Aldermen, and he was even the mayor elected from among the aldermen for 1678–1679.[57] An outspoken Koelmanite, he was so convinced of his preacher's theology that he was one of the four bakers known to have opened their shops instead of going to church on Easter Monday 1673.[58] In his will, Maertens bequeathed sums of money to various non-relatives, of whom the first to be mentioned is Koelman, who was to inherit a hundred guilders.

This legacy will have been the expression of Maerten Maertens' sympathy for his esteemed preacher's having been banned from Sluis and indeed from all Zeeland. His motives are therefore the same as those that drove Barbara's final dispositions of 1680. The only distinction between them, and a major one, was their social rank: Maertens was one of the city fathers and known as such to everyone in town, while Barbara was just a

---

53  M, ZA, ARWNZV., inv. no. 1935, 1 March 1672.
54  Oostburg, Gemeentearchief Sluis [Municipal Archive of Sluis], Oud archief Sluis [Sluis Old Archive], inv. no. 9.
55  M, ZA, ARWNZV., inv. no. 1944, 10 June 1690.
56  M, ZA, HGS , inv. nos. 3–8.
57  Dorrenboom [1893], 85b, 79b.
58  This study, 329, 335.

maid, one whose voice was never heard at public events. Precisely because of the extreme gap between the two in status, we can see how Koelman had penetrated the city's society from top to bottom with his doctrine. In that sense, the Further Reformation as a Reformed piety movement was a truly *popular* movement.

As we evaluate the evidence of this section, we should note that only two people are known to history to have felt sorry enough for Koelman and to have held him in high enough esteem to bequeath him a sum of money, and that both were residents of Sluis. Whether this phenomenon was a local peculiarity of Sluis cannot be determined until such time as researchers have systematically gone through the notarial archives of all the Dutch locations where Koelman had a followership. Given that his followers were dotted throughout the United Provinces, from Friesland down to States-Flanders, it will be a good long while before we have any clarity on that score.

The only conclusions we can draw in the present state of research is that the sometime mayor Maerten Maertens was rather late in following the example set by maid Barbara. It is not reasonable to assume that Barbara had told Maertens personally about her donation, nor would the notary Mattheeusen have taken such a liberty. I find it far more likely that it was Koelman himself who in 1681 confided in Maertens that he had received the generous sum of a hundred guilders from Barbara's estate, and that Maertens, his conscience touched, decided to match her bequest so as not to be outdone by a sister of much more limited means. It does, of course, remain a theoretical possibility that the two of them had the idea of remembering their beloved ex-preacher—and hit upon the identical amount—independently of each other.

One last question that this chapter might legitimately seek to address is this: Was the financial bequest to Koelman an idea that Barbara had thought up of her own creativity, or was she joining an existing tradition of testamentary generosity to clergy? In his dissertation on the Banbury Puritans in the period 1554–1660, Barton John Blankenfeld has demonstrated that there are few, if any, more reliable sources than a will as a touchstone of someone's Puritan sympathies (or lack thereof) in that Oxfordshire town. Puritans, in accordance with their financial means, left bequests to Puritan clergymen, particularly remembering those whose convictions had got them ejected from their livings or prevented them from ever obtaining one.[59] Although little has been written on this

---

59 Blankenfeld, 349–60; Wright, 163–167. That this was a widespread phenomenon within English Puritanism is seen from the fact that it was also practised elsewhere in the country: Reynolds, 75. This also applies to Thomas Brewer, an English Puritan resident in Leiden: Sprunger [1994], 135.

phenomenon,[60] it would be an unusual line of reasoning to conclude from this that remembering needy Puritan preachers in one's will was a practice quite confined to Banbury. It could well have become generalised in English Puritanism and become a practice in Scots Puritanism, too.[61] There is therefore a real chance that Barbara, in remembering the banned preacher of her city with a considerable sum, was propagating an existing tradition in a new land, followed by Maerten Maertens. There is one more similarity with the known English practice: in England, women bequeathed more than men to Puritan clergymen.[62] If this assumption as to the inspiration for Barbara's bequest to a hard-done-by Pietist preacher is correct, then it represents yet another entry in the already lengthy list of elements of Puritan influence on Dutch spirituality[63] and Barbara Jobs, the maid of Sluis, will (pending perhaps further discoveries) go down in the annals as the introducer of this practice in the Netherlands.

**Moral**
With the rise and rise of secularism in our day, even academics have become less inclined to take religion seriously as a factor in historical research. Yet the foregoing has shown that Barbara Jobs' religious convictions are the best key we have to understanding her wills. If we had not taken her beliefs as the basic premise of the above research, she would have remained another indistinguishable serving woman. As it is, however, she rises from the page, despite her social insignificance, as a woman who in her own way formed part of a network, encompassing all walks of life, of Koelmanites who expressed her religious ideals not merely abstractly but in pounds, shillings and pence. In future, she might even be noted as the importer to the Netherlands of a Puritan practice that others had not yet managed to introduce. If so, then she will have ended up being someone of far greater significance to history than anyone could have guessed.

The research subjects of specialists in Reformed Pietism in the Netherlands, and more particularly of the Further Reformation, are almost exclusively men. We always hear talk of the men of the Further Reformation, but seldom if ever of the women of the movement. Obviously, this has much to do with the infrequency in the seventeenth century with

---

60 Collinson [1980], 187; Cliffe [1993], 44–9, 52, 68, 116, 126, 128, 132.
61 Sadly, the literature on Scots Puritanism is silent on this matter.
62 Wright, 162–3.
63 Those wishing to scope that influence should consult the key literature on it: Graafland; Groenendijk [1984-1]; Op 't Hof [1987-1], [2001-1], 273–339.

which women left a documentary trace. In historical reality, at least as many women as men, and in all likelihood more—many more—women than men, will have adhered to and laboured for the ideals of that piety movement. One fact that is plain for all is that the Dutch Reformed Church had a female majority in membership.[64]

In the recent past, researchers such as Fred A. van Lieburg have sought to redress the imbalance found in conventional research on Dutch Reformed Pietism and the Further Reformation, and the typical image that people have of these movements, by deliberately focusing on women of those spiritual tendencies in Dutch history.[65] The disadvantage inherent in that approach is that the women on whom one can dig up data are all élite figures. What is known of Pietist women of the seventeenth-century middle and lower classes? Are such women even known to us by name? In amongst all the academic literature, there is one brief article that can provide us with an answer to those questions at local level. In the archive of a Dordrecht notary, J. van Voorst found an inventory of the chattels of one Wilhelmina van Loo, *alias* Wilhelmina van der Loo. Part of the inventory consists of a list of books, several of whose titles are Further Reformation standard reading. Van Voorst is quite right in her conclusion that the owner of these books can be reckoned among the adherents of that movement, as we can see from how van Loo is described in the church officers' minutes of the Reformed Church of Dordrecht, namely as an attender of conventicles.[66] It is seldom that legal sources are consulted to help confirm an historical subject's allegiance to Pietism or to the Further Reformation. Yet as we have seen from the previous chapter of the present work, legal documents can be a mine of such information, not just inventories but also sworn statements, and with the present chapter in mind, we can add wills to that list. Legal documents might not be the first source category that springs to mind when one turns one's hand to researching Dutch Reformed Pietism and the Further Reformation, but they can in the most unexpected way provide personal colour (although often only fragmentary hints) about the adherents. The particular value to researchers of these hints is that they often concern the lower orders of society.

---

64   Van Deursen [1974], 134–135; Abels and Wouters, 1: 259–264; Bergsma, 368–370.
65   F.A. van Lieburg dedicated an unfortunately unfinished series of articles to them: Van Lieburg [1985]. For a general overview of publications about women in Dutch Reformed Pietism and the Further Reformation, see Op 't Hof [2007], 131–133.
66   Van Voorst.

Clearly, a Barbara Jobs—a person whose religious convictions dictated her priorities—is the exception rather than the norm. Even so, she is a marker bobbing in the sea of historical research, whereby we may take warning not to ignore or trivialise religious motives, not even when we are looking at legal documents and particularly at wills.

# BIBLIOGRAPHY

**Pre-1801 publications**

Alleine [1717], Joseph, *Een alarm voor onbekeerde zondaren*. Rotterdam: Reinier van Doesburg, 1717

Baers [1648], Johannes, *Cornucopiæ, dat is: een boeck van allerley materien. Seer leersaem en aengenaem om te lesen, voor alle liefhebbers van vreemde ende fraye dingen*. Amsterdam: Johannes Baers, 1648

Beeltsnyder [1654/5], Johannes, *Euthanasia*. Amsterdam: the widow of Marten Janszoon Brandt and Abraham van den Burgh, 1654/5

Binning [1678], Hugh, *Ettelijcke gronden van de christelijcke religie*. Rotterdam: Pieter van Veen; Vlissingen: Abraham vam Laren; Amsterdam: Mercy Brouwning, 1678

Bois [1665], Mattheüs du, *Godts wonder-werck, voor en in de wedergeboorte, met een korte alleen-spraeck over 't selve. Door eygen bevindinge beschreven, en nu tot nut van anderen in 't licht gebracht*. Haarlem: Robbert Tinneken, 1665

Bois [1667], Mattheüs du, *Godts wonder-werck, voor en in de wedergeboorte*. Amsterdam: Abraham van den Burgh, 1667

Bois [1680], Mattheüs du, *Annotatien van veelderley christelyke sin en geestryke spreuken, en sententien*. Amsterdam: Johannes Boekholt, 1680

Bois [1681], Mattheüs du, *Geestelijck lusthofje, beplant met verscheyde christelijcke gezangen*. Amsterdam: Johannes Boekholt, 1681

Bois [1684], Mattheüs du, *Christelijke sin- en geest-rijke annotatien*. Amsterdam: Jacob van de Velde, 1684

Bois [1728], Mattheüs du, *Christelijke annotatien*. Rotterdam: Hermanus Kentlink, 1728

Borstius [1670], Jacobus, *Onderwys van het scheyden van de gereformeerde, en 't oprichten van een suyvere kercke*. Rotterdam: Johannes Borstius, 1670

Borstius [1696], Jacobus, *Vyftien predicatien*. Utrecht: Thomas Appels, 1696

Brown [1676], John, *Christus, de Wegh, de Waarheidt, ende het Leven*. Rotterdam: Henricus Goddaeus, 1676

Brown [1679], John, *Christus de Wegh, de Waarheidt, ende het Leven*. Amsterdam: Jan Bouman, 1679

Brown [1694], John, *Christ in believers the hope of glory*. Edinburg: John Reid, 1694

Burmannus [1671], Franciscus, *Synopsis theologiae, & speciatim oeconomiae foederum Dei, ab initio saeculorum usque ad consummationem eorum*, 2 vols. Utrecht: Cornelis Jacobszoon Noenaert and Willem Clerck, 1671

Christianus Parresius [Jacobus Koelman] [1677], *Vier zamenspraaken, over ettelijke kerkelyke zaaken*. Utrecht: Willem Clerk, 1677

Clarke [1662], Samuel, *A collection of the lives of ten eminent divines, famous in their generations for learning, prudence, piety, and painfullness in the work of the ministry*. London: William Miller, 1662

Clarke [1677], Samuel, *The lives of thirty-two English divines*. London: William Birch, 1677

Clarke [1683], Samuel, *The lives of sundry eminent persons in this later age*. London: Thomas Simmons, [1683]

Cotton [1633], John, *Salomons prophetie*. Middelburg: Anthony de Latre, 1633

Cuilemborgh [1683], Aemilius van, *Godtvruchtige sangh en rym-stoffe*, Utrecht: François Halma, 1683

Goodwin [1664], Thomas, *Opera ofte alle de theologische werken*. Amsterdam: Jan Hendrikszoon Boom, 1664

Hoffmann [1706], Johann Georg, *Geistlicher engelandis. Redner, worinne die Schrifften der engelandischen Prediger untersuchet, gegen die evangelische Prediger-Methode gehalten, und uberall, das es damit nicht allein auff euserliche Moden und Ohren-juckende Zierathen, sondern auff Beweisung des Geistes und der Krafft des gottlichen Worts ankomme, vermittelst der Theologiae exeget. & pathologicae bewiesen wird: wobey ein sonderbarer Vorbericht von der Beschaffenheit und Nutz solcher Schrifften, nebst etlichen nach engelandischer Art elaborirten Predigten zu finden*. Leipzig: the heirs of Friedrich Lanckischen, 1706

Hooker [1678], Thomas, *Ziels-vernedering, en heylzame wanhoop*. Amsterdam: Johanna Wasteliers, 1678

Hoornbeeck [1655], Johannes, *Des Heeren dags heiliging*. Leiden: Cornelis Banheining, 1655

Hoornbeeck [1659], Johannes, *Nader beweering van des Heeren dags heyliginge*. Leiden: Johannes Wagens, 1659

Koelman [1672], Jacobus, *De blijcken van godtzaligheydt, vertoont en open-geleydt, in het exemplaare leven en sterven van ettelijcke vroome. Zijnde een tweede aanhangsel van 't Groot interest eens christens*. Vlissingen: Abraham van Laren, 1672

Koelman [1675], Jacobus, *Reformatie nodigh ontrent de feest-dagen*. Rotterdam: Henricus Goddaeus, 1675

Koelman [1680], Jacobus, *De weeg-schaal des heyligdoms*. Amsterdam: Johanna Wasteliers, 1680

Koelman [1684], Jacobus, *Der labadisten dwalingen grondig ontdekt, en wederlegt*. Amsterdam: Johannes Boekholt, 1684

Leydecker [1707], Jacobus, *Eere van de Nationale Synode van Dordregt, in den jare 1618 en 1619*, vol. 2. Amsterdam: Isaak Stokmans, 1707, "Voor-af-spraak"

Love [1656], Christopher, *Den strijdt tusschen vleesch en geest*. Utrecht: Henricus Versteegh, 1656

[McWard] [1674], [Robert], *De wekker der leeraaren*. Vlissingen: Abraham van Laren, 1674

Oomius [1672], Simon, *Dissertatie van de onderwijsingen in de practycke der godgeleerdheid*. Bolsward: Samuel van Haringhouk, 1672

Quintius [1659], Johannes, *Wraeck-toneel handelende van de sonden van Neder-landt*. Utrecht: Simon de Vries, 1659

Ruë [1741], Pieter de la, *Geletterd Zeeland*. Middelburg: Michiel and Adam Callenfels, 1741

Schuttenius [1638], Everhardus, *Den christelicken ridder*, vol. 2. Amsterdam: Hendrick Laurenszoon, 1638

Stillingfleet [1690], Edward, *Origines sacrae, heilige oorsprongkelykheden. Of een redelijk bewijs van de gronden des christelijken geloofs*. Amsterdam: Ysbrand Haring, 1690

Teellinck [1624}, Willem, *Sleutel der devotie: ons openende de deure des hemels*. Amsterdam: Jan Evertszoon Cloppenburch, 1624

Teellinck [1631], Willem, *De worstelinghe eenes bekeerden sondaers*. Vlissingen: Samuel Claeys Versterre, 1631

Teellinck [1647], Willem, *Laetste predikatien*. Amsterdam: Theunis Jacobszoon, 1647

Teellinck [1648], Willem, *Timotheus*. Dordrecht: Françoys Boels, 1648

Theophilus Parresius [Jacobus Koelman] [1677], *Historisch verhael van de proceduuren tegen d. Jacobus Koelman, predicant tot Sluys in Vlaenderen. Wegens zijn debvoiren tot reformatie, ontrent het stuck der formulieren en feestdagen*. Rotterdam: Pieter Hendrickszoon, 1677

Thilenus [1668], Johannes, *Schat der princen*. Middelburg: Jaques Fierens, 1668

Vollenhove [1686], Joannes, *Poëzy*. Amsterdam: Hendrick Boom and the widow of Dirk Boom, 1686

Vrolikhert [1758], Godewardus, *Vlissingsche kerkhemel*. Vlissingen: Pieter de Paaynaar; Middelburg: Gabriel Clement, 1758

Wolseley [1695], Charles, *De redelykheid van't Schriftuur-geloof, of een redenering over de redelijke gronden op welke wy den Bijbel als Gods Woord aannemen*. Utrecht: Wilhelm Broedelet, 1695

Wtenbogaert [1621], Johannes, *Achabs biddagh*. S.l.: s.n., 1621

*Catalogus librorum, viri celeberrimi Joh. Thieleni. p.m. ecclesiae, Medioburg. Pastoris in duas partes divisus. Cujus una theologicos, (in his permulti Anglicé scripti) altera miscellaneos continet*. Middelburg: Aaron van Poulle, 1692

*Een waarachtige en volkomene copye van 't nieuw covenant*. S.l.: s.n., 1680

**Post-1800 publications**

Abels, P.H.A.M., and A.Ph.F Wouters, *Nieuw en ongezien. Kerk en samenleving in de classis Delft en Delfland 1572-1621* [Werken van de Vereniging voor Nederlandse Kerkgeschiedenis, 1-2], 2 vols. Delft: Eburon, 1994

Ady, C., *Pius II (Aeneas Silvius Piccolomini) the humanist pope*. London: Methuen, 1913

Akkerman, Fokke, and Arjo Vanderjagt (eds.), *Rodolphus Agricola Phrisius (1444-1485). Proceedings of the International Conference at the University of Groningen 28-30 October 1985*. Leiden: E.J. Brill, 1988

Akkerman, Fokke, *et al.* (eds.), *Wessel Gansfort (1419-1489) and Northern Humanism*. Leiden: Brill, 1993

Alblas, Jacob Baltus Huibert, *Johannes Boekholt (1656-1693). The first Dutch publisher of John Bunyan and other English authors* [Bibliotheca Bibliographica Neerlandica, 22]. Nieuwkoop: B. de Graaf, 1987

Anderson, Randall Louis, "'The Merit of a Manuscript Poem". The Case for Bodleian MS Rawlinson Poet. 85', in Arhur F. Marotti and Michael D. Bristol (eds.), *Print, Manuscript, & Performance. The Changing Relations of the Media in Early Modern England*. Columbus, OH: Ohio State University Press, 2000, 127-171

Archer, John, *De genezing van zondezieke zondaren*. Scherpenzeel: Robbers Reprints, 2010

Asselt [1997], W.J. van, *Johannes Coccejus: Portret van een zeventiende-eeuws theoloog op oude en nieuwe wegen*. Heerloog: Groen, 1997

Asselt [2001], Willem J. van, *The Federal Theology of Johannes Cocceius (1603-1669)* [Studies in the History of Christian Thought, 100]. Leiden: Brill, 2001

Axmacher, Elke, *Praxis Evangeliorum. Theologie und Frömmigkeit bei Martin Moller (1547-1606)* [Forschungen zur Kirchen- und Dogmengeschichte, 43]. Göttingen: Vandenhoeck & Ruprecht, 1989

Backhouse [1981], Marcel, 'De vlaamse vluchtelingenkerk in Sandwich in 1563. Twee manuscripten uit het British Museum', *Handelingen van de Koninklijke Commissie voor Geschiedenis*, 147 (1981), 75-113

Backhouse [1982], Marcel, 'De Vlaamse vluchtelingenkerk in Sandwich in 1573. Een derde manuscript uit het British Museum', *Handelingen van de Koninklijke Commissie voor Geschiedenis*, 148 (1982), 229-267

Backhouse [1985], M.F., *The Flemish and Walloon communities of Sandwich during the reign of Elizabeth I*. Brussels: Koninklijke Academie van België, 1985

Backus, Irena, and Philip Benedict (eds.), *Calvin and His Influence, 1509-2009*. Oxford: Oxford University Press, 2011

Barnett, Pamela R., *Theodore Haak, F.R.S. (1605-1690). The First German Translator of Paradise Lost* [Anglica Germanica. British Studies in Germanic Languages and Literatures, 3]. The Hague: Moulton & Co., 1962

Beal [1980], Peter (ed.), *Index of English Literary Manuscripts*. London: Mansell, 1980-1997

Beal [1998], Peter, *In Praise of Scribes. Manuscripts and their Makers in Seventeenth-Century England*. Oxford: Clarendon Press, 1998

Beck, Andreas J., *Gisbertus Voetius (1589-1676). Sein Theologieverständnis und seine Gotteslehre* [Forschungen zur Kirchen- und Dogmengeschichte, 92]. Göttingen: Vandenhoeck & Ruprecht, 2007

Beek, Pieta van, *The First Female University Student: Anna Maria van Schurman (1636)*. Utrecht: Igitur, 2010

Beeke [1991], Joel R., *Assurance of Faith. Calvin, English Puritanism, and the Dutch Second Reformation* [American University Studies. Series 7: Theology and Religion, 89]. New York: Lang, 1991

Beeke [2003], Joel R., 'Introduction', in Willem Teellinck, *The Path of True Godliness*, Annemie Godbehere (trans.) and Joel R. Beeke (ed.) [Classics of Reformed Spirituality]. Grand Rapids, MI: Baker Academic, 2003, 11-29

Benedict, Philip, *Christ's Churches Purely Reformed. A Social History of Calvinism*. New Haven: Yale University Press, 2002

Berge, Domien ten, *De hooggeleerde en zoetvloeiende dichter Jacob Cats*. The Hague: Martinus Nijhoff, 1979

Bergsma, W., *Tussen Gideonsbende en publieke kerk. Een studie over het gereformeerd protestantisme in Friesland, 1580-1650* [Fryske Histoaryske Rige, 17]. Hilversum: Verloren, 1999

Berkel [1983], Klaas van, *Isaac Beeckman (1588-1637) en de mechanisering van het wereldbeeld* [Nieuwe Nederlandse Bijdragen tot de Geschiedenis der Geneeskunde en der Natuurwetenschappen, 9]. Amsterdam: Rodopi, 1983

Berkel [2015], K. van, 'BEECKMAN, JACOB', in W.J. op 't Hof *et al.* (eds.), *Encyclopedie Nadere Reformatie*, vol. 1. Utrecht: De Groot Goudiaan, 2015, 74a-75b

Beyreuther, Erich, *August Hermann Francke 1663-1727. Zeuge des lebendigen Gottes*. Marburg an der Lahn: Verlag der Francke-Buchhandlung, 1956

Bie, J.P. de, and J. Loosjes (eds.), *Biographisch woordenboek van protestantsche godgeleerden in Nederland*, 5 vols. and the first part of vol. 6. The Hague: Martinus Nijhoff, 1903-1949

Bierma, Hessel, 'Samuel van Haringhouk', *Ut de smidte fan de Fryske Akademy*, 13-2 (1979), 21

Bijl, S.W., *Erasmus in het Nederlands tot 1617* [Bibliotheca Bibliographica Neerlandica, 10]. Nieuwkoop: B. de Graaf, 1978

Birken, William, 'Dr. John King (1614-1681) and Dr. Assuerus Regemorter (1615-1650), Brethren in the Dutch Church and in the Royal College of Physicians of London, with Added References to Other "Dutch" Congregants in the Royal College, Dr. Baldwin Hamey and Dr. George Ent', *Medical History. A Quaterly Journal Devoted to the History of Medicine and Related Sciences*, 20 (1976), 276-295

Blankenfeld, Barton John, *Puritans in the Provinces: Banbury, Oxfordshire, 1554-1660*, 2 vols. Unpublished dissertation, Yale University, 1985

Blekastad, Milada, *Comenius. Versuch eines Umrisses von Leben, Werk und Schicksal des Jan Amos Komenský*. Oslo: Universitetsforlaget, 1969

Boeles, W.B.S., *Frieslands Hoogeschool en het Rijks Atheneum te Franeker*, 2 vols. Leeuwarden: H. Kuipers, 1878-1889

Boer, C., *Hofpredikers van Prins Willem van Oranje. Jean Taffin en Pierre Loyseleur de Villiers* [Kerkhistorische Studiën behorende bij het Nederlands Archief voor Kerkgeschiedenis, 5]. The Hague: Martinus Nijhoff, 1952

Boersma, Owe, *Vluchtig voorbeeld. De Nederlandse, Franse en Italiaanse vluchtelingenkerken in Londen, 1568-1585*. S.l.: s.n., 1994

Borsius, J., 'Onuitgegeven brief van de afgevaardigden der Hervormde gemeenten in Vlaanderen tot de onderlinge zamenkomst te Gent, 1579', in H.M.C. van Oosterzee (ed), *Zeeland. Jaarboekje voor 1852*. Middelburg: De gebroeders Abrahams, 1852, 51-111

Bos, F.L., 'COCK, HENDRIK DE', in D. Nauta et al. (eds.), *Biografisch Lexicon voor de Geschiedenis van het Nederlandse Protestantisme*, vol. 2. Kampen: J.H. Kok, 1983, 129a-132a

Bos, J.M., 'Genealogische fragmenten uit Sluis N.H., 17e en 18e eeuw', *Zeeuwsche Stam. Contactblad van de nederlandse genealogische vereniging, afdeling Zeeland*, 1984, 101-117, 200-206; 1985, 111-117

Bostoen, K., *Bonis in bonum. Johan Radermacher de Oude (1538-1617), humanist en koopman*. Hilversum: Verloren, 1998

Bozeman, Theodore Dwight, *The Precisianist Strain. Disciplinary Religion & Antinomian Backlash in Puritanism to 1638*. Chapel Hill: University of North Carolina Press, 2004

Brecht [1993-1], Martin, 'Das Aufkommen der neuen Frömmigkeitsbewegung in Deutschland', in Martin Brecht (ed.), *Der Pietismus vom siebzehnten bis zum frühen achtzehnten Jahrhundert* [Geschichte des Pietismus, 1]. Göttingen: Vandenhoeck & Ruprecht, 1993, 113-203

Brecht [1993-2], Martin, 'Die deutschen Spiritualisten des 17. Jahrhunderts', in Martin Brecht (ed.), *Der Pietismus vom siebzehnten bis zum frühen achtzehnten Jahrhundert* [Geschichte des Pietismus, 1]. Göttingen: Vandenhoeck & Ruprecht, 1993, 205-240

Bremer, Francis J., *Congregational Communion. Clerical Friendship in the Anglo-American Puritan Community, 1610-1692*. Boston, Mass.: Northeastern University Press, 1994

Bremer [ODNB], Francis J., 'Cotton, John (1585-1652)', in *Oxford Dictionary of National Biography*, http.://www.oxforddnb.com/view/article/6416

Breuker [1989], Philippus, *It wurk fan Gysbert Japix*, 2 vols. Ljouwert: Fryske Akademy, 1989

Breuker [2015-1], Ph.H., 'BOËTIUS, GELLIUS', in W.J. op 't Hof *et al.* (eds.), *Encyclopedie Nadere Reformatie*, vol. 1. Utrecht: De Groot Goudiaan, 2015, 104a-105b

Breuker [2015-2], Ph.H., 'BRUNSVELT, SIXTUS', in W.J. op 't Hof *et al.* (eds.), *Encyclopedie Nadere Reformatie*, vol. 1. Utrecht: De Groot Goudiaan, 2015, 138a-141a

Breuker [2015-3], Ph.H., 'ELGERSMA, FRANCISCUS', in W.J. op 't Hof *et al.* (eds.), *Encyclopedie Nadere Reformatie*, vol. 1. Utrecht: De Groot Goudiaan, 2015, 233b-236b

Breuker [2015-4], Ph.H., 'HARINGHOUK, SAMUEL VAN', in W.J. op 't Hof *et al.* (eds.), *Encyclopedie Nadere Reformatie*, vol. 1. Utrecht: De Groot Goudiaan, 2015, 322b-225a

Breuker [2015-5], Ph.H., 'JOHANNES, FOCCO', in W.J. op 't Hof *et al.* (eds.), *Encyclopedie Nadere Reformatie*, vol. 1. Utrecht: De Groot Goudiaan, 2015, 400a-401b

Breuker, Ph.H., en W.J. op 't Hof, 'Een boekje vol nieuwe informatie over Johannes Baers, Paschasius Baers en Willem Lodewijk', *Documentatieblad Nadere Reformatie*, 43 (2019), 20-38

Briels [1972], J.G.C.A., 'Zuidnederlandse onderwijskrachten in Noordnederland 1570-1630', *Archief voor de Geschiedenis van de Katholieke Kerk in Nederland*, 14 (1972), 89-169, 277-298; 15 (1973), 103-149, 263-297

Briels [1974], J.G.C.A., *Zuidnederlandse boekdrukkers en boekverkopers in de Republiek der Verenigde Nederlanden omstreeks 1570-1630* [Bibliotheca Bibliographica Neerlandica, 6]. Nieuwkoop: B. de Graaf, 1974

Brienen [1974], T., *De prediking van de Nadere Reformatie. Een onderzoek naar het gebruik van de klassificatiemethode binnen de prediking van de Nadere Reformatie.* Amsterdam: Ton Bolland, 1974

Brienen [1990], T., 'Johannes Teellinck (ca. 1623-1674)', in T. Brienen *et al.*, *Figuren en thema's van de Nadere Reformatie*, vol. 2. Kampen: De Groot Goudriaan, 1990, 46-56

Brienen, [1993], T., 'Maximiliaan Teellinck (ca. 1606-1653)', in J.B.H. Alblas *et al.*, *Figuren en thema's van de Nadere Reformatie*, vol. 3. Rotterdam: Lindenberg Boeken&Muziek, 1993, 69-82

Briggs, Asa, and Peter Burke, *A Social History of the Media. From Gutenberg to the Internet.* Cambridge, GB: Polity Press, 2002

Broek Roelofs, Olchert Cornelis, *Wilhelmus Baudartius.* Kampen: Kok, 1947

Broeyer, F.G.M. [2015-1], 'BURMANNUS, FRANCISCUS', in W.J. op 't Hof *et al.* (eds.), *Encyclopedie Nadere Reformatie*, vol. 1. Utrecht: De Groot Goudriaan, 2015, 148b-152b

Broeyer, F.G.M. [2015-2], 'ESSENIUS, ANDREAS', in W.J. op 't Hof *et al.* (eds.), *Encyclopedie Nadere Reformatie*, vol. 1. Utrecht: De Groot Goudriaan, 2015, 236b-242a

Broeyer, F.G.M. [2016-1], 'MAETS, CAROLUS DE', in W.J. op 't Hof *et al.* (eds.), *Encyclopedie Nadere Reformatie*, vol. 2. Utrecht: De Groot Goudriaan, 2016, 83a-87b

Broeyer, F.G.M. [2016-2], 'NETHENUS, MATTHIAS', in W.J. op 't Hof *et al.* (eds.), *Encyclopedie Nadere Reformatie*, vol. 2. Utrecht: De Groot Goudriaan, 2016, 130a-135a

Broeyer, F.G.M. and E.G.E. van der Wall (eds.), *Een richtingenstrijd in de Gereformeerde Kerk. Voetianen en coccejanen 1650-1750.* Zoetermeer: Boekencentrum, 1994

Brown, Sylvia (ed.), *Women's Writing in Stuart England. The Mothers' Legacies of Dorothy Leigh, Elizabeth Joselin and Elizabeth Richardson.* Stroud: Sutton, 2000

Brummel, L., *Twee ballingen 's lands tijdens onze opstand tegen Spanje. Hugo Blotius (1534-1608). Emanuel van Meteren (1535-1612)*. The Hague: Martinus Nijhoff, 1972

Budé, E. de, *Vie de Jean Diodati, théologien Génevois, 1576-1649*. Lausanne: Bridel, 1869

Bunge, Wiep van, *et al.* (eds.), *The Continuum Companion to Spinoza*. London: Bloomsbury Academic, 2011

Burke [2005], Peter, *Lost (and Found) in Translation: A Cultural History of Translators and Translating in Early Modern Europe*. Wassenaar: NIAS, 2005

Burke [2007], Peter, 'Cultures of translation in early modern Europe', in Peter Burke and R. Po-Chia Hsia (eds.), *Cultural Translation in Early Modern Europe*. Cambridge: Cambridge University Press, 2007, 7-38

Bush, Sargent jr., *The Correspondence of John Cotton*. Chapel Hill: University of North Carolina Press, 2001

Cambers, Andrew, *Godly Reading. Print, Manuscript and Puritanism in England, 1580-1720* [Cambridge Studies in Early Modern British History]. Cambridge: Cambrige University Press, 2011

Cliffe [1984], J.T., *The Puritan Gentry. The Great Puritan Families of Early Stuart England*. London: Routledge & Kegan Paul, 1984

Cliffe [1993], J.T., *The Puritan Gentry Besieged*. London: Routledge & Kegan Paul, 1993

Coffey, John, 'The Problem of 'Scottish Puritanism', 1590-1638', in Elizabethanne Boran and Crawford Gribben (eds.), *Enforcing Reformation in Ireland and Scotland, 1550-1700*. [St. Andrews studies in Reformation history]. Aldershot: Ashgate, 2006, 66-90

Coffey, John, and Paul C.H. Lim (eds.), *The Cambridge Companion to Puritanism*. Cambridge, Eng.: Cambridge University Press, 2008

Collinson [1958], Patrick, 'The Elizabethan Puritans and the Foreign Reformed Churches in London', *Proceedings of the Huguenot Society of London*, 20 (1958-1964), 528-555

Collinson [1980], Patrick, 'Cranbrook and the Fletchers. Popular and Unpopular Religion in the Kentish Weald', in Peter N. Brooks (ed.), *Reformation Principle and Practice. Essays in Honour of Arthur Geoffrey Dickens*. London: Scolar, 1980

Collinson [1983], Patrick, *Godly People. Essays on English Protestantism and Puritanism*. London: Hambledon, 1983

Collinson [2002], Patrick, *et al.*, 'Religious publishing in England 1557-1640', in John Barnard en D.F. McKenzie (eds), *The Cambridge History of the Book in Britain*, vol. 4, 1557-1695. Cambridge: Cambridge University Press, 2002, 29-93

Crew, Phillis Mack, *Calvinist Preaching and Iconoclasm in the Netherlands 1544-1569*. Cambridge: Cambridge University Press, 1978

Cuno, Fr.W., *Franciscus Junius der Ältere, Professor der Theologie und Pastor (1545-1602). Sein Leben und Wirken, seine Schriften und Briefe*. Amsterdam: Scheffer & Co, 1891

Dankbaar, W.F., 'MICRON (MIKRON, MICRONIUS), MARTEN', in D. Nauta *et al*. (eds.), *Biografisch Lexicon voor de Geschiedenis van het Nederlandse Protestantisme*, vol. 2. Kampen: J.H. Kok, 1983, 327b-330b

Delft, M. van, and C. de Wolf (eds.), *Bibliopolis. Geschiedenis van het gedrukte boek in Nederland*. Zwolle: Waanders, 2003

Deppermann, Andreas, *Johann Jakob Schütz und die Anfänge des Pietismus* [Beiträge zur historischen Theologie, 119]. Tübingen: J.C.B. Mohr (Paul Siebeck), 2002

Deursen [1974], A.Th. van, *Bavianen en Slijkgeuzen. Kerk en kerkvolk ten tijde van Maurits en Oldebarnevelt* [Van Gorcum's Historische Bibliotheek, 92]. Assen: Van Gorcum & Comp., 1974

Deursen [2000], A.Th. van, *Maurits van Nassau 1567-1625. De winnaar die faalde*. Amsterdam: Bert Bakker, 2000

Dibbets, G.R.W., *Joannes Vollenhove (1631-1708), dominee-dichter. Een biografie*. Hilversum: Verloren, 2007

Dorrenboom [1886], J.A., 'Aantekeningen uit de trouwregisters te Sluis', *Algemeen Nederlandsch Familieblad. Tijdschrift voor Geschiedenis, Geslacht-, Wapen-, Zegelkunde, enz.*, 3 (1886), 39a-43a, 300b-303a; 4 (1887), 71a-74b, 178a-183a, 285a-288b; 5 (1888), 90b-92b, 273a-275b; 6 (1889), 17a-20b

Dorrenboom [1893], J.A., 'Lijst van de Magistraatspersonen die successievelijk van jaar tot jaar sedert de overgave der stad Sluis, dato 19 Augustus 1604, hebben geregeerd', *Algemeen Nederlandsch Familieblad. Tijdschrift voor Geschiedenis, Geslacht-, Wapen-, Zegelkunde, enz.*, 10 (1893), 85a-86b; 11 (1894), 78b-80a

Dorsten, J.A. van, "'I.C.O.' Het terugvinden van een bescheiden Nederlander in Londen: Jacobus Colius Ortelianus (1563-1628), koopman-schrijver', *Tijdschrift voor Nederlandse Taal- en Letterkunde*, 77 (1959/60), 17-32

Dorsten, J.A. van, and K. Schaap, 'Inleiding', in Jacob Cool, *Den staet van London in hare groote peste* [Leidse drukken en herdrukken, kleine reeks, 5]. Leiden: E.J. Brill, 1962, 1-11

Drummond, Andrew L., *The Kirk and the Continent*. Edinburgh: The Saint Andrew Press, 1956

Duker, A.C., *Gisbertus Voetius*, 3 vols. Leiden: Brill, 1897-1915

Dunthorne, Hugh, *Britain and the Dutch Revolt, 1560-1700*. Cambridge: Cambridge University Press, 2013

Eekhof, A, 'Jacobus Koelman te Sluis en de "nadere reformatie" in Zeeland', *Nederlandsch Archief voor Kerkgeschiedenis*, Nieuwe Serie, 14 (1918), 193-209

Eggermont, P.L., 'Samuel van Haringhouk als uitgever van de Nadere Reformatie', *Documentatieblad Nadere Reformatie*, 1 (1977), 90-102

Emerson, Everett H., *John Cotton*. New York: Twayne Publishers, 1965

Emmius, Ubbo, *Willem Lodewijk, graaf van Nassau (1560-1620). Stadhouder van Friesland, Groningen en Drenthe*. Hilversum: Verloren, 1994

End, G. van den, *Guiljelmus Saldenus (1627-1694), Een praktisch en irenisch theoloog uit de Nadere Reformatie*. Leiden: J.J. Groen en Zoon, 1991

Engelbrecht, E.A., *De vroedschap van Rotterdam 1572-1795* [Bronnen voor de geschiedenis van Rotterdam, 5]. Rotterdam: Gemeentelijke Archiefdienst, 1973

Eßer, Raingard, *Niederländische Exulanten im England des 16. und frühen 17. Jahrhunderts*. Berlin: Duncker & Humblot, 1996

Evenhuis [1965], R.B., *Ook dat was Amsterdam*, 4 vols. Amsterdam: W. ten Have, 1965-1974

Evenhuis [1978], R.B., 'ROTHE, JOHANNES', in D. Nauta *et al.* (eds.), *Biografisch Lexicon voor de Geschiedenis van het Nederlandse Protestantisme*, vol. 1. Kampen: J.H. Kok, 1978, 297a-298b

Exalto [1974-1], K., 'Rudolphus Petri en zijn 'Scherm en Schilt der Kinderen Gods' 1623', in K. Exalto, *Beleefd geloof. Acht schetsen van gereformeerde theologen uit de 17e eeuw*. Amsterdam: Ton Bolland, 1974, 2-31

Exalto 1974-2, K., 'Sixtus Brunsvelt en zijn 'Leevendige Christen' 1165', in K. Exalto, *Beleefd geloof. Acht schetsen van gereformeerde theologen uit de 17$^e$ eeuw*. Amsterdam: Ton Bolland, 1974, 54-73

Exalto [1975], K., *De dood ontmaskerd. De voorbereiding op de dood in de late middeleeuwen, in de reformatie en in de gereformeerde theologie in de 17$^e$ en begin 18$^e$ eeuw*. Amsterdam: Ton Bolland, 1975

Exalto [1976], K., *De kracht der religie. Tien schetsen van gereformeerde 'oude schrijvers' uit de 17e en 18e eeuw*. Urk: De Vuurtoren, 1976

Exalto [1989], K., 'Godefridus Udemans (1581/2-1649)', in T. Brienen *et al.*, *De Nadere Reformatie en het Gereformeerd Piëtisme*. The Hague: Boekencentrum, 1989, 87-121

Ezell, Margaret J.M., 'Ann Halkett's Morning Devotions: Posthumous Publication and the Culture of Writing in Late Seventeenth-Century Britain', in Arhur F. Marotti and Michael D. Bristol (eds.), *Print, Manuscript, & Performance. The Changing Relations of the Media in Early Modern England*. Columbus, OH: Ohio State University Press, 2000, 215-231

Fatio, Olivier, *Méthode et théologie. Lambert Daneau et les débuts de la scolastique réformée* [Travaux d'Humanisme et Renaissance, 147]. Genève: Droz, 1976

Félice, Paul de, *Lambert Daneau (de Baugency-sur-Loire), pasteur et professeur en théologie 1530-1595*. Paris: Fischbacher, 1881

Ferguson, James (ed.), *Papers Illustrating the History of the Scots Brigade in the Service of the United Netherlands 1572-1782*, vol. 1 [Publications of the Scottish History Society, 32]. Edinburgh: University Press, 1899

Fieret, W., *Udemans. Facetten van zijn leven en werk*. Houten: Den Hertog, 1985

Flinterman, R.A., 'MIGGRODE, JOHANNES VAN', in D. Nauta *et al.* (eds.), *Biografisch Lexicon voor de Geschiedenis van het Nederlandse Protestantisme*, vol. 2. Kampen: J.H. Kok, 1983, 332a-333a

Florijn [2015-1], H., 'ALARDIN, CASPARUS', in W.J. op 't Hof *et al.* (eds.), *Encyclopedie Nadere Reformatie*, vol. 1. Utrecht: De Groot Goudriaan, 2015, 19a-21a

Florijn [2015-2], H., 'BORSTIUS, JACOBUS', in W.J. op 't Hof *et al.* (eds.), *Encyclopedie Nadere Reformatie*, vol. 1. Utrecht: De Groot Goudriaan 2015, 114a-117b

Florijn [2015-3], H., 'EVERSDIJK, WILHELMUS', in W.J. op 't Hof *et al.* (eds.), *Encyclopedie Nadere Reformatie*, vol. 1. Utrecht: De Groot Goudriaan, 2015, 246a-249a

Fockema Andreae, S.J., and Th.J. Meijer (eds), *Album Studiosorum Academiae Franekerensis (1585-1811, 1816-1844)*. Franeker: T. Wever, 1968

Frank-van Westrienen, A., *De Groote Tour. Tekening van de educatiereis der Nederlanders in de zeventiende eeuw*. Amsterdam: Noord-Hollandse uitgeversmaatschappij, 1983

Frijhoff, Willem, *Fulfilling God's Mission: The Two Worlds of Dominie Everardus Bogardus, 1607-1647*. Leiden: Brill, 2007

Genderen, J. van, *Herman Witsius. Bijdrage tot de kennis der gereformeerde theologie*. The Hague: Guido de Brès, 1953

Gevers, A.J., and A.J. Mensema, *De havezaten in Salland en hun bewoners* [Werken Vereeniging tot beoefening van Overijsselsch regt en geschiedenis, 37]. Alphen aan den Rijn: Canaletto, 1983

Goeters, Johann Friedrich Gerhard, 'Der reformierte Pietismus in Deutschland 1650-1690', in Martin Brecht (ed.), *Der Pietismus vom siebzehnten bis zum frühen achtzehnten Jahrhundert* [Geschichte des Pietismus, 1]. Göttingen: Vandenhoeck& Ruprecht, 1993, 241-277

Graafland, C., 'De invloed van het Puritanisme op het ontstaan van het Gereformeerd Piëtisme in Nederland', *Documentatieblad Nadere Reformatie*, 7 (1983), 1-24 = Cornelis Graafland, 'Der Einfluß des Puritanismus auf die Enstehung des reformierten Pietismus besonders in Holland', *Monatshefte für Evangelische Kirchengeschichte des Rheinlandes*, 31 (1982), 73-92

Graafland, C., *et al.*, 'Nadere Reformatie: opnieuw een poging tot begripsbepaling', *Documentatieblad Nadere Reformatie*, 19 (1995), 105-184

Greengrass, M., ′Samuel Hartlib and the commonwealth of learning′, in John Barnard and D.F. McKenzie (eds.), *The Cambridge History of the Book in Britain*, vol. 4. Cambridge: Cambridge University Press, 2002, 304-322

Greengrass, Mark and Thomas S. Freeman, 'Scribal Communication and Scribal Publication in Early Calvinism. The Evidence of the the *Letters of the Martyrs*', in Irene Dingel and Herman J. Selderhuis (eds.), *Calvin und Calvinismus. Europäische Perspektiven* [Veröffentlichungen des Instituts für Europäische Geschichte Mainz. Abteilung für Abendländische Religionsgeschichte, 84]. Göttingen: Vandenhoeck & Ruprecht, 2011, 391-416

Grell [1986], Ole Peter, *Foreign Protestant Communities in Sixteenth-Century London* [Oxford Historical Monographs]. Oxford: Clarendon Press, 1986

Grell [1989], Ole Peter, *Dutch Calvinists in Early Stuart London. The Dutch Church in Austin Friars 1603-1642* [Publications of the Sir Thomas Browne Institute Leiden, New Series, 11]. Leiden: E.J. Brill, 1989

Grell [1996], Ole Peter, *Calvinist Exiles in Tudor and Stuart England*. Aldershot: Scolar Press, 1996

Greschat, Martin, *Martin Bucer: A Reformer and His Times*. Louisville, Kentucky: Westminster John Knox Press, 2004

Groenendijk [1977], L.F., 'De origine van Sixtus Brunsvelt's ontmaskering van 'de bijnachristen'', *Documentatieblad Nadere Reformatie*, 1 (1977), 133-136

Groenendijk [1978], L.F., 'Inhoud en oorsprong van de opvoedingsleer van Petrus Wittewrongel', *Documentatieblad Nadere* Reformatie, 2 (1978), 13-28

Groenendijk [1979], L.F., 'De huwelijksleer van Petrus Wittewrongel', *Documentatieblad Nadere* Reformatie, 3 (1979), 56-64, 101-110; 4 (1980), 104-108; 5 (1981), 17-22, 83-88; 6 (1982), 23-31; 7 (1983), 43-49

Groenendijk [1981], L.F., 'Guthrie's vademecum en de door Koelman toegevoegde illustraties', in William Guthrie, *Des christens groot interest*. Utrecht: Den Hertog, 1981, 475-512

Groenendijk [1983], L.F., 'Gezin en opvoeding in dienst van de theocratie bij Petrus Wittewrongel', *Theologia Reformata*, 26 (1983), 290-305 = L.F. Groenendijk, 'Gezin en opvoeding in dienst van de theocratie bij Petrus Wittewrongel', *Pedagogische verhandelingen*, 6-2/3 (1983), 85-94

Groenendijk [1984-1], L.F., *De nadere reformatie van het gezin. De visie van Petrus Wittewrongel op de christelijke huishouding*. Dordrecht: J.P. van den Tol, 1984

Groenendijk [1984-2], L.F., 'Een catalogus van Hofmanniana', *Documentatieblad Nadere Reformatie*, 8 (1984), 81-94

Groenendijk [1986], L.F., 'De puriteinse bronnen van Wittewrongels behandeling van "vergenoegdheid"', *Documentatieblad Nadere Reformatie*, 10 (1986), 126-142

Groenendijk [1990], L.F., 'Johannes de Swaef (1594-1653)', in T. Brienen et al., *Figuren en thema's van de Nadere Reformatie*, vol. 2. Kampen: De Groot Goudriaan, 1990, 11-18

Groenendijk [2017], L.F., *De pedagogiek van Jacobus Koelman. Inhoud en bronnen, grondslag en ambitie. 'Een klaare bestiering om de kinderen voor den HEERE op te voeden'*. Apeldoorn: Labarum Academic, 2017

Groenveld, S., *De winterkoning. Balling aan het Haagse hof*. The Hague: Atelier Rijksbouwmeester, 2003

Groot [1978], A. de, 'EEKHOF, ALBERT', in D. Nata et al. (eds.), *Biografisch Lexicon voor de Geschiedenis van het Nederlandse Protestantisme*, vol. 1. Kampen: J.H. Kok, 1978, 74b-76a

Grünberg, Paul., *Philipp Jakob Spener*, 3 vols. Göttingen: Vandenhoeck und Ruprecht 1893-1906

Haar [1978], J. van der, 'Puriteinse invloed uit Engeland (toegelicht uit een tweetal preken van resp. ds Joos van Laren en Dr Richard Sibbes)', *Documentatieblad Nadere Reformatie*, 2 (1978), 89-93

Haar [1980], J. van der, *From Abbadie to Young. A Bibliography of English, Most Puritan Works, Translated i/t Dutch Language*. Veenendaal: Kool, 1980

Haar [1984], J. van der, 'Welke geschriften van de oudvaders lazen de afgescheidenen?', *Documentatieblad Nadere Reformatie*, 8 (1984), 61-66
Haar [1986], J. van der, 'Nederlandse theologen onder Engelse puriteinen', *Documentatieblad Nadere Reformatie*, 10 (1986), 105-108
Haar [1987], J. van der, *Schatkamer van de gereformeerde theologie in Nederland (c. 1600 – c. 1800). Bibliografisch onderzoek*. Veenendaal: Antiquariaat Kool, 1987
Haar [1988], J. van der, ''n Merkwaardige verschuiving bij G. Boëtius', *Documentatieblad Nadere Reformatie*, 12 (1988), 140-141
Haar [1997], Jan van der, *Internationale ökumenische Beziehungen im 17. und 18. Jahrhundert. Bibliographie von aus dem Englischen, Niederländischen und Französischen ins Deutsche übersetzten theologischen Büchern von (1600-1800)*. Ederveen: Antiquariaat Kool Boeken, 1997
Haigh, Christopher, *The Plain Man's Pathway to Heaven. Kinds of Christianity in Post-Reformation England*. Oxford: Oxford University Press, 2007
Hambrick-Stowe [1982], Charles E., *The Practise of Piety. Puritan Devotional Disciplines in Seventeenth-Century New England*. Chapel Hill: University of North Carolina Press, 1982
Hambrick-Stowe [2008], Charles E., 'Practical divinity and spirituality', in John Coffey and Paul C.H. Lim (eds.), *The Cambridge Companion to Puritanism*. Cambridge, Eng.: Cambridge University Press, 2008, 191-205
Hamilton, Alastair, *The Family of Love*. Cambridge: James Clarke, 1981
Harris, L.E., *Vermuyden and the Fens. A Study of Sir Cornelius Vermuyden and the Great Level*. London: Cleaver-Hume Press, 1953
Hauck, Karl, *Karl Ludwig, Kurfürst von der Pfalz*. Leipzig: Breitkopf & Härtel, 1903
Heijting [1999], W., 'Voorsichtich ghelyck de slangen: en onnoosel als de duyven'. De Dordtse uitgever François Boels', *Documentatieblad Nadere Reformatie*, 23 (1999), 117-183
Heijting [2010], Willem, 'Beyond the Printed Book. The Media in Reformation Historiography', in Ulrike Hascher-Burger, *et al.* (eds.), *Between Lay Piety and Academic Theology. Studies Presented to Christoph Burger on the Occasion of his 65th Birthday*, Leiden: Brill, 2010, 415-432
Heijting [2011], Willem, 'François Boels en het piëtistisch-gereformeerde netwerk', *Documentatieblad Nadere Reformatie*, 35 (2011), 69-74

Heijting [2015], W., 'DOESBURG, REINIER VAN', in W.J. op 't Hof *et al.* (eds.), *Encyclopedie Nadere Reformatie*, vol. 1. Utrecht: De Groot Goudriaan, 2015, 217a-218b

Heppe, Heinrich, *Geschichte des Pietismus und der Mystik in der reformirten Kirche, namentlich der Niederlande*. Leiden: E.J. Brill, 1879

Hessels, Joannes Henricus (ed.), *Ecclesiae Londino-Batavae Archivvm*, 3 vols. Cambridge: Cambridge University Press, 1887-1897

Hildersam, Arthur, *De historie van des hovelings zoon*. Rumpt: De Schatkamer, 2011

Hinrichs, Carl, *Preußentum und Pietismus. Der Pietismus in Brandenburg-Preußen als religiös-soziale Reformbewegung*. Göttingen: Vandenhoeck & Ruprecht, 1971

Hoek, Pieter Cornelis, *Melchior Leydecker (1642-1721). Een onderzoek naar de structuur van de theologie van een gereformeerd scholasticus*. Amsterdam: VU, 2013

Hoenderdaal [1983], G.J., 'WTENBOGAERT (UYTENBOGAERT), JOHANNES', in D. Nauta *et al.*, *Biografisch Lexicon voor de Geschiedenis van het Nederlandse Protestantisme*, vol.2. Kampen: J.H. Kok, 1983, 464a-468a

Hof [1977], W.J. op 't, 'Willem Teellinck in het licht zijner geschriften (4)', *Documentatieblad Nadere Reformatie*, 1 (1977), 105-114

Hof [1978], W.J. op 't, 'Willem Teellinck in het licht zijner geschriften (5)', *Documentatieblad Nadere Reformatie*, 2 (1978), 1-11

Hof [1979], W.J. op 't, 'Johannes de Swaef als vertaler', *Documentatieblad Nadere Reformatie*, 3 (1979), 111-120

Hof [1981], W.J. op 't, 'Een apotheker in tweeërlei zin', *Documentatieblad Nadere Reformatie*, 5 (1981), 10-16

Hof [1983-1], W.J. op 't, 'Een fragment van een onbekende brief van Willem Teellinck', *Documentatieblad Nadere Reformatie*, 7 (1983), 63-67

Hof [1983-2], W.J. op 't, 'Johannes Polyander en Willem Teellinck. Een vergeten brief en nog meer', *Documentatieblad Nadere Reformatie*, 7 (1983), 126-143

Hof [1985], W.J. op 't, 'Een pamflet uit 1623 betreffende de bekering der Joden', *Nederlands Archief voor Kerkgeschiedenis*, 65 (1985), 35-45

Hof [1987-1], Willem Jan op 't, *Engelse piëtistische geschriften in het Nederlands, 1598-1622* [Monografieën Gereformeerd Piëtisme, 1]. Rotterdam: Lindenberg, 1987

Hof [1987-2], W.J. op 't, 'Frederick de Vry', in T. Brienen *et al.*, *Figuren en thema's van de Nadere Reformatie*, vol.1. Kampen: De Groot Goudriaan, 1987, 17-22

Hof [1987-3], W.J. op 't, 'De laatste dagen van G. Udemans', *Documentatieblad Nadere Reformatie*, 11 (1987), 6-11

Hof [1988-1], W.J. op 't, *Bibliografie van de werken van Eeuwout Teellinck*. Kampen: De Groot Goudriaan, 1988

Hof [1988-2], W.J. op 't, 'BACHILER (BATCHILER, BATCHELER, BATILER, BACHELOR, BAZILER), SAMUEL', in D. Nauta et al., *Biografisch Lexicon voor de Geschiedenis van het Nederlandse Protestantisme*, vol. 3. Kampen: J.H. Kok, 1988, 28a-29a

Hof [1989], W.J. op 't, 'Gisbertus Voetius en de gebroeders Willem en Eeuwout Teellinck', in J. van Oort et al. (eds.), *De onbekende Voetius. Voordrachten wetenschappelijk symposium Utrecht 3 maart 1989*. Kampen: J.H. Kok, 1989, 92-108

Hof [1991], W.J. op 't, *Voorbereiding en bestrijding. De oudste gereformeerde piëtistische voorbereidingspreken tot het Avondmaal en de eerste bestrijding van de Nadere Reformatie in druk*. Kampen: De Groot Goudriaan, 1991

Hof [1993-1], W.J. op 't, *Bibliografische lijst van de geschriften van Willem Teellinck*. Rotterdam: Lindenberg Boeken&Muziek, 1993

Hof [1993-2], W.J. op 't, 'The oldest Dutch commercial oeuvre lists in print', *Quærendo. A quarterly journal from the Low Countries devoted to manuscripts and printed books*, 23 (1993), 265-290

Hof [1993-3], W.J. op 't, 'Johan Fargharson: vaandeldrager in tweeërlei dienst', *Zwols Historisch Tijdschrift*, 10 (1993), 22-29

Hof [1995], W.J. op 't, 'De godsdienstige gezindheid van Zacharias Heyns', *Documentatieblad Nadere Reformatie*, 19 (1995), 2-16

Hof [1996-1], W.J. op 't, 'Piety in the wake of trade. The North Sea as an intermediary of Reformed piety up to 1700', in Juliette Roding and Lex Heerma van Voss (eds.), *The North Sea and Culture (1550-1800). Proceedings of the International Conference held at Leiden 21-22 April 1995*. Hilversum: Verloren, 1996, 248-265

Hof [1996-2], W.J. op 't, 'Een vergeten piëtistisch puriteins geschrift in het Nederlands uit 1612', *Documentatieblad Nadere Reformatie*, 20 (1996), 73-80

Hof [1996-3], W.J. op 't, 'Puriteinse preken in Friesland', *Documentatieblad Nadere Reformatie*, 20 (1996), 114-120

Hof [1997], W.J. op 't, 'De Nederlandse vertalingen van Henry [G]reenwood', in *Verzameld werk van Henry Greenwood in het Nederlands*. Geldermalsen: De Schatkamer, 1997, [3-24]

Hof [1998], W.J. op 't, 'TEGNEJUS, TOBIAS', in J. van den Berg et al. (eds.), *Biografisch Lexicon voor de Geschiedenis van het Nederlandse Protestantisme*, vol. 4. Kampen: Kok, 1998, 418a-b

Hof [1999-1], W.J. op 't, *Eeuwout Teellinck. Leven, werk en betekenis.* Rumpt: De Schatkamer, 1999

Hof [1999-2], W.J. op 't, 'Een uniek voorbeeld van Nadere Reformatie te Sluis', in *Verstilde passages* [Bijdragen tot de geschiedenis van West-Zeeuws-Vlaanderen, 27]. Aardenburg: Heemkundige Kring West-Zeeuws-Vlaanderen, 1999, 77-100

Hof [1999-3], W.J. op 't, 'In één kast, maar niet door één deur. De verhouding tussen twee Sluise oudvaders: Jacobus Koelman en Caspar Alardin', *Documentatieblad Nadere Reformatie,* 23 (1999), 73-98

Hof [2001-1], W.J. op 't, 'De internationale invloed van het puritanisme', in W. van 't Spijker et al., *Het puritanisme. Geschiedenis, theologie en invloed.* Zoetermeer: Boekencentrum 2001, 271-384

Hof [2001-2], W.J. op 't, 'Vertaalde puritanistica in Friesland vóór 1623', *Documentatieblad Nadere Reformatie,* 25 (2001), 43-54

Hof [2001-3], W.J. op 't, 'Jacobus Koelman in het licht van zijn eerste publicatie', *Documentatieblad Nadere Reformatie,* 25 (2001), 73-83

Hof [2001-4], W.J. op 't, 'Een onbekende zoon van Willem Teellinck', *Documentatieblad Nadere Reformatie,* 25 (2001), 84-89

Hof [2002], W.J. op 't, 'De Sluise dienstmaagd Barbara Jobs in het licht van haar testamenten', in *Aaneengeregen tijdankers* [Bijdragen tot de geschiedenis van West-Zeeuws-Vlaanderen, 30]. Aardenburg: Heemkundige Kring West-Zeeuws-Vlaanderen, 2002, 79-104

Hof [2003], W.J. op 't, 'Willem Teellinck in het licht zijner geschriften (48). *Cana Galileae, Documentatieblad Nadere Reformatie,* 27 (2003), 81-90

Hof [2004-1], W.J. op 't, 'De burgerbevolking van Sluis na de reductie in 1604 en 1605', in *Niemandsland in Staats verband. West-Zeeuws-Vlaanderen ten tijde van de Republiek en daarna* [Bijdragen tot de geschiedenis van West-Zeeuws-Vlaanderen, 32]. Aardenburg: Heemkundige Kring West-Zeeuws-Vlaanderen, 2004, 77-147

Hof, [2004-2], W.J. op 't, 'Nadere Reformatie in Friesland?', *De zeventiende eeuw. Cultuur in de Nederlanden in multidisciplinair perspectief,* 20 (2004), 53-65

Hof [2005-1], W.J. op 't, *Het gereformeerd Piëtisme* [Hersteld Hervormde Studies, 1]. Houten: Den Hertog, 2005

Hof [2005-2], W.J. op 't, 'De geschiedenis van *Fonteyne des levens* van Arthur Hildersam', *Documentatieblad Nadere Reformatie,* 29 (2005), 106-123

Hof [2005-3], W.J. op 't, 'Vertaling als misleiding', *Documentatieblad Nadere Reformatie,* 29 (2005), 155-160

Hof [2005-4], W.J. op 't, 'Daniël van Laren en de Engelse gemeente te Arnhem', *Arnhem de Genoeglijkste,* 25 (2005), 121-124

Hof [2007], W.J. op 't, 'Martha Greendon, de vrouw van Willem Teellinck en zijn visie op de vrouw', *Documentatieblad Nadere Reformatie*, 31 (2007), 131-143

Hof [2008-1], W.J. op 't, *Willem Teellinck. Leven, geschriften en invloed.* Kampen: De Groot Goudriaan 2008

Hof [2008-2], W.J. op 't, 'Zeeland en de Nadere Reformatie', *Documentatieblad Nadere Reformatie*, 32 (2008), 4-55

Hof [2009-1], W.J. op 't, 'De vertaler van *De practycke*: Everhardus Schuttenius', in W.J. op 't Hof *et al.* (eds.), *De praktijk der godzaligheid. Studies over* De practycke ofte oeffeninghe der godtzaligheydt *(1620) van Lewis Bayly*. Amstelveen: Eon Pers, 2009, 41-84

Hof [2009-2], W.J. op 't, 'De receptiegeschiedenis van *De practycke*', in W.J. op 't Hof *et al.* (eds.), *De praktijk der godzaligheid. Studies over* De practycke ofte oeffeninghe der godtzaligheydt *(1620) van Lewis Bayly*. Amstelveen: Eon Pers, 2009, 237-258

Hof [2011-1], W.J. op 't, *De theologische opvattingen van Willem Teellinck.* Kampen: De Groot Goudriaan, 2011

Hof [2011-2], W.J. op 't, 'Een interessante brief van Mattheüs du Bois aan Johannes Vollenhove en een spoorloze liedbundel van Du Bois boven water', *Voortgang. Jaarboek voor de Neerlandistiek*, 29 (2011), 69-99

Hof [2011-3], W.J. op 't, 'Puriteinse auteurs en Nederlandse vertalers', *Documentatieblad Nadere Reformatie*, 35 (2011), 23-68

Hof, [2011-4], W.J. op 't, 'Bayly in Beilen. De Beilense predikant Johannes Beeltsnyder citeert *De practycke ofte oeffeninghe der godtzaligheydt* van Lewis Bayly', *Documentatieblad Nadere Reformatie*, 35 (2011), 165-171

Hof [2013-1], W.J. op 't, 'De Nederlandse vertalers van het oeuvre van Christopher Love', in W.J. op 't Hof and F.W. Huisman (eds.), *Nederlandse liefde voor Christopher Love (1618-1651). Studies over het vertaalde werk van een presbyteriaanse puritein*. Amstelveen: Eon Pers, 2013, 235-292

Hof [2013-2], W.J. op 't, 'De editiegeschiedenis van Christopher Loves werken in het Nederlands', in W.J. op 't Hof and F.W. Huisman (eds.), *Nederlandse liefde voor Christopher Love (1618-1651). Studies over het vertaalde werk van een presbyteriaanse puritein*, Amstelveen: Eon Pers, 2013, 293-324

Hof [2013-3], W.J. op 't, 'Unique Information on a Seventeenth-Century Printing House in Arnhem. The dedication by the Arnhem printer Jacob van Biesen (d. 1677) in the 1669 edition of *Fonteyne des levens* by Arthur Hildersham (1563-1632) and its implications for the history of books', *Quærendo. A Journal Devoted to Manuscripts and Printed Books*, 43 (2013), 214-237

Hof [2013-4], W.J. op 't, 'Petrus Wittewrongel en zijn *Oeconomia christiana*', in Petrus Wittewrongel, *Oeconomia christiana of christelijke huishouding*, vol. 1. Wijk en Aalburg: Landelijke Stichting ter bevordering van de Staatkundig Gereformeerde beginselen, 2013, 13-53

Hof [2013-5], W.J. op 't, 'De boedelinventaris van Mattheüs du Bois (?-1695). Het boekenbezit van een stichtelijk auteur te Haarlem in de tweede helft van de zeventiende eeuw', *Documentatieblad Nadere Reformatie*, 37 (2013), 156-179

Hof [2014], Willem Jan op 't, 'Lusthof des Gemoets in Comparison and Competition with De Practycke ofte oeffeninghe der godtzaligheydt: Vredestad and Reformed Piety in Seventeenth-Century Dutch Culture', in A. den Hollander et al. (eds.), *Religious Minorities and Cultural Diversity in the Dutch Republic. Studies Presented to Piet Visser on the Occasion of his 65th Birthday* [Brill's Series in Church History, 67]. Leiden: Brill, 2014, 133-149.

Hof [2015-1], W.J. op 't, 'The eventful sojourn of Willem Teellinck (1579-1629) at Banbury in 1605', *Journal for the History of Reformed Pietism*, 1 (2015), 5-34

Hof [2015-2], W.J. op 't, 'APOLLONIUS, GUILIELMUS', in W.J. op 't Hof *et al.* (eds.), *Encyclopedie Nadere Reformatie*, vol. 1. Utrecht: De Groot Goudriaan, 2015, 47a-50a

Hof [2015-3], W.J. op 't, 'BARENZONIUS, NICOLAUS', in W.J. op 't Hof *et al.* (eds.), *Encyclopedie Nadere Reformatie*, vol. 1. Utrecht: De Groot Goudriaan, 2015, 62b-65a

Hof [2015-4], W.J. op 't, 'BAUDARTIUS, WILHELMUS', in W.J. op 't Hof *et al.* (eds.), *Encyclopedie Nadere Reformatie*, vol. 1. Utrecht: De Groot Goudriaan, 2015, 65a-68b

Hof [2015-5], W.J. op 't, 'BEELTSNYDER, JOHANNES', in W.J. op 't Hof *et al.* (eds.), *Encyclopedie Nadere Reformatie*, vol. 1. Utrecht: De Groot Goudriaan, 2015, 80b-83a

Hof [2015-6], W.J. op 't, 'BOERHAVE, MARCUS', in W.J. op 't Hof *et al.* (eds.), *Encyclopedie Nadere Reformatie*, vol. 1. Utrecht: De Groot Goudriaan, 2015, 102b-103b

Hof [2015-7], W.J. op 't, 'BRAKEL, WILHELMUS À', in W.J. op 't Hof *et al.* (eds.), *Encyclopedie Nadere Reformatie*, vol. 1. Utrecht: De Groot Goudriaan, 2015, 121b-129b

Hof [2015-8], W.J. op 't, 'BUCERUS, GERSON', in W.J. op 't Hof *et al.* (eds.), *Encyclopedie Nadere Reformatie*, vol. 1. Utrecht: De Groot Goudriaan, 2015, 141a-142b

Hof [2015-9], W.J. op 't, 'BURSIUS, JACOBUS', in W.J. op 't Hof *et al.* (eds.), *Encyclopedie Nadere Reformatie*, vol. 1. Utrecht: De Groot Goudriaan, 2015, 152b-154a

Hof [2015-10], W.J. op 't, 'BUSSCHOF, BERNARDUS', in W.J. op 't Hof *et al.* (eds.), *Encyclopedie Nadere Reformatie*, vol. 1. Utrecht: De Groot Goudriaan, 2015, 154a-158a

Hof [2015-11], W.J. op 't, 'CATS, JACOB', in W.J. op 't Hof *et al.* (eds.), *Encyclopedie Nadere Reformatie*, vol. 1. Utrecht: De Groot Goudriaan, 2015, 164a-168a

Hof [2015-12], W.J. op 't, 'COCQUIUS, ADRIANUS', in W.J. op 't Hof *et al.* (eds.), *Encyclopedie Nadere Reformatie*, vol. 1. Utrecht: De Groot Goudriaan, 2015, 180a-183a

Hof [2015-13], W.J. op 't, 'DELIËN, NICOLAUS VAN DER', in W.J. op 't Hof *et al.* (eds.), *Encyclopedie Nadere Reformatie*, vol. 1. Utrecht: De Groot Goudriaan, 2015, 213a-215a

Hof [2015-14], W.J. op 't, 'DONIUS, BARTHOLOMEÜS', in W.J. op 't Hof *et al.* (eds.), *Encyclopedie Nadere Reformatie*, vol. 1. Utrecht: De Groot Goudriaan, 2015, 218b-220a

Hof [2015-15], W.J. op 't, 'DORTH, JOHANNES VAN', in W.J. op 't Hof *et al.* (eds.), *Encyclopedie Nadere Reformatie*, vol. 1. Utrecht: De Groot Goudriaan, 2015, 220a-223b

Hof [2015-16], W.J. op 't, 'FAUKELIUS, HERMANNUS', in W.J. op 't Hof *et al.* (eds.), *Encyclopedie Nadere Reformatie*, vol. 1. Utrecht: De Groot Goudriaan, 2015, 259a-262a

Hof [2015-17], W.J. op 't, 'HOFMAN, JOHANNES', in W.J. op 't Hof *et al.* (eds.), *Encyclopedie Nadere Reformatie*, vol. 1. Utrecht: De Groot Goudriaan, 2015, 350b-357a

Hof [2015-18], W.J. op 't, 'HOORNBEECK, JOHANNES', in W.J. op 't Hof *et al.* (eds.), *Encyclopedie Nadere Reformatie*, vol. 1. Utrecht: De Groot Goudriaan, 2015, 372a-377a

Hof [2015-19], W.J. op 't, 'HOUTE, JOSIAS VAN DEN', in W.J. op 't Hof *et al.* (eds.), *Encyclopedie Nadere Reformatie*, vol. 1. Utrecht: De Groot Goudriaan, 2015, 377a-379b

Hof [2016-1], Willem J. op 't, 'Kommunikationsformen der reformierten Frömmigkeit im 16. und 17. Jahrhundert in internationaler und interkonfessioneller Sicht', in Pia Schmid and Christian Soboth (eds.), *>>Schrift soll leserlich seyn<< Der Pietismus und die Medien. Beiträge zum IV. Internationalen Kongress für Pietismusforschung 2013* [Hallesche Forschungen, 44]. Halle am Saale: Verlag der Franckeschen Stiftungen, 2016, 625-638

Hof [2016-2], W.J. op 't, 'LAREN, ABRAHAM VAN', in W.J. op 't Hof *et al.* (eds.), *Encyclopedie Nadere Reformatie*, vol. 2. Utrecht: De Groot Goudriaan, 2016, 35b-37b

Hof [2016-3], W.J. op 't, 'LAREN, DANIËL VAN', in W.J. op 't Hof *et al.* (eds.), *Encyclopedie Nadere Reformatie*, vol. 2. Utrecht: De Groot Goudriaan, 2016, 37b-41b

Hof [2016-4], W.J. op 't, 'LAREN, JOOS junior VAN', in W.J. op 't Hof *et al.* (eds.), *Encyclopedie Nadere Reformatie*, vol. 2. Utrecht: De Groot Goudriaan, 2016, 41b-43b

Hof [2016-5], W.J. op 't, 'MEUSEVOET, VINCENTIUS', in W.J. op 't Hof *et al.* (eds.), *Encyclopedie Nadere Reformatie*, vol. 2. Utrecht: De Groot Goudriaan, 2016, 111b-114b

Hof [2016-6], W.J. op 't, 'MONTANUS, DAVID', in W.J. op 't Hof *et al.* (eds.), *Encyclopedie Nadere Reformatie*, vol. 2. Utrecht: De Groot Goudriaan, 2016, 118b-122b

Hof [2016-7], W.J. op 't, 'OOSTERWIJCK, VOLCKERUS VAN', in W.J. op 't Hof *et al.* (eds.), *Encyclopedie Nadere Reformatie*, vol. 2. Utrecht: De Groot Goudriaan, 2016, 163b-165b

Hof [2016-8], W.J. op 't, 'PELT, HENDRIK VAN', in W.J. op 't Hof *et al.* (eds.), *Encyclopedie Nadere Reformatie*, vol. 2. Utrecht: De Groot Goudriaan, 2016, 182a-185a

Hof [2016-9], W.J. op 't, 'PIETERSZOON, ROELOF', in W.J. op 't Hof *et al.* (eds.), *Encyclopedie Nadere Reformatie*, vol. 2. Utrecht: De Groot Goudriaan, 2016, 185a-188b

Hof [2016-10], W.J. op 't, 'QUINTIUS, JOHANNES', in W.J. op 't Hof *et al.* (eds.), *Encyclopedie Nadere Reformatie*, vol. 2. Utrecht: De Groot Goudriaan, 2016, 199a-200b

Hof [2016-11], W.J. op 't, 'ROLDANUS, JOHANNES', in W.J. op 't Hof *et al.* (eds.), *Encyclopedie Nadere Reformatie*, vol. 2. Utrecht: De Groot Goudriaan, 2016, 229b-231b

Hof [2016-12], W.J. op 't, 'SPILJARDUS, JOHANNES senior', in W.J. op 't Hof *et al.* (eds.), *Encyclopedie Nadere Reformatie*, vol. 2. Utrecht: De Groot Goudriaan, 2016, 315a-318b

Hof [2016-13], W.J. op 't, 'SWAEF, JOHANNES DE', in W.J. op 't Hof *et al.* (eds.), *Encyclopedie Nadere Reformatie*, vol. 2. Utrecht: De Groot Goudriaan, 2016, 329a-332b

Hof [2016-14], W.J. op 't, 'TAFFIN, JEAN', in W.J. op 't Hof *et al.* (eds.), *Encyclopedie Nadere Reformatie*, vol. 2. Utrecht: De Groot Goudriaan, 2016, 337a-342a

Hof [2016-15], W.J. op 't, 'TEELLINCK, JOHANNES', in W.J. op 't Hof *et al.* (eds.), *Encyclopedie Nadere Reformatie*, vol. 2. Utrecht: De Groot Goudriaan, 2016, 346b-351a

Hof [2016-16], W.J. op 't, 'TEELLINCK, MAXIMILIAAN', in W.J. op 't Hof *et al.* (eds.), *Encyclopedie Nadere Reformatie*, vol. 2. Utrecht: De Groot Goudriaan, 2016, 353b-357b

Hof [2016-17], W.J. op 't, 'THILENUS, JOHANNES', in W.J. op 't Hof *et al.* (eds.), *Encyclopedie Nadere Reformatie*, vol. 2. Utrecht: De Groot Goudriaan, 2016, 377b-379a

Hof [2016-18], W.J. op 't, 'UBELMAN, JOHANNES', in W.J. op 't Hof *et al.* (eds.), *Encyclopedie Nadere Reformatie*, vol. 2. Utrecht: De Groot Goudriaan, 2016, 405a-408b

Hof [2016-19], W.J. op 't, 'UILENBROEK, HENDRIK', in W.J. op 't Hof *et al.* (eds.), *Encyclopedie Nadere Reformatie*, vol. 2. Utrecht: De Groot Goudriaan, 2016, 417a-421a

Hof [2016-20], W.J. op 't, 'VLETEREN, TIMOTHEÜS VAN', in W.J. op 't Hof *et al.* (eds.), *Encyclopedie Nadere Reformatie*, vol. 2. Utrecht: De Groot Goudriaan, 2016, 465a-467a

Hof [2016-21], W.J. op 't, 'WALAEUS, ANTONIUS', in W.J. op 't Hof *et al.* (eds.), *Encyclopedie Nadere Reformatie*, vol. 2. Utrecht: De Groot Goudriaan, 2016, 500b-503b

Hof [2016-22], W.J. op 't, 'WITTE, PETRUS DE', in W.J. op 't Hof *et al.* (eds.), *Encyclopedie Nadere Reformatie*, vol. 2. Utrecht: De Groot Goudriaan, 2016, 531b-534b

Hof [2016-23], W.J. op 't, 'WYCKENBURGIUS, THEODORUS', in W.J. op 't Hof *et al.* (eds.), *Encyclopedie Nadere Reformatie*, vol. 2. Utrecht: De Groot Goudriaan, 2016, 542a-544a

Hof [2016-24], W.J. op 't, 'De auctiecatalogus van het boekenbezit van de Gamerse predikant Michael Spranger (1627-1673). Een voorbeeld van de mogelijkheden die het onderzoek van gedrukte auctiecatalogi van particuliere boekenverzamelingen biedt', *Documentatievlad Nadere Reformatie*, 40 (2016), 170-189

Hof, W.J. op 't, and F.W. Huisman [2002], 'Vertalingen van werken van afgevaardigden', in *De Synode van Westminster 1643-1649*. Houten: Den Hertog, 2002, 195-202

Hof, W.J. op 't, and F.W. Huisman (eds.) [2013], *Nederlandse liefde voor Christopher Love (1618-1651). Studies over het vertaalde werk van een presbyteriaanse puritein*. Amstelveen: Eon Pers, 2013

Hof, W.J. op 't, and F.W. Huisman [2016], *Hendrik Versteeg (1630-1673). Een nader-reformatorische uitgever, werkzaam te Utrecht van 1654-1672*. Amstelveen: Eon Pers, 2016

Hof, W.J. op 't, *et al.* [1993], *Adrianus Hofferus (1589-1644). Drie opstellen over Hofferus' ambtelijke loopbaan, godsdienstige positie en literaire betekenis, alsmede gravures en een bloemlezing uit zijn Nederduytsche poëmata.* Amsterdam: Stichting Neerlandistiek VU, 1993

Hof, W.J. op 't, *et al.* (eds.) [2009], *De praktijk der godzaligheid. Studies over* De practycke ofte oeffeninghe der godtzaligheydt *(1620) van Lewis Bayly.* Amstelveen: Eon Pers, 2009

Hofmeyr, J.W., *Johannes Hoornbeeck as polemikus.* Kampen: J.H. Kok, 1975

Hoftijzer, P.G., 'Henry Hexham (c. 1585-1650), English Soldier, Author, Translator, Lexicographer, and Cultural Mediator in the Low Countries', in S.K. Barker and Brenda Hosington (eds.), *Renaissance Cultural Cross-roads. Translation, Print, and Culture in Britain, 1473-1640.* Leiden: Brill, 2013, 209-224

Houston [1985], R.A., *Scottish Literacy and the Scottish Identity. Illiteracy and Society in Scotland and Northern England, 1600-1800* [Cambridge Studies in Population, Economy and Society in Past Time, 4]. Cambridge: Cambridge University Press, 1985

Houston [1989], R.A., 'Women in the economy and society of Scotland, 1500-1800', in R.A. Houston and I.D. Whyte (eds.), *Scottish society, 1500-1800.* Cambridge: Cambrige University Press, 1989, 118-147

Howie, John, *The Sctots Worthies.* Glasgow: W.R. M'Phun, 1837

Hughes, Ann, 'The Frustrations of the Godly', in John Stephen Morrill (ed.), *Revolution and Restoration. England in the 1650s.* London: Collins & Brown, 1992, 70-90

Huisman [2008], F.W., 'Puriteins-piëtistische invloeden in het lutherse Denemarken tot 1800', *Documentatieblad Nadere Reformatie,* 32 (2008), 170-254

Huisman [2009-1], F.W., 'De bibliografie van *De practycke*', in W.J. op 't Hof *et al.* (eds.), *De praktijk der godzaligheid. Studies over* De practycke ofte oeffeninghe der godtzaligheydt *(1620) van Lewis Bayly.* Amstelveen: Eon Pers, 2009, 107-169

Huisman, [2009-2], Frans W., 'Danske oversættelser af engelske puritansk-pietistiske værker i det 17. og 18. Århundrede', *Kirkehistoriske samlinger* (2009), 83-187

Huisman [2010], F.W., 'De *Christelycke Morghen-wecker* als Nieuwjaarsgave. Een nader-reformatorisch geestelijk lied van Johannes Spiljardus (1624)', *Documentatieblad Nadere Reformatie,* 34 (2010), 45-57

Huisman [2011], F.W., 'Pietas Online! Pietas als schatkamer van gereformeerde vroomheidsliteratuur', *Documentatieblad Nadere Reformatie,* 35 (2011), 1-22

Huisman [2013], F.W., 'Het leven van Christopher Love (1618-1651)', in W.J. op 't Hof and F.W. Huisman (eds.), *Nederlandse liefde voor Christopher Love (1618-1651). Studies over het vertaalde werk van een prebyteriaanse puritein*. Amstelveen: Eon Pers, 2013, 11-78

Hull, William I., *Benjamin Furly and Quakerism in Rotterdam*. Swarthmore Pa: Swarthmore College, 1941

Hullu, J. de, 'De Waalse gemeente te Sluis', *Nederlandsch Archief voor Kerkgeschiedenis*, Nieuwe Serie, 11 (1914), 117-123

Hunt, Arnold, *The Art of Hearing. English Preachers and their Audiences, 1590-1640* [Cambridge Studies in Early Modern British History]. Cambridge: Cambridge University Press, 2010

Imminkhuizen, H., *De Nadere Reformatie. Primaire bibliografie van 19$^{de}$-eeuwse uitgaven*. Rotterdam: Lindenberg's boekhandel, 1985

Ingen, Ferdinand van, *Böhme und Böhmisten in den Niederlanden im 17. Jahrhundert* [Nachbarn, 29]. Bonn: Presse- und Kulturabteilung der Kgl. Niederländischen Botschaft, 1984

Israel, Jonathan I., *Radical Enlightenment: Philosophy and the Making of Modernity*. Oxford: Oxford University Press, 2001

Itterzon [1930], G.P. van, *Franciscus Gomarus*. The Hague: Martinus Nijhoff, 1930

Itterzon [1983-1], G.P. van, 'BOGERMAN(NUS), JOHANNES', in D. Nauta *et al.* (eds.), *Biografisch Lexicon voor de Geschiedenis van het Nederlandse Protestantisme*, vol. 2. Kampen: J.H. Kok 1983, 73b-76b

Itterzon [1983-2], G.P. van, 'HEYDEN (HEIDEN, HEIDANUS), GASPAR (CASPAR) VAN DER', in D. Nauta *et al.* (eds.), *Biografisch Lexicon voor de Geschiedenis van het Nederlandse Protestantisme*, vol. 2. Kampen: J.H. Kok 1983, 243a-246a

Jansen, Jeroen, *Imitatio: literaire navolging (imitatio auctorum) in de Europese letterkunde van de renaissance (1500-1700)*. Hilversum: Verloren, 2008

Janssen, A.E.M. and Kosterus G. van Manen, *Johannes Fontanus [1545-1615]. Een Gelders predikant in dienst van de orthodoxie*. Nijmegen: Valkhof Pers, 2015

Janssen, H.Q., *De kerkhervorming in Vlaanderen*, 2 vols. Arnhem: Swaan, 1868

Jelsma, A.J., *Adriaen van Haemstede en zijn martelaarsboek*. The Hague: Boekencentrum, 1970

Jong, Christiaan George Frederik de, *John Forbes (ca. 1568-1634)*. S.l.: s.n., 1987

Joosse, L.J., *Geloof in de Nieuwe Wereld. Ontmoetingen met Afrikanen en Indianen (1600-1700)*. Kampen: Kok, 2008

Juten, G.C.A., 'Grafschriften in de St. Janskerk te Sluis', *De Wapenheraut. Maandblad gewijd aan Geschiedenis, Geslacht-, Wapen-, Oudheidkunde, enz.*, 6 (1902), 49-56, 97-104, 145-152, 203-216

Kalma, J.J., *Mensen in en om de Grote Kerk. Beelden uit de Leeuwarder kerkgeschiedenis*. Drachten: Friese Pers Boekerij, 1987

Kamp [2007], Jan van de, 'Johannes Deusing Bremensis. Die Bedeutung zweier Übersetzer für den reformierten un den lutherischen Pietismus in Deutschland im 17. Jahrhundert', *Pietismus und Neuzeit. Ein Jahrbuch zur Geschichte des neueren Protestantismus*, 33 (2007), 13-47

Kamp [2009], J. van de, 'De vertaalmethoden van Everhardus Schuttenius en Gisbertus Voetius', in W.J. op 't Hof *et al.* (eds.), *De praktijk der godzaligheid. Studies over* De practycke ofte oeffeninghe der godtzaligheydt *(1620) van Lewis Bayly*. Amstelveen: Eon Pers, 2009, 215-235

Kamp [2010], Jan van de, 'John Cotton en de Nadere Reformatie', *Documentatieblad Nadere Reformatie*, 34 (2010), 36-44

Kamp [2012-1], Jan van de, *Op verzoek van vromen vertaald. Duitse vertalingen van gereformeerde stichtelijke lectuur 1667-1697 en de rol van netwerken*. Zoetermeer: Boekencentrum, 2012

Kamp [2012-2], Jan van de, 'Ein frühes reformiert-pietistisches Netzwerk in der Kurpfalz in der ersten Hälfte des 17. Jahrhunderts', *Archiv für Reformationsgeschichte*, 103 (2012), 182-209

Kamp [2013], J. van de, 'De vertaalstrategieën van de Nederlandse vertalers van de geschriften van Christopher Love', in W.J. op 't Hof and F.W. Huisman (eds.), *Nederlandse liefde voor Christopher Love (1618-1651). Studies over het vertaalde werk van een presbyteriaanse puritein*. Amstelveen: Eon Pers, 2013, 325-378

Kamp [2015], J. van de, 'GRIBIUS, PETRUS', in W.J. op 't Hof *et al.* (eds.), *Encyclopedie Nadere Reformatie*, vol.1. Utrecht: De Groot Goudriaan, 2015, 296a-297b

Kamp [2016], Jan van de, 'Internationale Vermittlung von Reformprogrammen. Die Rezeption von Willem Teellincks *Noodwendigh vertoogh* in Deutschland im 17. Jahrhundert', in Pia Schmid and Christian Soboth (eds.), >>*Schrift soll leserlich seyn*<< *Der Pietismus und die Medien. Beiträge zum IV. Internationalen Kongress für Pietismusforschung 2013*. Halle am Saale: Verlag der Franckeschen Stiftungen, 2016, 261-283

Kess, Alexandra, *Johann Sleidan and the Protestant vision of history*. Aldershot: Ashgate, 2008

Klink, Hubrecht, *Opstand, politiek en religie bij Willem van Oranje 1559-1568. Een thematische biografie*. Heerenveen: J.J. Groen en zoon, 1997

Kluiver, J.H., *De souvereine en independente staat Zeeland. De politiek van de provincie Zeeland inzake vredesonderhandelingen met Spanje tijdens de Tachtigjarige Oorlog tegen de achtergrond van de positie van Zeeland in de Republiek*. Middelburg: De Zwarte Arend, 1998

Knappen, M.M., *Two Elizabethan Puritan Diaries by Richard Rogers and Samuel Ward*. Gloucester, Mass.: Peter Smith, 1966

Knetsch, Frederik Reinier Jacob, *Pierre Jurieu, theoloog en politikus der refuge*. Kampen: J.H. Kok, 1967

Knuttel, W.P.C. (ed.), *Acta van de particuliere synoden van Zuid-Holland 1621-1700*, 6 vols. The Hague: Martinus Nijhoff, 1908-1916

Koopman, H., 'Wilhelmus Grasmeer (±1621-1678). Probleempredikant en Boltonvertaler', in *Documentatieblad Nadere Reformatie*, 42 (2018), 23-40

Korthals-Altes, J., *Sir Cornelius Vermuyden. The Lifework of a Great Anglo-Dutchman in Land-reclamation and Drainage*. London: Williams & Norgate, 1925

Krull, A.F., *Jacobus Koelman*. Sneek: Campen, 1901

Kwekkeboom, J., 'Een spoorloos boekje?', *Documentatieblad Nadere Reformatie*, 19 (1995), 67-68

Laan, Harry van der, *Het Groninger boekbedrijf. Drukkers, uitgevers en boekhandelaren in Groningen tot het eind van de negentiende eeuw*. Assen: Koninklijke Van Gorcum, 2005

Laasonen, Pennti, 'Erweckungsbewegungen im Norden im 19. und 20. Jahrhundert', in Ulrich Gäbler (ed.), *Der Pietismus im neunzehnten und zwanzigsten Jahrhunder* [Geschichte des Pietismus, 3]. Göttingen: Vandenhoeck & Ruprecht, 2000, 321-357

Lamping [1980], A.J., *Johannes Polyander* [Kerkhistorische Bijdragen, 9]. Leiden: E.J. Brill, 1980

Lamping [2001], A.J., 'THYSIUS, ANTONIUS', in C. Houtman et al. (eds.), *Biografisch Lexicon voor de Geschiedenis van het Nederlandse Protestantisme*, vol. 5. Kampen, Kok, 2001, 505a-508a

Lang, August, *Puritanismus und Pietismus. Studien zu ihrer Entwicklung von M. Butzer bis zum Methodismus* [Beiträge zur Geschichte und Lehre der Reformierten Kirche, 6]. Neukrichen: Neukirchener Verlag des Erziehungsvereins GmbH, 1941

Larminie, Vivienne, 'Johann Heinrich Hummel, the Penningtons and the London godly community: Anglo-Swiss networks 1634-1674', *Journal for the History of Reformed Piety*, 2-2 (2016), 1-26

Lemper, Ernst-Heinz, *Jacob Böhme. Levenswege (1575-1624)*. Görlitz: G. Oettel, 2000

Lennep, Maximiliaan Frederik van, *Gaspar van der Heyden 1530-1586*. Amsterdam: C.A. Spin & Zoon, 1884

Leurdijk [1987], G.H., 'Dionysius Spranckhuysen', in T. Brienen *et al.*, *Figuren en thema's van de Nadere Reformatie*, vol. 1. Kampen: De Groot Goudriaan, 1987, 27-42

Leurdijk [2013], G.H., 'Vroomheid van Bremen tot Berkel. Theodor Undereyck (1635-1693) en Simon Jodocus Krüger (ca. 1652-1706): hun betekenis voor een nadere reformatie in Holland', *Documentatieblad Nadere Reformatie*, 37 (2013), 23-75

Leurdijk [2015], G.H., 'KRÜGER, SIMON JODOCUS', in W.J. op 't Hof *et al.* (eds.), *Encyclopedie Nadere Reformatie*, vol. 1. Utrecht: De Groot Goudriaan, 2015, 427a-431a

Lieburg [1985], F.A. van, 'Vrouwen uit het gereformeerde piëtisme in Nederland (1-4)', *Documentatieblad Nadere Reformatie*, 9 (1985), 78-87, 119-127; 10 (1986), 94-104; 12 (1988), 116-127

Lieburg [1989], F.A. van, 'Piëtistische lectuur in de zeventiende en achttiende eeuw', *Documentatieblad Nadere Reformatie*, 13 (1989), 73-87

Lieburg [1990], F.A. van, 'Jacobus Koelman (1631-1695): jeugd en studietijd', in T. Brienen *et al.*, *Figuren en thema's van de Nadere Reformatie*, vol. 2. Kampen: De Groot Goudriaan, 1990, 57-62

Lieburg [1994], Fred A. van, 'From Pure Church to Pious Culture: The Further Reformation in the Seventeenth-Century Dutch Republic', in W. Fred Graham (ed.), *Later Calvinism: International Perspectives* [Sixteenth Century Essays and Studies, 22]. Kirksville, MO, Sixteenth Century Journal Publications, 1994, 409-429

Lieburg [1996], F.A. van, *Repertorium van Nederlandse hervormde predikanten tot 1816*, 2 vols. Dordrecht: F.A. van Lieburg, 1996

Lieburg [2011], Fed van, *Een eiland na de Reformatie. Schouwen-Duiveland 1572-1700*. Amsterdam: Bert Bakker, 2011

Lind van Wijngaarden, Jan Daniël de, *Antonius Walaeus*. Amsterdam: G. Los, 1891

Linde, S. van der, *Jean Taffin. Hofprediker en raadsheer van Willem van Oranje*. Amsterdam: Ton Bolland, 1982

Lindeboom, J., *Austin Friars. Geschiedenis van de Nederlandse Hervormde Gemeente te Londen, 1550-1950*. The Hague: Nijhoff, 1950

Lindner, Andreas, *Leben im Spannungsfeld von Orthodoxie, Pietismus und Frühaufklärung. Johann Martin Schamelius, Oberpfarrer in Naumburg*. Giessen: Brunnen Verlag, 1998

Loonen, P.L.M., *For to learne to buye and sell. Learning English in the Low Dutch area between 1500 and 1800. A critical survey* [Studies of the Pierre Bayle Institute, 22]. Amsterdam: APA-Holland University Press, 1991

Los, Frans Johannes, *Wilhelmus à Brakel*. Leiden: G. Los, 1892
Love [1993], Harold, *Scribal Publication in Seventeenth-century England*. Oxford: Clarendon Press, 1993
Love [2000], Harold, 'The Rapes of Lucina', in Arhur F. Marotti and Michael D. Bristol (eds.), *Print, Manuscript, & Performance. The Changing Relations of the Media in Early Modern England*. Columbus, OH: Ohio State University Press, 2000, 200-214
Love [2002], Harold, 'Oral and scribal texts in early modern England', in John Barnard en D.F. McKenzie (eds), *The Cambridge History of the Book in Britain*, vol. 4, 1557-1695. Cambridge: Cambridge University Press, 2002, 97-121
MacLean, J., *De huwelijksintekeningen van Schotse militairen in Nederland 1574-1665* [Werken uitgegeven door het Koninklijk Nederlandsch Genootschap voor Geslachts- en Wapenkunde, 4]. Zutphen: De Walburg Pers, 1976
Madsen, Victor, 'Karen brahes Bibliothek i Odense', *Nordisk tidskrift för Bok- och Biblioteksväsen*, 6 (1919), 171-185
Mann, Alastair J., *The Scottish Book Trade 1500-1700. Print, Commerce and Print Control in Early Modern Schotland. An historiographical survey of the early modern books in Scotland*. Phantassie: Tuckwell Press, 2000
Markham, Clements Rovert, *"The Fighting Veres". Lives of Sir Francis Vere, General of the Queen's Forces in the Low Countries, Governor of the Brill and of Portsmouth and of Sir Horace Vere, General of the English Forces in the Low Countries, Governor of the Brill, Master-General of Ordnance, and Baron Vere of Tilbury*. London: Sampson Low, Marston, Searle & Rivington, 1888
Marotti [1995], Arthur F., *Manuscript, Print and the English Renaissance Lyric*. Ithaca, NY: Cornell University Press, 1995
Marotti [2000], Arthur F., 'Manuscript Transmission and the Catholic Martyrdom Account in Early Modern England', in Arhur F. Marotti and Michael D. Bristol (eds.), *Print, Manuscript, & Performance. The Changing Relations of the Media in Early Modern England*. Columbus, OH: Ohio State University Press, 2000, 172-199
McKenzie, Edgar C., *A Catalogue of British Devotional and Religious Books in German Translation from the Reformation to 1750*. Berlin: Walter de Gruyter, 1997
Meertens, P.J., 'Godefridus Cornelisz Udemans', *Nederlandsch Archief voor Kerkgeschiedenis*, Nieuwe Serie, 28 (1936), 65-106
Meeus, H., *Zacharias Heyns, uitgever en toneelauteur. Bio-bibliografie en studie van zijn toneelwerk*. Kessel-Lo: H. Meeus, 1992

Meeuse [1990], C.J., 'Jacobus Koelman (1631-1695): leven en werken', in T. Brienen et al., *Figuren en thema's van de Nadere Reformatie*, vol. 2. Kampen: De Groot Goudriaan, 1990, 63-93

Meeuse [1996], C.J., 'De visie van Koelman op de puriteinen', *Documentatieblad Nadere Reformatie*, 20 (1996), 44-61

Meeuse [2008], C.J., *Jacobus Koelman*. Kampen: De Groot Goudriaan, 2008

Mett, Rudolf, *Regiomontanus. Wegbereiter des neuen Weltbildes*. Stuttgart: Teubner, 1996

Miert, Dirk van, *Humanism in an Age of Science. The Amsterdam Athenaeum in the Golden Age, 1632-1704*. Leiden: Brill, 2009

Milton, Anthony, 'Puritanism and the continental Reformed churches', in John Coffey and Pul C.H. Lim (eds.), *The Cambridge Companion to Puritanism*. Cambridge: Cambridge University Press, 2008, 109-126

Moens [1884], William John Charles (ed.), *The Marriage, Baptismal, and Burial Registers, 1571 to 1874, and Monumental Inscriptions, of the Dutch Reformed Church, Austin Friars, London. With a Short Account of the Strangers and Their Churches*. Lyminton: King and Sons, 1884

Moens [1905], William John Charles (ed.), *Registers of Baptisms in the Dutch Church of Colchester from 1645 to 1728* [Publications of the Huguenot Society of London, 12]. Lyminton: King and Sons, 1905

Morgan, John, *Godly Learning. Puritan Attitudes towards Reason, Learning, and Education, 1560-1640*. Cambridge, Eng.: Cambridge University Press, 1986

Moser [2003-1], Nelleke, 'Verspreid verzameld. Rederijkersteksten in vroegmoderne verzamelhandschriften', *Nederlandse Letterkunde*, 8-2 (2003), 101-115

Moser [2003-2], Nelleke, 'Van papier of uit het hoofd? De overlevering van een rederijkersrefrein', *Tijdschrift voor Nederlandse Taal- en Letterkunde*, 119 (2003), 187-203

Moser [2007], Nelleke, '"Poezijlust en vriendenliefd"'. Literaire sociabiliteit in handschrift en druk na 1600', *Spiegel der Letteren*, 49-2 (2007), 247-264

Moser [2008], Nelleke, 'Het merk van de maker. Auteursvermeldingen in autografen als teken van dichterlijk zelfbewustzijn', *Jaarboek De Fonteyne*, 2008, 147-178

Moser [2010], Nelleke, 'Migrants and Merchants. Two Early Modern Dutch Readers and Their English Entempories', *Huntington Library Quarterly*, 73 (2010), 471-490

Moser [2011], Nelleke, 'Manuscript Pamphlets and Made-Up Performances: New Sources and Challenges in the Study of Public Opinion', in J. Bloemendal et al., (eds.), *Literary Cultures and Public Opinion in the Low Countries, 1450-1650*. Leiden: Brill, 2011, 181-218

Moser [2013], Nelleke, 'Oorlog? Welke oorlog? Herinneringen en vergeten in het *Digt Memoriaal* (1762-1815) van Cornelis van der Schelling', in Nina Geerdink and Lotte Jensen (eds.), *Oorlogsliteratuur in de vroegmoderne tijd. Verbeelding, herinnering, identiteit.* Hilversum: Verloren, 2013, 163-181, 227-231

Moser [2015], Nelleke, 'Bedekte letters, betere lezers. Schijnbedriegers in boekvorm als vehikels voor verlichtingsdenken', *Jaarboek voor Nederlandse boekgeschiedenis*, 22 (2015), 160-186

Moser [2016-1], Nelleke, 'The Aura of the Letter. Cornelis Crul's ABC Poem in BL Sloane MS 1174 and Sixteenth Century Views on Form and Content', in Jessica Buskirk and Samuel Mareel (eds.), *The Aura of the Word in the Early Age of Print (1450-1600)*. Abington: Routledge, 2016, 151-179

Moser [2016-2], Nelleke, 'Performing Pietism in the Peatlands. Songs in the Manuscript Miscellany of a Village Schoolmaster in the Dutch Republic between 1750 and 1800', in Dieuwke van der Poel et al., *Identity, Intertextuality, and Performance in Early Modern Song Culture*. Leiden: Brill, 59-92

Müller, Jan-Dirk (ed.), *Sebastian Franck (1499-1542)*. Wiesbaden: Harrossowitz, 1993

Müller, Johannes Martin, *Exile Memories and the Dutch Revolt. The narrated diaspora, 1550-1750*, unpublished thesis, Leiden University 2014

Mullan, David George, *Scottish Puritanism 1590-1638*. Oxford: Oxford University Press, 2000

Murdock [2000], Graeme, *Calvinism on the Frontier 1600-1660. International Calvinism and the Reformed Church in Hungary and Transylvania* [Oxford Historical Monographs]. Oxford: Clarendon Press, 2000

Murdock [2004], Graeme, *Beyond Calvin. The Intellectual, Political and Cultural World of Europe's Reformed Churches, c. 1540-1620* [European History in Perspective]. Basingstoke: Palgrave MacMillan, 2004

Murphy, Daniel, *Comenius. A Critical Reassessment of his Life and Work*. Dublin: Irish Academic Press, 1995

Nagtglas [1860], F., *De algemeene kerkeraad der Nederduitsch-Hervormde Gemeente te Middelburg van 1574-1860*. Middelburg: J.C. & W. Altorffer, 1860

Nagtglas [1888], F., *Levensberichten van Zeeuwen*, 2 vols. Middelburg: J.C. & W. Altorffer, 1888-1893

Nauta [1983-1], D., 'AMAMA, SIXTINUS AB', in D. Nauta *et al.* (eds.), *Biografisch Lexicon voor de Geschiedenis van het Nederlandse Protestantisme*, vol. 2. Kampen: J.H. Kok, 1983, 27a-29a

Nauta [1983-2], D., 'SPANHEIM, FRI€DERICUS, filius', in D. Nauta *et al.* (eds.), *Biografisch Lexicon voor de Geschiedenis van het Nederlandse Protestantisme*, vol. 2. Kampen: J.H. Kok, 1983, 411b-413b

Nellen, Henk, *Hugo de Groot. Een leven in strijd om de vrede 1583-1645*. Amsterdam: Balans, 2007

Nielsen, Lauritz Martin, *Danske privatbiblioteker gennem tiderne*. Kopenhagen: Gyldendalske boghandel, 1946

Niet, Cornelis Adrianus de, *Gisbertus Voetius. De praktijk der godzaligheid (TA A?KHTIKA dive Exercitia pietatis – 1664). Tekstuitgave met inleiding, vertaling en commentaar* [Monografieën Gereformeerd Piëtisme, 2], 2 vols. Utrecht: De Banier, 1996

Nuttall, Geoffrey F., 'English dissenters in the Netherlands, 1640-1689', *Nederlands Archief voor Kerkgeschiedenis*, Nieuwe Serie, 59 (1978/9), 37-54

Obst, Helmut, *August Hermann Francke und sein Werk*. Wiesbaden: Harrassowitz, 2013

Oort, J. van, *et al.* (eds.), *De onbekende Voetius. Voordrachten wetenschappelijk symposium Utrecht 3 maart 1989*. Kampen: J.H. Kok, 1989

Ossolton, N.E., *The Dumb Linguists. A study of the earliest English and Dutch Dictionaries* [Publications of the Sir Thomas Browne Institute, Special Series, 5]. Leiden: University Press, 1973

Ouden, P. den, 'Hildersam bij Joos van Laren', *Documentatieblad Nadere Reformatie*, 27 (2003), 91-101

Packer, J.I., *A Quest for Godliness. The Puritan Vision of the Christian Life*. Wheaton, Il.: Crossway, 1990

Panhuysen, Luc, *De Ware Vrijheid, De levens van Johan en Cornelis de Witt*. Amsterdam: Atlas, 2005

Pettegree, Andrew, *Foreign Protestant Communities in Sixteenth-Century London*. Oxford: Clarendon Press, 1986

Pettegree, Andrew, and Arthur der Weduwen, *The Bookshop of the World. Making and Trading Books in the Dutch Golden Age*. New Haven: Yale University Press, 2019

Platt, J.E., 'Sixtinus Amama (1593-1629): Franeker professor and citizen of the Republic of Letters', in G.Th. Jensma *et al.* (eds.), *Universiteit te Franeker 1585-1811*. Leeuwarden: Fryse Akademie 1985, 136-248

Poelhekke, J.J., *Frederik Hendrik, Prins van Oranje. Een biografisch drieluik*. Zutphen: De Walburg Pers, 1978

Pol [1999], F. van der, 'Simon Oomius in reactie op zijn tijd', *Documentatieblad Nadere Reformatie*, 23 (1999), 44-62

Pol [2002], Frank van der, 'Religious Diversity and Everyday Ethics in the Seventeenth-Century Dutch City Kampen', *Church History*, 71-2 (2002), 16-62

Pol [2019], Frank van der, *De vliegende bij op zoek naar honing. Geestelijk leiderschap van Simon Oomius*. Kampen: Brevier, 2019

Pollard, A.W., et al. [eds.], *A Short-Title Catalogue of Books Printed in England, Scotland, and Ireland and of English Books Printed Abroad 1475-1640*, 3 vols. Londen: The Bibliographical Society, 1976-1991

Post, S.D., *Bernardus Smijtegelt, leven en werken*. Kampen: De Groot Goudriaan, 2006

Postema, H.J., *Strijder op de middenweg. Leven en werk van Franciscus Ridderus*. Kampen: De Groot Goudriaan, 2005

Postma, F., and J. van Sluis [eds.], *Auditorium Academiae Franekerensis. Bibliographie der Reden, Disputationen und Gelegenheitsdruckwerke der Universität und des Athenäums in Franeker 1585-1843*. Leeuwarden: Fryske Akademy, 1995

Priem, Ruud, 'Een 'begaeft en seer ijverich man'. Willem Thielen en zijn echtgenote Maria de Fraeye, geportretteerd door Cornelis Jonson van Ceulen', in *Face Book. Studies on Dutch and Flemish Portraiture of the 16th-18th Centuries. Liber Amicorum Presented to Rudolf E.O. Ekkart on the Occasion of his 65th Birthday*. Leiden: Primavera Pers, 2012, 215-226

Primus, John H., *Richard Greenham. Portrait of an Elizabethan Pastor*. Macon, Georgia: Mercer University Press, 1998

Raa, F.J.G. ten, et al., *Het Staatsche leger 1568-1795*, 8 vols. Breda: Koninklijke Militaire Acadcmie, 1911-1964

Regt, W.M.C., 'MANTEAU VAN DALEM (PIETER)', in P.C. Molhuysen and Fr.K.H. Kossmann (eds.), *Nieuw Nederlandsch Biografisch Woordenboek*, vol. 9. Leiden: A.W. Sijthoff, 1933, 647-648

Reitsma, J. and S.D. van Veen (eds.), *Acta der provinciale en particuliere synoden, gehouden in de Noordelijke Nederlanden gedurende de jaren 1572-1620*, 8 vols. Groningen: J.B. Wolters, 1892-1899

Reynolds, Matthew, *Godly Reformers and their Opponents in Early Modern England. Religion in Norwich, c.1560-1643*. Woodbridge: The Boydell Press, 2005

Riising, Anne [ed.], *Katalog over Karen Brahes Bibliothek i Landsarkivet for Fyn. Håndskiftsamlingen*. Kopenhagen: Munksgaard, 1956

Rimbault, Lucien, *Pierre du Moulin 1568-1658, un pasteur classique à l'âge classique. Étude de théologie pastorale sur des documents inédits* [De Pétrarque à Descartes, 10]. Paris: Librairie Philosophique J. Vrin, 1966

Rodgers, Dirk W., *John à Lasco in England*. New York: Lang, 1994

Rogge, H.C., 'Het Album van Emanuel van Meteren', *Oud-Holland*, 15 (1897), 159-192, 199-209

Roker, L.F., 'The Flemish and Dutch Community in Colchester in the Sixteenth and Seventeenth Centuries', *Proceedings of the Huguenot Society of London*, 21 (1966), 15-30

Romeijn, A., *De stadsregering van Tholen (1577-1795). Bestuur en bestuurders van de stad Tholen vanaf de Satisfactieovereenkomst met Prins Willem van Oranje in 1577 tot de val van de Republiek in 1795*, 2 vols. Tholen: Gemeente Tholen, 2012

Romein, T.A., *Naamlijst der predikanten, sedert de hervorming tot nu toe, in de hervormde gemeenten van Friesland*. Leeuwarden: Meijer, 1886

Ros [1995], A., 'David Montanus. Stichtelijk dichter tussen Renaissance en Nadere Reformatie', *Documentatieblad Nadere Reformatie*, 19 (1995), 37-58

Ros [2010], A., *Davids soete lier. Vijf eeuwen Nederlandse psalmberijmingen. Een overzicht van de Nederlandse psalmberijmingen van de zestiende tot de twintigste eeuw*. Apeldoorn: De Banier, 2010

Rosenkranz, Albert (ed.), IDas Evangelische Rheinland, ein rheinisches Gemeinde- und Pfarrerbuch, vol. 2. Düsseldorf: Presseverband der Evangelischen Kirche im Rheinland, 1958

Rotscheidt, Wilhelm, 'Peter von Streithagen', *Monats-Hefte für rheinische Kirchengeschichte*, 13 (1919), 165-169

Rowen, Herbert H., *John de Witt, Great Pensionary of Holland, 1625-1672*. Princeton, New Yersey: Princeton University Press, 1978

Ruler, Han van, and Hugo Verbrugh (eds.), *Desiderius Erasmus, filosoof en bruggenbouwer: historische en Rotterdamse perspectieven*. Rotterdam: Erasmus Academie, 2008

Ruytinck, Symeon, et al., *Gheschiedenissen ende handelingen die voornemelick aengaen de Nederduytsche natie ende gemeynten, wonende in Engelant ende int bysonder tot Londen* [Werken der Marnix-vereeniging, Series 3, Part 1], J.J. van Toorenenbergen (ed.). Utrecht: Kemink en Zoon, 1873

Saxby, T.J., *The Quest for the New Jerusalen. Jean de Labadie and the Labadists, 1610-1774*. Dordrecht: Nijhoff, 1987

Schalkwijk, Frank Leonard, *The Reformed Church in Dutch Brazil (1630-1654)*. Zoetermeer: Boekencentrum, 1986

Schelven [1909], A.A. van, *De Nederduitsche vluchtelingenkerken der XVIe eeuw in Engeland en Duitschland in hunne beteekenis voor de Reformatie in de Nederlanden*. The Hague: Martinus Nijhoff, 1909

Schelven [1918-1], A.A. van, 'REGIUS (Jacobus)', in P.C. Molhuysen and P.J. Blok (eds.), *Nieuw Nederlandsch Biografisch Woordenboek*, vol. 4. Leiden: A.W. Sijthoff, 1914, 1130-1132

Schelven [1918-2], A.A. van, 'REGIUS (Johannes)', in P.C. Molhuysen and P.J. Blok (eds.), *Nieuw Nederlandsch Biografisch Woordenboek*, vol. 4. Leiden: A.W. Sijthoff, 1914, 1132-1134

Schelven [1939], A.A. van, *Marnix van St. Aldegonde*. Utrecht: Oosthoek, 1939

Scheurweghs, G., 'English Grammars in Dutch and Dutch Grammars in English in the Netherlands Before 1800', *English Studies*, 41 (1960), 129-167

Schmidt [1951], Martin, 'Speners Pia Desideria. Versuch einer theologischen Interpretation', *Theologia viatorum*, 3 (1951), 70-112

Schmidt [1969], Martin, 'Die "Geistliche Bad-Cur" Wolfgang Mayers in Basel (1649) und ihr literarisches Vorbild: Thomas Taylors Traktat "A Man in Christ or a New Creature" (vor 1629)', in Martin Schmidt, *Wiedergeburt und neuer Mensch. Gesammelte Studien zur Geschichte des Pietismus* [Arbeiten zur Geschichte des Pietismus, 2]. Witten: Luther-Verlag, 1969, 24-50

Schneider, Hans, *Der fremde Arndt. Studien zu Leben, Werk und Wirkung Johann Arndts (1555-1621)*. Göttingen: Vandenhoeck & Ruprecht, 2006.

Schoneveld, Cornelis W., *Intertraffic of the mind. Studies in Seventeenth-Century Anglo-Dutch Translation with a Checklist of Books Translated from English into Dutch, 1600-1700* [Publications of the Sir Thomas Browne Institute Leiden, New Series, 3]. Leiden: E.J. Brill, 1983

Schotel [1840], G.D.J., *Geschied-, letter- en oudheidkundige uitspanningen*. Utrecht: L.E. Bosch en zoon, 1840

Schotel [1841], G.D.J., *Kerklijk Dordrecht, eene bijdrage tot de geschiedenis der Vaderlandsche Hervormde Kerk, sedert het jaar 1572*, 2 vols. Utrecht: N. van der Monde, 1841-1845

Schrader, Hans-Jürgen, *Literaturproduktion und Büchermarkt des radikalen Pietismus. Johann Henrich Reitz' "Historie Der Wiedergebohrnen" und ihr geschichtlicher Kontext* [Palaestra. Untersuchungen aus der deutschen, englischen und scandinavischen Philologie, 283]. Göttingen: Vandenhoeck & Ruprecht, 1989

Schutte [1980], O. [ed.], *Het album promotorum van de academie Harderwijk*. Arnhem: Vereniging "Gelre", 1980

Schutte [1989], O., 'De Vriese', in *De Nederlandsche Leeuw. Maandblad van het Koninklijk Nederlandsch Genootschap voor Geslacht- en Wapenkunde*, 106 (1989), 228-336

Schwanda, Tom, *Soul Recreation. The Contemplative-Mystical Piety of Puritanism*. Eugene: Pickwick Publications, 2012

Sluis, J. van, 'WAEYEN, JOHANNES VANDER', in J. van den Berg *et al.* (eds.), *Biografisch Lexicon voor de Geschiedenis van het Nederlandse Protestantisme*, vol. 4. Kampen: Kok, 1998, 442b-445b

Spaans, Joke, *Haarlem na de Reformatie. Stedelijke cultuur en kerkelijk leven, 1577-1620*. The Hague: Stichting Hollandse Historische Reeks, 1989

Spijker [1981], W. van 't, 'De acata van de synode van Middelburg (1581)', in *De nationale synode te Middeburg in 1581* [Werken uitgegeven door het Koninklijk Zeeuwsch Genootschap der Wetenschappen, 1]. Middelburg: Koninklijk Zeeuwsch Genootschap der Wetenschappen, 1981, 64-126

Spijker [2015], W. van 't, 'AMESIUS, GUILIELMUS', in W.J. op 't Hof *et al.* (eds.), *Encyclopedie Nadere Reformatie*, vol. 1. Utrecht: De Groot Goudriaan, 2015, 35a-44b

Spijker, W. van 't, *et al.*, *De Synode van Westminster 1643-1649*. Houten: Den Hertog, 2002

Sprunger [1972], Keith L., *The Learned Doctor William Ames. Dutch Backgrounds of English and American Puritanism*. Urbana, Il.: University of Illinois Press, 1972

Sprunger [1982], Keith L., *Dutch Puritanism. A History of English and Scottish Churches of the Netherlands in the Sixteenth and Seventeenth Centuries* [Studies in the History of Christian Thought, 31]. Leiden: E.J. Brill, 1982

Sprunger [1994], Keith L., *Trumpets from the Tower. English Puritan Printing in the Netherlands 1600-1640* [Brill's Studies in Intellectual History, 46]. Leiden: E.J. Brill, 1994

Spurr, John, 'Kroniek van het non-conformisme in de marge. Roger Morrice en het Engelse protestantisme, 1677-1691', *Transparant. Tijdschrift van de Vereniging van Christen-Historici*, 15-1 (2004), 7a-10b

Stamkot, Bert, *Het Gorcumse boek. Vijf eeuwen drukken, uitgeven, verzamelen, lezen en leren te Gorinchem*. Gorinchem: Gorcums Museum, 2004

Stearns, Raymond Phineas, *Congregationalism in the Dutch Netherlands. The Rise and Fall of the English Congregational Classis 1621-1635*. Chicago, Illinois: The American Society of Church History, 1940

Stenvall, Gunnar, *Peter Lorenz Sellergren. Minnesteckning.* Lund: Gleerup, 1943
Steven, William, *The History of the Scottish Church, Rotterdam. To which are subjoined, Notices of the Other British Churches in the Netherlands; and a Brief View of the Dutch Ecclesiastical Establisment.* Edinburgh: Waugh and Innes, 1833
Stilma, Astrid, *A King Translated. The Writings of King James VI and I and Their Interpretation in the Low Countries, 1593-1603* [St. Andrewes Studies in Reformation History]. Farnham: Ashgate, 2012
Stoeffler, F. Ernest, *The Rise of Evangelical Pietism* [Studies in the History of Religions, 9]. Leiden: E.J. Brill, 1965
Sträter, Udo, *Sonthom, Bayly, Dyke und Hall. Studien zur Rezeption der englischen Erbauungsliteratur in Deutschland im 17. Jahrhundert* [Beiträge zur historischen Theologie, 71]. Tübingen: J.C.B. Mohr (Paul Siebeck), 1987
Streiter, Jochen, 'Johannes Rulitius – Ein Kirchberger Theologe in den Wirren des 17. Jahrhunderts', *Hunsrücker Heimatblätter*, 51 (2011), 265-275, 396-412; 52 (2012), 516-532
Strom, Jonathan, *Orthodoxy and Reform. The Clergy in Seventeenth Century Rostock Jahrhundert* [Beiträge zur historischen Theologie, 111]. Tübingen: Mohr Siebeck, 1999
Stronks, Els, *Stichten of schitteren. De poëzie van zeventiende-eeuwse gereformeerde predikanten.* Houten: Den Hertog, 1996
Todd, Margo, 'The problem of Schotland's Puritans', in John Coffey and Paul C.H. Lim (eds.), *The Cambridge Companion to Puritanism.* Cambridge, Eng.: Cambridge University Press, 2008, 174-188
Todd, Richard, 'The Manuscript Sources for Constantijn Huygens's Translation of Four Poems by John Donne, 1630', in Peter Beal & Grace Ioppolo (eds.), *Manuscripts and their Makers in the English Renaissance* [English Manuscripts Studies 1100-1700, 11]. London: The British Library, 2002, 154-180
Toepke, Gustav (ed.), *Die Matrikel der Universität Heidelberg*, 7 vols. Heidelberg: Winter, 1884-1916
Toorenenbergen [1871], J.J. van (ed.), *Philips van Marnix van St. Aldegonde. Godsdienstige en Kerkelijke Geschriften*, 4 vols. The Hague: Nijhoff, 1871-1891
Toorenenbergen [1872], J.J. van (ed.), *Acta van de Colloquia der Nederlandsche Gemeenten in Engeland, 1575-1609* [Werken der Marnix-vereeniging, Series 2, Part 1]. Utrecht: Kemink en zoon, 1872

Trim, David J.B., 'English Military Émigrés and the Protestant Cause in Europe, 1603-c. 1640', in David Worthington (ed.), *British and Irish Emigrants and Exiles in Europe, 1603-1688* [The Northern World. North Europe and the Baltic c. 400-1700 A.D. Peoples, Economies and Cultures, 47]. Leiden: Brill, 2010, 237-258

Trimp, J.C., *Jodocus van Lodensteyn. Predikant en dichter*. Kampen: De Groot Goudriaan, 1987

Troost, Wout, *Stadhouder-koning Willem III. Een politieke biografie*. Hilversum: Verloren, 2001

Uil [2016-1], H., 'LEYDECKER, JACOBUS', in W.J. op 't Hof *et al.* (eds.), *Encyclopedie Nadere Reformatie*, vol. 2. Utrecht: De Groot Goudriaan, 2016, 55a-58b

Uil [2016-2], H., 'UDEMANS, GODEFRIDUS', in W.J. op 't Hof *et al.* (eds.), *Encyclopedie Nadere Reformatie*, vol. 2. Utrecht: De Groot Goudriaan, 2016, 408b-416b

Veenhoff, A., and M. Smolenaars, 'Hugh Goodyear and his papers', *Transactions of the Lancashire and Cheshire Antiquarian Society*, 95 (1999), 1-22

Veld, H. van 't, *Beminde broeder die ik vand op 's werelts pelgrims wegen. Jan Luyken (1649-1712) als illustrator en medereiziger van John Bunyan (1628-1688)*. Utrecht: De Banier, 2000

Venemans, Bernard Albert, *Franciscus Junius en zijn Eirenicum de pace ecclesiae catholicae*. Leiden: Elve/Labor vincit, 1977

Verwijs, A., 'BEELS, LEONARD', in W.J. op 't Hof *et al.* (eds.), *Encyclopedie Nadere Reformatie*, vol. 1. Utrecht: De Groot Goudriaan, 2015, 75b-80b

Visscher, Hugo, *Guilielmus Amesius. Zijn leven en werken*. Haarlem: J.M. Stap, 1894

Visser, Dirk, *Zacharias Ursinus the Reluctant Reformer. His Life and Times*. New York: United Church Press, 1983

Visser, H.B., *De geschiedenis van den Sabbatsstrijd onder de Gereformeerden in de zeventiende eeuw*. Utrecht: Kemink en Zoon, 1939

Vliet, Jan van, *The Rise of Reformed System. The Intellectual Heritage of William Ames* [Studies in Christian History and Thought]. Milton Keynes: Paternoster, 2013

Vogler, J.G., 'De leerlingen van het Middelburgsch Gymnasium van 1629 tot 1905', *Archief, uitgegeven door het Zeeuwsch Genootschap der Wetenschappen*, 1906, 1-82

Voorst, J. van, 'De nadere reformatie van een leesgierige vrouw? Sporen van Nadere Reformatie in een zeventiende-eeuwse boekenlijst', *Documentatieblad Nadere Reformatie*, 16 (1992), 35-42

Vooys, C.G.N. de, *Engelse invloed op de Nederlandse woordvoorraad* [Verhandelingen der Koninklijke Nederlandse Akademie van Wetenschappen, Afdeling Letterkunde, Nieuwe Reeks, 57-5]. Amsterdam: North-Holland Publishing Company, 1951
Vrijer, M.J.A. de, *Ds Bernardus Smytegelt en zijn "Gekrookte Riet"*. Amsterdam: H.J. Sprruyt, 1947
Waard, C. de, *Journal tenu par Isaac Beeckman de 1604 à 1634*, 4 vols. The Hague: Martinus Nijhoff, 1939-1953
Wagenaar, L.H., *Het leven van graaf Willem Lodewijk, een vader des vaderlands, "Uz Heit"*. Amsterdam: Boekhandel voorheen Höveker & Wormser, 1904
Wallmann, Johannes, *Philipp Jakob Spener und die Anfänge des Pietismus* [Beiträge zur historischen Theologie, 42]. Tübingen: J.C.B. Mohr (Paul Siebeck), 1986
Walser, Ernst, *Poggius Florentinus. Leben und Werke* [Beiträge zur Kulturgeschichte des Mittelalters und der Renaissance, 14]. Leipzig: B.G. Teubner, 1914
Watkins, Owen C., *The Puritan Experience. Studies in Spiritual Autobiography*. New York: Schocken Books, 1972
Webster [1997], Tom, *Godly Clergy in Early Stuart England. The Caroline Puritan Movement c.1620-1643* [Cambridge Studies in Early Modern British History]. Cambridge: Cambridge University Press, 1997
Webster [2006], Tom, 'Household Seminaries', in Francis J. Bremer and Tom Webster (eds.), *Puritans and Puritanism in Europe and America. A Comprehensive Encyclopedia*, 2 vols. Santa Barbara, California: ABC-CLIO, 2006, 1:416b-417a
Welti, Manfred Edwin, *Der Basler Buchdruck und Britannien. Die Rezeption britischen Gedankenguts in den Basler Pressen von den Anfängen bis zum Beginn des 17. Jahrhunderts* [Basler Beiträge zur Geschichtswissenschaft, 93], Basel: Helbing & Lichtenhahn, 1964
Westerink, Herman, *Met het oog van de ziel. Een godsdienstpsychologische en mentaliteitshistorische studie naar mensvisie, zelfonderzoek en geloofsbeleving in het werk van Willem Teellinck (1579-1629)*. Zoetermeer: Boekencentrum, 2002
Wijk [2004], B. van, 'In Veen hield men iedere dag kerk. Cornelius de Kranckel en de heiligheid des levens', *Historische Reeks Land van Heusden en Altena*, 13 (2004), 77-107
Wijk [2019], B. van (ed.), *Op deze woeste kusten, of een bloemlezing uit de gezangen en gedichten van Brabantse gereformeerde piëtisten uit de 17$^e$ en 18$^e$ eeuw*. Wijk: B. van Wijk, 2019

Wing, D. (ed.), *Short-Title Catalogue of Books Printed in England, Scotland, Ireland, Wales, and British America and of English Books Printed in Other Countries 1641-1700*, 4 vols. New York: Modern Language Association of America, 1994-1998

Wood, Anthony à, *Athenae Oxonienses. An Exact History of All the Writers and Bishops who have had their Education in the University of Oxford. To which are added the Fasti, or Annals of the said University*, 4 vols. London: F.C. and J. Rivington *et al.*, 1813-1820

Woude [1978-1], C. van der, 'RUYTINCK (RUYTINGIUS, RUTINCK, RUTINGIUS), SYMEON', in D. Nauta *et al.* (eds.), *Biografisch Lexicon voor de Geschiedenis van het Nederlandse Protestantisme*, vol. 1. Kampen: J.H. Kok, 1978, 305a-306b

Woude [1978-2], C. van der, 'VORSTIUS, CONRADUS', in D. Nauta *et al.* (eds.), *Biografisch Lexicon voor de Geschiedenis van het Nederlandse Protestantisme*, vol. 1. Kampen: J.H. Kok, 1978, 407b-410b

Wright, Katie, '*The Performance of Piety. Exploring Godly Culture and Identity in England c.1580-1640*. Unpublished dissertation, University of Birmingham, 2008

Wumkes, G.A., 'MEY, George de', in P.C. Molhuysen *et al.* (eds.), *Nieuw Nederlandsch Biografisch Woordenboek*, vol. 10. Leiden: A.W. Sijthoff, 1937, 625-626

Ziff, Larzer, *The Career of John Cotton. Puritanism and the American Experience*. Princeton NJ: Princeton University Press, 1962

Zwanenburg, L.G., 'BELCAMPIUS, OTTO', in W.J. op 't Hof *et al.* (eds.), *Encyclopedie Nadere Reformatie*, vol. 1. Utrecht: De Groot Goudriaan, 2015, 86a-87b

*Album Studiosorum Academiae Groninganae, uitgegeven door het Historisch Genootschap te Groningen*. Groningen: J.B. Wolters' U.M., 1915

*Album Studiosorum Academiae Lugduno Batavae MDLXXV-MDCCCLXXV. Accedunt nomina curatorum et professorum per eadem secula*. The Hague: Martinus Nijhoff, 1875

*Album Studiosorum Academiae Rheno-Traiectinae MDCXXXVI-MDCCCLXXXVI*. Utrecht: J.L. Beijers and J. van Boekhoven, 1886

*Revolt and emigration. Refugees from the Westkwartier in Sandwcch in the XVIthe century*. Dikkebus: Westhoek, 1988

# ACKNOWLEDGEMENTS OF PHOTOGRAPHS

| | |
|---|---|
| Bibliotheek Universiteit van Amsterdam | p. 257 |
| Bibliotheek Universiteit van Utrecht | p. 264 |
| Bibliotheek Vrije Universiteit, Amsterdam | pp. 27, 39, 46, 77, 84, 192, 241 |
| Bush, Sargent, jr., *The Correspondence of John Cotton*. Chapel Hill: University of North Carolina Press, 2001, 167 | p. 291 |
| Gemeentearchief Sluis-Aardenburg | pp. 314, 320, 348 |
| Gemeentebibliotheek Rotterdam | p. 62 |
| Gereformeerde Bijbelstichting, Leerdam | pp. 11, 12 |
| Heemkundige Kring West-Zeeuws-Vlaanderen, Aardenburg | p. 317 |
| Internet | pp. 115, 141, 143, 153, 162, 164, 166, 203 |
| Koninklijke Bibliotheek, The Hague | pp. 103, 304 |
| Museum Catharijneconvent, Utrecht | pp. 158, 159 |
| Private collections | pp. 32, 52, 89, 105, 119, 123, 138, 149, 151, 161, 194, 210, 213, 220, 231, 253, 260, 261, 279, 297, 300, 324 |
| Tresoar, Leeuwarden | p. 281 |
| Zeelandia Illustrata, Middelburg | p. 308 |
| Zeeuws Archief, Middelburg | pp. 330, 349, 351, 353 |

# INDEX OF PERSONS

*This index arranges names in the Dutch manner, with alphabetic order determined by the final element. Elements such as 'van' and 'de' should be disregarded for the purposes of searching alphabetically*

| | |
|---|---|
| Abernethy, John, | 226-227 |
| Abbot, Maurice, | 187 |
| Adam, Melchior, | 67 |
| Agricola, Rudolphus, | 66 |
| Alardin, Casparus, | 312 |
| Alberts, Ids, | 211-212 |
| Alberts, Marten, | 202 |
| Ablas, Jacob Baltus Huibert, | 230-231 |
| Alleine, Joseph, | 240, 242-243 |
| Althusius, Samuel, | 24 |
| Alva, | 68, 184, 189 |
| Amama, Sixtinus, | 129, 216 |
| Ames, William, | 131, 138, 144-145, 148, 173-176, 216, 256, 270-272, 292 |
| Ammodius, Conradus, | 179 |
| Andries, Elisabeth, | 347 |
| Angier, John, | 131, 133 |
| Arcerius, Johannes, | 211 |
| Archer, John, | 34-39, 69-71, 97, 126 |
| Arcularius, Johannes, | 179 |
| Arminius, Jacobus, | 202 |
| Arndt, Johann, | 57, 124 |
| Ashe, Simeon, | 133 |
| Athanasius, | 337 |
| Augustine, | 267 |
| | |
| Bachiler, Samuel, | 174, 209, 247, 295-296, 298 |
| Bacon, Francis, | 67 |
| Baerle, David van, | 155 |
| Baerle, Susanna van, | 155 |
| Baers, Johannes, | 177-178 |
| Baers, Paschasius, | 177-178 |

| | |
|---|---|
| Ball, John, | 133, 140 |
| Ball, Thomas, | 133, 179-180 |
| Barenzonius, Nicolaus, | 312-313, 321 |
| Barlow, John, | 134 |
| Barneveld, Henrik van, | 239 |
| Baudaert, Willem, | 201 |
| Baudartius, Willem, | 112, 126, 201-208 |
| Baxter, Richard, | 87, 242, 273 |
| Bayly, Lewis, | 92, 116, 254-256, 261-263, 265-266, 275, 294 |
| Baynes, Paul, | 76, 117-118, 227 |
| Beadle, John, | 132 |
| Beeckman, Isaac, | 143, 148 |
| Beeckman, Jacob, | 143, 148 |
| Beels, Leonard, | 153, 171 |
| Beeltsnyder, Johannes, | 254-256, 266-267 |
| Bellers, Fulk, | 188 |
| Below, Sophia, | 114, 116 |
| Benedict, Philip, | 14 |
| Benschop, T., | 56 |
| Benzon, Severinus, | 138-139, 149 |
| Berdenis, Henricus, | 319 |
| Bergerus, Jacobus, | 67 |
| Berghuyzen, Aernout van, | 349, 356 |
| Berkel, Klaas van, | 143 |
| Bernard, Nicholas, | 131 |
| Bethune, Archibald, | 292 |
| Beverley, John, | 151 |
| Beyerlandt, Abraham van, | 96 |
| Bezar, Willemijntje, | 209 |
| Biesen, Jacob van, | 38, 284 |
| Bille, Karen, | 116 |
| Binning, Hugh, | 50-51 |
| Bisschop, Isaac junior, | 169 |
| Bisschop, Isaac senior, | 79, 109-110, 139, 143-144, 168-170, 173-174, 210 |
| Bisschop, Samuel, | 169 |
| Blackerby, Richard, | 131-134, 137, 141-143, 174, 176, 186 |
| Blankenfeld, Barton John, | 359 |
| Bloody Mary, | 68, 183 |
| Böhme, Jacob, | 96, 100 |

| | |
|---|---|
| Boekholt, Johannes, | 227, 234-235, 284 |
| Boels, François, | 41-42 |
| Boenja, Philippus Sioerts, | 211 |
| Boesius, Clemens, | 179 |
| Bogerman, Johannes, | 204, 208 |
| Bois, Agatha du, | 223 |
| Bois, Dirk du, | 223 |
| Bois, Geertruyt du, | 223 |
| Bois, Hermanus du, | 223 |
| Bois, Jacob du, | 223 |
| Bois, Jacomina du, | 223 |
| Bois, Maria du, | 223 |
| Bois, Mattheus du, | 221-237, 247-249 |
| Bois, Susanna du, | 223 |
| Bois, Vincent du (grandfather), | 222 |
| Bois, Vincent du (grandson), | 222 |
| Bois, Vincent du (great-grandson), | 223 |
| Bois, Zeger du, | 222 |
| Bolton, Robert, | 118, 226-227, 270-272 |
| Boots, Isaacus, | 179 |
| Borstius, Jacobus junior, | 40, 45 |
| Borstius, Jacobus senior, | 40-45, 47, 69-70 |
| Borstius, Johannes, | 44, 49, 51 |
| Boswell, William, | 167, 287-288 |
| Bouchellion, Gillis, | 228 |
| Boudry, Cornelis, | 335 |
| Brahe, Karen, | 114, 124 |
| Brakel, Wilhelmus à, | 305 |
| Bremer, Francis J., | 132-133, 135, 137 |
| Breuker, Philippus H., | 280 footnote 13 |
| Brewer, Thomas, | 174 |
| Bridge, William, | 135 |
| Brienen, Pieter, | 320 |
| Brinsley, John, | 133 |
| Brößke, Johann Christoph, | 122, 127 |
| Bromley, Thomas, | 224 |
| Brooks, Thomas, | 273 |
| Broughton, Hugh, | 292 |
| Brown, John, | 40-50, 58, 70, 75, 83-97, 323 |
| Browne, Robert, | 131 |
| Brüggemann, Heinrich, | 121 |

Brüßken, Christoph, see Brößke, Johann Christoph
Brunga, Gellius, 211
Brunsvelt, Sixtus, 212, 258, 267, 275
Bruynvisch, Martinus, 210
Bryan, John, 133, 135
Bucer, Martin, 37, 60, 268
Bucerus, Gerson, 204, 207-210, 247, 249
Bucerus, Jacobus, 184, 207
Burlamachi, Philip, 216
Burmannus, Franciscus, 284
Burrell, Christopher, 134
Burroughs, Jeremiah, 132, 135
Bursius, Gillis, 260
Bursius, Jacobus, 260, 262
Burton, Henry, 179
Bush, Sargent, 82, 135, 139-140
Bussche, Maljard van den, 331-332
Busschof, Bernard, 233-234
Byfield, Adoniram, 179
Byfield, Nicholas, 76
Byland, Margarete van, 239

Calamy, Edmund, 135, 273
Calandrinus, Caesar, 155, 246
Calvin, John, 38, 68
Cambij, Cornelis, 346, 355-356
Cameron, Richard, 86, 303, 305
Campbell, Archibald, 302
Cant, Johan, 345, 355
Capnie, 66
Cargill, Donald, 303, 305
Carnier (Cunira), Hester, 211
Caryl, Joseph, 228
Cats, Jacob, 76, 78, 112, 152
Caulier, Jacob, 340, 342-343, 345-348, 352-357
Cawdrey, Daniel, 134
Cawton, Thomas, 43, 131
Ceulen, Cornelis Jonson van, 157
Charles I, 71, 147
Charles II, 58, 303, 305
Charles Louis, 147, 269

| | |
|---|---|
| Chauncey, Charles, | 131 |
| Citters, Arnoud van, | 245 |
| Claeszoon, Cornelis, | 193, 248 |
| Clarke, Samuel, | 138, 140, 142, 150-153, 157, 167-168, 187, 273-274 |
| Cleaver, Robert, | 272 |
| C.M.R., | 116 |
| Coccejus, Johannes, | 311, 326 |
| Cock, Hendrik de, | 56 |
| Cocquius, Adriaan, | 312-313, 331 |
| Coffey, John, | 16 |
| Collins, Samuel, | 134, 188 |
| Collinson, Patrick, | 182 |
| Comenius, Jan Amos, | 145, 148 |
| Compton, Henry, | 244 |
| Coninck, Maria de, | 348 |
| Coninck, Pieter de, | 329 |
| Cool, Jacob, | 195-196, 199-200 |
| Coolman, Levinus, | 109 |
| Cotton, John, | 76-83, 93-95, 97, 107, 109-113, 131-133, 135, 137-141, 143-149, 168-170, 173-177, 210, 247 |
| Cotton, Seaborn, | 135 |
| Cousemaker, Balduinus, | 313 |
| Cowper, William, | 111-112, 126, 205-206, 221, 227 |
| Crane, Leendert van de, | 330 |
| Cranmer, Thomas, | 183, 268 |
| Crantzius, Albertus, | 64 |
| Crespin, Jean, | 289 |
| Croix, Pieter de la, | 335 |
| Cromwell, Oliver, | 131, 296 |
| Cuilemborgh, Aemilius van, | 243-249 |
| Cuilemborgh, Hermannus van, | 243 |
| Cullen, John, | 134 |
| Culverwell, Ezekiel, | 290 |
| Culverwell, Richard, | 179 |
| | |
| Dallens, Clasina, | 221 |
| Dallens, Jaques, | 221 |
| Daneau, Lambert, | 76 |
| Darrell, John, | 133 |

Deliën, Nicolaas Anthony van der, 104, 107, 198
Demetrius, Andreas, 138-139, 149-150, 168
Demetrius, Daniel, 149
Dent, Arthur, 116
Dern, Thomas, 179
Deusing, Johann, 270-271
Diodati, Giovanni, 216
Dibbets, Henricus, 43
Dod, John, 131, 134, 221, 272
Doesburg, Reinier van, 240, 243
Dorsius, Petrus Henricus, 55-56
Dorth, Johannes van, 312-313
Downham, George, 209
Downham, John, 179, 227, 272
Drake, John, 174-175
Drummond, Andrew L., 75
Durham, James, 43
Durie, John, 145, 148, 151, 179-180
Dyke, Daniel, 113-114, 116, 165, 221, 226-227
Dyke, Jeremiah, 238, 242-243

Echten, Salomon van, 229
Eck, Catharina van, 294-295
Edward VI, 183, 268
Eekhof, Albert, 321
Elcoma, Elconius, 212
Elgersma, Franciscus, 280, 282-283, 285
Eliot, John, 134
Elizabeth I, 64, 183-184, 204
E.M., 236
Episcopius, see Bisschop
Erasmus, Desiderius, 66, 293, 295
Erberfeld, Philipp, 120-122, 126-127
Ernest Casimir, 301
Essen, Hillegond van, 244
Essenius, Andreas, 244-245
Eversdijk, Wilhelmus, 236-237

Façon, Jan, 348, 355
Fairclough, Samuel, 131, 133
Fargharson, John, 292-295, 298, 301

| | |
|---|---|
| Faukelius, Hermannus, | 208 |
| Fenner, Dudley, | 26 |
| Felton, Nicholas, | 135 |
| Fisher, | 139, 164-166 |
| Fleming, Robert, | 58-71, 93, 97, 126 |
| Fontanus, Johannes, | 202, 206 |
| Fonteyne, Claude, | 212 |
| Forbes, John, | 296 |
| Foxe, John, | 226-227, 289 |
| Fraeye, Maria de, | 157, 159 |
| Franck, Sebastiaan, | 212, 214 |
| Francke, August Hermann, | 57 |
| Fraye, Jan de, | 157 |
| Frederik V, | 146-147, 167, 179, 269 |
| Frederick Hendrik, | 298-299, 301 |
| Fuller, John, | 134 |
| | |
| Galama, Hero, | 212 |
| Gansfort, Wessel, | 66 |
| Gardiner, James, | 40-49, 69-71, 93, 97 |
| Gataker, Thomas, | 120, 127, 132-133, 137-141, 149-150, 152-154, 156, 160, 171-178, 186, 272 |
| Geer, Louis de, | 148 |
| Gerbens, Jan, | 212 |
| Gilpin, Bernard, | 133 |
| Gipson, Martinus, | 332 |
| Glazemaker, Jan Hendrik, | 101 |
| Gløe, Falck, | 116 |
| Glover, Hugh, | 134 |
| Godfrey, Christopher, | 106 footnote 17 |
| Gomarus, Franciscus, | 156, 202 |
| Goodwin, John, | 188 |
| Goodwin, Thomas, | 12-13, 35, 127 |
| Goodyear, Hugh, | 41, 144-145, 174, 176 |
| Goring, George, | 288 |
| Gouge, William, | 179, 188, 272 |
| Gøye, Anne, | 114-115 |
| Grayle, John, | 133 |
| Greenham, John, | 134 |
| Greenham, Richard, | 131, 133, 135 |

INDEX OF PERSONS · 411

| | |
|---|---|
| Grell, Ole Peter, | 136, 138-139, 142, 167, 185-186 |
| Gribius, Petrus, | 106-107, 138, 143-145, 147, 168-170, 173-174, 255 |
| Grim, Egbert, | 138, 143, 145-146, 168, 170, 173 |
| Grindal, Edmund, | 184 |
| Groenendijk, Leendert F., | 172, 272-273 |
| Groot, Hugo de, | 67 |
| Großgebauer, Theophilus, | 57, 269-270 |
| Gruterus, Daniel, | 240 |
| Gruterus, Samuel, | 239 |
| Gustavus Adolphus of Sweden, | 147, 167 |
| Guthrie, William, | 85, 236, 273 |
| | |
| Haack, Josina, | 156 |
| Haak, Theodore, | 139, 147, 164-167, 173 |
| Haar, J. van der, | 138-139, 278, 280 |
| Haemstede, Adriaan van, | 183, 289 |
| Haes, François de, | 335 |
| Haes, Sara de, | 347 |
| Hajonides, Nollius, | 212 |
| Hall, Henry, | 303 |
| Hall, Joseph, | 116, 165, 270-271, 290, 295 |
| Hamilton, | 302 |
| Hamilton, Robert, | 302, 305 |
| Haringhouk, Anthony van, | 211 |
| Haringhouk, Matheus van, | 211 |
| Haringhouk, Samuel van, | 211-215, 247, 284 |
| Harmens, Aeltje, | 282 |
| Harris, Robert, | 131, 134 |
| Hartlib, Samuel, | 127, 140, 145, 148, 170, 179 |
| Harwood, Edward, | 290-292 |
| Hauchepied, Cornelius, | 313 |
| Heermans, Franciscus, | 225, 229, 234 |
| Heijting, Willem, | 18, 100 |
| Hemeryck, Geleyn, | 330 |
| Hendricx, Steven, | 347, 355 |
| Hendrik Casimir of Nassau, | 301 |
| Henry III, | 204 |
| Henry VIII, | 183 |
| Hexham, Henry, | 288-290, 292 |
| Heyden, Gaspar van der, | 190 |

| | |
|---|---|
| Heydon, Christopher, | 288 |
| Heyns, Zacharias, | 294-295 |
| Higginson, Francis, | 133 |
| Higginson, John, | 135 |
| Hildersham, Arthur, | 34, 39, 131, 133, 210, 214, 272-273, 280 |
| Hill, Thomas, | 131 |
| Hille, Thomas junior, | 135 |
| Hof, Willem J. op 't, | 7 |
| Hofferus, Adrianus, | 199 |
| Hoffmann, Johann Georg, | 33, 121 |
| Hofman, Johannes, | 240, 242, 246 |
| Hofstede, Petrus, | 255 |
| Hofstede, Willem, | 255 |
| Hog, John, | 40-49, 69-71, 93, 97 |
| Holbeach, Martin, | 135 |
| Holles, Thomas, | 294-295, 298, 301 |
| Holsaert, Johannes, | 348, 356 |
| Holwarda, Johannes Phocyclides, | 212 |
| Hondius, Johannes, | 289 |
| Honeywood, Thomas, | 187 |
| Hooker, Thomas, | 113, 131-132, 134 |
| Hoornbeeck, Isaac, | 210 |
| Hoornbeeck, Johannes, | 138-139, 147, 149-152, 168, 171, 177, 226 |
| Hopf, | 139, 164-166 |
| Hopsius, Johannes Conradus, | 179 |
| Hottingerus, Johan Hendrik, | 66 |
| Houte, Josias van den, | 199 |
| Howe, Edward, | 133 |
| Hughes, Georges, | 179 |
| Huisman, Frans W., | 17-18, 99, 113, 114 footnote 46, 125 |
| Hummel, Johann Heinrich, | 157 |
| Hus, Anna, | 319, 357-358 |
| Irenaeus Philalethius, | see Teellinck, Eeuwout |
| Irlin, Johannes, | 179 |
| Ixem, Jacomina van, | 356 |
| Jacobszoon, Laurens, | 193, 248 |

INDEX OF PERSONS · 413

| | |
|---|---|
| James VI/I, | 191-192, 193-194, 209, 219, 248, 268, 291, 340 |
| Janeway, James, | 273 |
| Janse, Wim, | 9 |
| Jansen, Jeroen, | 266 |
| Japicx, Gysbert, | 212 |
| J.D., | see Deusing, Johann |
| J.K., | see Koelman, Jacobus |
| Jessey, Henry, | 273 |
| Jobs, Barbara, | 339-362 |
| Johannes, Focco, | 212 |
| Jonge, Jacob de, | 332 |
| Jonge, Maria de, | 222 |
| Josselin, Ralph, | 187 |
| Juel, Jens, | 116 |
| Juel, Susanne, | 116 |
| Junius, Franciscus, | 142, 201 |
| Junius, Roberts, | 217-218 |
| Jurieu, Pierre, | 67 |
| Jurissen, Frans, | 293 |
| | |
| Kamp, Jan van de, | 18, 93, 99, 102, 120, 175, 269-271 |
| Kanu, Jan, | 348, 356 |
| Kentlinck, Hermanus, | 236-237 |
| Kerrebroeck, Gillis van, | 332 |
| Kimedoncius, Jacob, | 201 |
| Koelman, Jacobus, | 12-13, 43-45, 48-51, 55-57, 69-72, 83, 85-88, 90-96, 113, 126, 171, 200, 235-236, 267, 272-276, 302-303, 305, 312-314, 318-337, 339-340, 344-345, 349-360 |
| Kranckel, Cornelius de, | 244 |
| Krüger, Simon Jodocus, | 118 |
| | |
| Labadie, Jean de, | 40, 44-45, 47-49, 70, 86 |
| Lamotius, Johannes junior, | 111-112, 117, 200-201, 205, 221, 247-249, 284 |
| Lamotius, Johannes senior, | 200 |
| Lanckischen, Friedrich, | 33, 121 |
| Lange, Petrus de, | 229 |
| Laren, Abraham van, | 326 |

| | |
|---|---|
| Laren, Daniel van, | 34-36, 38, 69-71, 126, 210, 280 |
| Laren, Joos van, | 210, 278-280, 284-285 |
| Larminie, Vivienne, | 19 |
| Lasco, Johannes à, | 183 |
| Laud, William, | 35, 147, 287, 289 |
| Laurentius, Georg Michael, | 57 |
| Leech, Jeremy, | 157 |
| Leurelius, Theodorus, | 179 |
| Levett, Ralph, | 135 |
| Leydecker, Jacobus, | 129, 177 |
| Leydecker, Melchior, | 240 |
| Lieburg, Fred A. van, | 91, 109 footnote 22, 361 |
| Lieftinck, Jacob, | 238 |
| Liens, Joachim, | 219 |
| Liens, Johan, | 219 |
| Liens, Maria, | 219 |
| Lignon, Pierre du, | 49 |
| Lingen, Cornelius van der, | 313 |
| Livingstone, John, | 40-49, 69-71, 93, 97 |
| Lodensteyn, Jodocus van, | 233-234, 312-313 |
| Loo, Wilhelmina van, | 361 |
| Louis XIV, | 245 |
| Love, Christopher, | 257-258, 269, 273, 276 |
| Lucianus, | 293 |
| Luther, Martin, | 61, 64-65 |
| | |
| Maertens, Adriaen, | 345-346, 355-356 |
| Maertens, Gideon, | 335 |
| Maertens, Maerten, | 329, 335, 358-360 |
| Maertens, Martina, | 344, 346, 356 |
| Maes, Pieter, | 341-342 |
| Maets, Carolus de, | 198 |
| Mangelaer, Cornelis, | 357-358 |
| Mann, Alastair J., | 75 |
| Manteau van Dalem, Pieter, | 339-340 |
| Marinissoon, Erasmus, | 335 |
| Marnix, Philips of, | 190 |
| Marshall, Stephen, | 132, 134 |
| Marten, Henry, | 188 |
| Mattheeusen, Abraham, | 332 |
| Mattheeusen, Thomas, | 329, 344-346, 355, 359 |

| | |
|---|---|
| Maurice of Nassau, | 178, 290, 292-293 |
| Maurice Louis I van Nassau la Leck, | 323 |
| McWard, Robert, | 43, 50-58, 69-72, 86, 88, 97 |
| M.D.B., | see Bois, Mattheus du |
| Mead, Matthew, | 258, 267 |
| Meerbottius, Henricus, | 179 |
| Melanchthon, Philip, | 65 |
| Mellinga, Catharina van, | 212 |
| Mercator, Gerardus, | 289 |
| Meriton, John, | 245-246 |
| Meteren, Emanuel van, | 195-196, 205-206 |
| Meusevoet, Reinier, | 189 |
| Meusevoet, Vincentius, | 88-190, 193-194, 200-201, 247-248, 259, 284 |
| Mey, George de, | 138-139, 149, 152-153, 168, 171, 177-178 |
| Mey, Jean de, | 152 |
| Meyer, Jacob, | 124 |
| Meyer, Wolfgang, | 178, 268-269 |
| Micron, Marten, | 183 |
| Middleton, Thomas, | 188 |
| Miggrode, Johannes van, | 191 |
| Milton, Anthony A., | 8, 14, 140 |
| Milton, John, | 132 |
| Moerman, Johannes, | 357 |
| Moerman, Maria, | 357-358 |
| Moller, Martin, | 124 |
| Montanus, David, | 86, 312-313, 325, 331, 339-340 |
| Montgomery, Hugh, | 298, 301 |
| Moonen, Arnold, | 240, 243 |
| Moore, | 273 |
| Moreta, Olympia Fulvia, | 67 |
| Morgan, Charles, | 295-296 |
| Morgan, John, | 130, 132, 135, 137, 142 |
| Moriae, Johannes, | 179 |
| Morn, Josina, | 204 |
| Morton, Nicholas, | 179 |
| Moser, Nelleke, | 18 |
| Mosselanus, Petrus, | 66 |
| Motte, Elisabeth de la, | 187 |
| Motte, Hester de la, | 187 |

416 - INDEX OF PERSONS

| | |
|---|---|
| Motte, John de la, | 187-188 |
| Moulin, Pierre du, | 124, 212-213 |
| Mulder, T.E., | 56 |
| Mullan, David George, | 16 |
| Murdock, Graeme, | 168 |
| | |
| Napier, John, | 191, 193-194 |
| N.B., | see Barenzonius, Nicolaus |
| Negeman, Jacob, | 335 |
| Nemegeer, Laurens, | 349 |
| Nemegeer, Maria, | 345, 349, 356 |
| Nethenus, Matthias, | 218 |
| Nevay, John, | 40-49, 69-71, 93, 97 |
| Newcomen, Matthew, | 135 |
| Niet, Cornelis Adrianus de, | 254, 263 |
| Nye, Philip, | 35 |
| | |
| Offspring, Charles, | 131, 133 |
| Oldenbarnevelt, Johan van, | 207 |
| Oomius, Simon, | 214, 278, 284 |
| Oosterwijck, Volckerus van, | 216 |
| Ouden, Pieter den, | 280 |
| | |
| Paget, Robert, | 41, 147 |
| Palmer, Herbert, | 131-132, 140, 167 |
| Panneel, Gerson, | 191 |
| Panneel, Johannes, | 191 |
| Panneel, Josintgen, | 191 |
| Panneel, Michiel, | 189-194, 247-248 |
| Paraeus, Philippus, | 179 |
| Parent, Abraham, | 319 |
| Parker, Matthew, | 184, 186 |
| Pelt, Hendrik van, | 55-56 |
| Perkins, William, | 25, 131, 137, 178, 225-226, 256-259, 268, 270-273, 276 |
| Peter, Hugh, | 132 |
| Peters, | 138, 149, 154 |
| Petri, Alexander, | 43, 288-289 |
| Philips II, | 68 |
| Pieterszoon, Roelof, | 197 |
| Piscator, Johannes, | 202, 204, 206 |

| | |
|---|---|
| Pius II, | 67 |
| Poel, Christiaan van den, | 56 |
| Poele, Elisabeth van, | 187 |
| Poggius, | 67 |
| Polyander, Johannes, | 288-289 |
| Poole, Matthew, | 240, 243 |
| Pownall, Nathaniel, | 218 |
| Poynter, John, | 134 |
| Preston, John, | 133, 146, 174, 227 |
| Preusses, Jacob, | 57 |
| Primrose, David, | 23-24 |
| Primrose, Gilbert, | 23 |
| Proost, Jonas junior, | 132, 134, 137, 141-143, 168, 174, 186 |
| Proost, Jonas senior, | 142-143, 174, 186 |
| Putte, Abraham van de, | 348, 356 |
| Putte, Egidia van de, | 348 |
| Pythius, Johannes, | 237 |
| | |
| Quick, John, | 171 |
| Quintius, Johannes, | 257-258, 267, 276 |
| | |
| Raap, Adriaan, | 239 |
| Radermacher, Johan, | 157 |
| Radermacher, Maria, | 157 |
| Raedt, Catharina de, | 207 |
| Raet, Franciscus de, | 332 |
| Regemortius, Ambrosius, | 157 |
| Regiomontanus, | 66 |
| Regius, Jacobus, | 197 |
| Regius, Johannes junior, | 157 |
| Regius, Johannes senior, | 157, 197-198 |
| Regius, Samuel, | 157 |
| Reid, John, | 90-91 |
| Rentsen, Anna Catharina, | 244 |
| Renwick, James, | 305 |
| Reynolds, Edward, | 214 |
| Rich, | see Rijcke |
| Richardson, Alexander, | 131, 134 |
| Richardson, Edward, | 224-225, 227, 229-230, 233 |
| Richardson, Richard, | 133 |
| Rieu, Philips du, | 335 |

## 418 · INDEX OF PERSONS

| | |
|---|---|
| Rijcke, Arnoldus de, | 139, 149, 154, 168, 177 |
| Rintjes, Hendrik, | 212 |
| Ripperda, Mechteld, | 294 |
| Rob, Isabella, | 341 |
| Robinson, John, | 174 |
| Roelinck, Herman, | 294 |
| Rogers, Daniel, | 135 |
| Rogers, John, | 132-135 |
| Rogers, Nathaniel, | 132 |
| Rogers, Richard, | 134 |
| Rooseboom, Pieter, | 348, 356 |
| Rosenkrantz, Holger, | 114 |
| Rothe, Johannes, | 224, 230 |
| Rous, Francis, | 274 |
| Rowyer, Matthaeus, | 179 |
| Rozendaal, Jan, | 18 |
| Rulice, John, | 133, 137, 140, 143-144, 146-148, 168, 170, 174 |
| Rutherford, Samuel, | 43, 240 |
| Ruurds, Abbe, | 211 |
| Ruytinck, Jan, | 215 |
| Ruytinck, Johannes, | 215 |
| Ruytinck, Simeon junior, | 215-218, 247, 249 |
| Ruytinck, Simeon senior, | 136, 196, 215, 246 |
| | |
| Saldenus, Guiljelmus, | 120 |
| Schamelius, Johann Martin, | 33-34, 122 |
| Schepers, Willem, | 58 |
| Schieux, Jan, | 335 |
| Schloer, Friedrich, | 166-167 |
| Schlüter, Heinrich, | 47 |
| Schmidt, Martin, | 269 |
| Schotanus Rinckema, Wilhelmus, | 214 |
| Schurman, Anna Maria van, | 49 |
| Schuttenius, Everhardus, | 263, 266, 294-295, 298-302 |
| Sclaer, | 167 |
| Scott, Thomas, | 298 |
| Seaman, Lazarus, | 133 |
| Sedgwick, Obadiah, | 179 |
| Sedgwick, William, | 211 |
| Selden, John, | 67 |
| Sellergren, Peter Lorenz, | 57 |

INDEX OF PERSONS · 419

| | |
|---|---|
| Shepard, Thomas, | 134, 173 |
| Sibbes, Richard, | 270-271, 279-280 |
| Sierxma, Lamcke Gysberts, | 211 |
| Silvius, Aeneas, | 67 |
| Simpson, Sidrach, | 179 |
| Skelton, Anne, | 273 |
| Sleer, | 139, 164-167 |
| Sleidanus, Johannes, | 66 |
| Sluymer, Willem, | 325, 333 |
| Smijtegelt, Bernardus, | 155 |
| Smith, Henry, | 135, 272 |
| Smith, Samuel, | 214, 218 |
| Snabelius, Philippus, | 179 |
| Snijer, Elsken, | 347 |
| Sohnius, Georgius, | 243 |
| Spanheim, Friedrich, | 66 |
| Sparehemius, Rixtie, | 283 |
| Spener, Philipp Jakob, | 57, 121, 270 |
| Spiljardus, Johannes, | 209-210, 298 |
| Spinoza, Baruch, | 100 |
| Spira, Franciscus, | 67 |
| Spranchuysen, Dionysius, | 213, 288 |
| Sprat, Thomas, | 278, 284 |
| Sprint, John, | 248 |
| Sprunger, Keith L., | 14, 36, 138 |
| Spruyt, Margaretha, | 292 |
| Stalenus, Johannes, | 146 |
| Steenbarch, Jacob Roelofsen, | 293 |
| Steven, William, | 75 |
| Stillingfleet, Edward, | 239-240, 242-243 |
| Stippius, Casparus, | 179 |
| Stock, Richard, | 293 |
| Stone, Samuel, | 131 |
| Stoughton, John, | 179, 188 |
| Strathnaver, Lady, | 87 |
| Streithagen, Petrus, | 179, 269 |
| Strom, Jonathan, | 269 |
| Stronks, Els, | 234 |
| Swaef, Johannes de, | 76, 78-83, 93-96, 112, 126, 169, 191 |
| Swancke, Nicolaes, | 332 |
| Sweerde, Jacobus van de, | 138, 149, 154, 168, 174, 176 |
| Symonds, Joseph, | 132, 179 |

| | |
|---|---|
| Taffin, Jean, | 227 |
| Taylor, Thomas, | 117-118, 133, 212, 214, 269 |
| Teellinck, Eeuwout, | 30-31, 71, 76, 78-79, 95, 169, 198-200, 227, 229, 248, 252-254, 256, 258-261, 263, 265, 275-276 |
| Teellinck, Johanna, | 106-107, 170 |
| Teellinck, Johannes, | 170 |
| Teellinck, Justus, | 255 |
| Teellinck, Maximiliaan, | 78-79, 82, 93, 106-110, 133, 137, 139, 143, 148-149, 163, 168-170, 173-177, 198, 210, 248, 255 |
| Teellinck, Willem, | 25-26, 30-31, 33-34, 42, 51, 69-70, 72, 76, 78-79, 81, 83, 93-95, 102, 104, 106-111, 120-122, 126-127, 133-134, 148, 155-156, 162-163, 169, 171-176, 194-200, 202, 206, 208-210, 226-227, 247-248, 252, 254-255, 259-263, 265, 267, 269-270, 275-276, 296, 313-314 |
| Tegnejus, Tobias, | 280 |
| Terence, | 201 |
| Terwisca, Isbrant, | 347, 355 |
| Thielen, Joachim van, | 156 |
| Thilenus, Johannes, | 139, 149, 154-156, 168, 171, 177 |
| Thilenus, Willem, | 132, 137-139, 149, 154, 156-158, 168, 173-174, 186, 196-197, 217 |
| Thomson, Alexander, | 18 |
| Thott, Birgitte, | 114, 116, 124 |
| Thott, Sophie, | 116 |
| Thysius, Anthonius, | 205 |
| Tillotson, John, | 240, 242-243 |
| Todd, Margo, | 15-16 |
| Tol, J. van, | 242 |
| Tossanus, Paulus, | 179 |
| Trail, Robert, | 40-49, 69-71, 93, 97 |
| Trelcatius, Lucas, | 163 |
| Treschovius, | 138-139, 149, 152, 157 |
| Tronchin, Théodore, | 156 |
| Tuckney, Anthony, | 131, 135 |
| Tuke, Thomas, | 289-290 |
| Turenout, Niclaas van, | 147 |

INDEX OF PERSONS · 421

| | |
|---|---|
| Twisse, William, | 175 |
| Ubelman, Johannes, | 237-244, 247, 249 |
| Udemans, Godefridus, | 41-42, 121, 124, 126, 199, 210, 227, 255 |
| Uilenbroek, Hendrik, | 235 |
| Ursinus, Zacharias, | 227 |
| Ussher, James, | 131, 217 |
| Valen, Leen van, | 18, 45 footnote 47, 86 footnote 39 |
| Velsen, Franciscus van, | 283 |
| Velsen, Gerhardus van, | 280-284 |
| Velsen, Lambertus van, | 280, 282-283 |
| Verbeke, Adriana, | 348 |
| Vere, Francis, | 288 |
| Vere, Horace, | 288-289 |
| Vereecke, Mayken, | 222 |
| Vermuyden, Bartel, | 219 |
| Vermuyden, Cornelis, | 219 |
| Vermuyden, Johan, | 219-221, 233, 247-248 |
| Versteeg, Hendrik, | 284 |
| Veth, Jacob, | 155 |
| Vincent, Thomas, | 273 |
| Vlaardingerwoud, Maarten, | 55 |
| Vleteren, Timotheüs van, | 78-79, 93, 109-110, 169-171, 175, 197-199, 210-211, 247-249 |
| Voetius, Gisbertus, | 31, 33, 71, 150-151, 169, 171, 199, 226, 236, 245, 252, 254, 256, 263-266, 275-276, 296, 311 |
| Vollenhove, Johannes, | 229-230, 235-236, 239-240, 243 |
| Vondel, Joost van den, | 160 |
| Voorst, J. van, | 361 |
| Vorstius, Conradus, | 268 |
| Vrij, Frederick de, | 207 |
| Waeyen, Johannes vander, | 155 |
| Walaeus, Antonius, | 197-198 |
| Walker, George, | 134, 179 |
| Walker, Henry, | 273 |
| Wallace, James, | 302 |
| Walsingham, Francis, | 64, 182 |
| Ward, Samuel, | 188 |
| Webster, Tom, | 133-135, 137, 142, 162-163 |

| | |
|---|---|
| Weld, Thomas, | 134 |
| Welle, Apollonia van der, | 160 |
| Wenden, Johannes Theodori van der, | 113 |
| Westhovius, F.G., | 238 |
| Whately, William, | 25-34, 69-71, 94, 102-109, 122, 126, 134, 137, 141, 162-164, 172, 252, 254-256, 258-259, 261-263, 265, 272, 275-276 |
| White, John, | 139, 141, 146, 164-167, 173, 188 |
| White, Thomas, | 273 |
| Whitfield, Henry, | 147 |
| Wijngaarden, Agatha Dirksdochter, | 223 |
| Wijngaarden, Bernardus van, | 24 |
| Wildius, Joannes Daniel, | 179 |
| Willem II, | 229 |
| Willem III, | 155, 229-230, 235-236, 244-246 |
| Willem Lodewijk of Nassau, | 178, 293 |
| Willem of Orange, | 190 |
| Wilmot, John, | 67 |
| Wilson, John, | 134-135 |
| Winslow, Ludvig, | 113-114 |
| Winstanly, Ellen, | 133 |
| Winter, Samuel, | 131, 133 |
| Witsius, Hermannus, | 319 |
| Witt, John de, | 43 |
| Wittewrongel, Petrus, | 138, 149, 160, 168, 171-172, 174, 176, 272-276 |
| Wolseley, Charles, | 239-240, 242-243 |
| Wood, Anthony à, | 150 |
| Woodbridge, Benjamin, | 135 |
| Wright, Robert, | 146 |
| Wtenbogaert, Johannes, | 259 |
| Wyckenburgius, Theodorus, | 225-226 |
| | |
| Yates, John, | 131, 134 |
| Young, Thomas, | 132 |
| Ytegem, Susanna van, | 348 |
| | |
| Zachmortel, Maria, | 201 |
| Ziff, Larzer, | 137 |
| Zoelen, Herman van, | 58 |
| Zunnern, Joh. David, | 122 |

# INDEX OF SUBJECTS

| | |
|---|---|
| Adultery, | 103 |
| Affidavit, | 329-331, 333, 335-336 |
| Affliction, | 37, 63, 124, 294 |
| *Afscheiding* [Secession], | 56, 72, 91 |
| *Agape*, | 136 |
| Anabaptism, | 48, 299 |
| Anointing of the sick, | 36 |
| Antichrist, | 60, 63, 66, 191, 193 |
| Antonomianism, | 48, 175-176 |
| Apocalyptic, | 95, 193 |
| Arminianism, | see Remonstrantism |
| Army chaplain, | 131-132, 144-145, 167, 174, 209, 287-289, 295-296 |
| *Ars moriendi*, | 41, 255 |
| Assurance of faith, | 59, 61, 63, 65, 273, 290 |
| Atheism, | 59, 64, 67, 240, 243 |
| Auction catalogue, | 156 |
| Austin Friars, | 132, 136, 138-139, 183-185, 187-188 |
| Autobiography, | 112, 205, 223-224, 233-234, 236 |
| Baptism, | 29, 47, 256, 322-323, 328 |
| Bible, | see Scripture |
| Bible translation, | 165, 202, 204, 206, 216 |
| Book of Common Prayer, | 53, 55, 144, 244, 246, 289, 296 |
| Borrowing, | 10, 31, 251-285 |
| Calvinisation, | 307-309 |
| Capital punishment, | 103 |
| Cards, | 173, 321 |
| Catechesis, | 42, 50, 59, 76, 109-110, 127, 169, 218, 233, 246 |
| Ceremonies of the Church of England, | 35, 144-145, 289, 296, 323 |
| Charity, | 140, 188 |
| Christian liberty, | 54, 63 |
| Christocentrism, | 92, 95 |

424 · INDEX OF SUBJECTS

| | |
|---|---|
| Christology, | 83 |
| Church, | 63, 66 |
| Church covenant, | 36 |
| Church of England, | 35, 145, 168, 176, 182-183, 246, 289, 296 |
| Church registration, | 223 |
| Classical antiquity, | 225 |
| Cloisters, | 42, 48 |
| *Collegium qualificatum*, | 316, 318-319 |
| Coming to Christ, | 36-37 |
| Common grace, | 110, 175 |
| Commonplace book, | 276 |
| Communion sermons, | 214, 221 |
| Communion with God, | 53, 61, 63, 187 |
| Community of goods, | 48 |
| Confess, | 59, 61, 65, 67 |
| Confirmation, | 211, 342, 356 |
| Congregationalism, | 36, 82, 296, 323 |
| Congregation for the Propagation of the Faith, | 64 |
| Conscience, | 63, 272 |
| Contra-Remonstrantism, | 202, 206-207, 259, 290, 293, 309-311, 316 |
| Controvers, | 23, 35, 40, 51, 69, 96, 175, 309-311, 316, 355 |
| Conventicle, | 54-55, 85, 92, 96, 229, 233-235, 237, 248, 303, 361 |
| Conversion, | 25, 57, 110-111, 132, 175, 195, 224-225, 227, 229-230, 236, 308-309 |
| Conversion of the Jews, | 64, 81, 145 |
| Copying manuscripts, | 82, 112-113, 135-136, 140 |
| Covenanters, | 43-45, 48, 51, 86, 94-95, 302-303, 305 |
| Covenant of grace, | 48, 179 |
| Covenant with Abraham, | 48 |
| Dancing, | 45, 49, 86, 320 |
| Danish Lutheran Pietism, | 57, 117, 124, 177 |
| Danish translations of Puritan writings, | 57, 72, 99, 113-117, 120, 125-126 |
| Death, | 36, 65, 68, 111, 120, 195, 255-256, 273 |
| Deathbed, | 43, 63-64, 67, 155 |

| | |
|---|---|
| Dedham Conference, | 131 |
| Deism, | 243 |
| Desertion, | 103 |
| Devotion, | 9, 12-13, 17, 24-25, 34, 41-42, 51, 79, 91-92, 95, 114, 162, 179, 195, 214, 218, 221, 226-227, 234, 246, 252, 254, 275, 285, 287, 293, 305 |
| Dialogue, | 111-112, 126, 195-196, 205, 293 |
| Dice, | 173, 321 |
| Discipline, | 61, 208, 320, 350 |
| Divorce, | 48, 103 |
| Dogmatics, | 15, 93, 125, 127, 214, 218, 277, 290, 295, 311 |
| Dort Church Order, | 311, 325 |
| Dress, | 326 |
| Drinking, | 320, 325 |
| Dutch East India Company, | 58, 217 |
| Dutch Reformed Pietism, | 16, 100, 125, 127, 278, 357, 360-361 |
| Dutch Revolt, | 204-206 |
| Dutch translations of Puritan works, | 7, 9-12, 17-19, 23-127, 129, 156, 179, 181-251, 259, 277 |
| Dutch West India Company, | 59, 155 |
| Ecclesiastical festivals, | 23, 53-54, 83, 86, 188, 206, 208, 323, 326-329, 332, 336-337, 349 |
| Ecclesiastical goods, | 205 |
| Education, | 145, 208, 254, 275, 308 |
| Election, | 16, 37, 289, 311 |
| Emotion, | 53, 206, 233-234, 290 |
| English Manuscript Studies 1100-1700, | 100 |
| English Synod, | 145, 296 |
| Enlightenment, | 91-92, 242 |
| Episcopalism, | 92, 111, 135, 146, 165, 167, 183-184, 200, 205, 209, 217, 244, 246, 263, 268, 278, 287, 289-290 |
| Eschatology, | 71 |
| European Pietism, | 127, 129-130 |
| Evangelicalism, | 57 |
| Exegesis, | 79, 94-95 |

| | |
|---|---|
| Fair, | 206, 320 |
| Faith, | 13, 37-38, 47, 59-60, 63-67, 85-86, 104, 110, 125, 150, 182, 195, 224-227, 232-234, 239, 242, 290, 309, 311 |
| Falling-away, | 50, 59-60 |
| Fall of Rome, | 59, 68 |
| Family of Love, | 196 |
| Family worship, | 25-26, 76, 162, 172, 237, 245 |
| Fasting, | 16, 28-29, 53, 163, 254, 256, 329 |
| Fear of death, | 68, 273 |
| Female, | 117, 330, 361 |
| Formularies, | 145, 289, 323, 325-328, 341, 349-350 |
| Formulary prayers, | 51, 53, 325 |
| Fourth Commandment, | see Sabbath |
| Franckesche Stiftungen, | 117 |
| Frankfurt Book Fair, | 122 |
| Free offer of grace, | 38 |
| Fundraising for Protestants in and from the Palatinate, | 147, 165, 188 |
| Funeral sermon, | 153, 167, 188, 214 |
| Further Reformation, | 16-17, 25, 31, 41-42, 44, 51, 70-71, 76, 79, 82, 94-95, 100, 120, 124, 126, 140, 155-156, 162, 164, 196-197, 199-200, 206-209, 218, 224, 226, 233-234, 251-252, 255, 258, 260, 262, 269, 272, 278, 288, 305, 309, 312-314, 319-323, 325, 332, 336-337, 350, 354-355, 357-361 |
| Further reformation, | 30-31, 71, 307-337 |
| Further Reformation Study Foundation, | 17 |
| Future, | 60, 65, 68, 95 |
| Games of chance, | 323 |
| German translations of Puritan writings, | 33-34, 72, 117-118, 122, 125, 147, 179, 268, 271 |
| German Further Reformation, | 17, 199 |
| German Lutheranism, | 33-34, 57, 96 |
| German Lutheran Pietism, | 57, 72, 121, 124, 269-270 |
| Glory, | 63 |

| | |
|---|---|
| Godliness, | 14, 41, 53-54, 63, 65, 129, 179, 236, 272, 295 |
| Godly conversation, | 16, 28, 109, 169, 236 |
| Gospel, | 37-38, 48, 53, 59-61, 63, 85, 87, 179 |
| Great Church Assembly at 's-Hertogenbosch, | 150 |
| Heavenly academy, | 55, 274 |
| Hearing of the Word, | 28, 54-55, 226, 254 |
| Hebrew, | 142, 201, 208 |
| Hell, | 53, 63 |
| Herrnhuter Brethren, | 57 |
| Holy Communion, | 36, 42, 45, 48, 221, 226, 327, 331 |
| Holy Ghost, | 36, 53-55, 59-60, 63, 67, 85, 225, 227-228, 232, 258, 290, 325 |
| Holy kiss, | 36, 45, 49, 86 |
| Holy Writ, | see Scripture |
| Household seminary, | 78-79, 82, 107, 109-110, 129-180, 186, 272 |
| Humiliation, | 113, 118, 187 |
| Hungarian Puritanism, | 17, 140 |
| Hymns, | 86, 230, 232-235, 237 |
| Idolatry, | 60, 63, 80 |
| Image-worship, | 60 |
| Independentism, | 36, 44, 151, 171, 177, 288 |
| Indifference, | 64, 295, 309 |
| Indulgence, | 303 |
| Infralapsarism, | 311 |
| Inner life of faith, | 25, 63, 71, 85, 126, 227, 232, 283 |
| Inquisition, | 189 |
| Intellect, | 12, 59, 66 |
| Interconfessionalism, | 72, 117 |
| Invisible church, | 47 |
| Jews, | 64 |
| Journal of spiritual experiences, | 64 |
| Judgement of a person's spiritual state, | 47 |
| Justification, | 37, 85 |

| | |
|---|---|
| Karen Brahes Library, | 114, 124 |
| Kingdom of God, | 63-65, 191, 274 |
| Knowledge, | 28, 37-38, 53, 55, 59, 65, 195, 293-294, 323, 326 |
| | |
| Labadism, | 44-45 |
| Latent citations, | 251-276 |
| Latitudinarianism, | 242 |
| Law of God, | 37, 53 |
| Laying-on of hands, | 36, 303 |
| League of Piety, | 140 |
| Learned game, | 266, 274, 276 |
| Lecturership, | 133-134 |
| Legalism, | 57, 85, 87, 225 |
| Libertinism, | 240 |
| Life to come, | 38 |
| Lombards, | 321 |
| Long Parliament, | 182 |
| Lord's Day, | see Sabbath |
| Lord's Supper, | 29, 42, 212, 263, 326, 331, 356 |
| Lukewarmness, | 64-65, 71 |
| Lutheran Pietism, | 57, 72-73, 121, 125 |
| | |
| Magistracy, | 61 |
| Malay, | 42 |
| Manner of life, | 53, 249, 255 |
| Manuscripts, | 23-127 |
| Marriage, | 102-104, 106, 133, 272, 325 |
| Massachusetts Bay Company, | 146 |
| Mastery of English, | 41, 129, 140, 150, 154, 177, 214, 221, 237, 242, 282-283, 285 |
| Meditation, | 16, 28, 34, 42, 53, 104, 114, 191, 194, 235, 252, 254, 277, 298, 327 |
| Men's hair, | 41 |
| Millenarianism, | 35-36, 48, 224 |
| Military, | 287-305 |
| Ministerial preparation, | 160, 172 |
| Mission, | 42, 64-65, 134, 208, 217 |
| Mohammedanism, | 60 |
| Moral law, | 29 |
| Mysticism, | 196, 205-206, 224, 232 |

| | |
|---|---|
| National Covenant, | 303 |
| Natural theology, | 242 |
| Navigation Act, | 152 |
| New birth, | 65, 224, 269 |
| New covenant, | 48, 303 |
| Nonconformism, | 10, 35, 60-61, 82, 131-132, 134, 146, 167, 174, 176-177, 243, 287-288, 294, 296 |
| | |
| Orange, | 43, 190, 205, 219, 229, 245-246, 299 |
| Organ, | 323 |
| Original sin, | 152 |
| Orthodoxy, | 47, 311 |
| Orthopraxy, | 311 |
| Oxford Dictionary of National Biography [ODNB], | 24, 75, 135, 167 |
| | |
| Parousia of Christ, | 48 |
| Pastoral care, | 7, 26, 53, 130, 136, 163, 177-178, 236, 312, 350 |
| Peace of Münster, | 147 |
| Pedagogy, | 76, 148, 237, 272 |
| Persecution, | 54, 60, 65-66, 85, 94, 152, 189, 204, 222, 245, 309 |
| Pietas, | 17-19, 69, 277 |
| Pietism, | 10, 12, 14-17, 24, 57, 72, 76, 78, 91-92, 95, 99-180, 186-187, 194 199, 205-206, 214-215, 218, 224, 232, 234, 236, 249, 251-276, 278, 282, 287, 289-290, 293, 295, 309, 312-313, 360-361 |
| Piety, | 13-16, 18, 28, 43-44, 57, 75, 92, 99-127, 148, 156, 181-251, 254, 256, 261, 263, 265-266, 272, 275, 287-305, 309, 312-313 |
| Piety movement, | 16, 25, 71, 120, 140, 180, 186, 199, 234, 337, 350, 359, 361 |
| Poetry, | 76, 78, 212, 215, 221, 229-230, 232-235, 238-240, 243, 245-246, 339 |
| Polemics, | 23, 30, 41, 59-60, 64, 66-67, 71, 83, 100, 127, 204, 206, 224, 240, 242-243, 260, 262, 289-290, 302, 311 |

| | |
|---|---|
| Popery, | 60-61, 194 |
| Portrait, | 157, 204 |
| Practical divinity, | 9, 15, 26, 145, 178 |
| Piety movement, | 16, 25, 71, 120, 140, 180, 186, 199, 234, 337, 350, 359, 361 |
| Practice of piety, | 12, 15-16, 33, 59, 76, 85, 92, 126, 148, 168, 188, 232, 254-256, 261, 263, 265, 294 |
| Prayer, | 16, 28, 53, 64, 163, 227, 233, 244-246, 254, 325, 327, 329 |
| Preaching, | 7, 26, 28-29, 33, 53-55, 57, 67, 72, 85, 120-121, 125, 130, 132, 136, 139-140, 154-155, 163, 177-178, 242, 254, 277-285, 303, 312, 329, 336 |
| Preciseness, | 54, 154 |
| Predestination, | 110, 169, 290 |
| Preparation for the Lord's Supper, | 42, 212, 221 |
| Presbyterianism, | 58, 61, 131, 257, 296, 302, 323 |
| Primary manuscripts, | 101-111 |
| Proverbs, | 204, 206-207, 225, 227-229, 236-237 |
| Promises, | 38, 63-64, 68, 147 |
| Prophecy, | 36 |
| Puritanising, | 248, 288, 292, 302 |
| Puritanism, | 1-362 |
| | |
| Qur'ān, | 60 |
| | |
| Ramism, | 26 |
| Rationalism, | 239, 242 |
| Reading of the Word, | 28-29, 226, 294 |
| Reason, | 64, 96, 240, 242 |
| Rebellion, | 303, 305 |
| Reformation, | 66-68, 194, 222, 255, 268, 316 |
| Reformation of morals, | 86, 299, 301, 303, 311, 314, 321, 323, 350 |
| Reformation programme, | 17, 120, 206, 270, 301, 313, 322-323, 326, 332, 337 |
| Reformed Pietism, | 17, 73, 312-314, 360-361 |
| Regeneration, | 47, 224-225, 269 |

| | |
|---|---|
| Relationship between church and state, | 61, 310, 314-316, 350 |
| Religious vows, | 28-29, 254 |
| Remonstrantism, | 30, 129, 175, 202, 207, 242, 259, 268, 290, 309-310 |
| Repentance, | 36-37, 116, 118, 214, 256, 293-294, 299 |
| Reprobation, | 37, 226 |
| Restored Reformed Church of the Netherlands, | 4, 18 |
| Resurrection, | 256 |
| Revelation, | 59 |
| Romanism, | 30, 42, 48, 54, 59-60, 64, 66-67, 146-147, 152, 183, 204, 206, 208, 243, 307-309, 316, 322-323, 328, 333, 337 |
| Royal Society, | 165 |
| Sabbath, | 23-25, 28-29, 54, 85-86, 171, 173, 184, 186, 188, 200, 208-209, 224, 254, 256, 270, 307, 311, 321, 323, 326, 329 |
| Sacraments, | 28-29, 254 |
| Salvation history, | 78 |
| Sanctification, | 16, 61, 85, 87-88, 92, 196, 298 |
| Saracen, | 60 |
| Satan, | 51, 53, 65, 67, 117 |
| Savoy Declaration of the Faith and Order, | 150 |
| Scholasticism, | 64 |
| Scots Puritanism, | 15-16, 50, 71, 95, 200, 205, 226-227, 247, 323, 350, 360 |
| Scripture, | 16, 28-29, 36, 42, 49, 53, 59-61, 63, 65-66, 78, 85, 95, 142, 155, 165, 193, 201-202, 204, 206, 216, 227-228, 235, 240, 242, 259, 289, 292-293, 340-341, 344 |
| Secondary manuscripts, | 102, 111-118, 120 |
| Separatism, | 40, 44, 47, 61, 64-65, 70, 80, 85, 185, 195 |
| Service of God, | 59, 63-64 |
| Sex, | 103 |
| Short-Title Catalogue Netherlands (STCN), | 17-18 |

| | |
|---|---|
| Sin, | 34, 36-38, 63, 66, 108, 227, 240, 258, 294, 298-299, 301, 311, 320, 325, 350 |
| Sin against the Holy Ghost, | 225-227 |
| Socinianism, | 59 |
| Solo-singing, | 36 |
| Soul, | 36 |
| Spirit of God, | see Holy Ghost |
| Spiritual abandonment, | 226, 232 |
| Spiritual biography, | 40, 138, 167, 234, 236, 242, 273-274 |
| Spiritual conflict, | 273 |
| Spiritual example, | 26, 53, 63, 67, 87, 155, 182, 197, 228-229, 234, 285, 294, 359 |
| Spiritual experience, | 17, 26, 53-54, 59, 61, 66-67, 94, 155, 224, 227, 232, 234, 249, 273, 290 |
| Spiritual hallmarks, | 36-37 |
| Spiritual preparation, | 29, 37, 42, 104, 195 |
| Spiritual testament, | 232 |
| Spouses, | 103-104 |
| Statenvertaling, | 165, 205-209 |
| Stichting Deddens-Koppefonds, | 4, 18 |
| Supralapsarism, | 311 |
| Swedish Lutheran Pietism, | 57, 72 |
| Synod of Dort, | 129, 156, 178, 202, 216, 268, 310-311, 316 |
| | |
| Temptation, | 54, 221, 227 |
| Theatre, | 160 |
| Theocracy, | 155, 162, 209, 309, 313, 318, 320 |
| Theological training, | 54, 131-132, 134-135, 168-169 |
| Truth of Christianity, | 60, 63, 65 |
| | |
| Union with Christ, | 37, 59 |
| United Societies, | 302, 305 |
| University of Groningen, | 56 |
| University of Leiden, | 56, 142, 144-145, 148, 150-152, 154, 160, 165, 208, 215 |
| University of Utrecht, | 169, 237, 244 |
| Unregenerate Christians: | 59 |
| Usury, | 321, 323 |

| | |
|---|---|
| Visible church, | 47 |
| VU University Amsterdam, | 9, 17 |
| | |
| Wedding sermon, | 102-104, 106-108, 126 |
| Weigelian heresy, | 147 |
| Westminster Assembly, | 36, 131 |
| Wstminster Shorter Catechism, | 273 |
| Will, | 59 |
| Wills, | 339-362 |
| Witness, | 60, 63-65 |
| Woman Pope, | 146 |
| Women's hairstyle, | 155 |
| | |
| Yearning for heaven, | 232 |
| | |
| Zeeland Church Order, | 315, 318 |

# INDEX OF PLACES

| | |
|---|---|
| Aagtekerke, | 139, 154 |
| Aardenburg, | 307 |
| Abbega, | 280 |
| Aberdeen, | 340-341 |
| Akersloot, | 142 |
| Amersfoort, | 144, 211 |
| Amsterdam, | 45, 47-49, 86-87, 96, 139, 144, 147-148, 155, 160, 170, 193, 197, 202, 211, 217, 224, 230, 235, 237-238, 248, 260, 272-273, 284, 298 |
| Antwerp, | 157, 193 |
| Arnhem, | 34-36, 38, 69, 202, 284 |
| Ashby-de-la-Zouch, | 133 |
| Ashen, | 134 |
| | |
| Banbury, | 25-26, 69, 108, 162-164, 359-360 |
| Bangor, | 263 |
| Barking, | 134 |
| Basel, | 178, 268 |
| Batenburg, | 244 |
| Beilen, | 255 |
| Bergum, | 283 |
| Bolsward, | 211-212, 214, 284, 322 |
| Boston (Engl.), | 76, 78, 80, 93, 109-110, 131, 133, 169-170, 173, 175-176 |
| Boston (USA), | 76, 80, 131 |
| Brakel, | 204 |
| Bruges, | 190-191, 320 |
| Bruinisse, | 144 |
| Brussels, | 318 |
| Burgh, | 25 |
| | |
| Cambridge, | 113, 130-135, 140, 146, 165, 173-174, 178, 268 |
| Canterbury, | 183-184, 201, 268, 289 |
| Canvvey Island, | 170, 185, 245 |

INDEX OF PLACES · 435

| | |
|---|---|
| Coggeshall, | 187 |
| Colchester, | 142-143, 174, 182, 184-187, 200 |
| Cologne, | 152, 165 |
| Copenhagen, | 57, 113, 318 |
| Coventry, | 185 |
| | |
| Dedham, | 131-132 |
| Deinze, | 201 |
| Delft, | 224, 288, 292, 296 |
| Dokkum, | 322 |
| Dorchester, | 146, 165-166 |
| Dordrecht, | 30, 41-43, 112, 143, 149, 288, 292, 361 |
| Dover, | 185 |
| Dublin, | 131 |
| | |
| Earls Colne, | 187 |
| Edinburgh, | 85, 87, 90-91 |
| Eeklo, | 189-190 |
| Epe, | 255 |
| | |
| Folsgara, | 280 |
| Franeker, | 106, 120, 131, 138, 144-145, 148, 169-170, 173, 178, 201, 211-212, 216, 255-256, 280, 285, 292, 322 |
| Frankfurt, | 122 |
| | |
| Gauw, | 280 |
| Geneva, | 66, 156, 166, 215-216 |
| Ghent, | 190, 200-201, 215 |
| Giessen-Nieuwkerk, | 200 |
| Goënga, | 280 |
| Goes, | 154-155 |
| Gorinchem, | 152, 209, 238-240, 295-296 |
| Gotha, | 57 |
| Gouda, | 152, 171 |
| 's-Gravenzande, | 200 |
| Great Yarmouth, | 185, 222, 237, 240, 248 |
| Grijpskerke, | 139, 150, 156 |
| Groningen, | 156 |
| Grouw, | 282 |

| | |
|---|---|
| Haamstede, | 25 |
| Haarlem, | 40, 151, 222-225, 229-230, 232, 237, 239 |
| Hälleberg, | 57 |
| The Hague, | 111, 146, 166, 200, 202, 205, 219, 230, 269, 314-315, 318, 332-333, 351 |
| Halle, | 57, 117 |
| Halstead, | 184 |
| Harderwijk, | 205, 244 |
| Harlingen, | 212 |
| Heidelberg, | 142, 147, 165-166, 168, 200-201 |
| Herborn, | 146 |
| Herford, | 40, 45-46, 48-49, 86 |
| 's-Hertogenbosch, | 40-41 |
| Herwijnen, | 257-258 |
| Heusden, | 244, 295-296 |
| Hoek, | 139, 154 |
| Hontenisse, | 139, 150 |
| Ipswich (Engl.), | 185, 189-190 |
| Ipswich (USA), | 132 |
| Izegem, | 191 |
| Kampen, | 200-202, 293 |
| Kessel, | 150 |
| King's Lynn, | 185 |
| Kirchberg, | 146-147 |
| Koudekerke, | 139, 154-155 |
| Leeuwarden, | 178, 212, 280, 282, 302, 322 |
| Leiden, | 24-25, 33, 40-41, 56, 139, 142, 144-146, 148, 150-152, 154, 160, 163, 165, 173-174, 189, 197, 201, 204, 207-209, 215-216, 224, 288 |
| Leidschendam, | 139, 152 |
| Leipzig, | 33, 121 |
| Lisse, | 202 |
| Little Baddows, | 134 |

INDEX OF PLACES · 437

| | |
|---|---|
| London, | 23, 78, 80, 87, 93, 109-110, 131, 133, 138, 140, 142-143, 145, 147, 150, 152, 154-157, 169-171, 179, 181, 183-189, 193, 195-200, 208, 210-211, 214-217, 219, 222-223, 242, 244-248, 293, 296, 298 |
| Lopik, | 56 |
| Maastricht, | 193, 217, 291 |
| Maidstone, | 170, 185 |
| Middelburg, | 25-26, 44, 76, 81, 93, 102, 104, 107, 112, 120, 129, 139, 144, 149-150, 154-157, 160, 163, 169, 171, 173-174, 176-177, 190-191, 193, 195-198, 248, 254, 260, 292, 313, 326, 341-343 |
| Mortlake, | 185 |
| Mülheim, | 152 |
| Nantes, | 216 |
| Naumburg, | 122 |
| Nazeing, | 134 |
| Neckerau, | 122 |
| Nieuw- en Sint-Joosland, | 169 |
| Nieuweschoot, | 282 |
| Nieuwpoort, | 238 |
| Nijmegen, | 217-218 |
| Norfolk, | 131, 184-185 |
| Northampton, | 133 |
| Norwich, | 152, 184-185, 189-191, 215, 248 |
| Odense, | 114 |
| Offenbach, | 122 |
| Offingawier, | 280 |
| Oosthem, | 212, 280 |
| Ostend, | 288, 309 |
| Oudeschoot, | 282 |
| Oudkerk, | 282 |
| Oxford, | 130-131, 145, 156, 165, 167, 216, 245, 268 |

| | |
|---|---|
| Paraíba, | 295-296 |
| Paris, | 216 |
| Purmerland, | 40 |
| | |
| Queensferry, | 303 |
| | |
| Ravensteyn, | 150 |
| Reading, | 133 |
| Recife, | 295 |
| Rees, | 146 |
| Renesse, | 160 |
| Ritthem, | 154 |
| La Rochelle, | 216 |
| Rochester, | 278 |
| Roeselare, | 222 |
| Roodkerk, | 282 |
| Rotterdam, | 36, 40-44, 50-51, 55, 58-59, 67-69, 75, 83, 85-86, 131-132, 143, 148, 152, 236, 240, 296, 302-303 |
| Rouen, | 23 |
| | |
| Salem (USA), | 133 |
| Sandwich, | 184, 186, 197, 201, 207-208, 211, 247 |
| Sanquhar, | 303 |
| Saumur, | 156, 215-216 |
| Schagen, | 189, 259 |
| Scherpenisse, | 198, 219 |
| Serooskerke, | 154 |
| Sint-Maartensdijk, | 219 |
| Sluis, | 10, 12, 50, 83, 86, 90, 302, 307-337, 339-362 |
| Sneek, | 201, 280, 282, 322 |
| South Benfleet, | 245 |
| Stad aan 't Haringvliet, | 198 |
| Stamford, | 185 |
| Steenvoorde, | 211 |
| Steenwijk, | 152 |
| Strasbourg, | 216, 268 |
| | |
| Thetford, | 185 |
| Tholen, | 219, 221, 260 |

INDEX OF PLACES · 439

| | |
|---|---|
| Thurlby, | 290 |
| Tidworth, | 133 |
| Tiel, | 167 |
| Tüttleben, | 57 |
| | |
| Utrecht, | 31, 35, 50-51, 55, 70, 87, 90, 113, 139, 150-152, 154, 169, 218, 237-238, 240, 244, 252, 257, 284, 321 |
| | |
| Veen, | 244 |
| Veendam, | 56 |
| Veere, | 154, 169, 208, 342 |
| Venice, | 216 |
| Vianen, | 35 |
| Vlissingen (Flushing), | 50, 139, 144, 148, 169-170, 198, 208, 279, 313, 326 |
| Vollenhove, | 319 |
| | |
| Wageningen, | 243 |
| Wesel, | 44, 146, 168 |
| Wormer, | 319 |
| Wormerveer, | 41 |
| | |
| Yerseke, | 56 |
| Ypres, | 207 |
| | |
| Zaandijk, | 41 |
| Zevenhoven, | 189 |
| Zevenhuizen, | 243 |
| Zevenwolde, | 322 |
| Zierikzee, | 41, 149, 160 |
| Zoutelande, | 79, 109, 144, 169-170, 198-199 |
| Zurich, | 193 |
| Zutphen, | 112, 202, 204, 206 |
| Zwolle, | 255, 292, 294-295, 298-299, 301-302 |

# INDEX OF BIBLE TEXTS

| | |
|---|---|
| Exodus 15:20, | 49 |
| Deuteronomy 23:9,14, | 298 |
| Joshua, | 296 |
| Joshua 24:15, | 58 |
| II Samuel 6:14, | 49 |
| I Chronicles 21:24, | 325 |
| Esther, | 76 |
| Psalm 1, | 218 |
| Psalm 51, | 210 |
| Canticles, | 78-79, 83, 94, 110, 112-113, 169, 175 |
| Canticles 1:5-9, | 80 |
| Canticles 1:10-17, | 80 |
| Canticles 3, | 81 |
| Canticles 4:7-11, | 81 |
| Canticles 5:2, | 82 |
| Jeremiah 31:20, | 81 |
| Ezekiel, | 209 |
| Matthew 5:6, | 54 |
| Luke 5:31-32, | 36 |
| John 4, | 210 |
| John 6:35, | 36-37 |
| John 14:6, | 88 |
| John 19:30, | 116 |
| Acts, | 195 |
| Acts 2:37, | 118 |
| 1 Corinthians 11:14, | 41 |
| I Corinthians 11:23-29, | 327 |
| II Corinthians 5:17, | 117 |
| Galatians 4:9-11, | 325 |
| Ephesians 5:23, | 103 |
| Ephesians 6:10, | 117 |
| Colossians 1:27 | 90 |
| II Timothy 4:17, | 279 |
| James 2:5, | 38 |
| I Peter 4:17, | 65 |
| I John 4:9, | 280 |

| | |
|---|---|
| I John 4:10, | 280 |
| Jude:20, | 325 |
| Revelation, | 60, 111, 191, 193 |
| Revelation 2:4-5, | 197 |
| Revelation 9:14, | 60 |
| Revelation 16, | 193 |
| Revelation 20:7-10, | 191 |

CPSIA information can be obtained
at www.ICGtesting.com
Printed in the USA
BVHW040524030820
585257BV00008B/14